SOCIAL FOUNDATIONS OF EDUCATIONAL DECISIONS

SOCIAL FOUNDATIONS OF EDUCATIONAL DECISIONS

Louis Fischer and Donald R. Thomas

San Fernando Valley State College

WADSWORTH PUBLISHING COMPANY, INC.
BELMONT, CALIFORNIA

To My Father, Hugh W. Thomas

D.R.T.

L.C. Cat. Card No.: 65-21114

Printed in the United States of America

PREFACE

The purpose of this work is to acquaint students with the social bases of educational processes and institutions. In order to understand the educational process and be able to make intelligent decisions about and within it, one must look systematically at the social forces bearing upon it—some just emerging, some vigorously with us, and some fading into the past.

The social foundations of education, like the similarly important psychological foundations, assist the serious student of education in constructing for himself an overarching theoretical framework for his work. Drawing upon these theories and understandings, the educator, we believe, will make more effective decisions in his day-by-day encounters with the educational process.

The point of view held throughout this work is that education is an occupation aspiring to become a mature profession; as such, it must draw upon significant bodies of theoretical analysis. The systematic utilization of theory is a crucial distinguishing characteristic of a profession. Knowledge of the social foundations of education, like that of the other bases of education, does not offer the teacher a set of techniques, tricks, or rules of thumb to be used on prescribed occasions. On the contrary: sound understanding of the foundations of education makes one realize that it is indefensible to propose a "cookbook" approach to the educational process.

Neither can any single volume dealing with the social foundations of education include a detailed report of the extensive array of data and materials available in the field. There is the constant danger also, which we recognize, that the rapidly changing social scene will produce significant developments which will supersede materials in this volume. We believe, therefore, that serious students will pursue the search for more extensive details by using our suggested bibliographies and by constantly researching the many problems we will pose. The content presented herein, then, is a broad picture of the field and the problems confronting education in its social setting and should help one to achieve a better understanding of the social bases of educational decisions. Behavior based upon such a perspective will be more intelligent, and thus more effective, than behavior taking place in the absence of such understandings.

A professional teacher functions both in and out of the classroom. The theoretical materials on the social foundations of education will enable him to work more effectively in such out-of-class roles as his work with parents, with various lay groups in the community, with teacher groups building curricula and with various professional organizations. His classroom work with individual students and with student groups likewise will be enhanced. The relevance of the theoretical materials for the various roles of the teacher will be noted in the appropriate places.

The book is divided into four parts. Part I provides an overview of how educational decision-making processes work in our *culture.* The dimensions of decision making are explored, and the relevance of scientific as well as nonscientific considerations in this process is developed.

In Part II we consider various specific aspects of the American culture that relate to educational decisions. Some of these have been with us for many decades or even centuries, like the issues relating to "education and religion" and "federal aid to education." Others are relative newcomers on the changing cultural scene, as "education and cultural deprivation," "the education of the gifted," and the relevance of the "new leisure" to education.

Part III deals with the significant changes that have occurred in the occupational status of teaching; with the teachers, who are members of the largest "professional" group in our society; and with past and current efforts to develop a more mature profession. Part IV gives a brief review of the volume and presents an outline of actual situations calling for decisions. These cases are presented to underline the thesis of the volume—namely, that educators are repeatedly called upon to make significant decisions, and that such decisions must be based upon sound analysis of both the culture and the society that support the schools.

The student might be wise to read Chapters 1 and 16 first, and then to commence systematic study of this volume.

The reader who considers teaching to be a craft or craft-like occupation will be impatient with our explorations. The professionally oriented student, however, will appreciate the guiding function of theorizing. When the urge arises to ask: "How can I use this in my classroom at 9 A.M. next Monday?" let us realize that many important concepts may be irrelevant at that *particular* time and place; other important concepts might be of only indirect relevance. The impatient student, representing an unsophisticated brand of pragmatism often found in the American culture, should be reminded that leading pragmatic philosophers would assert that, in the long run, nothing is as practical as careful, systematic theorizing.

L.F.
D.R.T.

CONTENTS

PART ONE EDUCATIONAL DECISION MAKING

1. The Complexity of Educational Decisions 3
2. Education and Culture 21
3. Value Conflicts and Education 48
4. Science and the Social Foundations of Education 61
5. Philosophy and the Social Foundations of Education 100

PART TWO AMERICAN SOCIETY AND EDUCATION

6. American Mass Society and Education 131
7. The New Leisure, Automation, and Education 151
8. Education and Religion 176
9. Education and the Culture of Deprivation 204
10. Education and the Gifted Child 231
11. Expanded Federal Aid to Education 246
12. Controversial Issues in the Classroom 263

PART THREE TEACHERS AND TEACHING

13. Teaching in the United States 281
14. Teachers 308
15. Professionalism in Education 324

PART FOUR CONCLUSIONS AND CASES

16. Concluding Remarks 351

PART I

EDUCATIONAL DECISION MAKING

CHAPTER 1

THE COMPLEXITY OF EDUCATIONAL DECISIONS

The process of education is a highly complex, all-inclusive one. Many facets of life—many situations, relationships, institutions, and persons—exercise educative influence on children, youth, and adults. Although we recognize this breadth, the systematic use of the term *education* in this book will be restricted to the formal, institutional processes wherein teaching and learning occur. Similarly, the term *educator* will be used to refer to persons who occupy various positions in educational institutions by virtue of certain prescribed, specialized training, licensure, and experience.

To illustrate the distinction offered here, let us compare the role of the father and that of a fifth-grade teacher in an elementary school. Clearly, a young boy learns from both of these adults. In the sense that they are both educating him, the label "educator" would apply to each of them. But, according to our stipulated definition, only the fifth-grade teacher will here be referred to as an educator. To carry our illustration further, a speaker on television, a newspaper reporter, a billboard, the neon signs of our cities, city zoning, etc., would not be "educators," though the educational influence of each could be readily demonstrated. For present purposes let us simply note that human beings learn both in school and out. Thus, education is a concept more encompassing than *schooling,* which refers specifically to the institutions created for the purposes of teaching and learning.

Educators, then, are people who, by virtue of special preparation, occupy various positions in our complex systems of schooling. The important distinction between education and schooling will be further analyzed in Chapter 2.

The man on the street, upon hearing the word "educator," immediately thinks of a teacher—since, by and large, his contact has been with teachers or perhaps, on rare occasions, with principals. But those who want to understand the educational enterprise more thoroughly must be aware of the range of important positions, other than that of the teacher, included in the term *educator:* principals, assistant principals, department heads, supervisors, curriculum consultants, superintendents, visiting teachers, school psychologists, county and state personnel, professors of education, even representatives of the United States Office of Education.

All of these positions are occupied by people who continually must make the countless decisions necessary for the functioning of our schools. Whatever occurs in our schools, concerning the curriculum and its implementation, does so because someone, somewhere, made a decision. It is no longer useful or possible to conceive of educators as kind, patient persons whose sole task is that of passing on ready-made knowledge in neat packages to young minds eager to learn. It is doubtful that this simple formulation was ever an accurate description, however popularly held. A more accurate description of educators would propose that they are constantly involved in the making of important decisions. In their daily work, most of which is *not* routine, they inevitably face problems that must somehow be solved by choices among alternative courses of action. Upon making a choice and following the selected course of action, they are led to new situations, where again choices must be made. When a choice is made concerning a goal to be reached or an end sought, alternative means are often available to reach the goal. Educators must decide which of the available means should be used to gain the agreed-upon end. Consequently, we may look at the work of educators as a continuous process of interlocking decisions related to the ends and means of education.

An educator cannot avoid making decisions. Whether he works in the classroom, with parents, in the principal's chair, at the central office of the school system, or in the State Department of Education, various alternatives will face him. At the minimal level, he might choose to continue doing today what he did yesterday. As a new situation arises, he might choose to ignore it or to let someone else choose a course of action. Notice that the educator who was reluctant to choose a new course of action has nevertheless made a decision. Although it might sound like verbal gymnastics, the choice not to make a decision is itself a decision. The choice to have someone else make a decision also involves the making of that decision.

LEVELS OF DECISION MAKING

Even a cursory glance at the organization of a school system will reveal its hierarchic structure—from the classroom teachers on up through the principals, supervisors, curriculum consultants, and other central-office personnel to the superintendent and the governing board of education.

Each school system has its own governing board, chosen in a manner acceptable to its voters. This board, with the advice of the local superintendent of schools, determines the over-all policies for the schools. The local system operates within a broad framework established by each state, with a very few but significant requirements imposed by our federal constitution. It is the chief duty of the superintendent to see that these overarching policy decisions are carried out. In this process, he has to make many significant decisions which have consequences throughout the school system.[1]

The naive observer often assumes that educators below the level of the superintendent do not make decisions, but merely carry out those fashioned above and handed down. This belief is mistaken. It is more accurate to say that the decisions made at the higher levels of the educational hierarchy have consequences broader in scope than those made at lower levels. Nevertheless, although narrower in scope, the decisions made by individual principals or teachers are bound to be very important, because they are more immediate to the teaching-learning process—which is, of course, the *raison d'être* of the educational enterprise.

EXAMPLES OF DECISIONS AT DIFFERENT LEVELS

The following list of some typical problems faced by educators also illustrates the various levels at which important decisions are made.

Decisions Made by Local School Board (with advice of Superintendent and/or Business Manager)

Should the schools open on a day designated by a teachers' organization as a strike day?

Should the schools offer Russian as a modern language in the school system?

Should U.S. History be taught at the fifth, eighth, and eleventh grades or in some other sequence?

Should all ninth graders take algebra?

Should the new high school have a vinyl or carpet floor cover?

Should we force migrant workers' children to attend school?

[1] In recent years, this level of decision making has received systematic attention in various publications dealing with educational administration. See Daniel E. Griffiths, *Human Relations in School Administration* (New York: Appleton-Century-Crofts, 1956), and Kimball Wiles, "How Should Decisions Be Reached?" in *Supervision for Better Schools*, 2nd ed. (Englewood Cliffs, N.J.: Prentice-Hall, 1955), pp. 173–180.

Decisions Made by Principal (with advice of Department Chairman and/or Teachers)

Should Mr. Brown be recommended for tenure?

Should student X be suspended from school?

Which classrooms should certain visitors observe?

Should a certain local service club be allowed time to present a program during a student assembly?

Decisions Made by Teacher

In a homeroom, how much voice should the students have in managing their affairs?

Should Negro and Caucasian children work together on small-group projects?

How do I have an effective conference with the parents of Mary?

Should I teach world history in a chronological approach or through current problems?

Just how should I teach division of fractions to this specific group of individual children?

Do I give Dan the extra attention he seems to need when he stays around daily after school?

The list could continue indefinitely. The variety of situations calling for decisions is great. Some require careful long-term study, while others need quick analysis and immediate action. Some have consequences for an entire school system, others for a single school, others for one classroom within a school, and still others for a small group or even an individual. The decisions are all important ones, even though they relate to problems different in substance and scope.

INDIVIDUAL AND GROUP DECISIONS

A glance at the list of questions posed above shows that some educational decisions are made by individuals and others by groups. Further analysis also reveals that the individual educator, whatever position he occupies, makes his decisions while functioning within policies fashioned by groups.[2]

[2] The importance of the group in decision making was recognized by Chester I. Barnard (*The Functions of the Executive* [Cambridge, Mass.: Harvard University Press, 1938], p. 180), who distinguished between "personal" and "organizational" decisions. According to Barnard, "organizational" decisions can be delegated to others, whereas "personal" decisions cannot.

Barnard, as well as Daniel R. Davies and Kenneth F. Herrold (*Problem Solving for the Executive* [New London, Conn.: Arthur C. Croft, 1954], pp. 18–19), considered only *administrators* as decision makers. In contrast, we regard *all educators* as decision makers—a position also developed by John I. Goodlad ("The Teacher Selects, Plans, Organizes," in *Learning and the Teacher* [Washington, D.C.: Association for Supervision and

For example, decisions on construction, scope, and sequence of the curriculum; provision of various psychological services; use of textbooks; and purchase of teaching machines are generally made after systematic study by groups of educators. However, most crucial of all educational activities are the relationships between the individual teacher and a particular student; the individual principal and a teacher or a student; or the individual guidance worker and a teacher or a student. In short, we are back at the point where the individual educator must make situational decisions to achieve stated objectives.

To illustrate the foregoing, let us take a local community of laymen and educators who have decided to make a significant concerted effort to educate the children of migrant bean pickers who spend six weeks in town each fall. This is a very important decision. Equally important are the situational decisions made by the teacher who works with the youngster of a migrant farm worker. *How* he works with this child or youth is a consequence of choices he makes within the broad choice made by the larger community. The teacher would have to decide, for example, whether or not the child needs remedial work in reading; whether or not to refer him to the school psychologist for testing; whether or not to have a conference with his parents and what information to gather in such a conference; and countless other questions. The fact that the *scope* of the teacher's activity is narrower than that of a principal, superintendent, or school-board member does not make his decisions any less important.

INGREDIENTS OF DECISION MAKING

What goes into the making of a decision? What are its ingredients? What ought to be the ingredients?

Not too long ago, educators could rely on the guiding forces of tradition to direct their activities. In some of the nonindustrial cultures today, where the rate of cultural change is very slow, this is still possible. In the technological culture of the second half of the twentieth century, however, where "change is the only thing constant," we cannot place substantial reliance on the way things were done in the past.[3] The rapidity of change

---

Curriculum Development, National Education Association, 1959]; see also "The Organizing Center in Curriculum Theory and Practice," *Theory into Practice,* 1, No. 4 [October 1962], 215–221).

[3] For a delightful satire which, nonetheless, is a classic analysis of this problem see H. Benjamin, *The Sabre Tooth Curriculum* (New York: McGraw-Hill Book Company, Inc., 1939).

demands constant re-evaluation of existing situations and new perspectives. The past is not ignored; the wisdom gained from the long centuries of human experience must be used to shed light on the present and the future. But this wisdom must be used with care, by selection of relevant aspects that can be used to achieve a fruitful synthesis. (Since the cultural context of decision making is a broad and complex subject, it will be given detailed attention in Chapter 2.)

FACTS

If one can no longer look to a significant past for guidance when faced with a choice, with a decision, where does one look? The first suggestion likely to be offered is that we look at the facts of the case, particularly as "science" gives us the facts. There are serious problems with this kind of a suggestion, but for our immediate purpose let us agree that facts are very important. But are they enough? While they may enable us to come up with a sound diagnosis of a problem, facts do not speak for themselves, no matter how thorough, objective, and exhaustive they are. The same set of facts can be used differently by equally intelligent persons. A set of facts provided for us by chemists and botanists can be used to create plants or to destroy them. Information about population growth and mobility may lead different persons to varied solutions concerning the financing of public schools. Sound understanding of the "facts" concerning the intelligence of women does not lead to general agreement regarding their education.

PURPOSES

These illustrations lead us to conclude that facts are necessary but insufficient ingredients in the decision-making process. It is apparent from the foregoing examples that their individual purposes will lead two or more people to use the same facts differently. Consequently, when educational decisions are to be made, the purposes advocated by each of the educators involved must be carefully considered.

By an educational purpose, we mean the end sought, which directs or guides a particular activity. A purpose held is a fact. Whether or not it *should* be held raises a question of value.

VALUES

In addition to the factual information assembled, and the purposes to which it is applied, we must consider the values of the individual or the group making a decision. Values are related to purposes, but go beyond them. At times we strive to attain a certain purpose; yet, upon further analysis, we are convinced that we ought to be striving for some other purpose. The latter indicates a value held, while the former is simply a statement of fact. Since values or convictions about what ought to be done influence behavior, they must be considered an important dimension of decision making.

OUTLOOK ON LIFE

One's outlook on life, or what has been popularly called one's philosophy of life, also enters the picture. People approach life's problems with different *sets of assumptions.* One may assume, as Rousseau did, that people are "inherently good" or that they are "inherently bad" and "depraved"—a notion held by John Calvin. One may look upon the learning process as painful and unpleasant, or as an exciting and pleasant adventure. One may look on society as an evil that is constantly encroaching upon one's freedom; or one can assume that man attains his status as a human being only through association with other men and that he is free to carry on some activities in society which would be impossible in a Robinson Crusoe setting. In short, we may formulate different sets of assumptions concerning any significant aspect of life. Similarly, educators act upon different assumptions in the analysis and solution of their problems.

Facts, purposes, values, and an outlook on life based on assumptions are all fed into the decision-making mill. They should all be considered carefully and systematically. This decision-making process is fantastically complex because each of the many persons involved in it—and in the consequences of decisions—individually interprets facts, has his own values and purposes, and acts upon his own assumptions. This complexity calls for great care in understanding the way in which we approach the decision-making process. We need to understand each other's points of view even though we may disagree with them. The better we understand the values, purposes, and basic assumptions of our co-workers, the more likely that we shall enlarge our areas of agreement and thus minimize conflict and confusion.

As we look at the several dimensions of the decision-making process, we cannot help but be impressed by its complexity and comprehensiveness. Coladarci, among others, has suggested that we look at the teacher as a "hypothesis maker." The following diagram is a modification of his analysis of the educative act.[4]

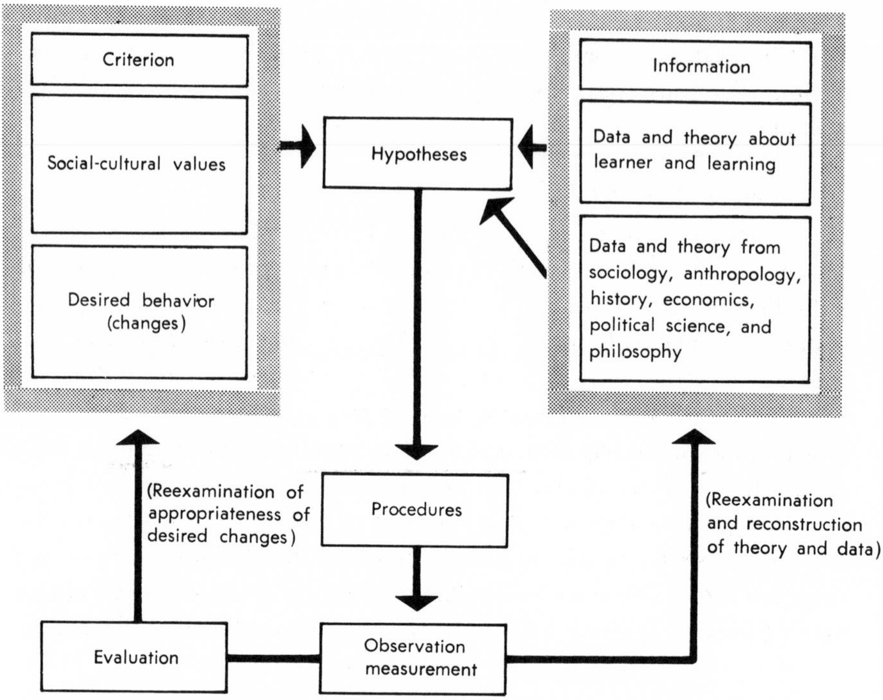

The Total Cultural Setting within Which the Continuous Teaching Process Occurs

The focus of Coladarci's presentation is on the problem of measurement and evaluation as a part of the teaching process. He is concerned, and soundly so, with the relevance of psychology to the several phases of the process.

Our concern in the analysis of the teaching act, based on the same diagram, has three foci: (1) the social-cultural values from which criteria are derived by the teacher and the learner; (2) the relevant data and theory from sociology, anthropology, history, economics, political science and philosophy; and (3) the total cultural setting which supports the educa-

[4] Arthur P. Coladarci, "The Teacher as Hypothesis-Maker," *California Journal for Instructional Improvement*, 2, No. 1 (March 1959), 5.

tional enterprise and which forms the changing milieu wherein the activities represented by the diagram take place. It is the conviction of the authors that educators will be more effective decision makers only when they have a sound understanding of these three foci as well as of the psychological dimensions of their decisions.

THE CHANGING PATTERN OF DECISION MAKING

The work of social historians provides documented evidence that historically, in almost all phases of human activities, decisions, in the form of orders, were handed down from a select few to the many. The imperial command was long the single modus operandi of societies. The accepted mode of behavior for the bulk of the workers in any field was to carry out decisions made by others, in an unquestioning manner and often without any understanding of the reasons for, or probable consequences of, their actions. It was quite simple for behavior thus originated to become the traditional, institutionalized way of doing things. Once part of a culture, the behavior was repeated without specific commands from "above."

For varied and complex reasons this pattern has been more or less modified. Three of the most important reasons for this change away from autocratic decisions have been (1) the significant rise in the general level of education of the population; (2) the tremendous impact of the industrial revolution and the subsequent rise of technological societies, which demand for their effective functioning a great deal of independent judgment applied in new and changing situations; and (3) the slow but steady diffusion of democratic ideas, which include a healthy respect for the intelligence and educability of the "common man."

The changes in the direction of more democratic decision making are supported by the mounting evidence supplied by research in social psychology that speaks in favor of including workers in the making of decisions concerning their work. When decisions are arrived at through cooperative effort, productivity rises, morale improves, and the workers become more strongly committed to the purposes of the organization. Similarly, when teachers have had a hand in determining educational procedures and curricular goals, their morale is higher and they work much harder and with more enthusiasm. By contrast, in an authoritarian setting —where decisions are handed down in a hierarchic structure and where communication is limited and occurs mainly in one direction—morale and productivity tend to be low, and the accumulated resentment and hostility find outlets in various undesirable ways.[5]

As we shall see in Chapter 14, there is a further important consideration we must face on the issue of "decisions handed down from above." It will be made clear in our discussion that professional workers, in whatever profession, constantly face unique problems, which cannot be approached in a fixed, cookbook manner. A professional worker draws upon an increasing body of theory as well as tested procedures in his approach to a current problem. Thus, to the extent that teachers are attempting to become professional workers, they must exercise situational judgments and make decisions in their daily work. Those persons who propose complete uniformity imposed by orders from some central source of authority, which attempts to eliminate or minimize the need for educators to make situational decisions, are working against the achievement of professional maturity by educators, as well as defying the needs of a technological world and the spirit of democratic ideals.

LIMITATIONS OF SCIENTIFIC FINDINGS

We have so far established that educators cannot avoid making decisions. We have also indicated, though briefly, the several components of a decision. For a more thorough understanding, we should now take a new and different look at the role of science and scientific "facts" in this process.

DANGERS OF SCIENTISM

Can we rely on scientific "facts" alone for the making of decisions? If not, what is their relevance to the over-all process?

This point is repeated for emphasis, because the cult of scientism is growing fast in Western civilization. The rallying cry of the cult is that science alone is sufficient to guide our life. The cure for the ills around us is more science. This is a faith no scientist who soundly understands the possibilities and limitations of science should advocate or hold.[6]

The finding of a scientific experiment may illuminate a hitherto dark

[5] While these generalizations are widely accepted by educators, the need for more definitive research is well stated in a summary analysis of existing studies in N. L. Gage, ed., *Handbook of Research on Teaching* (Chicago: Rand McNally & Company, 1963), pp. 781–785.

[6] See John W. N. Sullivan, *The Limitations of Science* (New York: New American Library, 1949).

or obscure set of relationships. Popularly stated, it may give us knowledge. If the experiment is well done, the knowledge or information gained is reliable. Any new bit or body of knowledge, however, makes us aware of the limits of our current knowledge and of the tremendous and apparently expanding areas of our ignorance. Herman Melville, in *Moby Dick,* offers a beautiful and useful analogy. He likens a scientific finding to a lighthouse in a sea of darkness. As each new lighthouse turns on its revealing beam of light, we become aware of a new, vast area of darkness. Similarly, in the educational process, the more we learn about the teaching-learning process, the more we become conscious of its as yet unexplored complexities.

How does man behave in such a predicament? Does he turn his back on this never ending search for reliable knowledge through the sciences? Does he turn to the certainty offered by folklore, by tradition, or by common sense? These latter alternatives, unfortunately, happen all too often. Happily, they are not the only alternatives. The mature person is capable of using the findings of science, though they be incomplete and always tentative. But he needs more than scientific generalizations.

EXAMPLES OF LIMITATIONS

Examples of generalizations which may be valid and reliable yet insufficient for decision making are legion. We can start with almost any of the haunting problems of the current human scene. Physicists offer us a host of generalizations about the atomic structure of matter, and the consequences of the splitting of atoms under various conditions. Do these "facts" readily answer the vexing questions about the possible uses and abuses of atomic energy? We know that millions of persons in the world today are malnourished; at the same time, we know how to produce more than sufficient foodstuffs to feed all human beings everywhere. Has this knowledge enabled us to solve the malnutrition problem? Sociologists and social psychologists have told us why over 40 per cent of our youth drop out before completing high school. Do these reliable "facts" automatically point to a course of action? Children at the age of six, we are told, can learn certain symbolic manipulations referred to as "logic"; does this per se suggest that they *ought* to do so? An infinite number of examples could be offered to support the statement that scientific conclusions alone are insufficient to guide our behavior.

Though patently insufficient to guide our behavior, nevertheless the methods and conclusions of scientific inquiry must play an important role in decision making. We also need various beliefs and assumptions, which we use together with science as we face each problem. The beliefs and assumptions we hold may need to be changed, just as our conclusions based on scientific evidence change. Thus, from time to time, we should reexamine our beliefs and assumptions to ascertain their relevance in light of current conditions. This idea will be further developed after we have seen what beliefs are and how they influence behavior.

THE ROLE OF BELIEFS IN DECISION MAKING

We frequently use expressions like "I believe," "I know that . . . ," "I think" to express varying degrees of conviction. Each of these expressions indicates some degree of readiness to act. A belief refers to a willingness to act. According to Larrabee, "A believer . . . is one who is consciously prepared to accept the risk of action."[7] Beliefs, then, guide behavior—even though some beliefs are fleeting impulses, while others are held firmly and over long periods of time; some are clearly expressed, while others are only incompletely verbalized or not at all.

Technically speaking, philosophers categorize assertions of beliefs under two headings: *synthetic* and *analytic* assertions. A synthetic assertion makes a prediction or description that is, *in principle,* testable in human experience, by means of the methods of scientific inquiry. Examples of synthetic assertions are all around us:

> Mary reads above grade level.
> If it rains on Friday, the game will be postponed.
> Children who study comparative governments will make better citizens than those who do not.
> The team method is more effective than the platoon system in the teaching of junior high school children.
> Harvard University was founded for the purpose of training religious leaders.
> There are no Russians on the moon.

A synthetic assertion may refer to the present, past, or future. *In principle,* each of these beliefs can be investigated in actual situations within a time-space matrix.[8]

[7] Harold A. Larrabee, *Reliable Knowledge* (Cambridge, Mass.: The Riverside Press, 1945), p. 67.

[8] For a systematic development of the meaning of belief and the differences between synthetic and analytic assertions, see H. Gordon Hullfish and Philip Smith, *Reflective Thinking: The Method of Education* (New York: Dodd, Mead & Company, 1961), Chapters 4, 5, 6.

An analytic assertion contains only relationships of meaning among words and other intellectual symbols. Verbal definitions are the most common examples of analytic statements. Note the following examples:

> A gifted child is one who scores 130 or more points on the Stanford-Binet test.
> Man is basically good.
> Parallel lines do not cross.
> Team teaching consists of a hierarchic arrangement of teachers, teacher aids, and clerks who work together with an identifiable group of students.
> Liberal education consists of studying the Great Books, mathematics, and French.
> Individuals are inherently valuable.

The foregoing statements, though they may be very important for certain purposes, cannot be proved or disproved with the methods of science. They either state the meaning of a concept or are part of a conceptual system and derived by logic from some other stated assumptions, postulates, or axioms.

To illustrate the difference between a synthetic and an analytic proposition, let us examine the statement "There are four gifted students in my classroom." Whether or not this is true depends upon prior agreement on the meaning of "giftedness." If we accept the analytic statement that "a gifted child is one who scores 130 or more points on the Stanford-Binet test," then we can proceed to find out whether or not there are four such students in the classroom. The prediction that four gifted students are in the room is a synthetic statement. The truth or falsity of such a statement can be determined only if agreement is first reached on the meaning of giftedness. We cannot find the *meaning* of giftedness by experimentation alone, but observation and experimentation are necessary to test whether or not there are gifted students in this particular room.

The above is a brief discussion of the relevance of both synthetic and analytic statements to the solution of educational problems. Let us also note that both kinds of statements can be true or false. However, the methods of determining their truth or falsity differ significantly. The truth or falsity of synthetic assertions is tested in experience through what is popularly called scientific methodology, whereas the truth or falsity of analytic statements is tested by logical consistency with other accepted assumptions, axioms, or postulates.

As we established previously, educational decisions are not determined entirely by synthetic beliefs supported by facts or scientific findings. The goals we seek, what we consider to be important enough to strive for, what we believe to be the nature and purposes of man, of society, and perhaps even of the universe will influence what we do and how we do it. In light of the rapidly accumulating body of scientific information, however, long-held beliefs often ought to be re-examined and altered. But we still find businessmen who continue to behave in a set pattern because they've "always done things that way." The steady flow of new and proven information from the Department of Agriculture does not change the behavior of certain marginal farmers, who tenaciously cling to the ways of their ancestors in their methods of farming. There are classroom teachers who follow the dictates of tradition, in spite of more appropriate approaches suggested by well-designed and executed research studies.

Even the most careful person acts on the basis of nonscientific beliefs.[9] For example, let us grant that, in general, there is no significant difference in intelligence between males and females. This is a highly useful bit of information. How we use it, however, depends on other information and on some nonscientific beliefs we hold. If we propose that both sexes should have equal opportunities in education and in our occupational structure, our proposal goes beyond the findings of science. It entails certain assumptions concerning the nature of society, the connection between education and society, a conception of the good life and the purposes of man. We cannot escape our presuppositions and our value judgments by a systematic reliance on science. We *can*, however, refashion them. At one period in history, it was accepted by intelligent men that "woman is the unreasoning animal and pokes the fire from on top."[10] Our beliefs concerning women's intelligence must be changed if we are to use science to guide our behavior. We obviously hold other beliefs concerning women. Some fly in the face of scientific evidence; others are major premises underlying the current organization of our society. Still others are, at least for the time being, reasonable, but as yet not verified by scientific evidence. There is no way of knowing whether they ever will be. Although the body of scientific knowledge is growing at a rapidly accelerating pace, it is never complete and, it is safe to assert, never will be. Therefore, decisions will

[9] In order to economize on space, we shall use the expression *scientific beliefs* to indicate synthetic assertions, because they are "grounded" or "proved" by the general methods of science; and the expression *nonscientific beliefs* for analytic assertions, which may be assumptions, postulates, axioms, or other beliefs that are *in principle* not testable by scientific inquiry.

[10] W. James, *Principles of Psychology* (New York: Henry Holt, 1890), Vol. II.

have to be made through reliance on verified information when it is available, and on other sources of knowledge and wisdom when it is not.

CATEGORIES OF BELIEF

Educators, as well as persons in other walks of life, continue to base the conduct of their affairs on various kinds of beliefs. One way to categorize beliefs is by indicating their sources:

1. *Authority.* The truth of a proposition is accepted because a special person or a person in a special office made it. The authoritarian person usually has power, or attempts to use power, to force others to accept his conclusion.

2. *Revelation.* The truth of a statement is accepted because it originated from a supernatural source. There is some variation in the way in which the revelation occurs.

3. *Tradition.* The truth of a statement is established by the claim that "things were always done this way." Other indications of unquestioning reliance on tradition are phrases such as "there is nothing new under the sun" and "if it was good enough for my grandparents, it's good enough for me."

4. *Tenacity* (wishful thinking). The truth of a statement is asserted by a person who is convinced that it will become true if he believes it strongly enough: "It's true because I want it to be true."

5. *Intuition.* The truth of a statement is asserted on the basis of an unanalyzed feeling or hunch, or an "extra sense." This differs from the hunch or intuition of the scientist, who proceeds to test his proposition.

6. *Common Sense.* The truth of a statement is asserted on the basis that it is "obviously so," that "it should be clear to everyone," or that it is the "only natural way of looking at the thing." One must continuously adjust his "common sense," however. It is "common sense" today to speak of the earth's revolving and moving around the sun; yet our eyes and sense of direction seem to indicate that this is not so. We deny the perceptions of our senses as a result of scientific evidence; yet we assert that it is "common sense" to believe the new scientific finding. It is also no longer "common sense" to conceive of the world as flat or to suggest that all fifth graders within a city should be studying multiplication of decimal fractions on May 17.

7. *Rational Analysis.* The truth of a statement is asserted on the basis of systematic analysis of the language used, with regard to (a) the meanings of the words involved, (b) the consistency or inconsistency of

the propositions made, and (c) the reasonableness of the basic premises.

8. *Scientific Method.* The truth of a statement is asserted on the basis of careful, systematic observation and experimentation.

Since there are at least these eight different sources from which people derive their various beliefs, the ultimate validity of any statement is relative to the criteria used to determine its truth or falsity. Educators who work together must agree upon the method or methods they will use in their attempts to determine what is true and what is false. Deliberations will not bear fruit unless substantial agreement is reached on the methods whereby the validity of beliefs is established.

RELATION OF BELIEFS AND THE FINDINGS OF SCIENCE

Granting that both nonscientific beliefs and the offerings of science are relevant to decision making, what is the proper relationship of one to the other? Since *all* the facts are never available in the complex human relationships which make up the educator's arena, he must act while still lacking some facts. Must his action then be arbitrary? This is not the only choice. The recommended course of action would be to rely on a set of beliefs which are *consistent* with the currently available conclusions of science, but of necessity go beyond them. The beliefs held should be subjected to rigorous intellectual analysis. The assumptions upon which they are based need to be clearly understood and the beliefs held should be consistent with each other as well as with the offerings of valid empirical research.

From time to time a re-examination of beliefs would be desirable. Changing conditions, changes in the individual, as well as new scientific evidence, would suggest that it is intelligent behavior to re-examine our beliefs about education. It would appear, then, that well-examined beliefs and the findings of science are organically related. They do not constitute alternative, disjointed directives for behavior. They are, at once, supplementary and dependent upon one another. They help shape each other and, in turn, shape our progress toward an increasingly defensible basis for decision making.

Unless there is a continuous and deliberate re-examination of our beliefs about education in light of the growing offerings of empirical research, on what bases can we proceed? The alternative would be use of the "truths" provided by common sense, untested intuition, revelation, tenacity, or authoritarian imposition of directives. The explicit assumption of the present work, however, has been that intelligent educators in a modern democracy cannot function effectively on any of these platforms. Intelligent decision making in a democratic society requires open, critical examination of ideas and their deliberate reshaping with the aid of modern science.

CULTURAL CONTEXT OF DECISIONS

Decisions do not occur in a vacuum. As a matter of fact, they do not occur as discrete, isolated activities. They are part of the warp and woof of life, and we lift one out here and there in an artificial manner for purposes of analysis. Such a lifting out, such momentary isolation is necessary, for we cannot look at all the factors at the same time in a thorough, systematic fashion. We also know that the component parts of a complex whole will influence each other in various ways. A thorough understanding of a complex phenomenon requires an understanding of the dynamic, functioning whole, of each separate part, and of the relationship of the segments.

Therefore, before we proceed to analyze the specific factors which feed into our decisions, we must stress the overarching cultural setting that constantly influences not only the situations the educator faces, but also his perceptions of them and reactions to them.

SUMMARY

Educators, up and down the organizational ladder of educational institutions, are of necessity decision makers. Their daily work calls for the use of judgment and the exercise of discretion in ever changing situations. In order to make intelligent decisions and be able to explain or defend one's behavior, one needs to evaluate all the major dimensions of decision making. Various kinds of beliefs, as well as scientific information, purposes, values, and assumptions enter this process. All of these factors are necessary for sound decisions. They are, in fact, relatable and, in the best instances, related. Beliefs need to be systematically submitted to rational analysis and modified in light of the best evidence currently offered by empirical research. The continuing processes of education and of decision making occur in varied cultural settings. The processes themselves, as well as the culture supporting and influencing them, must be understood by educators if they are to become more effective participants in them.

SELECTED BIBLIOGRAPHY

Association for Supervision and Curriculum Development. *Learning and the Teacher.* Washington, D.C.: National Education Association, 1959.

Bailey, Stephen K., et al. *Schoolmen and Politics.* Syracuse, N.Y.: Syracuse University Press, 1962.

Barnard, Chester I. "The Environment of Decision," in *The Function of the Executive.* Cambridge, Mass.: Harvard University Press, 1938, pp. 185–199.

Churchman, C. West. *Prediction and Optimal Decision.* Englewood Cliffs, N.J.: Prentice-Hall, Inc., 1961.

Counts, George S. *Decision Making and American Values in School Administration.* New York: Teachers College Bureau of Publications, 1954.

Dahl, Robert A. *Who Governs?* New Haven: Yale University Press, 1961.

Dewey, John. *How We Think.* Boston: D. C. Heath & Company, 1910; revised, 1933.

Griffiths, Daniel E. *Human Relations in School Administration.* New York: Appleton-Century-Crofts, Inc., 1955.

Hullfish, Gordon H., and Philip G. Smith. *Reflective Thinking: The Method of Education.* New York: Dodd, Mead and Company, 1961.

Raup, Bruce R., Kenneth D. Benne, George Axtelle, and Othanel B. Smith. *The Improvement of Practical Intelligence.* New York: Harper & Brothers, 1950.

Schools for the 60's. Report of the Project on Instruction, National Educational Association. New York: McGraw-Hill Book Company, Inc., 1963.

Taba, Hilda. *Curriculum Development: Theory and Practice.* New York: Harcourt, Brace and World, Inc., 1962.

Thelen, Herbert A. *Dynamics of Groups at Work.* Chicago: The University of Chicago Press, 1954.

__________. *Education and the Human Quest.* New York: Harper, 1960.

Willner, Dorothy, ed. *Decisions, Values and Groups,* Reports from the First Interdisciplinary Conference in the Behavioral Science Division held at the University of New Mexico. New York: Pergamon Press, 1960.

CHAPTER 2

EDUCATION AND CULTURE

We have stated that it is necessary to study a culture in order to understand the various functions of education and of educational beliefs as they operate in the cultural context. A brief definition of culture, with its seven basic components, will lay the groundwork for substantiation of that assertion.

DEFINITION OF CULTURE

Culture, states Merrill,[1]

> (1) is the characteristically human product of social interaction; (2) it provides socially acceptable patterns for meeting biological and social needs; (3) it is cumulative as it is handed down from generation to generation in a given society; (4) it is meaningful to human beings because of its symbolic quality; (5) it is learned by each person in the course of his development in a particular society; (6) it is, therefore, a basic determinant of personality; and (7) it depends for its existence upon the continued functioning of the society but it is independent of any individual or group.

Significant to education is the fact that many of the basic components of culture depend upon the educative process for their existence, just as the educative process becomes meaningless without the substance of culture. The handing down of culture from generation to generation is an educative process; the symbolic quality of culture is learned, as culture is learned, by the individual as he grows, develops, and "is educated" into the ways of his particular society. Education, being a process of cultural transmission, is enjoined to pass on cultural values and all of the knowledges

[1] Francis E. Merrill, *Society and Culture: An Introduction to Sociology,* 2nd ed. (Englewood Cliffs, N.J.: Prentice-Hall, Inc., 1961), p. 116. With permission.

and understandings attendant to those values. Education, then, is like the fingers of a hand, at once dependent and yet capable of supplementation.

Malinowski[2] states that "culture comprises inherited artifacts, goods, technical processes, ideas, habits and values." Surely, these are the primary subject matters of education in any society, whether under the direction of formal authority or more simply transmitted from father to son, mother to daughter, group to individual. Thus the educator, whom some have called the cultural "gatekeeper," to understand his task more adequately and to improve the quality of his decisions, needs to have intimate acquaintanceship with the structure and complexities of his culture.

CULTURE AND SOCIETY

C. Wright Mills opens his book *The Power Elite* with the statement that "the powers of ordinary men are circumscribed by the everyday worlds in which they live, yet even in these rounds of job, family, and neighborhood, they often seem driven by forces they can neither understand nor govern."[3] In a far less foreboding way, in order to embark upon an examination of the social basis of educational decisions, we must construct the context which circumscribes the entire adventure of life.

Let us start from the notion that inexorably in this world, human beings will be forced to interact with one another, and this interaction will assume some pattern or system (because it happens regularly) which has both structure and process. This is asserted merely to gain recognition that such an idea is fundamental to the study of cultures and societies and any of their special aspects. The study of cultures and societies means no more or less than an examination of the ways in which people interact, and particularly those ways which produce identifiable, predictable and thus regular behavior. People engaging in significant activities seem to follow certain consistent behavior patterns, and all behaviors which are a part of such patterns make up the whole, the structure of which is called "society," while the dynamic element of it is called "culture."

We have said that a society is a complex of behavior patterns of a given group of human beings who interact with one another, and that this society has structure and process. It was also suggested that human interaction is inevitable because, simply in order to survive and to achieve any

[2] Bronislaw Malinowski, "Culture," in E. R. A. Seligman, ed., *The Encyclopedia of the Social Sciences* (New York: The Macmillan Co., 1930), p. 621.

[3] C. Wright Mills, *The Power Elite* (New York: Oxford University Press, 1957), p. 3.

ends or goals, human beings must have some kind of relationship with others of their kind. No man can live without becoming an item in his environment. He is a regular customer at the cleaners, a sale to the merchant, and an occupied seat in a theater. Motorists will slow down for him in the street, and dogs will bark at him as he passes in the night. Should he depart, his absence would be felt by the newsboy and the postman on his route, and there would be a vacancy where he lived. We are, of course, speaking of average people who intend to live, reproduce if possible, and remain on earth. We suggest, therefore, that human society sees some value in survival and achievement. There is "value" because people *choose* to survive and achieve. All human societies are, in this sense, value-oriented. All societies are, therefore, alike in this way. Differentiation between one society and another can be measured by the differences in value orientations and their subsequent implementing decisions. A group of interacting human beings in Tasmania develops a distinctive value system which is different in some specific ways from the value system evolved by a group in New Mexico. A subgroup in Greenwich Village may differ sharply from the Dartmouth crowd. Local perception, then, influences the specific nature of values, for a value orientation is a particular set of criteria a group uses to respond to its environment and to make choices on how to achieve its ends and its survival. The dynamic functions involved are called "the culture."

Obviously, then, cultures differ. But if we all accept the primary value of survival—and there is considerable evidence that most cultures try to survive—then the people in any culture find it necessary to engage in certain basic activities. For example, they must obtain food and shelter. Also, they must construct some rules governing their relationships with one another as they pursue the enterprise of seeking food and shelter. Both the functions and the rules tend to become fixed, in order that the culture may have some stability.

INSTITUTIONS

As the group attains greater complexity through its desire to achieve a greater diversity of ends, the fixed functions and rules become even more necessary, and thus become "institutionalized." This is to say that patterns of behavior, appropriate to certain functions or rules, become predictable and can be evoked consistently if normal conditions prevail. The people engaged in a particular institutionalized function can correctly predict certain behavior on their own part, and can have equal expectations of their colleagues who are similarly engaged, with the further knowledge that this behavior will normally be perceived as "right" and useful to the basic existence of the culture in which they live. The great majority of the group, therefore, reasons that such institutionalized behavior is "normal" and that any major violation of the expected pattern of behavior would, in some fashion, impair the achievement of the culture's values. Such a comfortable belief tends to stabilize human relationships within a culture, for any major change in institutionalized behavior would of necessity imply a prior change in the culture's basic value orientation. And basic value orientations, as history will testify, are slow to change, having evolved gradually out of common needs and goals.

A culture, then, has institutions and therefore a culture defines a great deal of human behavior. Malinowski points out that "a pure-blooded Negro infant, transported to France and brought up there, would differ profoundly from what he would have been if reared in the jungle of his native land. He would have been given a different social heritage: a different language, different habits, ideas, and beliefs; he would have been incorporated into a different social organization and cultural setting."[4] A culture defines the manner in which people will do the things that maintain the culture. The culture defines limits for behavior which are never consciously in violation of its basic goals and values. For a culture perpetuates itself by so ordering enough of existence that the values of succeeding generations will be those nurtured in the confines of the present culture.

It is this final process, the nurturing of the future, which is education, and education is therefore an institutionalized function in any culture. As Spindler has said: ". . . education is a continuous process, beginning at birth and operating with cumulative intensity as the child grows, develops, and learns to live in the symbolic world of his group traditions and to participate in the social order of which he is a member."[5] The outward trappings of the process of education may differ considerably from society to society, but the structure of education is everywhere based upon the same end—the perpetuation of the particular culture and its basic value system. The aim of education, then, is to produce human beings who, at best, will perpetuate and improve the present culture, or who, at worst, will not destroy the culture and its values, for "culture is idealized in the educative process."[6]

4 Malinowski, "Culture" (see note 2).

5 George D. Spindler, ed., *Education and Anthropology* (Stanford, Calif.: Stanford University Press, 1955), p. viii. With permission.

6 Spindler, *Education and Anthropology,* p. 14.

There are, naturally, other institutions that have evolved out of the needs of a society to survive. E. Merle Adams, Jr.,[7] identifies eight institutions commonly observed in the local community system: kinship (or family), occupation, exchange, property, authority, stratification, religion, and education. Education is, of course, the eighth institution on his list.

These institutions are not mere accumulations of men and women; neither do they exist in splendid isolation from one another—although observers, because of their particular interest in one such institution, often treat other institutions as if they existed in separate compartments. Thus, people will say, "You educators want this or that," as if they themselves were not a part of the institutionalized function of education. Or conversely, some school people will say, "Teaching is not an occupation, but a way of life," as if teachers could somehow survive outside the limits of other social institutions.

As Adams's definitions[8] make clear, each institution has fundamental interrelationships with all other institutions in both structure and process.

> 1. *Kinship or family* takes account of the basic human factors of age, sex, biological relatedness, and the considerable care necessitated by the helplessness and plasticity of the newborn child.
> 2. *Occupation* refers to the organization of work or "job" roles in the community.
> 3. *Exchange* represents the manner in which things of value are regularly transferred from one individual or group to another.
> 4. *Property* refers to the way in which individuals or groups hold and exercise rights in things of value.
> 5. *Authority* refers to the recognized right exercised by certain individuals in controlling or influencing the behavior of other individuals.
> 6. *Stratification* refers to the differential distribution of prestige among persons in the community.
> 7. *Religion* refers to the pattern of beliefs and rites to which community members adhere.

The institution of education has dependent interrelationships with all of these other institutionalized functions.

A clear avenue of inquiry into the nature of any of these institutions is suggested by Brim:

[7] E. Merle Adams, Jr., "New Viewpoints in Sociology," in Roy A. Price, ed., *New Viewpoints in the Social Sciences,* 28th Yearbook, National Council for the Social Studies (Washington, D.C.: National Education Association, 1958), pp. 101–103. With permission.

[8] Adams, *New Viewpoints,* p. 103.

> The five major problems in institutional analysis might be described as follows. First, an institutionalized activity (such as education) is designed to achieve certain ends for its members and/or for society at large or its sub-groups, and hence is regulated toward the pursuit of institutionalized aims. Second, natural resources (money and other goods) must be allocated to the institution as a whole from those available to society, and subsequently, must be allocated within the institution. Third, personnel must be recruited into the institution to carry out the activities necessary to achieve the aims. Fourth, the appropriate attitudes and behavior for the members of the institution must be specified and the performance of those roles assured. Finally, the institutional activity has results in fact, both for members and for society, which may or may not be recognized and which may or may not be consonant with the avowed aims.[9]

SUBCULTURES

If the aim of a society is to perpetuate itself and achieve certain ends, then it systematically allocates materials, personnel, roles, and functions to accomplish these aims. Subgroups, or individuals within the society, find themselves so allocated in some way to more than one institution, and are, in the process of living, involved in the interdependent relationships between institutions. As a person is inducted into various roles in various institutions, he follows certain behavior patterns, not merely out of conformity to authority, but because he too possesses the values of the culture which created the institutions. "The goals, motivations to secure and express the goals and the ways of attaining them, are internalized by the individual as they are transmitted to him by the *agents* of culture (parents, teachers, elders, etc.) so that he supports and behaves within the norms of the culture as though they were his own."[10]

Definition. Naturally, these "agents" of the culture also have a location in time and space, so we must now conceive of American culture as having some distinctive subcultures and a persuasive element of local perception. A subculture may be defined as a group within the main culture which displays in its organized or patterned behavior some elements which differentiate it from the main cultural pattern sufficiently to be recognized as a special subgroup. Such things as language, race, occupational pattern, or religion may cause a group to exhibit the characteristics

[9] Orville G. Brim, Jr., *Sociology and the Field of Education* (New York: Russell Sage Foundation, 1958), pp. 12–13. With permission.

[10] George D. Spindler, "New Trends and Applications in Anthropology," in *New Viewpoints in the Social Sciences* (see note 7), p. 135.

of a subculture. Local perception, on the other hand, may not be sufficiently different from the national cultural pattern to warrant the title of "subculture," but it may, and usually does, reflect some peculiarities which have local origins, which are products of the very particular response of a given community to its environment. These particular responses often have a distinct influence on the educational process.

THE PROBLEM OF COMMUNITY

What is a community? What is its relationship to a total society? Where are the borders, the barricades that separate local from regional, regional from national, national from international?

Kingsley Davis[11] suggested that a definition of community must include both physical and social criteria. He attempted to define community in terms of territorial proximity and social completeness. Territorial proximity refers to various clusters of residences. A particular community is defined as those residences which are closer to its center cluster than to any other such cluster. Accepting this, we see that communities have geographical relationship because people need to interact and seem to find it desirable to cluster together geographically in order to interact more conveniently. Social completeness describes the ability to embrace all aspects of social life, to include all of the major institutions, all of the statuses and interests, that make a society. "A community," Davis concludes, "is the smallest local (geographical) group that can be, and often is, a complete society."

It is difficult, in the light of conditions in the 1960s, to accept Davis's definition of community at face value. Since World War II, the "expanding metropolis" and the blooming of suburbia have dislocated the concepts of both territorial proximity and social completeness. Urban development clashes with any concept of social completeness, and old concepts of community must wither away under the impact of an exploding population which is both mobile and increasingly urban. For example, is Evanston, Illinois, a community in itself, or a suburb of Chicago? Are the peninsula towns south of San Francisco separate communities or merely bedrooms for the larger urban center? Where does New York City end?

A man works for a company in the heart of Chicago. He lives in Glencoe. His friends are his company associates and their wives and children, and his interests are surely influenced by what happens during his

[11] Kingsley Davis, *Human Society* (New York: Macmillan, 1948), pp. 310–312.

working hours. But his associates may live in Oak Park, Skokie, or Des Plains. His relationship to the institutions of his society are thus spread out over the entire urban center, and he has little intimate identification with this broad and highly complex unit called Chicago. What is community to this man? He works in one area, lives in another, socializes in still others. He travels to and from work with strangers, and he cannot recognize his neighbors. When he and his friends discuss the education of their children, they may be talking about school systems which are miles and miles apart with almost nothing in common, each operating without knowledge of the other. Yet the very nature of this urban complex may make its inhabitants have perceptions of cultural values different from those people who live, say, in New Mexico, or along the South Carolina coast. What those perceptions are and how they differ is, of course, a complex problem. But certainly the consummate fragmentation of the big metropolis is the reason why urban sociology is "probably the most unclearly defined of all the sociological fields."[12]

As the concept of "community" becomes indistinguishable, other perspectives, dependent upon a clear definition of community, waver and are often discarded as no longer useful tools for examining society. Warner's social-class research, for example, seems particularly susceptible to revaluation, since, before a researcher can stratify a community along Warner's social-class lines, the "community" must hold still long enough to be examined, and, indeed, it must be a living, definable, identifiable body. The only way out, of course, is to redefine "community" and in the process admit that people who live in the same general area may have similar perceptions, and that these perceptions may differ in some degree from those of people elsewhere. It follows, then, that children who go to school in one area receive their perceptions of cultural values from their particular environment. If that environment is changed by a move to another place, there can be a change of perception. The school's franchise for the transmission of cultural values is therefore complicated, and the first major task educators face, as the lid of our Pandora's box is opened, is to decide how we select and implement the *crucial* attitudes, behaviors, knowledge, and skills demanded by our total society and, at the same time, recognize that local perceptions will be at work to modify those all-culture values, as will the distinct characteristics of subcultures.

[12] Noel P. Gist, "The Urban Community," in J. B. Gittler, ed., *Review of Sociology* (New York: John Wiley and Sons, Inc.), p. 159.

INTEREST GROUPS

As we narrow our focus from the total culture to subcultures to local perception, we approach the "real life" of the institution of education. At the point of application, it is clear that education is a local affair, pulsating on a local level in considerable collaboration with the particular visions of individuals, neighborhoods, and, most influentially, *special-interest groups.* R. M. MacIver has pointed the way in the analysis of interest groups.[13]

When each individual in a group pursues a personal interest, which, however, is similar to that of every other member of the group (for instance, in an occupation such as teaching), MacIver calls it a *like* interest. On the other hand, when all of the group pursue one single comprehensive interest (such as the success of some group enterprise), MacIver would call that a *common* interest.

He goes on to make further distinctions. When several persons pursue personal or discrete interests which differ in type, we have *unlike* interests. A plumber and a teacher, for instance, have unlike interests. Between the extremes of like and unlike interests are *complementary* interests, which are partly alike and partly unlike. These interests of two or more individuals, while not wholly similar, nevertheless are interrelated and call for reciprocal service—as in teaching and, say, school administration. But when two or more individuals pursue some goal that only *one* of them can attain, then we have *conflicting* interests. Finally, some goals can be obtained only—or at least more efficiently—through cooperative acts. These goals, MacIver asserts, develop *concordant* interests.

MacIver, then, is admitting that "community" is a matter of degree within some loose territorial boundaries. The unifying agent is interests. Various communities may exist within a territory, one overlapping another, one tangent to one, and others superimposed, until there may even be the possibility of discovering some matrix of community interests. Institutional relationships are interwoven and interdependent with such community interests, and the various interest groupings have social relationship and influence upon each other as well as upon institutions, which are, of course, the common elements.

In other words, people living in a society may have widely different interests because of factors such as sex, age, or occupational specialty.

[13] R. M. MacIver, "Classes of Social Interest," in V. F. Calverton, ed., *The Making of Society* (New York: The Modern Library, Random House, Inc., 1937), pp. 681–684. With permission.

Society in part integrates these differences, but specialized interests are fundamental to people, each according to some special differentiating principle. Interestingly enough, such groupings can both support and disrupt the institutions to which all people need to conform. When special interest groups tend to support societal institutions, they enrich and strengthen those institutions. When they clash with institutions, they force individuals to erect a hierarchy and thereby diminish discord. If the resolution of disagreements between special interest groups and society's institutions proves impossible, social disorganization results.

Angell[14] injects a moral note into his discussion of the decline of the community when he points out that now individuals have little "sense of obligation to local community standards," since such standards are increasingly difficult to identify, due to the lack of definition of a "community." "A man may feel the direct influence of his family or his church," says Angell, but he can lose himself in a group and excuse himself from responsibility for the group's actions, just as the group may disclaim responsibility for the actions of one of its members. Coupled with each individual's inability to have first-hand knowledge of the behaviors of all possible interest groups operating within the broad community, a certain degree of moral disintegration seems almost inevitable. Thomas and Znaniecki[15] conclude that ". . . society is gradually losing all its old machinery for the determination and stabilization of individual characters."

The notable exceptions to this pattern seem to be occupations which traditionally have been highly stereotyped. Such occupations are apparently little influenced by social upheaval, and people engaged in such occupations continue to be primarily governed by the stereotype. Doctors, schoolteachers, nurses, and clergymen are surely examples of occupations which kindle patterned responses.

It is clear, then, that any current considerations of "community" must call attention to the increasing significance of interest groupings as they operate in the determination of social policy. Institutions of a society are no longer the result of the hammering out of common goals in a community or town meeting. Rather they are the net result of the interplay of power among a variety of special interest groupings. In MacIver's structure, institutional behavior is the product of common interests, or concordant,

[14] Robert Angell, "The Decline of the Local Community," in William O. Stanley et al., eds., *Social Foundations of Education* (New York: The Dryden Press, 1956), p. 89.

[15] W. I. Thomas and Florian Znaniecki, "Building Stable Character in a Multigroup Society," in William O. Stanley et al., eds., *Social Foundations of Education* (see note 14), pp. 100–101.

like, discrete interests. For the institution of education, this observation has a special meaning.

IMPACT OF FRAGMENTATION ON EDUCATION

If the aims of education are to be determined by the society, and the institution of education must evolve from those culturally determined aims and goals, the personnel, the material resources and the appropriate attitudes and behavior for members of the institution are also dependent upon the collaboration of all the elements of a society which can determine or influence social policy. The translation of social policy into viable classroom experiences is therefore a complex and difficult task. If the climate of opinion in the society is foggy, a corresponding haze envelops education. If the pavilions of the culture resound with controversy, the echo is soon heard in the hallways of the schools. Education, in other words, cannot pursue some narrow course to fulfillment, impervious to the stresses and strains of the society which sponsors its existence. The fable of the ivory tower with leaves of ivy is precisely a myth, a storybook concept conscripted from fairyland, where elves and goblins live apart, guided by another destiny or dark energy incomprehensible to men.

Education, then, is both a process and a product of culture. "A culture," states Lewin, "is not a static affair but a live process, like a river which moves but still keeps a recognizable form."[16] Siegel[17] found this analogy useful when he proposed an educational-process model to show the "variety of converging forces" which educate a child.

The value systems which motivate each of Siegel's channels originate in the structure and process of the general society. Channel 3, "The Home," reflects the patchwork of interest groups and interrelationships of which the home is a part. Channel 2, "Peer Groups and Cliques," is drenched with the influence of every conceivable combination of social forces reflected in the student body of an average school. Channel 1, "Educational Institutions," by definition is a selected pattern of behaviors and attitudes promulgated by whatever strident forces are in ascendancy in the total society. Each of the channels has direction and purpose, although conflicts

[16] Kurt Lewin, as quoted in Bernard J. Siegel, "Models for the Analysis of the Educative Process in American Communities," in George D. Spindler, ed., *Education and Anthropology* (see note 5), p. 45.

[17] Siegel (see note 16), p. 46. Figure 2–1, from Siegel's article, is reprinted with the permission of the publishers, Stanford University Press. © Copyright 1955 by the Board of Trustees of the Leland Stanford Junior University.

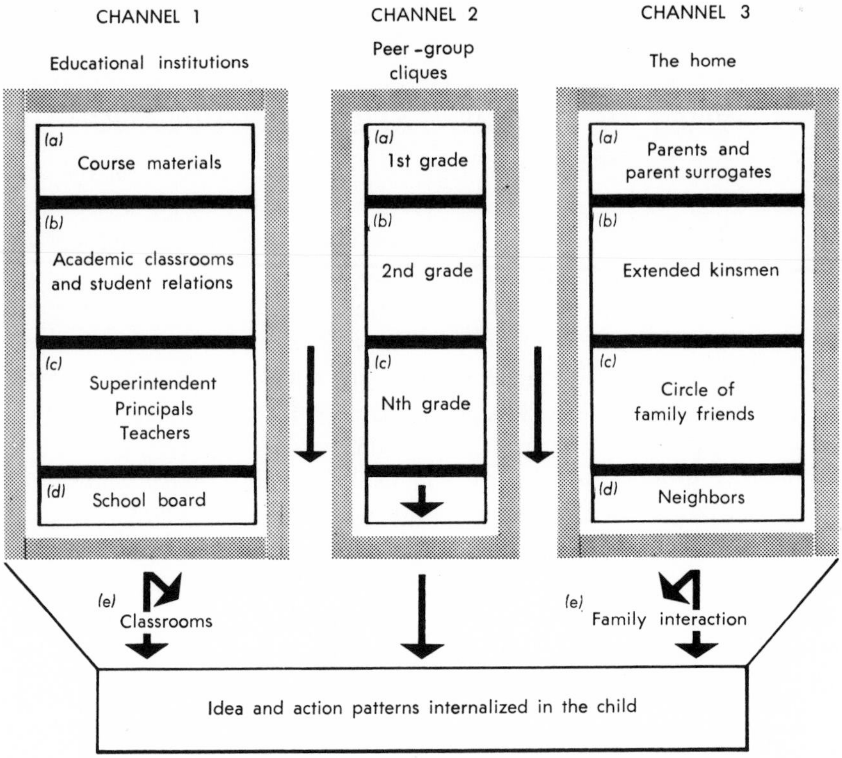

LEGEND:
1. Solid lines within each channel mark off sections through which cultural content must pass
2. Arrows indicate the direction of stimuli and socio-cultural forces
3. Small letters indicate sections within the channel

may exist between channels and within channels. All in all, in a complex society, the process of education is a labyrinth of pressures and counter pressures, only raftered by some vague common goals or basic framework of common belief in order that the society may continue to exist.

The urgent dilemma confronting American education, operating as it is in the most complex of all complex societies, is the problem of selecting the appropriate timbers for its primary structure. Stanley[18] states:

> It is exceedingly difficult to establish or to maintain a consistent program of education in a society characterized by fundamental confusion and conflict. For, in such societies, there is no conclusive standard of the public welfare, and hence, no certain conception of the kind of character

[18] William O. Stanley, "The Present Dilemma of Education," in Stanley, *Social Foundations* (see note 14), p. 442.

which the school should undertake to build. Consequently, the educator has no clear definition of the ends and purposes of education which is generally acknowledged or taken for granted by all parties to the educational enterprise. Moreover—and for the same reason—there is no common perception of the function and role of the school or of the nature and scope of pedagogical authority. Obviously in constructing a consistent program of study and instruction for the public schools, the educational profession cannot ignore the confusion and conflict in the contemporary culture nor can it arbitrarily impose either a common set of values or a unified way of life on the society which it serves.

Encircled by bonfires of feelings concerning the aims of education, which Butts[19] has identified as "to fit the individual into his culture; to pass on the heritage; to make good citizens for the state; to achieve salvation for the soul; to develop character; to train the intellect; to develop the whole personality; to prepare for earning a living; to develop the individual's capacities; to develop critical thinking; to develop social responsibility; and to aid in social change," the wary educator soon realizes that each aim or combination of aims may mean a variety of things to a variety of people. He may inquire, as Alice asked the Cheshire Cat:

> "Would you tell me, please, which way I ought to go from here?"
>
> "That depends a good deal on where you want to get to," said the Cat.
>
> "I don't much care where . . ." said Alice.
>
> ". . . so long as I get somewhere," Alice added as an explanation.
>
> "Oh, you're sure to do that," said the Cat, "if you only walk long enough."

But Alice as educator cannot merely walk along. Her questions need answers. Brim[20] begins to approach the problem when he states:

> While the descriptive study of the objectives of education held by different groups may seem of little importance, there are at least two ways in which such information would be of value. First, the descriptive data are a necessary foundation for research on the relation of aims to other aspects of the culture—and for research on intra-institutional relations—Second, by virtue of the fact that educational aims reflect one's values, express his fundamental beliefs regarding the desirable attributes of man, such descriptive data provide an insight into the basic values held by society's members. It is an extremely sad commentary on current social science

19 R. Freeman Butts, *A Cultural History of Western Education,* 2nd ed. (New York: McGraw-Hill Book Co., 1955), p. 5.

20 Brim (see note 9), p. 21.

> that we know almost nothing of the aspirations of man for the kind of person he wants to become, and wants his children to become. Even the literature on socialization, where one would expect to find these facts, has emphasized the description of parent behavior and presents fewer than a half-dozen studies of the characteristics parents desire for their children.

Some tentative propositions on the objectives of American education have been made, based upon either logical reality or primary research. Many other propositions exist, obviously, but they are often stated with glib optimism and alarming naïveté, or are perched upon generalization levels which are so abstract as to be utterly meaningless. To build a proper argument, it seems necessary to examine further the questions surrounding values, which we shall do in Chapter 3.

FORMAL AND INFORMAL ASPECTS OF EDUCATION

The institution of education has both its formal and informal aspects, a fact that may account for some measure of the existing conflicts. *Informal education,* or all those aspects of the socialization process which occur outside of the formal school, accounts for a wide range of differences in the educational process. The variations in child-rearing practices, the child's response to his particular environment and all its various components—the social, political, economic, and psychological atmospheres in which he lives—all are part of his informal education.

In addition, there is the *formal educational process,* or *schooling,* provided, even required, by the society to promote systematic transmission of all of the knowledge and values attendant to the culture. In an open, democratic society, the extent of such an assignment is staggering, and would be impossible if it were not for the general but shaky agreement that the professionals who inhabit the institution shall have primary responsibility for attempting to organize such knowledge and values into a manageable sequence of learning. Schools in the United States are organized in a sequence to educate children from as early as age five through the doctoral degree. The common pattern of state laws requiring school attendance covers ages seven to seventeen. Schools in the United States are both private and public. Public schools are supported by taxation of the entire population at local, state, and federal levels. Private schools support their particular interests by drawing upon tuition fees, grants from like-minded people, or levies upon all members of the group which created the school. Often, private schools are aided by government in that they are exempted from normal property or corporate taxes usually levied upon private enterprises. Tax exemption is, in these cases, the real equivalent of cash support, as any nonexempt organization will be quick to testify. Public schools operate in self-governing units and their governing boards, usually elected by the general society, have legislative, executive, and in some cases, even judicial powers which have the full impact of law. Autonomous as this may seem to be, schools are nevertheless completely enmeshed in the fabric of social-policy decision making and must, therefore, conform to the same procedures found in the decision-making processes of other social institutions.

THE HISTORY OF SCHOOLING

How all of this came about is another long and interesting tale. The curious student will find innumerable sources he will want to investigate.[21] It is enough to say here that education as a function of social organization began in the most primitive of societies, for it was necessary to the preservation of tribal folkways and culture. As social organizations grew more complex, as more and more societies required systematic organization because of increasingly complex technology and the development of language, there developed bodies of knowledge and doctrine which needed transmission in an organized fashion. As youth needed more training to cope with the world and as a society developed the need for more systematic inculcation of the technology and doctrines it had developed, informal educative procedures gave way to formalized education, or schooling.

But it was soon discovered that there is an intimate relationship between education and social control. The man who was educated was the man who possessed vitally needed skills, and the man who possessed the needed skills was soon the man of power. A man's power in society was directly related to the degree of skill he possessed or the need the society had for his skill. Thus, men in power in societies recognized early that a substantial portion of their power rested upon their possession of the fruits of education, and history well records their reaction to this insight. Men in power, wanting to perpetuate that power and the privileges which accompanied it, began to limit access of education to all those outside their power

[21] See Butts (note 19); R. Freeman Butts and Lawrence A. Cremin, *A History of Education in American Culture* (New York: Holt, Rinehart and Winston, 1953); and Robert Ulich, ed., *The Education of Nations* (Cambridge, Mass.: Harvard University Press, 1961).

group. By limiting access to education, they automatically limited access to power, to the ruling class, to the priesthood, or whatever group possessed final power in a particular society.

One of the essentials of Plato's ideal state was differential access to education. Only the ruling group, the Guardians, were to have full access—and yet even they were to be restricted from considering some aspects of knowledge—while the Warriors were to have only military preparation, the Freemen vocational training, and the slaves no education at all. Plato is clear in his argument that unrestricted access to education for the general population means unrestricted access to power, and he argued further that in a society where there is unlimited access to power, political stability is an impossibility; therefore, such a state cannot be ideal.

Formal education, therefore, was restricted to privileged groups in societies for many, many centuries. During the middle ages, access to education was largely restricted to the priesthood, and since theological dogma was in the main fixed, the evolution of Western societies seemed to grind to a halt, until the excesses of this system brought about an inevitable reaction. What started primarily as a theological question, the right of the priesthood to interject themselves between man and God, spawned a social and educational revolution. When Protestants insisted upon a direct relationship between man and God and His Holy Word, they set loose the power of education, for a man must learn to read if he is going to interpret the Bible for himself. But once a man has learned to read, *all* written language is available to him, and discovering this, he is limited in his educational potential only by his own capacity and the materials available to him.

As Western civilization bloomed in the Renaissance and Reformation periods, so did formal education; for there were now many who sought knowledge, and the social changes required a more broadly educated and sophisticated populace. Commerce, now burgeoning, needed workers who could use their heads as well as their hands. Even the church needed to recruit greater numbers to send to the far corners of the earth, to propagate the faith. Everywhere, the needs of societies were pressing for increased education.

While advanced formal education was still largely restricted to the privileged, now economically as well as politically privileged, the case for a basic rudimentary education for the general population had gained sufficient footholds never to be displaced. In the United States, although education was still a luxury and was severely controlled by the alliance of religious and political power, the conception of universal education had been born. Thomas Jefferson, in his *Bill for the More General Diffusion of*

Knowledge (1779), had argued that only when people in general are educated can tyranny be prevented. A democracy is dependent upon wise legislation to maintain itself, and wise legislation cannot come from unenlightened or uneducated peoples. James Madison wrote: "A popular Government, without popular information, or the means of acquiring it, is but a Prologue to a Farce or a tragedy or, perhaps both. Knowledge will forever govern ignorance; and a people who mean to be their own Governors, must arm themselves with the power which knowledge gives." These clear statements of the vital link between democracy and mass formal schooling constitute one of America's most authentic contributions to Western civilization, and the success this alliance has enjoyed is unparalleled.

These simple statements of principle were, of course, not enough to overcome the opposition of those who had for centuries restricted access to education. The chronicles of Horace Mann in Massachusetts and Henry Barnard in Connecticut give us ample illustration of the monumental struggle which occured as the principles began to be turned into practice. For Mann and Barnard, as well as other leaders, faced the bitter opposition of both powerful religious groups and political-economic pressure groups. Religious organizations had long ago recognized the need to control education if what they considered "secularism" was to be excluded. Political-economic pressure groups opposed mass education because it threatened both their power and their pocketbooks. Even a cursory glance at the history of American education indicates that neither side has ever won a clear-cut victory, even though mass education has clearly established itself as an integral part of American culture. But the debate over the separation of Church and State as applied to education still persists today, and public mass education must constantly fight for its existence as political conservatives question its need, and economic conservatives challenge its expenditures. The low prestige and rewards system often accorded modern educators in the United States may be traced back directly to the same essential groups which first opposed the installation of mass education in our society. Their continued opposition has always had a significant impact upon the degree of support granted mass formal schooling.

THE ORGANIZATION OF SCHOOLS

Despite such opposition, almost every American child today has the opportunity to attend a free public school from the first through the twelfth grades, or schooling from approximately his sixth or seventh to his seventeenth or eighteenth year. Almost all land in the United States, excepting Federal and State lands, lies within the boundaries of an organized school district and is therefore subject to taxation for the support of the public schools located within the district. Each of these nearly 40,000 school districts is controlled by the voters residing in the district, and, in accordance with the principle of representative government, is usually administered by an elected lay board of trustees of three to seven members. Pittenger suggests the following sketch of the organization of local school districts in the United States, although some districts may not provide all of the services that his sketch implies:

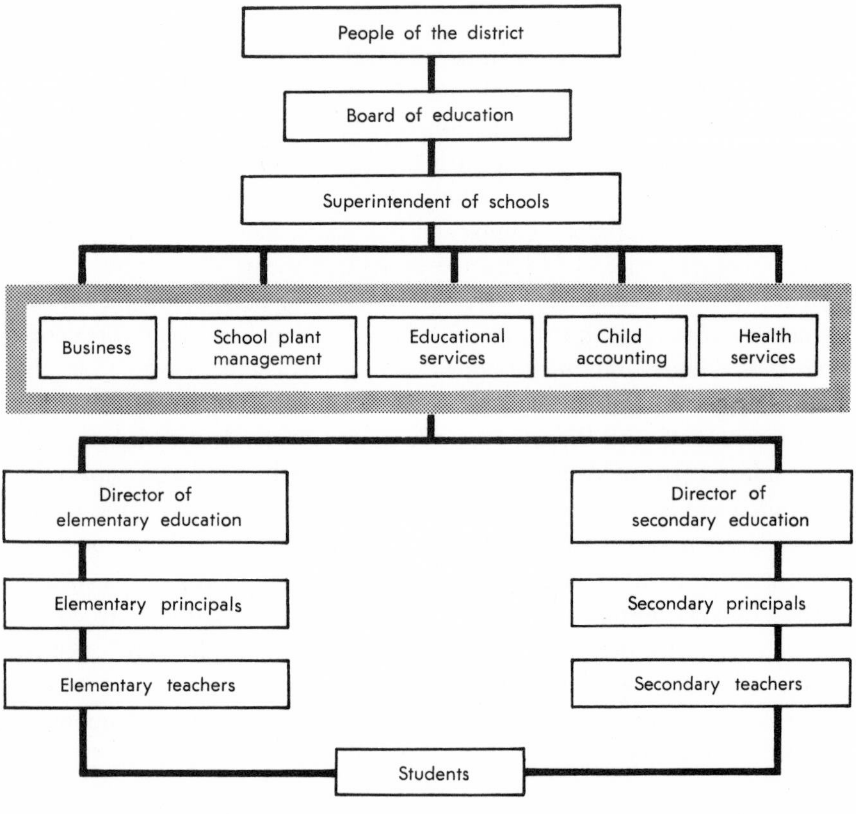

From Benjamin F. Pittenger, *Local Public School Administration* (New York: McGraw-Hill Co., Inc., 1951), p. 47. With permission. Note that the power of decision flows from the top of the chart downward. If one perceives the main business of education as the transactions between students and teachers, the distance between such transactions and the source of decision-making power raises some interesting questions.

In some parts of the United States, elementary schools are not under the same administration as secondary schools. In such cases, a specific plot of land may be under the separate jurisdiction and taxation of an elementary school district, a secondary school district, and even a junior college district. Such arrangements reflect the evolution of public education from widespread acceptance of the need for elementary education to recognition of the need for secondary education to the current trend toward public provision for junior colleges. Currently, efforts are widespread to unify the different levels of schooling into single administrative and tax-fixing units.

The pattern of schooling developed in the United States assigned the first eight years to the elementary schools, and the next four years to the secondary schools. This arrangement has often been modified until the most common pattern today is to conclude elementary at the end of the sixth year. This pattern often includes a pre-first-grade year of kindergarten, and some school districts even provide nursery schools. After elementary school, there is a junior high school of two or three years, covering the designated seventh and eighth grades; in the three-year junior high school, the ninth grade is included. High school is then either ninth through twelfth or tenth through twelfth. United States schools have maintained the grade organization in name, although many schools are now recognizing that the single criterion of age upon which the grade system is based does not adequately provide for the wide range of abilities found within a given age group. Not all ten-year-olds, for example, are equally able; therefore, a typical fifth grade must deal with content material which may have been designed for as low as an average first grader and each subsequent level to as high as an average ninth grader. As more professional educators recognize the organizational implications of children's individual differences, and as the educators receive approval from the public, so organizational patterns will change.

EDUCATION AND CULTURAL CHANGE

While changes in the theories and practices of educators may affect the organization of public schools in the United States, changes within the culture are occuring all the time and are thereby modifying the process of education. A modern literate culture is in a constant state of flux as new challenges call for new responses. This dynamic quality, characteristic of all cultures, is more apparent in literate cultures, and the changes come quickly since the mechanisms are available to effect changes rapidly. Nonliterate cultures, lacking the complexity and available change mechanisms, tend to change more slowly, but when changes occur they are often major upheavals, in response to some dire change in the environment. Nonliterate cultures are not as prone to make changes of their own volition for, like the Navajo, they have institutionalized and ritualized so many facets of the simple status quo, that change comes painfully. The Navajo regard present survival as proof that they are "in tune" with nature, so change must mean getting "out of tune" with nature, or getting "back in tune" if survival under present conditions seems impossible. Such religious adherence to the perpetuation of the specific structures and functions of a culture makes change difficult.

Literate societies, with their level of complexity extended far beyond that of nonliterate ones, have infinite possibilities for the making of adjustments to the realities of life. Changes can be made quickly and often easily and are, therefore, characteristically a series of small changes rather than major revolutions. To understand theories of cultural change, it may be useful here to introduce the idea of all cultures being engaged in what has been termed the basic functions of human living. Briefly, these functions, which span the basic social institutions and are engaged in by all cultures in all times, give us a more specific focus on *what* changes in a culture.

Basic Functions of Human Living

1. Protecting and conserving life, resources, and property
2. Producing, distributing, and consuming goods and services
3. Transporting people and goods
4. Communicating ideas and feelings
5. Providing education
6. Providing recreation
7. Organizing and governing
8. Expressing spiritual and esthetic impulses
9. Creating new tools and techniques

THEORIES OF CULTURAL CHANGE

Studies in cultural change tend to fall into three major approaches. The first theory, a cyclical theory, proposes that changes occur in cycles at three different levels or orders: (1) material changes; (2) nonmaterial; (3) changes which are a composite of both material and nonmaterial.

In a modern literate culture, each of these basic functions has become highly complex, and an intricate network of relationships exists between the systems and institutions developed around each basic function. Thus, a comparatively minor change in one function—say, the development of jet aircraft—changes the patterns of transportation and, like the proverbial stone in the pool of water, begins to change activities associated with other functions.

It is appropriate here to introduce another useful scheme, which may clarify the process of cultural change. The *cultural pyramid* proposes to demonstrate that the base of any culture lies in the basic tools it employs to wrest its living from its natural environment:

> Then, layer by layer, the cultural pyramid builds on this base, through the development of techniques and processes of production, to social, political and economic arrangements, through an emerging and powerful climate of opinion concerning many aspects of life, to a final capstone of values which then permeate the total pyramid and regulate human behavior in the society.[22]

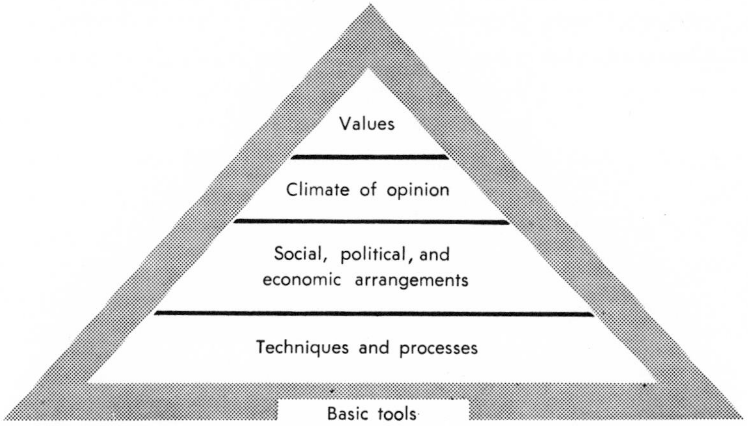

Cultural Pyramid. From I. J. Quillen and Lavonne Hanna, as modified in Sowards and Scobey (see note 22), p. 102.

The cyclical theory, therefore, asserts that first-order changes are most influential.

Herbert Spencer, the nineteenth-century sociologist, asserted a different theory. He regarded change as a uniform, gradual, and progressive *evolutionary* process. Implicit in his theory was the idea of progress, which implied that change always moves toward a more desirable state. Many

[22] G. Wesley Sowards and Mary-Margaret Scobey, *The Changing Curriculum and the Elementary Teacher* (Belmont, Calif.: Wadsworth Publishing Co., Inc., 1961), pp. 102–103.

social scientists have rejected Spencer's biologically oriented theory on the grounds that science cannot possibly support the crucial value position inherent in the theory.

Lester Ward, an early American sociologist, contended that man, as an intelligent being, is not hopelessly trapped in a preordained evolutionary process, but rather can guide change toward desirable ends. John Dewey carried Ward's assertions further with his insistence that cultural change could and should be *purposive.* That is, cultural change could be the result of applied intelligence so that there would be planned direction of the natural and social forces toward the achievement of some purpose. This latter theory has had much currency in the twentieth century, and in the United States it is not uncommon to find the government or other agencies deliberately interceding to promote change in an agreed-upon direction. Certainly, such activities as flood control, mass polio inoculations, establishment of regulatory agencies, and reforestation are a few examples of intelligent social planning, or man imposing his will upon a whimsical nature.

Obviously, the process of education is vital to the success of purposive cultural change theory, and in 1932 a leading educator, George S. Counts, had audaciously asked the question: "Dare the Schools Build a New Social Order?" While Counts was not actually advocating that the schools should attempt such a monumental task, the question he raised had many reverberations. Fundamentally, it posed the question of just what is the function of the schools in a modern society. Should the schools attempt to lead the society (purposive change)? Or should they simply reflect society (reinforce the status quo)? Or should they be citadels of the past (conservation)?

To some these questions seemed irrelevant, for they pointed out that an institutionalized activity can only be reflective, on the one hand, and must be contemporary, on the other. To these thinkers, there were no such alternatives as conservation or purposive change for both of these were contained, in part, in the reflective modern school. The problem, as they saw it, was rather to keep schools as current as possible and avoid a "cultural lag."

CULTURAL LAG

The problem of *cultural lag* can be defined simply. It is a condition where tools and techniques, or technology, have advanced so rapidly that the value structure, or the climate of opinion, or perhaps the complementary basic functions of living lag behind, or fail to make simultaneous adjustments. The "cultural-lag" theorists contend that man's inventive powers in tools and technology outstrip his ability to adjust his behavior to the new conditions created by such technological advances. The function of education, they assert, is to cut down this inevitable gap more efficiently. Or, as Carl Becker puts it: "Mankind has entered a new phase of human progress—a time in which the acquisition of new implements of power too swiftly outruns the necessary adjustment of habits and ideas to the novel conditions created by their use."[23]

There have been numerous challenges to the theory of "cultural lag." Opponents of the theory point out a number of defects they see in it. For example, use of the word *progress* (as by Becker above) again seems to imply movement toward a *desirable* goal, and thus the insertion of a subjective value position invalidates the theory as scientifically useful. And, too, change does not necessarily imply progress; some changes may be retrogressive or even neutral, pushing the culture neither forward nor backward along some value scale. It seems evident, too, that technical changes and value changes cannot be measured by any comparable units; thus, the "lag" is not a useful concept. Probably the most significant argument offered by the opponents of the "cultural lag" theory is simply to say that culture, being composed of all of the elements of technology and values, cannot, by definition, lag behind itself. Presumably no action can be taken, particularly on any mass scale, unless it is perceived to be consonant with the existing value structure or its logical extensions. The *creators* of new technology and new implements of power are themselves a part and product of the culture. Therefore, the interrelationships between the various elements of the culture are so complexly interwoven that it is impossible to extricate one aspect as a discrete function and claim it leads or follows another aspect.

Lest this argument also seem to suggest that change is not possible at all, it is appropriate to note that nature may evoke changes not conceived by man which require his response, and purposive change by man can occur when specific desirable (value) goals are sought. Without a doubt, the process of education is intimately involved in man's responses to cultural change; and, in some cases, education may promote change. Nonliterate societies wishing to become literate societies use the schools consciously to build their new social orders.

[23] C. Becker, as quoted in Harold L. Hodgkinson, *Education in Social and Cultural Perspectives* (Englewood Cliffs, N.J.: Prentice-Hall, Inc., 1962), p. 140.

DECISION MAKING AS CULTURAL CHANGE

Whatever the role of the school in cultural change, the origin of change most frequently lies in some kind of decision-making process. Cultures choose between alternatives because not all alternatives are compatible, nor do they all achieve desired goals. Thus, cultures must constantly face the task of making choices; and, to do so, a culture sets up some regular mechanisms whereby choices can be processed efficiently. The usual decision-making mechanisms are contained within the various institutionalized activities as they reflect the basic functions of living. In effect, the task of such mechanisms is to select those elements of the culture which should be perpetuated.

The function of education is, therefore, selective cultural transmission. Out of all the possible knowledge, skills, and values which may exist, the school deliberately chooses to transmit only those which seem to perpetuate the supporting culture and move it toward its goals. United States education, for example, does not instruct American youth in the skills of lion-hunting, though the youth of the Masai tribe in Africa may find this skill an important part of their education. Similarly, American youth are specifically forbidden in most states from being indoctrinated with Communist theories and methodology, while Soviet youth are protected from what their culture believes to be the corrosive influence of American capitalist ideas.

It becomes a crucial problem in a culture to decide just what groups or individuals should have the power of decision invested in them. Since education in the United States, by constitutional omission, is a state rather than a federal function, the mechanisms for choice may differ from state to state. In any increasingly unified nation, such diversity in procedures sometimes promotes serious problems, such as the racial segregation policies which were practiced for so long by some states, in direct contradiction to integrative practices in the majority of states. Intervention by the federal government, using other constitutional prerogatives, has attempted to resolve this conflict in the culture. Different states grant different decision-making powers to state boards of education, county boards of education, and local school district boards. The relative uniformity of programs within a state largely depends upon the distribution of such decision-making power among these three organizational levels.

Selective cultural transmission, as a process, is formalized by the schools into a set of prescriptions for which the school takes responsibility.

These prescriptions are called "the curriculum." The curriculum of a school classroom is determined by (1) broad policies enunciated at a statewide level by the legislature and/or appropriate commissions specifically assigned these responsibilities; (2) county boards of education or their representatives; (3) school-district boards of education or their representatives; (4) individual school policies enunciated by the administrator as an individual or in conjunction with the faculty of the school; and (5) choices made by the individual teacher. Again, practices vary as emphasis is placed upon one level or another as the key decision maker. Selective cultural transmission, it is clear, is also a highly structured process in American schools, and, as such, reveals a degree of rigidity inherent in highly structured activities which often causes conflicts not easily arbitrated.

PROBLEMS OF CONFLICT

In a complex, open society like the United States, conflicts arise with the regularity of the sun. Such conflicts inevitably impinge upon the arena of education, since education is presumably responsible for cultural transmission and most conflicts originate in value differences where decisions must be made before the transmission process can proceed. Conflicts over the proper elements of the curriculum may arise because differences in perception of problems may occur at the different levels of decision making. A classroom teacher, in other words, may not perceive a problem in the same way as her school board, just as a school board in one particular place in a state may not see a problem in quite the same fashion as the state legislature. These are natural differences in perception, because the natural interests and responsibilities of each level differ. In many cases, there is an inherent conflict between these natural interests; but, more important, there is inherent conflict in interests in the society which each level of decision making perceives it is serving.

Needless to say, the solution of conflicts depends upon adequate communications between the disputing interests as well as well-designed mechanisms, agreed upon in advance by all parties, which can resolve the differences, or, at least make a decision which all parties will respect. It is apparent, as one explores the conflict problems facing American education, that neither of these conditions has been adequately fulfilled. Some channels of communication (for instance, between the public and the teacher-training institutions on matters of teacher education) are nonexistent. Other channels seem hopelessly clogged, such as in a dispute on curricular matters between a special-interest group and a specific school. Some observers have noted that one condition which contributes to weakness in the communications system is the increasingly technical and professional nature of the educational process, which makes it difficult for educational practitioners and laymen to understand each other. Another condition is the frequent structuring of the decision-making bodies to include a majority of individuals who do not have sufficient knowledge of their task to perform it successfully. Many school boards and most state legislatures fall into this category. Such groups are often composed of honest, conscientious men and women who do not understand either the complexities of curricular decisions or the limitations of their own competence and power. And yet they are constantly enjoined to make complex decisions which involve the most subtle understanding of inherent conflicts of interest in the society and within the formal structure of education.

SUMMARY

Culture is the product of man's unique ability to communicate by language. It is learned in the social environment and consists of knowledges, artifacts, beliefs, and values which human beings in a particular culture have developed to establish rules for social living and methods of adapting, and adapting to, nature. Culture, being a product of human beings, may be modified, slowly or rapidly to fit new conditions, by its creators.

The organization of human beings into groups is a society, and the basic activities of human societies are carried on in organized groups. Membership in any group requires an individual to assume various roles, which, in turn, imply various rights, responsibilities, and opportunities. Groups, of course, vary as their purposes, histories, and locations in society vary.

The organization of society and the impact of its culture upon individuals tends to standardize behavior, and therefore stabilizes life in a particular society by the development of interrelated and complex institutions.

Every individual inevitably has membership in many groups; groups thus overlap. But an individual's membership in various groups may cause him conflicts as group purposes and procedures differ. An individual may, therefore, be involved in several roles which have differing, and sometimes conflicting, responsibilities and opportunities.

Education is one of the eight major institutions of society. As such, it has a specific purpose—that of transmitting culture, or inducting youth into the society, a specific history, and specific allocations by society to achieve its purpose. Part of its heritage is that it is subject to all of the conflicts inherent in the culture, just as it has available all of the opportunities such a key institutional role promises. Consequently, education is everywhere and constantly confronted by the necessity of making choices.

It follows, then, that educators need to know and understand their culture, its conflicts and opportunities, in order to make effective choices from available alternatives.

SELECTED BIBLIOGRAPHY

Berkson, I. B. *The Ideal and the Community.* New York: Harper & Brothers, 1958.

Brameld, Theodore. *Cultural Foundations of Education.* New York: Harper & Brothers, 1957.

Brim, Orville G., Jr. *Sociology and the Field of Education.* New York: The Russell Sage Foundation, 1958.

Calverton, V. F., ed. *The Making of Society.* New York: The Modern Library, 1937.

Dewey, John. *Democracy and Education.* New York: The Macmillan Company, 1916.

Hanna, Paul R., ed. *Education: An Instrument of National Goals.* New York: McGraw-Hill Book Company, 1962.

Hodgkinson, Harold L. *Education in Social and Cultural Perspectives.* Englewood Cliffs, N.J.: Prentice-Hall, Inc., 1962.

Lee, Dorothy. *Freedom and Culture.* Englewood Cliffs, N. J.: Prentice-Hall, Inc., 1959.

Mercer, Blaine E., and Edwin R. Carr. *Education and the Social Order.* New York: Rinehart and Company, 1957.

Merrill, Francis E. *Society and Culture,* 2nd ed. Englewood Cliffs, N.J.: Prentice-Hall, Inc., 1961.

National Society for the Study of Education. *Social Forces Influencing American Education.* Chicago: University of Chicago Press, 1961.

Spindler, George D., ed. *Education and Anthropology.* Stanford, Calif.: Stanford University Press, 1955.

__________. *Education and Culture.* New York: Holt, Rinehart and Winston, 1963.

Stanley, William O., et al. *Social Foundations of Education.* New York: The Dryden Press, Inc., 1956.

CHAPTER 3

VALUE CONFLICTS AND EDUCATION

At any point in history, the popular and the technical literature of the times present a wide sample of conflicting prescriptions for the youth of the nation. The schools are given a prominent place in these statements, for they are used by society as instruments to change children and youth in the directions the culture considers desirable. To assert that something is desirable is to assert a *value* held.

What are values? Though the term is commonly used, there is much disagreement concerning its meaning. According to Redfield,[1] "A value is a conception, explicit or implicit, distinctive of an individual or characteristic of a group, of the desirable which influences the selection of modes, means, and ends of action." Kahl[2] gives both a technical and a more general definition. On the one hand, he states, "Technically speaking, values are constructs in the mind of the scientific observer that summarize the general principles used by his subjects to guide their behavior." On the other hand, he writes, "Whenever people behave according to their standards of what ought to be done, whenever they act according to what they believe is right, proper, decent, or moral, then they are expressing their values,"[3] a definition in which he seems to agree with Redfield.

Any discussion of values must clearly distinguish them from mere likes, or *preferences*. The statement that "Mr. Jones supports the public schools" is a statement of fact; it simply asserts Mr. Jones's preference. By contrast, "Mr. Jones should support the public schools" is a statement of value. It is significantly different in meaning from a mere assertion of fact.

[1] Robert Redfield, "Values," in Sol Tax et al., *An Appraisal of Anthropology Today* (Chicago: University of Chicago Press, 1953), p. 322.

[2] Joseph A. Kahl, *The American Class Structure* (New York: Rinehart and Company, 1960), p. 185.

[3] Kahl, p. 184.

Normal human beings prefer some things and reject others; prefer some ideas and reject others. In short, they have preferences.

Preferences may represent values, or they may not. For example, one may prefer spending his leisure hours examining sports cars and still not propose that he or anyone else *should* spend his leisure time in such fashion. This is a preference that does not represent a value position. Someone else may prefer to spend his leisure hours reading and asserts that he, as well as others, *ought* to read for recreation. This is a preference that does represent a value position. The distinction between "the desired" and "the desirable" further points to the distinction between preferences and values. An individual's preferences are generally more inclusive than his values; his values are among his preferences, but not all his preferences are values.

How do we then distinguish a value from a mere preference? A value is a belief representing a preference which an individual—after examining the probable consequences of this preference and of alternative preferences he may have adopted—considers important enough to be maintained, supported, and perpetuated.

Social values are values shared by groups of persons. Examples of social values are legion: The United Nations should be strengthened; the United Nations should be abolished; publicly supported schools should be available to all children and youth; libraries should be conveniently available to all residents of a community; the schools ought to teach about religion; schools must not teach about religion; limitations ought not be placed on freedom of belief; the schools ought to teach the importance of wildlife conservation; the schools should not teach students to drive cars.

It is evident from the foregoing that the entire web of our life is directed, controlled, enhanced, limited, and in other ways influenced by social values. It may even be proposed that social change, as well as resistance to it, is the result of behavior motivated by the preferences and values one holds individually or in association with other persons, and the hierarchy of those preferences and values.

IMPACT OF VALUES ON CHANGE

If values are more than fleeting preferences based on whim or on the random operations of one's intellectual taste buds, what are their functions or their meaning in our daily living? To state it simply, values provide the direction for social change. As indicated in Chapter 2, all cultures change, although the rate and direction of change vary considerably. Values and value systems, to the extent that they are well developed and organized, provide a conceptual road map for this change. With the help of such a map, daily decisions may be faced and resolved consistently with long-range destinations. However, even when they are thoroughly examined and firmly held, values do not automatically guide behavior. They do not provide recipes for daily living. Careful reflection and deliberation cannot be avoided, but general guiding principles are available to assist the process of deliberation. To continue the analogy to the road map, the traveler who possesses a map is not thereby freed from the many decisions involved in a long journey. Situational decisions must be faced time and time again, but the long-range goal or purpose assists in the making of each individual choice and provides a rationale for it.

It is also true that repeated choice of the same or similar alternatives tends to develop in an individual (or even in a group) a certain attitude or psychological set to continue making the same choice. In this sense, an *attitude* is a predisposition to acting a certain way, to make a certain decision rather than another one. A choice which was once based upon a value might become simply an entrenched habit, beyond examination and alteration, in which case it is more properly labeled a strong preference. The foregoing points up the rational ingredient in value formation; that is, to have a value, one must examine the various choices present in the situation as well as the probable consequences of these alternative choices.

IDEAL AND OPERATIONAL VALUES

One objection to the foregoing analysis readily appears: that one may hold on to a value or a system of values but not act according to them. Ready examples of such inconsistency are available in the files of our criminal courts and penal institutions in the form of individuals who kill although they profess to respect and value the lives of others, who steal or embezzle while proclaiming an unqualified commitment to honesty. A humorous anecdote relevant to this point is often cited by lawyers:

> A lawyer was pleading before an English judge that his client had had an "irresistible impulse" to steal a coat; whereupon the judge asked the defendant whether he would have taken it in the presence of a policeman. On receiving a negative reply, the judge remarked, "In other words, the impulse was irresistible in the absence of a policeman."

More subtle but legally acceptable inconsistencies occur in discriminations against, or in favor of, particular racial, religious, or ethnic groups by persons professing to respect and value all men.[4] Such inconsistencies occur in the classroom where a teacher espouses the value of creativity yet prevents it through subtle but powerful means; they are present in the high school or college that creates elaborate machinery for student self-government but permits the faculty, through this screen of student officers, to continue to make all the important decisions; and they also occur where the school-district policies call for equal educational opportunities for all children within the district, while the schools located in the poorer section of the city are systematically deprived of the means to implement these policies.[5]

Such apparent inconsistencies in human behavior in no way disprove the validity of our analysis. A lag may be found in any facet of human behavior. Long-range goals necessarily imply a gap between the actual situation and what the situation might be. In this sense, values held serve the same function as carefully considered ideals. By definition, a gap will be found between the ideal and the existential situation. Change should occur in the direction of the ideal. Unless the ideal functions in this way, it becomes but excess baggage, a speculative daydream.

Consequently, whenever one finds a significant difference, a gap, between his stated values and the operational ones, he can follow one of two courses. (1) He can treat values as nonfunctional and thus ignore the gap and continue operating, behaving, as before. This choice, in effect, indicates the acceptance of another value position—a position of complete expediency. As a conscious decision, this alternative is here rejected as intellectually and morally indefensible. (2) He can examine the stated value and, if he still finds it desirable and defensible, work toward its achievement. In this sense people are constantly working to achieve their ideals. As they approach their ideals, or as their goals come nearer to realization, new ones are fashioned and used to guide human progress. Progress has always been the result of this type of leap-frogging. According to this analysis, it makes sense to say that he who has no ideals is not a realist.

Yesterday's dreams and ideals are today's realities. Whether we

[4] For a competent analysis of this problem, see Gunnar Myrdal, *An American Dilemma* (New York: Harper & Brothers, 1944), Vols. I and II.

[5] See Patricia C. Sexton, *Education and Income* (New York: The Viking Press, 1961).

look at man's efforts to fly, to extend the length of human life, or to make more and better schooling available to an increasing percentage of the population, the sequence of progress always starts with a concept of something "better" than what we now have. The ideal represents an unrealized potential of the present and the realist, in this sense, is the person who clarifies his ideals and then systematically works toward their realization.

VALUE CONFLICTS IN CULTURE

Value conflicts are likely to occur in all cultures. A value conflict is present in any situation where persons or groups of persons have arrived at two or more value positions which lead to imcompatible consequences. When one group agrees that property taxes must be maintained at present levels and another group is convinced that more funds are needed to operate local institutions that derive their revenue from taxes on real property, we have a clear example of a conflict in social values. In a highly pluralistic culture, such as that of the United States, organized groups are found representing alternative, conflicting positions on most, if not all, social values. Sharp illustrations of this fact can be found around election times, both in the speeches of candidates and in the voting on the many proposed courses of social action facing the voter at the local, state, and national levels.

As was seen in the previous chapter, more homogeneous, tradition-oriented cultures have fewer value conflicts than the pluralistic ones. This is true, almost by definition. However, value conflicts are never completely absent in any culture. Members of a highly tradition-oriented culture, for instance, might have to face the conflict of abandoning the land of their ancestors, which they have inhabited for many generations, or of learning new ways of making a living, giving up time-honored occupational patterns. Or they might have to choose between lucrative opportunities in the employ of members of another group or continue their earlier ways at a near-starvation level.

How are these and other value conflicts resolved?

RESOLUTION OF VALUE CONFLICTS

First of all, we must realize that not all conflicts get resolved. It is possible for institutions to function and "do daily business" in the midst of vigorous disagreement. One such example of what seems to be a perennial conflict in social values—a conflict that has continued to demand the attention of serious men at least since the time of Aristotle—is the disagreement over the proper aims of education. With appropriate editorial changes in the *form,* but not the *content,* of the following quotation, it would be relevant to almost any decade in the history of man. It was in Athens, about 300 B.C., that Aristotle expressed this note of concern in Book VIII of *The Politics:*

> There are doubts concerning the business (of education) since all people do not agree in those things which they would have a child taught, both with respect to improvement in virtue and a happy life: nor is it clear whether the object of it should be to improve the reason or rectify the morals. From the present mode of education we cannot determine with certainty to which men incline, whether to instruct a child in which will be useful to him in life, or what tends to virtue, or what is excellent; for all these things have their separate defenders.

Disagreements on the aims of education will be with us into the indefinite future. Although substantial agreements have been reached on the local and even on the national scene, vigorous disagreement and conflict continue.

Another persistent social conflict concerns the appropriate relationships between religious and secular institutions. Questions concerning the separation of church and state lie dormant some years and in other years are in the forefront of social concern and conflict (see Chapter 2). It seems reasonable to conclude that in a pluralistic culture, there are certain recurring conflicts in social values—conflicts that will periodically demand our serious attention. It is unlikely that these conflicts will ever disappear, considering the very makeup of a pluralistic culture.

It is almost tautologous to propose that any value conflict is difficult to resolve. It is also well known that the machinery for the peaceful solution of value conflicts has often failed. We may offer as examples for such failures the many civil wars in the history of man; wars between and among nations; bloodshed in labor-management disputes; Negroes boycotting the public schools of Chicago, New York, and elsewhere; teachers' strikes; gang fights.

Wars and other forms of naked force aside, various means have been employed for the resolution and adjudication of value conflicts. In order to understand these variations and our current difficulties, we should indicate briefly the differences that are likely to be found between the traditional, homogeneous cultures and the more complex, heterogeneous ones.

Members of a homogeneous culture tend to rely either on tradition or on the decision of a power figure or group to resolve conflicts in social values. The tradition orientation in effect proposes that things ought to be done today as they have been done in the past. The old ways were and are the good ways. *What* the old ways were, however, and in what manner they are to apply to the present situation, is not always obvious. A special person or a special group might be necessary to interpret and to apply the wisdom of the past. When this happens, this method of resolution becomes very similar to the second one—namely, a decision by a power figure or power groups.

The power figure or group may be a military or warrior group, a priesthood or other religious hierarchy, the elders of the tribe, or a strong and talented individual who can manipulate the others. The decision is made, and the conflict in social values is resolved by the particular person or group that occupies the power position. Thus, there are not likely to be complex public debates or competing pressure groups working toward their own separate convictions and carrying on disparate styles of life. There are occasions where substantial segments of the total group will not accept the conclusion of the power elite, but these are rare. In such situations, a group may secede from the rest, there may be a civil war, the leaders of the dissenting faction may be purged, or the unaccepted point of view might merely lie dormant and appear again at a later occasion.

In a pluralistic culture the process or processes for the resolution of conflicts in social values become amazingly complex. When we consider, for example, the conflicting social values to be found in a culture such as that of the United States, England, or France—internal conflicts as well as those posed by international commitments, interests, and threats—the demands placed upon those who seek peaceful resolution of conflicts become awesome. Let us, therefore, briefly explore some of the processes whereby value conflicts are resolved in pluralistic cultures.

Within a pluralistic culture there exist a number of subcultures. We must differentiate between the methods and processes for the resolution of conflicts used within a subculture and the methods and processes used in the overarching culture which includes the various subcultures. The processes used by the subcultures must, of course, comply with the legal limitations set forth by the dominant culture. Within such broad limits, however, much variation occurs. We may find subcultures which function as the more traditional cultures described earlier do. This would be exemplified by a Spanish enclave in the Pacific Southwest, by a tightly knit Hungarian or Polish subculture in a Midwestern city, by the many tribes of American Indians who are attempting to perpetuate their ancestral modes of life, or by a Portuguese group in New York. On the other hand, we may find subcultures which operate upon highly refined, rational procedures, or parliamentary processes such as the well-known Roberts Rules of Order. It was even suggested by one astute observer of the social scene that the political machine of the modern city serves a valuable function as a *broker* of social value conflicts, and that the cost of graft might well be worth the service rendered in avoiding outright chaos or perhaps even violent revolution.[6] While value conflicts are avoided or rather simply resolved in a traditional, homogeneous culture, their peaceful solutions present more of a challenge in heterogeneous, pluralistic cultures—particularly in a complex democracy, which precludes the role of a ruling elite, whether military, religious, or secular.

What would be the guidelines for the resolution of conflicting social values in a democratic pluralistic culture?

As will be developed in more detail in Chapter 5, the authors' conception of democracy includes, among other beliefs, a commitment to the rational examination of all available points of view. In any conflict of social values, two or more courses of action compete for our favor. It is not at all sufficient to list the alternatives and proceed to a quick vote. This approach is often used by clever politicians and sly parliamentarians in all walks of life. It is contended here, however, that this is a highly undemocratic procedure. A more defensible approach would first of all explore whether other, heretofore unthought-of, alternatives might also be available. Once the various possible courses of action are clearly in mind, the pros and cons of each should receive fair hearing. The probable consequences of each line of action, the ends sought as well as the means needed to reach them, must be examined with care.

In this process it is very important to distinguish questions of fact from other kinds of questions. There is no use debating matters which can be satisfactorily resolved by gathering reliable factual information. Assumptions based upon inadequate or inaccurate facts can also be corrected this way. At times, what appear to be questions of value are really straightforward empirical questions phrased in value terms. "Is the core curriculum good?" or "Should we teach about the Hopi culture in the third grade?" are examples of questions which could be easily rephrased to remove their immediate value flavor. Let us rephrase the second question

[6] David Riesman, *Individualism Reconsidered* (New York: Doubleday and Company, Inc., 1955), p. 2.

as an example: Very often when we say "X is desirable" we mean that "X is good or useful for the purpose of attaining our goal Y under conditions Z." If we apply this reasoning to the question about study of Hopi culture in the third grade, we will have to ask: "Is studying the Hopi culture in the third grade likely to develop certain understandings and attitudes in the children of our community?" By rephrasing our question, we have now shifted to a more verifiable approach, although the value element has not been completely eliminated by this restatement. The understandings and attitudes we plan to attain still represent values expressed as goals of instruction. These goals, in turn, can be further restated to explore their relationships to still further goals, but as long as the stated goals are expressed in naturalistic terms they can be constantly restated in ways that can be investigated with the aid of factual evidence.

Due to practical limitations of time, money, and human energy, we do not keep pushing for a continuous restatement of goals and their justifications but tend to agree that, on the basis of careful analysis of past experience, certain goals are desirable for our children and youth. It is only when serious disagreement arises or when environmental conditions change substantially that we are forced to re-examine goals and reach new agreements on serious value questions. Educators must, therefore, become skilled in restating questions and assertions in a way that will stress the relevance of factual information, for it is more likely that issues will be resolved with the aid of facts than without them.[7]

In the final analysis, however, it is naive to believe that if all the available facts are examined by everyone participating in a decision, agreement will follow. Reasonable people acting in good faith can, and often do, disagree on what course of action to take, even though they work with the same facts. The legislative process is fraught with examples of such honest and reasonable disagreements. It is tempting to put horns on the heads of one's opponents or to impute ill motives to them. But can't they, by the same logic, make you the devil's advocate? The democratic process requires that one make a genuine effort to put himself in the other fellow's shoes, to try to understand the conflicting alternatives and strive for consensus before deciding the issue by voting or by other parliamentary means.

[7] A challenging minority position is expressed by Lawrence G. Thomas, who proposes that by a careful restatement of value assertions and by separating the "valuing" act into its three phases, we have a defensible empirical approach to the resolution of value problems. See his "The Prospects of Scientific Research into Values," *Educational Theory,* 6, No. 4 (October 1956), 193–205.

RELATION OF VALUES TO THE EDUCATIONAL PROCESSES

Whether we look on education in the broadest sense, as occurring constantly everywhere, or in its narrower sense of schooling, we cannot overstate the importance of values in the educational process.

Why do we have schools? What should the schools teach? What are the goals of education? Who shall be educated? Should all children study the same courses and materials? How much of the tax dollar will be spent on education? Should we teach foreign languages? To whom? Why? Who is the gifted child? What shall we do with him? Should our most talented teachers work with the "gifted," the "retarded," or with the "average" students? None of these questions can be thoroughly explored and answered without our running into some serious value questions. There are countless other questions we could raise, but the foregoing sample should suffice to illustrate that the educational process is fraught with questions and conflicts involving social values.

VALUES AND THE CURRICULUM

Popular discussion tends to stop when someone asserts that a particular point of view "is a matter of value." The popular assumption seems to be that intelligent persons do not discuss or "argue over" "matters of taste" or values. If this were true, could the process of education or of schooling continue? Could there be a functioning curriculum?

The term *curriculum* can be defined in several ways. According to the most restrictive definition, the curriculum consists of the logically organized bodies of subject matter to be studied in a school. Some people have gone further and said, "Curriculum is all the experiences a child has in school." This is, of course, not a workable definition. The most inclusive conception of curriculum can, after all, include only the activities provided for students by their school or all the experiences the students partake in under the aegis of a school.

The curriculum, however defined, represents the conclusions and decisions reached on a series of value conflicts. Any subject to be included, any method to be used, any experience the child is offered in school represents one alternative among the several possible ones. For any activity that takes place in a school, we may point to several going on outside the school that could, according to a different value judgment, replace the in-school activity or find a place in the curriculum alongside the existing subjects and activities. This is what is meant, in part, by the expression that education involves the selective transmission of a culture. As developed in Chapter 2, the schools cannot nor would want to transmit the culture in its entirety; consequently, a process of selection must operate. As we educators select, as we choose among competing possibilities, we are making value judgments. We, in effect, assert that it is desired (a preference) and desirable (a value assertion) for our students to undergo certain experiences. As such, the curriculum of a particular school at any one time represents a significant portion of the social values held by the community which supports that school.

VALUES BEYOND THE CURRICULUM

All the activities in an educational enterprise must ultimately be justifiable in relation to the curriculum and to the students. There are countless decisions which, strictly speaking, are of a noncurricular nature but nevertheless are necessary for the functioning of schools. Decisions must be made on school boundaries, the location and design of buildings, the purchase of equipment, the sizes of classes at different age levels, and support of various "extra- or co-curricular" activities. All of these decisions in some way or other include value judgments.

The community, with the cooperation of its educators, must make still further decisions when value conflicts are involved. For example, defeat of a proposal for a local bond issue would reduce the operating funds available for existing school programs. In that case, difficult decisions will have to be made: Should parts of the curriculum be eliminated, and which? Should the community cut out instruction in foreign languages, the advanced programs in mathematics and sciences, the industrial arts program, music, or literature? These complex and difficult questions call for decisions based on meticulous consideration of all relevant facts and careful analysis of competing social values. Although many of these problems can be avoided or solved by wealthy school districts, no amount of wealth can eliminate all conflicts of social values from a community's processes of education.

SUMMARY

In this chapter we distinguished values from mere preference and developed the thesis that the entire fabric of life is permeated by individual and social values. Since gaps constantly appear between existing conditions and values held that reflect heretofore unrealized potentialities, values indicate the direction of social change.

Value conflicts are found in all cultures. After discussion of the various approaches to the peaceful resolution of conflicts in social values, we highlighted the democratic emphasis in the resolution of such conflicts in a pluralistic culture.

Educational processes and institutions, reflecting the cultural setting, are also permeated by values and value conflicts. The curriculum represents the tentative decisions reached in attempts to solve such conflicts, both substantive and methodological. The historic changes in the American curriculum are symptoms of the changing value positions that are bound to arise in a culture in transition. The midcentury conflict and confusion over education in the United States is, in effect, a serious symptom of significant transformations occurring in the core culture, as well as in its many subcultures. The school, as a significant social institution, is at once the focal point of conflict in social values and an instrument for the transmission of agreed upon values.

SELECTED BIBLIOGRAPHY

Broudy, Harry S. *Paradox and Promise.* Englewood Cliffs, N.J.: Prentice-Hall, Inc. (a Spectrum Book), 1961.

Brubacher, John S. *A History of the Problems of Education.* New York: McGraw-Hill Book Company, Inc., 1947.

Childs, John L. *Education and Morals.* New York: Appleton-Century-Crofts, Inc., 1950.

Dahlke, Otto H. *Values in Culture and Classroom.* New York: Harper & Brothers, 1958.

Dewey, John, *Theory of Valuation.* Chicago: The University of Chicago Press, 1939.

Ehlers, Henry, and Gordon C. Lee. *Crucial Issues in Education,* 2nd ed. New York: Holt, Rinehart and Winston, 1959.

Hook, Sidney. *Education for Modern Man: A New Perspective.* New York: Alfred A. Knopf, 1963.

Hutchins, Robert M. *The Conflict in Education in a Democratic Society.* New York: Harper & Brothers, 1953.

Kerber, August, and Wilfred Smith. *Educational Issues in a Changing Society.* Detroit: Wayne University Press, 1962.

Nelson, Jack, and Gene Roberts, Jr. *The Censors and the Schools.* Boston: Little, Brown and Company, 1963.

Rafferty, Max. *Suffer Little Children.* New York: The Devin-Adair Company, 1962.

Raywid, Mary Anne. *The Ax-Grinders.* New York: The Macmillan Company, 1963.

CHAPTER 4

SCIENCE AND THE SOCIAL FOUNDATIONS OF EDUCATION

THE SOURCES OF OUR FACTS

The underlying thesis of this volume is that the process of education necessarily entails an endless series of decisions. In order to reach adequate and defensible decisions, educators must have reliable factual information. Like other citizens who claim to possess a sound general education, they must be able to distinguish statements of fact from other types of statements, and they must be equipped to distinguish the relevant from the irrelevant.

The term "fact" is difficult to define with precision.[1] For the purposes of this work, however, a fact is an occurrence, a quality, or a relationship manifest in experience: an actual happening or relationship in time or space that can be openly investigated.

What are the sources of facts that are useful to educators? Where do we search for them?

Well-known educators throughout history seem to have relied on facts in their decision-making processes. Famous teachers like Plato, Quintilian, and Comenius gathered their facts by the method of common sense and by reflecting upon their observations and intellectually criticizing and reshaping their common-sense conclusions.

It was not until the twentieth century that the inductive emphasis of Sir Francis Bacon achieved much of a foothold in our efforts to learn about human behavior. Except for the biological sciences, systematic empirical observation of, and controlled experimentation with, human behavior on a significant scale is still in its infancy. At this stage of its development, education as a field of study is primarily a derived discipline. During the first four decades of the twentieth century, the rapidly developing field of

[1] See Morris R. Cohen and Ernest Nagel, *An Introduction to Logic and Scientific Method* (New York: Harcourt, Brace and World, Inc., 1934), pp. 217–219.

psychology produced most of the facts, conclusions, and generalizations upon which educators based their decisions. Since then, however, important developments in sociology, anthropology, and social psychology have steadily gained recognition. Contributions have been gleaned also from other disciplines, such as history, political science, and economics.

In time, a somewhat autonomous discipline may emerge, generating and testing its own theories and principles in order to guide the development of the educative process; but the discipline will undoubtedly still be related to sociology, history, economics, etc. Consequently, the more thorough grounding an educator has in these fields, the better he will be in his professional work.[2]

For reasons that have been explained, this volume does not deal in any systematic way with the relevance of psychology to education. The relevance is admitted, its importance is urged, but it cannot be explored here in any detail. Practically all teacher-education programs in the United States include some, though rarely enough, work in this area. Our focus will be on other sources of information. Even here we can only highlight some of the important areas relevant to the educator and perhaps start him on his road toward mastery in depth through formal study or through self-education. Of the many areas of systematic study, perhaps the most fruitful one for educators has been the exploration of social stratification. Consequently, it makes sense to start with this topic.

STUDIES OF AMERICAN SOCIAL STRATIFICATION

There was a time in the not too distant past when the very idea of social classes brought forth vigorous protests in the United States. Because the ideal of equality is strongly embedded in the American tradition, people objected to the social scientist's attempts to make explicit the system of social stratification that implicitly existed. Today the protests are not so vigorous, and even the popular literature speaks of upper, middle, and lower classes. Only election times bring forth vehement denials of social differentiation, as our office-seeking orators proclaim that we are all equal and that we are all "the common man."

It is true that one cannot see, touch, feel, or hear social classes any more than we see culture, or motivation, or that $\pi = 22/7$. These are all

[2] See John Dewey, *The Sources of a Science of Education* (New York: Horace Liveright and Company), 1929.

intellectual constructs or ideas, which man invents to use as tools in his efforts to understand himself, others, and his relationships to his human as well as nonhuman environment.[3]

Every human group studied by social scientists has used some system of valuing certain traits, attributes, or characteristics more than others. The symbols of prestige are never distributed evenly throughout the population. The social scientist categorizes people into various classes in an attempt to make explicit the implicit beliefs and convictions of a society; namely, that for various reasons certain persons are rated higher on a comparative scale than others. He does not impose a class system on a particular society. He describes and clarifies, with the aid of intellectual tools, what is there—existing and functioning.

THE DISTINCTION BETWEEN CLASS AND CASTE

An important reason for the general resistance to the concept of a class system in America is the lack of clear distinction between class and caste in the understanding of the general population. The term "class" brings to mind some characteristics of the well-known caste system of India or of the caste-like systems associated with the various types of feudalisms in European history.

To offer a simplified definition, social class consists of an aggregate of people differentiated from others by certain recognized qualifications. Social stratification indicates a ranking of social classes in a systematic hierarchy of higher and lower prestige groups. The vernacular often expresses this common recognition of levels in society: "He married beneath himself," "He lives on the right side of the tracks," "Aren't your folks good enough for you?" There is substantial mobility across class lines, and there are no formal or customary indicia of class membership. Intermarriage across class lines is frequent, and one may achieve membership in a class other than the one ascribed to him at birth.

A caste consists of a group of people separated from other groups by rigid social barriers enforced by law, custom, or both. By contrast to social classes, no movement is possible from one caste into another, intermarriage is forbidden, and a person lives his entire life within the caste imposed upon him by the fortuitous circumstances of his birth. The

[3] One must be on guard against the danger of reifying "social class." To reify is to attach a noun to a process or relationship and then assume that it exists as a "thing." Speed, beauty, government, love, power are examples of processes or relationships often reified. Reification has been referred to as "thingification."

Hungarian gypsy is a functioning example of a caste group in contemporary Europe.

Analysis of American society shows that there are caste-like groupings in the United States, the American Negro being the most extreme example. Negroes are said to be a caste-*like* group—rather than an actual caste—because there is no universal prohibition against intermarriage of races throughout our culture, although intermarriage is outlawed in many places and generally frowned upon in others. Other caste-like groups in the United States are the American-Indians, the Japanese-Americans, the Chinese-Americans, and the Mexican-Americans.

Once the distinctions between caste and class become sufficiently clear, the popular resistance to the phenomenon of a class system tends to disappear or at least diminish.

METHODS OF DETERMINING CLASS MEMBERSHIP

How do social scientists decide whom to place into which class? While the approaches of research workers have varied a great deal, only two widely used methodologies will be highlighted here.[4]

"EVALUATED SOCIAL PARTICIPATION." The earlier studies, of which the most widely read were the Yankee City studies[5] and *Elmtown's Youth,*[6] used a method commonly known as "evaluated social participation." By this method, long-time residents of the community are carefully interviewed in order to ascertain the outlines of the social structure. Several names are noted of persons who, according to the interviewees, occupy given positions up and down the social structure. Next, the research workers determine whom these known people associate with in service organizations, social clubs, and churches. Other people are thus placed in relation to people on the original list. Eventually all of the residents can be plotted on the social map.

This method is time consuming and expensive, and calls for highly skilled interviewers. Moreover, larger cities and metropolitan areas cannot be studied by this technique, since a city dweller does not know most of the members of his own social class. Social scientists have, therefore, been

[4] For a thorough treatment see Joseph A. Kahl, *The American Class Structure* (New York: Holt, Rinehart and Winston, Inc., 1957); and Reinhard Bendix, and Seymour Martin Lipset, *Class, Status and Power* (Glencoe, Ill.: The Free Press, 1953).

[5] W. Lloyd Warner and Paul S. Lunt, *The Social Life of a Modern Community* (New Haven: Yale University Press, 1941).

[6] August B. Hollingshead, *Elmtown's Youth* (New York: John Wiley and Sons, 1949).

searching for a reliable instrument that is easily applied and relatively inexpensive.

"INDEX OF STATUS CHARACTERISTICS." Among the many attempts to develop a scientific instrument for the assessment of social-class membership, perhaps the most widely recognized and used method is the "Index of Status Characteristics" (ISC).[7] The ISC is a rating instrument by which scores are assigned on the following six items:

Occupation.
Amount of income.
Source of income (charity, wages, salary, profits, or inherited wealth).
Amount of education.
Type of house lived in (size, style, condition).
Area of community lived in (rated on local desirability).

A numerical score from 1 (highest) through 7 (lowest) is assigned to a person on each item. When the total score is compared to a standardized scale, the social-class status of the person rated is indicated. This is a useful and relatively quick method of judging social-class position and has been widely used in recent studies. However, of the six categories constituting the ISC, two require the opinion of local residents and particularly of persons well acquainted with real-estate values. The fact that local opinion enters the evaluation has raised serious questions about the objectivity of the ISC as an instrument of science.

Further investigations have disclosed that three categories are fairly standard throughout the United States: amount of education, occupation, and source of income. For various reasons, not the least of which is the rise of a mass culture with its attendant mass communication and population mobility, American adults tend to agree on these criteria regardless of where they live. Regardless of the particular community one studies, a professional is ranked higher socially than a bank clerk, and a college degree is ranked higher than a diploma from a high school or trade school.

Furthermore, although a single criterion generally is not as accurate as the composite picture, if one must reach a quick judgment, occupation seems to be the most accurate single indicator of a person's social class. This makes sense when one realizes that in the United States occupations tend to reflect amount of education and also indicate source of income—and, to some extent, amount of income and choice of residence.

[7] W. Lloyd Warner, Marchia Meeker, and Kenneth Eels, *Social Class in America*, new ed. (New York: Harper Torchbooks, 1960). For a description of the revised scale, see *Social Class in America*, Chapters 8 and 9.

What we now know about social-class composition and its relevance to various aspects of life is quite accurate and reliable for our *small* and *medium-sized* communities of the East, Midwest, and South. The fast-growing West, as well as the large cities and metropolitan centers, await further study. In these areas of substantial recent growth, the lines of social differentiation have not crystallized as in the older, tradition-oriented communities. Social class in these communities is probably based more on wealth, occupation, and education than on other criteria. In these localities, *achieved* status is much more important than *ascribed* status: "It's what you can do that counts, not who you are." A recent study of Kansas City confirms the difficulties involved in assessing social class in a large city and points up the need for continued careful investigation of this phenomenon.[8]

POPULATION DISTRIBUTION IN SOCIAL CLASSES

Studies indicate that some communities are more highly stratified than others. Some contain six clearly identifiable classes: upper-upper, lower-upper, upper-middle, lower-middle, upper-lower, and lower-lower. Others, such as the so-called "bedroom communities" of the West, might be composed exclusively of upper-middle-class executives and professionals, all of whom purchased their homes from the same "tract" builder, and all of whom commute to work in the same nearby metropolis. In between these two extreme types of communities, a wide range of possibilities is found. The most common type is the three-class system: the upper-, middle-, and lower-class variety or the upper-middle, lower-middle, and lower-class type, depending upon the local community. In all of these types, there is no clear break, similar to layers in a layer cake, between classes. They tend to blend into each other on a continuum, and the criteria for clear separation of classes are very complex.[9]

Approximately how many Americans do we find in each of the social classes? It is impossible to offer a simple, direct answer. However, taking occupation as a single index of class, and relying on information available from the 1960 federal census, we estimate that nearly 43 per cent of the population is middle or upper class; 57 per cent belongs to the upper-lower and lower-lower classes.

These figures must be treated with great caution. Serious students

[8] Richard P. Coleman, "Social Class in Kansas City." Unpublished Ph.D. dissertation, University of Chicago, 1959.

[9] For an excellent analysis, see Talcott Parsons, "A Revised Analytical Approach to the Theory of Social Stratification," in R. Bendix and S. Lipset, *Class, Status and Power* (see note 4), p. 124.

of social stratification disagree on percentage distribution of the population in the several classes. Variations arise from differences in methodology used to reach the conclusion. The only general agreement discerned in the many available sources seems to indicate that the population of the United States is most heavily concentrated in the lower-middle and upper-lower classes; the next-largest group is the lower-lower class; the smallest proportion falls into the upper-middle and upper-class categories. Without proceeding in great detail, educators must be cognizant of the fact that substantial numbers of students come to them from each of the social classes.[10]

TWO-WAY MOBILITY WITHIN THE CLASS SYSTEM

As indicated earlier, one difference between a class system and a caste system is the possibility of movement from one class to another. The term *social mobility,* as used by social scientists, refers to a vertical change in position within the class structure. Such mobility may occur either upward or downward. The possibility of mobility is a characteristic of a democratic society, which values equality of opportunity. However, due to a pervasive optimism and a historic orientation toward success and achievement, not much is said in the United States about downward mobility. Nonetheless, the existence of the phenomenon must be recognized, and serious students of the field must study the conditions which lead to downward movement.

It should be further noted that class systems can and do exist *within* the caste-like groupings mentioned earlier. Studies indicate that the stratification of our caste-like groups is similar to that of our larger culture, although there is a difference in the percentages of people who fall into the several classes. By and large, the more disadvantaged the caste-like group happens to be, the larger the proportion of its members falling into the lower categories of the class structure.[11]

Upward mobility may occur because of chance circumstances that were intelligently used by the recipient. Such cases, however, are rare and sufficiently unusual to find their way into the popular movies or newspapers. Of more general concern are the means by which large numbers of

[10] For a more specific breakdown, see Robert J. Havighurst and Bernice Neugarten, *Society and Education,* rev. ed. (Boston: Allyn and Bacon, Inc., 1962), pp. 20–21. A cautious analysis is presented by Joseph Kahl, *The American Class Structure* (New York: Holt, Rinehart and Winston, 1957).

[11] See Allison Davis, Burleigh B. Gardner, and Mary R. Gardner, *Deep South* (Chicago: University of Chicago Press, 1941); John Dollard, *Caste and Class in a Southern Town,* 2nd ed. (New York: Harper & Brothers, 1949); and St. Clair Drake and Horace R. Clayton, *Black Metropolis* (New York: Harcourt Brace and Co., 1945).

individuals achieve upward mobility. The most widely used and increasingly most important is the process of formal education. In spite of the many ways we fall short of our ideal of equal opportunity, the publicly supported educational enterprise has served as a social ladder for millions of able students.

It is safe to propose that education is becoming more important than ever before to maintain status, and certainly to improve it. This is so because one's occupation is an important determinant of one's status; and increasingly, in today's complex industrial civilizations, more and more formal schooling is prerequisite for higher-prestige occupations. Even a cursory glance at how our population ranks various occupations will substantiate this analysis.[12]

In addition to education, upward mobility may be achieved through such factors as marriage, outstanding athletic ability, peculiar talent leading to success in one of the fields of the performing arts, intelligence coupled with "business sense" and hard work. However, for the bulk of the population, education is the most readily available means to achieve upward mobility.

Whereas case histories of upward mobility are legion (any one of the readers can easily identify a successful public figure or a personal acquaintance who began life in an upper-lower or lower-middle-class family but who now has an achieved status in the upper-middle class), it is more difficult to point to persons who have "achieved" downward mobility. Such cases do exist, often as a result of lack of success in formal education. There are numerous examples of children of professional people or high-powered business executives who, from lack of academic ability or because of personality problems, are unable to succeed in our schools. These people might drop out from high school or may begin but not complete their college education. As a consequence, higher-status occupations generally will be closed to them, and, as they become heads of families, their status is likely to be below that of their family of birth.

STUDIES OF CLASS VALUES AND BEHAVIOR

The various social classes tend to embody identifiable configurations of behavior sufficiently clearly, so as to be similar to subcultures. The types of behavior in each of the classes have been described extensively in

[12] See Bendix and Lipset, *Class, Status and Power* (note 4).

various studies. Kahl[13] formulated a set of descriptive categories that capture the key characteristics of the classes. They are:

Graceful living	upper class
Career	upper-middle class
Respectability	lower-middle class
Get by	upper-lower[14] class
Apathy	lower-lower class

He briefly describes the value orientations, the "class way of life," in the following summary statement:[15]

> Although there is a great deal of controversy over details, and considerable variation from one part of the country to another and from small towns to large cities, many researchers agree that contemporary American urban society can usefully be described as having five social classes. No single variable defines a class; instead, the interaction between several variables creates the total way of life which characterizes a class. Value orientations emerge from, integrate, and symbolize the class way of life. The classes can be labeled as follows:
>
> 1. *Upper Class.* Wealthy families who strive for a stable pattern of refined and gracious living. In its ancient form an upper class is based on inherited property and fixed traditions, and the earning of more money takes second place to the spending of income from property. But our upper class is mixed, and contains many newly successful persons who learn the gracious way of life and become accepted by their peers.
>
> 2. *Upper-Middle Class.* The successful business and professional men (but not those at the very top), and their families. Income is mostly from current occupation, thus the emphasis is on long-term careers. These people live in large houses in good suburbs or in the best apartment houses; most are college graduates; they dominate industry and community organizations.
>
> 3. *Lower-Middle Class.* The less successful members of government, business, and the professions, and the more successful manual workers. This is the least clearly defined level, shading imperceptibly into the working class. These people live in small houses or in multiple-family dwellings. Most are high-school graduates, and some have had a little additional training. They are the model for the popular stereotype of America's "Common man." They emphasize respectability.
>
> 4. *Working Class.* Factory and similar semiskilled workers. These are the people who work from day to day; they live adequately but on a

[13] *The American Class Structure* (see note 10), Chapter 7. With permission.

[14] Kahl, as well as other writers, uses the term "working class." This is avoided here because of the unfortunate implication that lawyers, physicians, teachers, etc., are not workers.

[15] Kahl, *American Class Structure,* pp. 215–216. With permission.

small margin, have little hope of rising, aim at getting by. They are graduates of grammar schools, with often some high-school training.

5. *Lower Class.* People who have the lowest paid jobs, work irregularly (especially in bad times), live in slums. They usually have not gone beyond grammar school (and often have not finished it), their family life is unstable, their reputations poor, and their values are based on apathy or aggression, for they have no hope.

STUDIES OF THE RELATION BETWEEN EDUCATION AND SOCIAL CLASS

It was indicated earlier that industrialization in America, with its attendant urbanization, brought about many changes in the occupational structure. Higher-paid and otherwise prestigious occupations have gradually increased their educational requirements. The close relationship between formal education, occupations available to one, and the income he will earn is clearly documented by a special report based on data of the United States Bureau of the Census.[16]

The report indicates, for example, that 82 per cent of men with only an elementary school education were found in manual labor and farm labor, and that 90 per cent of those with less than five years of elementary schooling were so occupied. High school graduates more or less straddled the fence dividing white-collar and blue-collar occupations; 57 per cent held manual jobs, often as skilled workers and foremen, but 21 per cent of them were in clerical and 15 per cent in managerial positions. Those with some college education but without an earned degree were primarily in managerial and clerical positions—about 25 per cent of them in technical or professional work, about 33 per cent in blue-collar work (with half of this group being highly skilled craftsmen). By contrast, 55 per cent of college graduates were in professional and technical occupations, and another 18 per cent worked as proprietors or business managers.

The positive relationship between years of school completed and average income is well established (see Table 4–1).

In light of the foregoing data and analysis, it is clear that equal opportunity in the American open-class system must presuppose equal access to education regardless of social origin. Equality of opportunity is denied if educators permit social origin or social-class conditioning to in-

[16] United States Bureau of the Census, *Education,* Special Report P-E No. 5B (Washington, D.C.: Bureau of Census, 1953).

TABLE 4–1. Relationship between amount of schooling and income.

	Average income of males 25–64 years old in the experienced civilian labor force in 1959
All males	$ 5,850
0–7 years of elementary school	3,660
8 years of elementary school	4,730
1–3 years of high school	5,380
4 years of high school	6,130
1–3 years of college	7,400
4 years of college	9,260
5 years of college or more	11,140

Computed from the U.S. Census of Population: 1960, Final Report PC(2)–7B, *Occupation by Earnings and Education,* Table 1 (Washington, D.C.: Bureau of the Census, 1963). Figures are rounded out to the nearest tens.

fluence a student's chances for success in our schools and, especially in recent years, in institutions of higher education.

Are educational opportunities equally available to all American youth? The answer is not easy to come by. Earlier studies concluded that youngsters from the lower classes are systematically disadvantaged in the schools.[17] Later, Warner, Havighurst, and Loeb leveled the same charge, as evidenced in the following bold statements:

> This book describes how our schools, functioning in a society with basic inequalities, facilitate the rise of a few from lower to higher levels but continue to serve the social system by keeping down many people who try for higher places. The teacher, the school administrator, the school board, as well as the students themselves, play their roles to hold people in their places in our social structure. . . .
>
> The young people are inspected not only for brains and learning ability, but also for skin color, pronunciation, cut of clothes, table manners, parental bank account. . . .
>
> The evidence is clear that the social class system of Yankee City definitely exercises a control over the pupils' choice of curricula. . . . The children of the two upper and the upper-middle classes, in overwhelming percentages, were learning and being taught a way of life which would fit them into higher statuses. On the other hand, the lower-middle and the lower-class children, in their studies in the high school, were learning a way of life which would help adjust them to the rank in which they were born. . . .
>
> Teachers represent middle-class attitudes and enforce middle-class

[17] See L. W. Warner and S. P. Lunt, *The Social Life of a Modern Community* (note 5); and Davis, Gardner, and Gardner, *Deep South* (note 11).

> values and manners. In playing this role, teachers do two things. They train or seek to train children in middle-class manners and skills. And they select those children from the middle and lower classes who appear to be the best candidates for promotion in the social hierarchy. . . .[18]

Hollingshead, in his widely read report on *Elmtown's Youth,*[19] reached the same conclusions.

More recent research indicates, however, that the earlier studies overemphasized social class as the all-important variable in equality of educational opportunity.[20] Analysis of the data in *Growing Up in River City*[21] discloses that the *gross* number of students from lower-class homes who attend college is greater than the *gross* number who attend from upper-class homes, *but* the percentage of college attendance is heavily in favor of the upper classes. Estimates from the national scene are in accord with this. "A study of graduate students in a sample of United States universities revealed that approximately two-thirds of the graduate students in natural science, social science, and the humanities came from lower-middle and lower-class backgrounds."[22]

There is an increasing amount of evidence that education provides a major avenue for social mobility in the United States. It is not unreasonable to suppose that today's teachers are more knowledgeable about the relevance of social class to motivation, discipline, and occupational aspirations, and consequently are better able to work with children and youth from the various social classes. It is also reasonable to suggest that the mass media, particularly television, have brought into lower-class homes many experiences (however vicarious these may be) that help to motivate students and add to the experiential background necessary for success in our middle-class-oriented school programs.

This is not to suggest that social class is irrelevant to one's probable success in our schools and consequently in the occupational and social hierarchies. At best it is a suggestion that large numbers of American youth

[18] W. Lloyd Warner, Robert J. Havighurst, and Martin B. Loeb, *Who Shall Be Educated?* (New York: Harper & Brothers, 1944), pp. xi, 50, 61, 107. With permission.

[19] See note 6.

[20] See S. J. Coleman, "Academic Achievement and the Structure of Competition," *Harvard Educational Review,* 29 (1959), 330–351; D. Gottlieb, "Processes of Socialization in the American Graduate School" (unpublished doctoral dissertation, University of Chicago, 1960), cited in W. B. Brookover and D. Gottlieb, "Social Class and Education," in W. W. Charters and N. L. Gage, eds., *Readings in the Social Psychology of Education* (Boston: Allyn and Bacon, Inc., 1963), p. 8.

[21] Robert J. Havighurst et al., *Growing Up in River City* (New York: John Wiley and Sons, Inc., 1962), Chapter 8.

[22] D. Gottlieb, in Charters and Gage (see note 20), p. 10.

achieve upward mobility with the aid of education. Statistically speaking, the "life chances" for success or achievement are still more favorable for children who "choose their parents wisely"—that is to say, who are born into middle- and upper-middle-class homes. The various studies conducted on the "drop-out" problem in our culture bear out the conclusion that the father's occupation is the most reliable single predictive factor in estimating a student's chances to graduate from high school and attend a college-level institution.[23]

Recognition of this relationship is widespread in our culture as a result of the genuine concern of the federal government; of top-level management; and of the leaders in education, science, industry, and the military. Some are concerned because of a serious commitment to the ideals of democracy, while others are motivated by less noble concerns reflecting a utilitarian approach to the worth of man. Their position is, in a nutshell, that our expanding economy, business, and government require an increasing number of highly educated, bright, and capable people to operate their various demanding enterprises. Current developments have made the *unskilled worker* fairly obsolete, and reliable signs point to a future where the *unskilled thinker* will be obsolete. Since we are not now producing enough people to fill the demanding upper-echelon positions, let us look to hitherto untapped population sources for talent.

Although the initial motivations differ, various persons can, and do, cooperate to encourage the educational development of talent from groups who, up to now, were substantially disadvantaged. Such disadvantaged groups were the lower social classes; certain ethnic groups such as the Mexican-Americans, Puerto-Rican Americans, Oriental-Americans; Negroes;[24] and, in some respects, the female population. While the obstacles in the way of equality of educational opportunity have not been completely eradicated, they have been diminished. This has been achieved by various scholarship, fellowship, and grant-in-aid programs; by substantial loan programs, the best known of which is the National Defense Education Act; and by the widespread concern for the education of the so-called "culturally deprived children." The long-range consequences of these programs will have to be assessed in the future, but intermediate results have been sufficiently impressive to win the support of intelligent critics. While the most

[23] Raymond A. Mulligan, "Socio-Economic Background and College Enrollment," *American Sociological Review*, 16 (April 1951), 188–196; James S. Davie, "Social Class Factor and School Attendance," *Harvard Educational Review*, 23 (Summer 1953), 175–185.

[24] See James B. Conant, *Slums and Suburbs* (New York: McGraw-Hill Book Company, Inc., 1961).

effective and efficient approach to the education of the "culturally deprived" is yet to be distilled, it is clear that we have wasted, and are wasting, much valuable human potential by bowing to the fortuitous circumstances of birth. (One does not choose his parents or the color of his skin.) Recognition of this has led to experimental and exploratory programs in most urban centers in the United States. The best known of these are the "Higher Horizons" program of New York and the "Great Cities Improvement Project" of Detroit, Michigan.[25]

Independently of these special programs, a classroom teacher can do much to help children grow toward their educational potential. The teacher, in effect, must become sufficiently objective to shake off her own social-class biases as she works with children. She must act like a clinician. The clinician, when faced with a problem, attempts to gather the relevant information needed to proceed toward stated objectives. The teacher must proceed in a clinical instead of a judgmental fashion. This is not to say that the teacher perpetuates the status quo, for she has no moral right to do so. She does not choose the objectives of education, but accepts those of the school system. In her professional role, as a member of the teaching group, she might attempt to change these objectives, but at any given day in school she must use her best talents to help *all* her children develop toward currently held goals.

It is, indeed, a demanding task for the middle-class-oriented teacher to work effectively with children from the lower as well as the upper classes. Experience has taught us that the more understanding a teacher has of our complex culture and the stratification within it, the more effective she is likely to be in working with children as individual learners, regardless of social origin. A physician gathers data about his patient but also works from the context of substantial knowledge about disease. His private moral judgments are irrelevant to, and are kept out of, his professional role.

In the same way, the teacher must use all relevant information to *change* her students in the directions specified by the goals or objectives of education. The more she knows about such factors as the styles of life, motivations, aspirations, and levels of language development of children at different ages and in different sociocultural settings, the more effective she should be with a particular group and with individual children within that group. In the final analysis, the task of a teacher is to help individuals learn; all else becomes instrumental to this task. Information about social

[25] Other programs of significance are to be found in Frank Reissman, *The Culturally Deprived Child* (New York: Harper & Row, 1962). See also Chapter 10.

class becomes relevant to educators if, and only if, it is used in some way to influence their decisions as educators.

There are many reports of teachers who have functioned well, and of some who have failed, in working with lower-class youngsters.[26] The worst cases point up the fact that many lower-class children leave school, become "drop outs" because they have been poorly handled by teachers. Examples of similar inadequacies with upper-class children are fewer because there are very few such children and these few often attend private schools.[27] The following is an example in point:

> Mike was a second-grade student in an elementary school of a very wealthy suburb. Analysis of Mike's family places them clearly in an upper-class position. Mike received a paper from his teacher containing exercises in word recognition, wherein the students chose the correct word of three alternatives to complete a sentence. One, which he missed, was the following: "Last night we had ________ for dinner." (splash, hash, flash) Mike chose "flash." When asked by one of the writers why he chose "flash," Mike replied: " 'Splash' is something we do in our pool, 'hash' is a word that sounds funny but doesn't mean a thing, so it must be 'flash' because that comes closest to 'fish.' "

Interestingly enough, Mike's family never, within his memory, ate anything called hash, but his teacher did. Perhaps a better knowledge of the upper-class style of life would lead Mike's teacher to use different examples or exercises to reach the same curricular goals.

STUDIES OF THE CHANGING FAMILY IN OUR CULTURE

The human infant slowly becomes a functioning member of a group. He undergoes the processes of enculturation and socialization; that is to say, he learns the folkways and mores of the human group into which he was born, and learns to differentiate the various statuses and roles within it. A *status* (sex status, age status, student status, religious status, soldier

[26] A powerful case history is poignantly presented in a film entitled *A Desk for Billy,* produced by the National Education Association on occasion of its 100th Anniversary. A more realistic picture emerges from the study of Donald R. Thomas, "No Desk for Carmen," *Teachers College Record,* 61, No. 3 (December 1959), 143–150.

[27] This is not to imply that private schools are better than public schools. Some are, while others are worse. By and large, a myth is perpetuated in the United States that ascribes better quality to private schools. There are no defensible bases for comparing the quality of instruction in private schools in *general* to that in public schools in *general.*

status) is a position in a social structure. *Role* signifies the pattern of behavior expected of one occupying a particular status.[28]

In a complex culture such as that of the United States, the processes of socialization and enculturation are intricate and accomplished under the continuing impact of several agencies. The more important of these are the family, the school, the peer group, the church, and the mass media. Although the relative importance of these agencies is not easily assessed and is not uniform in the lives of all individuals, it is generally agreed that, by and large, the family is the most important socializing agency. There are obvious variations in this general rule, as in the case of children growing up in institutions of various kinds, and even cultural variations, such as the Kibbutz system of the state of Israel.[29] In spite of these exceptions, the conclusion of Charles H. Cooley still stands: "the family is primary" in the shaping of the child's interests, values, commitments, and personality in general.

The growing volume of literature regarding the family as an institution is a valuable source of information for educators (as well as others). Therefore, an understanding of significant changes that have occurred and are still occurring should contribute to our ability to deal with educational problems more intelligently.

THE TRADITIONAL FAMILY

A pessimistic view of the changing American family asserts that a deterioration has been taking place, and that our culture is doomed because its basic supporting institution, the family, is doomed. This point of view assumes, of course, that any change away from the extended patriarchal family type is undesirable and that the family organization could, and should, remain the same in the midst of significant social changes. More objective analyses describe the changes taking place without assuming the fixed value position implicit in the foregoing pessimistic view. Burgess and Locke, for example, reflect this objectivity even in the subtitle of their excellent analysis of the family—*From Institution to Companionship;*[30] others characterize the changes as a general movement from an authoritarian toward a democratic style of family life.

[28] For a sound discussion of "Role Theory" see Neal Gross, W. S. Mason, and A. W. McEachern, *Explorations in Role Analysis: Studies of the School Superintendency Role* (New York: Wiley, 1958), Chapters 5 and 6.

[29] The reader will find an introduction to this topic in Bruno Bettelheim, "Does Communal Education Work? The Case of the Kibbutz," *Commentary,* 33, No. 2 (February 1962).

[30] E. W. Burgess and H. J. Locke, *The Family: From Institution to Companionship* (New York: The American Book Company, 1953).

The broadly held, idealized picture of the American family comes to us from a rural-agricultural past. Many writers point nostalgically to the extended family of a preindustrial culture, living happily in a small town, village, or even in relative isolation from other families. The various needs of the family members were satisfied by other family members, since there were always several children as well as a number of adults immediately available to anyone. The youngsters learned the accepted ways of behaving more or less by direct imitation—ways of life that changed but slowly. Religion and ritual occupied places of importance in this setting, with the elders acting as interpreters and authority figures.[31] The family often had to provide for all of its needs, though a limited amount of specialization appeared here and there, leading to the practice of bartering between families or in the open market.

While a more critical analysis might disclose that the historic, agrarian setting was never as idyllic as when described in retrospect through the rose-colored glasses of hindsight, we need not concern ourselves with this disagreement. We do not have a choice of living a hundred years ago, or actually re-creating the past. We must function today; consequently, we need to look at the current concept of the family.

THE MODERN FAMILY

One must recognize, of course, that there is fantastic diversity in American families, consistent with our cultural pluralism. However, it is still possible and useful to discern a concept of the American family representing current trends. Ernest W. Burgess,[32] a recognized authority in the field, notes the following as characteristic of the concept:

1. *Modifiability and adaptability,* in response to conditions of rapid social change.
2. *Urbanization,* not merely in the sense that the proportion of families living in cities is increasing but that rural, as well as urban, families are adopting the urban way of life.
3. *Secularization,* with the declining control of religion and with the increasing role of material comforts, labor-saving devices, and other mechanical contrivances like the automobile, the radio, and television.

[31] A well-written, insightful presentation of this setting appears in Joseph Krumgold's description of life on a sheep ranch in New Mexico, *And Now Miguel* (New York: Crowell, 1953).

[32] Ernest W. Burgess, "The Family in a Changing Society," *American Journal of Sociology,* 53, No. 6 (May 1948), 417–422. With permission of University of Chicago Press.

4. *Instability,* as evidenced by the continuing increase in divorce, reaching in 1945 the proportion of one for every three marriages.
5. *Specialization,* on the functions of the giving and receiving of affection, bearing and rearing of children, and personality development, which followed the loss of extrinsic functions, such as economic production, education, religious training, and protection.
6. The *trend to companionship,* with emphasis upon consensus, common interests, democratic relations, and personal happiness of family members.

THE DEMOCRATIZATION OF THE AMERICAN FAMILY

For the most part, the American family is based on a Western heritage of patriarchal family organization. The influence of diverse backgrounds is traceable in the American pattern—among them that of the Hebrew, the Greek, the Roman, the Christian, the Anglo-Saxon, and the Germanic family.[33] These European patterns were modified by several developments in the "New World."

The American frontier, with its scarcity of women, placed high status on them and altered many of the legal restrictions that had kept them in subordinate status. The freedom of women was also influenced by the self-reliance necessary on the frontier, where life was in constant danger and the husband often away from home. The man of the house often became the casualty of unfriendly animals, nature, or people; at times he also simply deserted the home, since the opportunities for desertion were high. All of these factors tended to strengthen the position of the female in the family.

The Industrial Revolution produced further significant changes in the family life in America. With industrialization and the attendant rise of the factory system of production, there was a linear increase through the decades in the proportion of women in the labor force. The data in Table 4–2 show the growing proportion of married women gainfully employed outside of the home.

The early years of the Industrial Revolution saw much exploitation of women and children in our factories, mines, and sweatshops. In the long run, however, many of these ills were remedied by laws regulating child labor as well as the hours and conditions of the employment of women. Along with these laws, a sizable amount of social legislation altered the

[33] For a brief but excellent treatment, see C. Kirkpatrick, *The Family: As Process and Institution* (New York: The Ronald Press, 1955), Chapter 5.

TABLE 4–2. Gainfully employed married women, 1890–1960.

Year	Number of married working women	Per cent increase over previous report		Per cent all married working women are of	
		Married working women	All married women	All married women	All working women
1890	515,260	....	....	4.6	13.9
1900	769,477	49.3	24.1	5.6	15.4
1910	1,890,661	145.7	28.1	10.7	24.7
1920	1,920,281	15.7	20.6	9.0	23.0
1930	3,071,302	59.9	22.8	11.7	28.9
1940	4,560,835	48.5	15.0	15.2	35.5
1950	9,273,000	103.3	24.5	24.8	52.1
1960	12,250,000	32.1	35.0	31.0	55.0

Bureau of the Census, *Fifteenth Census of the United States, 1930,* "Population," 5, "General Report on Occupations," p. 272; *Sixteenth Census of the United States, 1940,* "Population," 3, "Labor Force," Part I, p. 22. Data for 1950 from Bureau of the Census, *Current Population Reports,* "Labor Force," Series P-50, No. 37, December 26, 1951; 1960 data from the United States Department of Labor, *Women Workers in 1960,* Bulletin 284, 1962.

social status of women toward equality and, it has been charged, in some cases even toward preferential treatment. (California laws governing the property of husband and wife would be a case in point, where legal presumptions tend to run heavily in favor of the wife.)

Independently of other consequences, industrialization did make an impact on the American family. The employment of women tended to take them out of the home, thus making them less available to the children, and giving them a new taste of freedom in the occupational world. Equality of occupational opportunity for women is yet to come. Women by now have proven their value in high-status technical and professional occupations; yet, justifiably or not, in very many instances the male still holds the higher status and has easier access to desired jobs than females equally qualified. It was not until 1964 that the U.S. Congress enacted the so-called "equal pay for equal work" law, further protecting our "working women."

Along with the increase in the proportion of women in the labor force there has been a corresponding decline in the size of the family (see Table 4–3).

One important factor in this decline has been the steady shift of our population from the rural setting, with its ample space and where many

TABLE 4–3. Average number of persons per family household in the United States, 1790–1950, together with projections to 1980.

Year	Persons per family	Year	Persons per family	Year	Persons per family
1790	5.7	1880	5.0	1920	4.3
1850	5.6	1890	4.9	1930	4.1
1860	5.3	1900	4.7	1940	3.8
1870	5.1	1910	4.5	1950	3.4
				1965	3.32
				1980	3.45

Figure for 1790 from Bureau of the Census, *A Century of Population Growth from the First Census of the United States to the Twelfth, 1790–1900,* 1909, p. 96; 1850–1920, from *Fourteenth Census, 1920, Population, General Report and Analytical Tables,* 2, p. 1266; 1930 and 1940, from *Sixteenth Census of the United States, 1940, Population, Families, Size of Families, and Age of Head, Regions and Cities of 1,000,000 or More, 1944,* p. 4; 1950, from Bureau of the Census, *United States Census of Population, 1950, Characteristics of the Population,* Series P-B, No. 1 (U.S. Summary), Table 47; 1965 and 1980 are projections of the Bureau of Census, *Statistical Abstracts of the United States,* 1962, p. 42.

hands were needed for the daily chores, to the urban centers with their crowded residential areas and inadequate recreational facilities, where children often are considered liabilities.

The slow but steady development of our culture toward its democratic ideals brought about further changes within the family. The old common-law principle that, "Man and wife are one and he is it" gave way to an egalitarian ideal which, in 1920, produced the 19th amendment to the United States Constitution. (It is interesting to note that most of the work to accomplish this result went on while "the men were overseas or in the army" during World War I.) However, not for several years after 1920 did women gain equal treatment on a host of other matters, ranging from eligibility for jury service to penalties for sex offenses.[34] There is vigorous in-group fighting among the members of the fair sex who disagree on whether women should have "equivalent rights" (National League of Women Voters) or "identical rights" (National Women's Party). It might be well here to paraphrase the late Justice Oliver Wendell Holmes, Jr., to the effect that it would take more than legislative action to prove that there are no differences between men and women. However, the relevant point to make here is that all of these forces have interacted and been influential

[34] Ethel M. Smith, *Toward Equal Rights for Men and Women* (Washington, D.C.: Committee on the Legal Status of Women, National League of Women Voters, 1929).

in changing the American family from the earlier patriarchal type to an emerging pattern of democratic relationships.

THE MODERN FAMILY AND THE SCHOOLS

The transition affecting the family has had reverberations in our various educational institutions. In Colonial America, the child was in school three months of the year, as contrasted with the current practice of nine to ten months. Character education and personality formation—once functions of the family—have been increasingly turned over to the schools. With the rise of an industrial civilization, where the life of the student is generally removed from the world of work, the schools have become more important in vocational guidance. As the extended family disappeared and the shrinking conjugal family became less and less secure in a rapidly changing world fraught with conflict, the guidance functions of each teacher, as well as of the guidance specialists, have taken on increased significance. This situation is further complicated by a rising divorce rate that tends to remove the male influence from many homes. At the same time, our marriages have been taking place at an earlier and earlier age. According to the census information, between 1890 and 1960 the median age at first marriage has declined for males from 26.1 to 22.6 and for females from 21.0 to 20.4 years.

In the rural-agricultural setting of the extended family, the functions of the school and of the family were each clear and distinct. As the American family changed through the decades, the school and other institutions in society have taken over some of the functions previously reserved to the family. Whether or not the schools should be responsible for personality formation, character development, driver training, typing, music, art, sewing, health, and so forth, are important issues that are difficult to settle. The *fact* remains, however, that the American culture in its process of transition saw fit to turn many of these tasks over to the schools. The more or less agonizing process of reappraisal our culture is undergoing in the decade between 1960 and 1970 may reaffirm existing educational goals, or may suggest the need for drastic surgery on the curriculum. Either of these outcomes, or a compromise between them, should be done after careful appraisal of the changes that have occurred in the American family.

We now know that the school should cooperate with the family for the optimal development of children and youth. The "wall of separation" that historically often existed between these two very important institutions, and to some extent still is with us, cannot be defended on educational grounds. This is not to suggest that lay persons from the family should take over the professional roles of the educators or that educators should "invade" the home life of the student. It does mean that the schools should make a continuous, systematic effort to inform the parents and, in a sense, to educate the parents; and that educators should know about the changes in the American family. The next section explores some of these changes further as we look at the implications of industrialization, population growth, and population mobility.

STUDIES OF INDUSTRIALIZATION AND POPULATION MOBILITY

INDUSTRIALIZATION

Today's America is an advanced technological civilization. Although this development has its roots in man's earliest efforts to fashion tools, the real impetus came when James Watt perfected a working steam engine in the late eighteenth century. During the ensuing eighty or ninety years, a proliferation of steam, electrical, mechanical, and chemical devices has completely revolutionized man's efforts to produce and transport goods and services. The impact of science and technology is rapidly making even recent developments obsolete under the magic-like accomplishment and promises of electronic and nuclear developments.

In our "change-oriented" culture, each innovation quickly leads to a dozen or more other innovations, inventions, and changes. This process inspires the oft-repeated statement that today "the only thing constant is change." The dramatic accomplishment of spaceships and satellites suggests future developments that, heretofore, actually lay beyond the imagination of the boldest speculators. Writers of science fiction must strain to keep ahead of the actual accomplishments of science and technology.[35]

With the rise of technology, the process by which science is used in the solution of man's problems, several key developments occurred. New and effective systems of mass transportation and communication came into being, which later gave rise to urban developments. New communities sprang up as the railroads formed a giant web, making most of the country accessible. The concentration of machinery under one roof, made possible

[35] For an authoritative and comprehensive account of human history leading to the scientific revolution, see Carleton S. Coon, *The Story of Man* (New York: Knopf, 1955); for a narrower focus on science, see Frank S. Taylor, *A Short History of Science and Scientific Thought* (New York: W. W. Norton, 1949).

and necessary by the development of steam as the source of power, led to the factory system, mass production, and specialization. All this in time brought about the huge industrial centers, electronic and nuclear combines, and the concentration of manpower necessary for them to function effectively. There is no doubting the proposition that within less than a century America has changed from a predominantly rural-agricultural civilization to an overwhelmingly urban-industrial one.

Industrialization has had a profound impact upon most aspects of our society and its culture. It is very difficult to point to a significant human activity—be it economic, social, intellectual, or even aesthetic—that has totally escaped the impact of science and technology. We have seen part of the impact on the family as an institution, on stratification, on various aspects of the culture as pointed out in Chapter 2. Next we shall highlight the influence of modern science and technology on population movements, on education, leisure, and occupations; this analysis could be extended to all aspects of life.

POPULATION GROWTH AND MOBILITY

It is generally known that today most Americans live in urban centers. Along with the process of our becoming an industrial nation, our population by and large left the farms, and many of those who remained are no longer farm workers. Table 4–4 presents the statistical evidence documenting this rural-urban shift.

The rise of the city and of the metropolis and the "megalopolis" is a fascinating and controversial story which is still being written.[36] The decade between 1960 and 1970 is one of urban renewal, slum clearance, and beautification. The suburban dweller who works in the heart of the city is also reconsidering his conflicting preferences and often trades the comforts and demands of suburban living for the more convenient city apartment.

The population is not only shifting but rapidly expanding. The 1960 Census registered a population of over 180,000,000, which, by 1970, will increase to approximately 208,000,000, up 28,000,000 or a 15 per cent increase in one decade.[37] Along with this growth in numbers, there has been a steady westward shift in the statistical center of the population (see Table 4–5 and Figure 4–1).

[36] For a historical account, see Lewis Mumford, *The City in History* (New York: Harcourt, Brace and World, Inc., 1961).

[37] United States Department of Labor, *Manpower: Challenge of the 1960's.*

TABLE 4–4. Urban and rural places and population, by size of place: 1910 to 1960.

Class and Size	1910	1920	1930	1940	1950 Previous urban definition	1950 Current urban definition	1960 Previous urban definition	1960 Current urban definition
PLACES								
Urban	2,262	2,722	3,165	3,464	4,054	4,741	5,022	6,041
Places of 1,000,000 or more	3	3	5	5	5	5	5	5
Places of 500,000 to 1,000,000	5	9	8	9	13	13	16	16
Places of 250,000 to 500,000	11	13	24	23	23	23	30	30
Places of 100,000 to 250,000	31	43	56	55	67	65	80	81
Places of 50,000 to 100,000	59	76	98	107	129	126	203	201
Places of 25,000 to 50,000	119	143	185	213	283	252	427	432
Places of 10,000 to 25,000	369	465	606	665	831	778	1,146	1,134
Places of 5,000 to 10,000	605	715	851	965	1,129	1,176	1,326	1,394
Places of 2,500 to 5,000	1,060	1,255	1,332	1,422	1,574	1,846	1,789	2,152
Places under 2,500	—	—	—	—	—	457	—	596
Rural	11,830	12,855	13,433	13,288	13,235	13,807	13,418	13,749
Places of 1,000 to 2,500	2,717	3,030	3,087	3,205	3,404	4,158	3,545	4,151
Places under 1,000	9,113	9,825	10,346	10,083	9,831	9,649	9,873	9,598
POPULATION (1,000)								
United States	*91,972*	*105,711*	*122,775*	*131,669*	*150,697*	*150,697*	*179,323*	*179,323*
Urban	41,999	54,158	68,955	74,424	89,749	96,468	113,056	125,269
Places of 1,000,000 or more	8,501	10,146	15,065	15,911	17,404	17,404	17,484	17,484
Places of 500,000 to 1,000,000	3,011	6,224	5,764	6,457	9,187	9,187	11,111	11,111
Places of 250,000 to 500,000	3,950	4,541	7,956	7,828	8,242	8,242	10,766	10,766
Places of 100,000 to 250,000	4,840	6,519	7,541	7,793	9,724	9,479	11,548	11,652
Places of 50,000 to 100,000	4,179	5,265	6,491	7,344	9,138	8,931	13,959	13,836
Places of 25,000 to 50,000	4,023	5,075	6,426	7,417	9,876	8,808	14,776	14,951
Places of 10,000 to 25,000	5,549	7,035	9,097	9,967	12,768	11,867	17,731	17,568

Class and Size	1910	1920	1930	1940	1950		1960	
					Previous urban definition	Current urban definition	Previous urban definition	Current urban definition
Places of 5,000 to 10,000	4,217	4,968	5,897	6,682	7,832	8,139	9,350	9,780
Places of 2,500 to 5,000	3,728	4,386	4,718	5,026	5,579	6,490	6,332	7,580
Places under 2,500	—	—	—	—	—	578	—	690
Unincorporated parts of urbanized areas	—	—	—	—	—	7,344	—	9,851
Rural	49,973	51,553	53,820	57,246	60,948	54,230	66,267	54,054
Places of 1,000 to 2,500	4,234	4,712	4,821	5,027	5,383	6,473	5,616	6,497
Places under 1,000	3,930	4,255	4,363	4,316	4,129	4,031	4,032	3,894
Other rural	41,809	42,586	44,637	47,903	51,437	43,725	56,619	43,664
PERCENT OF TOTAL POPULATION								
United States	*100.0*	*100.0*	*100.0*	*100.0*	*100.0*	*100.0*	*100.0*	*100.0*
Urban	45.7	51.2	56.2	56.5	59.6	64.0	63.0	69.9
Places of 1,000,000 or more	9.2	9.6	12.3	12.1	11.5	11.5	9.8	9.8
Places of 500,000 to 1,000,000	3.3	5.9	4.7	4.9	6.1	6.1	6.2	6.2
Places of 250,000 to 500,000	4.3	4.3	6.5	5.9	5.5	5.5	6.0	6.0
Places of 100,000 to 250,000	5.3	6.2	6.1	5.9	6.5	6.3	6.4	6.5
Places of 50,000 to 100,000	4.5	5.0	5.3	5.6	6.1	5.9	7.8	7.7
Places of 25,000 to 50,000	4.4	4.8	5.2	5.6	6.6	5.8	8.2	8.3
Places of 10,000 to 25,000	6.0	6.7	7.4	7.6	8.5	7.9	9.9	9.8
Places of 5,000 to 10,000	4.6	4.7	4.8	5.1	5.2	5.4	5.2	5.5
Places of 2,500 to 5,000	4.1	4.1	3.8	3.8	3.7	4.3	3.5	4.2
Places under 2,500	—	—	—	—	—	0.4	—	0.4
Unincorporated parts of urbanized areas	—	—	—	—	—	4.9	—	5.5
Rural	54.3	48.8	43.8	43.5	40.4	36.0	37.0	30.1
Places of 1,000 to 2,500	4.6	4.5	3.9	3.8	3.6	4.3	3.1	3.6
Places under 1,000	4.3	4.0	3.6	3.3	2.7	2.7	2.2	2.2
Other rural	45.5	40.3	36.4	36.4	34.1	29.0	31.6	24.3

Beginning 1960, includes Alaska and Hawaii. Source: Department of Commerce, Bureau of the Census; *U.S. Census of Population: 1960*, Vol. I.

TABLE 4–5. Center of population: 1790 to 1960.*

Year	North latitude			West longitude			Approximate location
CONTERMINOUS U.S.[1]	°	′	″	°	′	″	
1790	39	16	30	76	11	12	23 miles east of Baltimore, Md.
1800	39	16	6	76	56	30	18 miles west of Baltimore, Md.
1810	39	11	30	77	37	12	40 miles northwest by west of Washington, D. C. (in Virginia).
1820	39	5	42	78	33	0	16 miles east of Moorefield, W. Va.[2]
1830	38	57	54	79	16	54	19 miles west-southwest of Moorefield, W. Va.[2]
1840	39	2	0	80	18	0	16 miles south of Clarksburg, W. Va.[2]
1850	38	59	0	81	19	0	23 miles southeast of Parkersburg, W. Va.[2]
1860	39	0	24	82	48	48	20 miles south by east of Chillicothe, Ohio.
1870	39	12	0	83	35	42	48 miles east by north of Cincinnati, Ohio.
1880	39	4	8	84	39	40	8 miles west by south of Cincinnati, Ohio (in Kentucky).
1890	39	11	56	85	32	53	20 miles east of Columbus, Ind.
1900	39	9	36	85	48	54	6 miles southeast of Columbus, Ind.
1910	39	10	12	86	32	20	In the city of Bloomington, Ind.
1920	39	10	21	86	43	15	8 miles south-southeast of Spencer, Owen County, Ind.
1930	39	3	45	87	8	6	3 miles northeast of Linton, Greene County, Ind.
1940	38	56	54	87	22	35	2 miles southeast by east of Carlisle, Haddon township, Sullivan County, Ind.
1950	38	50	21	88	9	33	8 miles north-northwest of Olney, Richland County, Ill.
1960	38	37	57	88	52	23	4 miles east of Salem in Marion County, Ill.
UNITED STATES[3]							
1950	38	48	15	88	22	8	About 3 miles northeast of Louisville, in Clay County, Ill.
1960	38	35	58	89	12	35	6½ miles northwest of Centralia, Ill., and approximately 50 miles east of East St. Louis, Ill.

* "Center of population" is that point which may be considered as center of population gravity of the U.S. or that point upon which the U.S. would balance if it were a rigid plane without weight and the population distributed thereon with each individual being assumed to have equal weight and to exert an influence on a central point proportional to his distance from that point.

[1] Excludes Alaska and Hawaii.

[2] West Virginia was set off from Virginia Dec. 31, 1862, and admitted as a State June 19, 1863.

[3] Includes Alaska and Hawaii.

Source: Department of Commerce, Bureau of the Census; *U.S. Census of Population: 1960,* Vol. I.

"The major trends in our population are by now quite familiar. We are living longer, getting married earlier, having our children sooner and more often."[38] Although the total population will increase, the greatest in-

[38] N. B. Ryder, "Demography and Education: Variability and Convergence in the American Population," *Phi Delta Kappan,* 41, No. 9 (June 1960), 381.

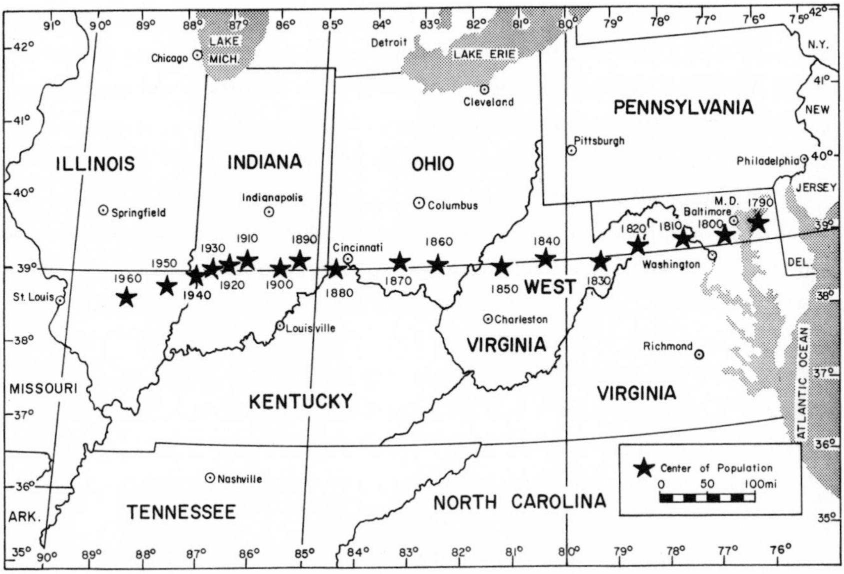

FIGURE 4–1. Center of population for conterminous U.S.: 1790 to 1960. (From Department of Commerce, Bureau of the Census.)

creases—*if present trends continue*—will be among the young and the old, with the middle age groups hardly increasing at all. It is predicted, for example, that "workers under 25 will account for nearly half of the labor force growth during the 1960's, even though they will stay in school longer." There will be "a relatively small increase among workers 25–34 and actually fewer workers age 35–44. More workers will be 45 years and over in 1970 than in 1960, despite earlier retirement." . . . The number of women workers will increase at nearly twice the rate for men. By 1970 there will be about 30 million women workers, six million more than in 1960."[39]

EFFECTS OF INDUSTRIALIZATION AND POPULATION GROWTH UPON EDUCATION

Demography—the systematic study of population composition, changes, and trends—became important to educators after World War II. This was brought about by the fact that many school systems were unprepared for a bumper crop of postwar babies, who inundated the schools five

39 United States Department of Labor (see note 37), pp. 6, 7.

years later. Since then, the harvest has been a rich one every year without letup. By now, careful educators conduct yearly surveys in their communities to anticipate the various needs of their school district. Others attempt to plan permanent and systematic study of Census figures, statistical abstracts, and other reliable, up-to-date sources of information.[40]

Although the Census data, as well as data from the N.E.A. and the U.S. Office of Education, are relevant for a general perspective of national, regional, and statewide trends, local educators must go beyond these sources. In order to plan and to make decisions for the local scene, educators must gather population data that present the facts and characteristics of their respective school districts. At times these can be extrapolated from the Census reports,[41] but often periodic local surveys must be conducted. In many fast-growing suburban communities, P.T.A.'s as well as local service organizations conduct these surveys under the guidance of the central administrative offices of the local schools.

The intelligent educator cannot make long-range decisions without being aware of demographic changes and trends. Some of the implications for educators are highlighted by Thomas,[42] who raises serious questions about the appropriate sources for needed funds to finance the tremendous educational tasks ahead. He points up the problem of the rural-urban shift in the population without a similar shift in political power; the problems of stability, conformity, and disintegration; and the problem of encouraging uniqueness and individuality in a population which is becoming increasingly similar in many important respects.[43]

When we examine some of the statistics relevant to the tasks of the schools, a staggering picture emerges before us. During the 1963–1964 school year, close to 42,000,000 pupils enrolled in our public elementary and secondary schools, taught by a staff of nearly 1,750,000.[44] The school-age population increased about 50 per cent between 1950 and 1964. As

[40] One highly recommended source is the *Statistical Abstracts of the United States,* United States Department of Commerce, Bureau of Census (yearly editions). Another one, focusing on material relevant to educators, is the National Education Association's *Research Bulletin.*

[41] See, for example, Marchia Meeker and Joan R. Harris, *Background for Planning,* Research Report No. 17, Research Department, Welfare Planning Council, Los Angeles Region, 731 South Hope St., Los Angeles 17, California, February 1964.

[42] Donald R. Thomas, "Implications of Demographic Changes for Education," *Phi Delta Kappan,* 41, No. 9 (June 1960), 383–385.

[43] See Ryder, *Demography and Education* (note 38), pp. 381–382.

[44] National Education Association, *Research Bulletin,* 39, No. 1 (February 1961), 4.

indicated in Figure 4–2, this population is growing faster than the total population of our country.

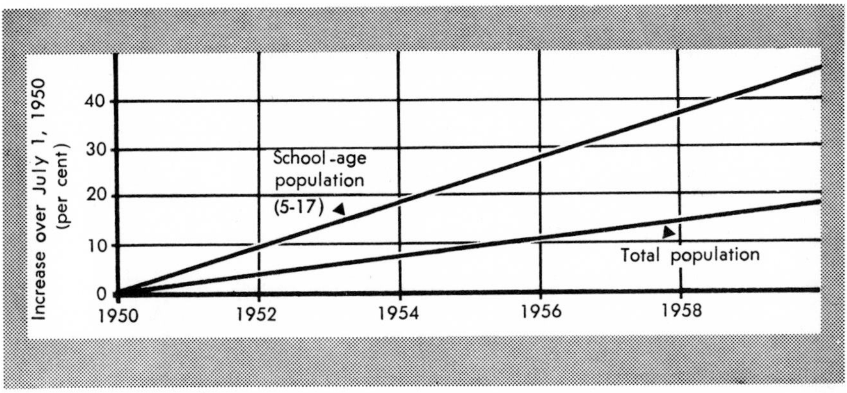

FIGURE 4–2. School-age population and total population.

Considering the changes occurring in the occupational structure of the United States, it can be predicted that future increases will be the greatest in occupations requiring the most education and training. Currently, of every ten children who enter grade school, seven will earn a high school diploma; of the seven, four will continue education beyond the high school, and only two will finish four years of college.

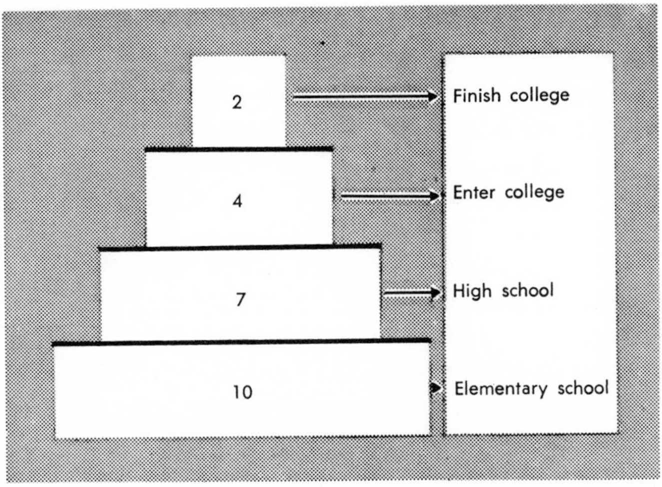

FIGURE 4–3

The prevailing relationship between the level of education attained and one's occupational status will be accentuated in the future. Table 4–6 reflects this trend.[45]

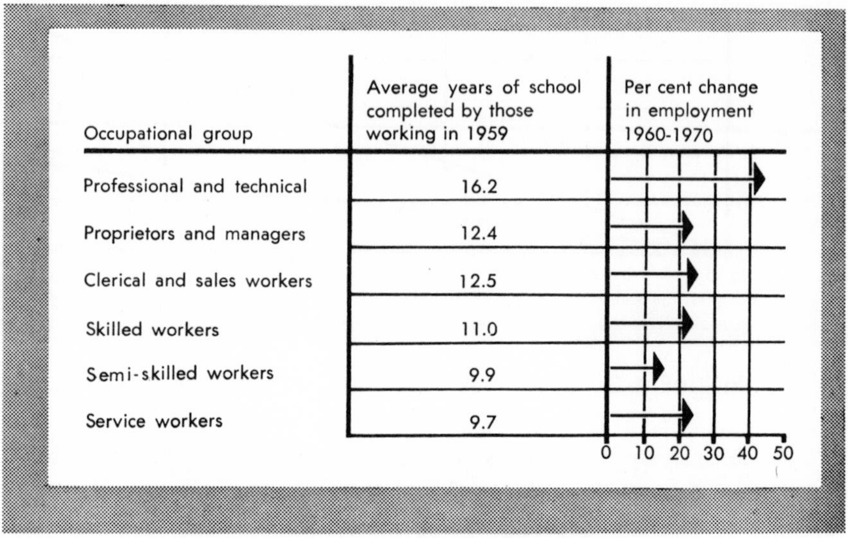

FIGURE 4–4. Education and occupational status.

It is generally agreed that the world of tomorrow will require more and better education of its aspirants for the higher-status occupations. Consequently, it should be easy to understand the prediction that "high school enrollment will increase by nearly 50 per cent during the 1960's—on top of a 40% increase during the 1950's, and that college enrollments will increase by 70% during the 1960's as compared with 40% during the 1950's."[46]

Nevertheless, the school "drop out" is still a serious problem in America. A group of advisers to the President predicts that "70% of new entrants to the labor force in the 1960's will be high school graduates or better, as compared with 60% in the 1950's" but that "7.5 million young people entering the labor force during the 1960's will not have completed high school and 2.5 million of these will not have completed even a grade

[45] *Education: For a Changing World of Work,* a Summary Report of the Panel of Consultants on Vocational Education Requested by the President of the United States (Washington, D.C.: United States Government Printing Office, 1962), 0-665976.

[46] United States Department of Labor, *Manpower: Challenge of the 1960's* (see note 37).

school education."[47] The magnitude of this problem is sufficient to deserve careful examination by educators as well as by other agencies in society.

Moreover, class sizes are still inadequate. In 1961, urban elementary schools had 380,000 children in classes of more than 40 pupils each; furthermore, in 1960, about 18,000 school districts in the United States enrolled less than 50 pupils each; in 1958–59, approximately 400,000 children attended one-teacher schools.[48] Regardless of the factors giving rise to such conditions, the quality of education is likely to leave much to be desired under each of these circumstances.

Although the problems facing our schools are formidable, past accomplishments can be fairly characterized as tremendous. Our schools have contributed significantly to the task of welding one nation from the stream of immigrants coming to our shores from dozens of different lands. Of the many possible measures of the accomplishments of American education, let us note only two: the illiteracy rate even during the current century dropped from 10.7 per cent of the adult population in 1900 to 2.2 per cent in 1959, while college enrollment climbed from 4 per cent of college-age population (18–21 years) in 1900 to 37 per cent in 1962. It should also be noted that 50–60 per cent of those who enter college eventually graduate. There can be no doubt, looking at the picture from a historical perspective, that the accomplishments have been enormous, in light of the problems to be surmounted.

PROBLEMS OF COMMUNICATION IN AN URBAN MASS SOCIETY

In an up-to-date nursery school in a suburban setting in California, whose clientele came from middle and upper-middle-class families, the children were "playing house." A round-faced little four-year-old boy was assigned the role of the father. As the "members of the family" went to perform their various roles, the "mother" and the "sisters" found appropriate tasks in and around the house, the "brother" did, too, and even the "baby" boy lay down with a cuddly toy and made gurgling sounds. But what did the "father" do? With an old hat on his head and a discarded briefcase in his hand, "father" left the "house" and *sat down* on a nearby box. After sitting still, almost bewildered for a while, "father" came home for dinner.

47 United States Department of Labor, *Manpower: Challenge of the 1960's*, p. 15.
48 National Education Association, *Research Bulletin* (see note 44), p. 27.

In a very real sense this episode from the play of children indicates the modern-day fact that the father's occupation is a mystery to most members of the household, and certainly for its young. Complex and all-pervasive changes in occupations accompanied the shift from a rural-agricultural to an urban-industrial society. Before the transformation of our way of life by the modern factory system and its attendant developments, most men were self-employed. Today, however, the overwhelming majority are employed by others; that is to say, they have shifted from "making a living to earning a living."

The occupational world at once became fantastically complex and at the same time removed from the proximity of the home. The rise of urban centers also brought with it specialized areas such as industrial sections, financial and banking centers, shopping areas, recreational areas, and residential areas. Even these break down further into heavy industries separated from light industries, certain kinds of recreational areas separated from others, and residential areas separated at times simply by economic factors and at times by religious, ethnic, and racial barriers.

Under such circumstances, where the father is typically away from home from early morning until 5 or 6 o'clock in the evening, several problems arise. One important one has to do with the psychological problems arising for girls and boys, as well as for the mothers, from living in a world where the adult authority figures are predominantly females. Our schools have an important role to play here, but this problem should be carefully considered by psychologists and by educators under the guidance of qualified psychologists.

Another relevant problem arises from the inability of the children and youth to have direct contact with the work world of the father. This is further complicated by the fact that an increasingly higher percentage of our married women also work away from home, with their number expected to rise to one third of the total labor force by 1970.

One only needs to spend ten minutes with the Want-Ad section of a Sunday edition of any metropolitan newspaper to reach utter bewilderment. Of the amazing number of occupational categories listed and advertised, probably nine tenths will be meaningless to the average reader. The gradual rise of industrial specialization has produced a fantastic array of occupational labels and sublabels that are meaningful only to the specialists and a small circle of workers in related fields. These labels disappear as fast as they appear, as the rapid pace of technological change dislocates workers and makes relatively recent discoveries and developments obsolete.

Is it any wonder that the young boy today wants to be a garbage man, fireman, milkman, policeman, or—perhaps later, when television moves in on him—a cowboy? These occupations are real and meaningful to him; they seem to deal with important things in life and are not complicated by a maze of abstract ideas far removed from the daily lives of the young. As the child becomes a youth, these so-called fantasy choices of occupation give way under the steady pressure of the culture to decide "what'll you be when you grow up?" But on what bases can the youth choose? On the bases of factual information and attitudes and insights gained from systematic exposure to the occupation? Or on the bases of empty labels that sound attractive or even glamourous? Or on the inadequate grounds of imitating an uncle, a father, a neighbor, or some television idol? It is, indeed, very risky to take the advice of those who themselves are not pleased with their own vocational choices, and survey after survey has indicated that most people are not.

We have reached the stage of complexity in our human development where expert vocational guidance is almost an absolute necessity. It is true that most adults are willing to "help." These "helpers," however, themselves act on the basis of inadequate knowledge or lack of knowledge; consequently, a kind of pervasive ignorance of, and misinformation about, occupations is the plight of modern youth.

In the face of this bewildering complexity, the educator can offer important help. His twin roles of counselor and occupational-guidance expert should be recognized as more important than ever before. The vocational aspects involved must be considered from a broader perspective than immediate employment opportunity. Carefully mapped out programs are needed to help youth gain insight into the tremendous range of occupational possibilities, the attitudes and skills relevant to them, and the kinds of rewards and satisfactions available through them. All this should be done by the schools in a spirit of inquiry, as in other areas of school work, and not with the sense of mission to recruit so many workers for each occupation that currently happens to need them.

Educators must also reexamine the existing vocational programs in the curriculum. The pace of current social and technological developments is such that narrow vocational preparation is likely to be disastrous. Today's graduates must be well equipped to enter a wide range of possible occupations, all of which are based upon the same or similar skills, understandings, and attitudes. Modern developments, even in an age of specialization, call for individuals with a sound general education that facilitates specialization and a subsequent shift to a different but related specialty. It is clear that for educators, as well as for commerce, government, and industry, the social problem of reeducating the dislocated worker will loom larger and larger in the years ahead.

Related to the foregoing problem of misinformation concerning occupations, we find a broader cultural phenomenon—namely, the attenuation of the meaning of symbols. *Symbol,* as used here, refers to any word, expression, or object used to represent something other than itself. For instance, the word *apple* may be used to represent a piece of fruit, a Biblical concept, an apple growers' association, or anything else we choose to have it represent. Symbols are necessary tools for communication and for the construction of the conceptual schemes men use to understand and control their environment. In fact, one very important ability that distinguishes man from lower forms of organisms is his ability, with the use of symbols, to represent both the past and the future in the present situation. Man creates cultures and plans for the future by means of the symbols and systems of symbols he has invented.

The significance of symbols depends upon the social context in which they are used. Communication presupposes that the individual shares with others the meanings attached to the symbols they use.[49] If shared meanings are based on experiences, direct and vicarious, which groups of people have had in common, a culture undergoing rapid change will suffer from attenuation of its symbols. This has to some extent occurred in the United States, due to factors implicit in the rapid rise of an industrialized mass society.

In any society, age tends to promote natural separation between generations. This gap turns into group isolation in an industrial culture that separates the work world of the adults from the home. As a result, youth is pushed to form subcultures of its own with values, interests, and a language that differ from those of the adults. Furthermore, adults in occupational specialties also tend to develop unique subcultures, with symbols shared only by members of their own circle of specialists.

The problem of attenuation of the meanings of symbols has further complications. We increasingly live in specialized communities and work at specialized tasks. At the same time, however, mass media bring into our homes reports from all corners of our land and of the world. We are asked

[49] There are important differences among various theories concerning symbols. For our purposes, we have assumed a functional, or instrumental theory of symbols. For a thorough analysis of this topic, see Charles Morris, *Signs, Language and Behavior* (New York: G. Braziller, 1955).

to express opinions and to help formulate decisions that will have consequences ranging far and wide. Those symbols that are based upon vicarious experiences derived from the mass media and are often carefully manipulated, in light of hidden purposes, do not have the same relevance and reliability as those based upon direct experiences.

The foregoing presents a twofold danger: (1) we can manipulate, at the verbal level, many symbols which have for us little or no meaning or to which we attach meanings that differ from meanings held by others all around us; or (2) we are called upon to make important decisions with worldwide consequences in matters for which we have only predigested, and often carefully censored, symbolic information.

When symbols are not rooted in direct experience, or in carefully analyzed vicarious experience, they become easily distorted and manipulated. The very core of the democratic process is threatened by this situation since this process, among other considerations, is based on the notion of a well-informed electorate capable of contributing intelligent voices to the decision-making processes of society. When symbols become attenuated, the demagogue, the authoritarian leader, or the amoral manipulator is in a better position to use the mass media to control the minds of men.[50]

The implication for educators is clear but very difficult to translate into action. Our times call for citizens who, better than ever before in history, can analyze, define, draw inferences, recognize fallacies and inconsistencies, differentiate between descriptive and emotive uses of language, and who possess a host of other skills and attitudes necessary to deal adequately with symbols. Students must understand the relationship of symbols, abstractions, constructs, and theories to the daily processes of human activity.

It is one of the tasks of education to move students toward defensible biases and away from prejudices. The objection is often raised that "analysis" leads to "paralysis"; that is, there is fear that careful examination of known relevant factors will immobilize one and prevent decision making. While this danger must be acknowledged, it need not materialize. More detailed discussion will follow in Chapter 5, but for present purposes, let us simply indicate the crucial difference between a prejudice and a bias. "Prejudice," as suggested by its etymology, refers to a decision reached without considering other possible alternatives, relevant evidence, or in spite of sufficient evidence to the contrary. "Bias," however,

[50] This analysis is based upon various speeches delivered by Dean I. James Quillen of the School of Education, Stanford, Calif.

operates when a decision is reached after due consideration of the relevant facts as well as of all the available alternative points of view.

In our complex industrial civilization, decisions must constantly be made. It is the task of the teacher to educate his students in the use of symbols and thus to help them to develop defensible biases and systematically eliminate prejudice as a factor in decision making. This is, indeed, a heavy assignment in a culture in which some agencies, such as advertising in the mass media, bombard our children and youth with symbols and push them toward an uncritical acceptance of the symbols and the products these symbols represent. The tasks of the schools become unbelievably difficult, if not impossible, in such a cultural milieu.

SCIENTIFIC METHOD AND EDUCATION

At the beginning of this chapter, we stated that the systematic, scientific study of man, of his behavior and his institutions, is relatively new. The *Novum Organum* (1620) of Sir Francis Bacon is generally credited with the launching of the *inductive method* of inquiry. This method, popularly known as the scientific method, was further clarified by John Stuart Mill and labeled the method of *experimental inquiry*. Bacon's view, which regarded science as systematic observation and inductive generalization from observed data, has been superseded by more accurate and sophisticated explanations of what science is.[51] It took the work of Charles Darwin, however, particularly his publication of *On the Origin of Species* (1859) and *The Descent of Man* (1871) to focus man's efforts on the scientific study of man and human behavior.

> It has now grown clear that the fundamental importance of evolutionary thought . . . lay primarily in its methodological significance: there was to be no sharp difference in intellectual methods in treating man and the other aspects of the nature of which he was taken to be a part.[52]

The latter part of the nineteenth century and the first half of the twentieth found American intellectual thought highly influenced by evolutionary naturalism. Adherents can be found in fields as divergent as law,

[51] See for example, Ernest Nagel, "Philosophy in Educational Research," *Educational Research,* Phi Delta Kappa, 1960; for a more thorough treatment by the same author, see his *The Structure of Science* (New York: Harcourt, Brace and World, Inc., 1961); for a presentation aimed at lay understanding, see James B. Conant, *On Understanding Science* (New Haven: Yale University Press, 1947).

[52] John Herman Randall, Jr., "The Nature of Naturalism," in Y. H. Kirkorian, ed., *Naturalism and the Human Spirit* (New York: Columbia University Press, 1944), p. 357.

sociology, history, and, of course, the physical sciences. As would be expected, the content and the methodology of education were influenced by these developments, particularly under the influence of key educational theorists such as G. Stanley Hall, William James, John Dewey, William H. Kilpatrick, R. Bruce Raup, John L. Childs, Boyd H. Bode, and others.

The "new science of man" proceeded from the assumption that "nature" is a category that includes the universe, man, and anything or any relationship knowable to man. The theory of the universe consistent with this view is one of constant change and development but without a specific beginning or an ultimate end. It is an open-ended universe within which man is continuous with nature and in which he is a complex product of organic biological evolution. Values, moral as well as aesthetic, are the products of systematic criticism of experience and are constructed by men rather than given to him or discovered by him. This point of view, relying on the methods of science, can neither affirm or deny the existence of supernatural entities, since first causes or ultimate purposes cannot be investigated by empirical methods.

Serious scholars confine use of the scientific method to its legitimate purposes and grant that other concerns of life are understandable only through reason or revelation. Adherents of a strictly naturalistic point of view tend to claim that statements about supernatural phenomena are either meaningless or, at best, poetry. Reliable knowledge is the result of open investigation and not of private intuition or revelation. A new idea, a hunch, or a hypothesis may originate from some intuitive leap or creative act of the imagination, but it cannot claim the status of knowledge or truth until sufficiently tested in shareable experience. In this open-ended universe, the key question is not "What are the purposes of man?" or of life but "What shall we make the purpose of life?" thus shifting the responsibility for the future to the shoulders of man.[53]

From what we now know about the possibilities and limitations of the "new science," it is safe to state that a complete or even near-complete science of human behavior is not yet visible on the horizon. This reservation, however, must not lead us to belittle the admittedly powerful and constantly growing contributions of the scientific method to the understanding of man. They are not likely to replace human judgments about values, beauty, and the aesthetic qualities in experience, although they will make an impact even there.

[53] For an analysis of the impact of Darwinian evolution on intellectual developments, see John Dewey, *The Influence of Darwin on Philosophy* (New York: Holt, 1910).

Today, the quality of education is generally better, thanks to the influence of the scientific method. The method itself is of great significance even in highly complex human enterprises, even when accurate measurement is not yet possible. For we can still carefully state our purpose, formulate a plan which we propose to test out (a hypothesis), gather our data pursuant to the plan, test out our hunch in action, and evaluate the consequences. Knowledge thus acquired is a result of systematically criticized action and prior to such action cannot be asserted on some basis of intuition, unquestioned authority, or revelation. The power of this method resides to a great extent in the fact that it is self-correcting—i.e., that its errors are corrected through constant open criticism and repetition of the experiment. Just as the cure for the ills of democracy is said to be more democracy, so the cure for the errors of scientific inquiry is further inquiry.

SUMMARY

This chapter presents some of the contributions of the social sciences (other than psychology) that are relevant to the processes and institutions of education: the relevance to education of (1) social stratification, (2) the American family in transition, (3) industrialization and population growth and mobility, and (4) the impact of industrialization on an understanding of occupational categories and the common understanding of cultural symbols. There are enormous areas not even touched upon.

Although limitations of space do not permit full discussion of the broad topics of this chapter, we have presented sufficient material to point up the importance of science and the implications of its method for the decisions educators must constantly make. The methods and results of scientific inquiry thus must be among the ingredients used by educators in their decision-making processes, along with other, nonempirical types of knowledge. This will be explored in the next chapter and elsewhere in this volume.

SELECTED BIBLIOGRAPHY

Brookover, Wilbur, and David Gottlieb. *A Sociology of Education,* 2nd ed. New York: American Book Company, 1964.

Cicourel, Aaron V., and John I. Kitsuse. *The Educational Decision-Makers.* New York: The Bobbs-Merrill Company, Inc., 1963.

Cohen, Morris R., and Ernest Nagel. *Logic and the Scientific Method.* New York: Harcourt, Brace and World, Inc., 1934.

Coleman, James S. *The Adolescent Society.* Glencoe. Ill.: The Free Press, 1961.

Conant, James B. *Slums and Suburbs.* New York: McGraw-Hill Book Company, 1961.

Davis, Allison. *Social-Class Influences upon Learning.* Cambridge, Mass.: Harvard University Press, 1948.

__________, Burleigh B. Gardner, and Mary R. Gardner. *Deep South.* Chicago: University of Chicago Press, 1941.

Dewhurst, J. Frederic, and Associates. *America's Needs and Resources: A New Survey.* New York: The Twentieth Century Fund, 1955.

Dollard, John. *Caste and Class in a Southern Town.* New Haven, Conn.: Yale University Press, 1937.

Farber, Bernard. *Family: Organization and Interaction.* San Francisco, Calif.: Chandler Publishing Co., 1964.

Gordon, C. Wayne. *The Social System of the High School.* Glencoe, Ill.: The Free Press, 1957.

Havighurst, Robert J., et al. *Growing Up in River City.* New York: John Wiley and Sons, 1962.

Hollingshead, August B. *Elmtown's Youth.* New York: John Wiley and Sons, 1949.

Kahl, Joseph A. *The American Class Structure.* New York: Holt, Rinehart, and Winston, Inc., 1957.

Lipset, Seymour M., and Reinhard Bendix. *Social Mobility in Industrial Society.* Berkeley and Los Angeles: University of California Press, 1959.

National Society for the Study of Education. *Social Forces Influencing American Education.* Sixtieth Yearbook, Part II. Chicago: University of Chicago Press, 1961.

Sexton, Patricia C. *Education and Income.* New York: The Viking Press, 1961.

Sirjamaki, John. *The American Family in the Twentieth Century.* Cambridge, Mass.: Harvard University Press, 1953.

Stanley, William O., et al. *Social Foundations of Education.* New York: The Dryden Press, 1956.

United States Bureau of the Census. *Illustrative Projections of the Population of the United States, by Age and Sex, 1960 to 1980.* Series P-25, No. 187. Washington, D.C.: U.S. Government Printing Office, November 1958.

United States Office of Education. *Progress of Public Education in the United States of America, 1960–61.* Washington, D.C.: U.S. Government Printing Office, 1961.

Warner, W. Lloyd, Marchia Meeker, and Kenneth Eells. *Social Class in America,* new ed. New York: Harper Torchbooks, 1960.

Wolfle, Dael. *American Resources of Specialized Talent.* New York: Harper & Brothers, 1954.

CHAPTER 5

PHILOSOPHY AND THE SOCIAL FOUNDATIONS OF EDUCATION

In Chapter 1 we established the point of view that educators are inevitably decision makers; that decision making has several dimensions; that the contributions of science are necessary but not sufficient for the formulation of these decisions. Our analysis also disclosed that *descriptions* derived by empirical methodology do not of themselves become *prescriptions;* in other words, knowing what the situation is does not automatically tell us what we should do about it. In this chapter we shall explore selected systems of nonscientific beliefs that educators rely upon in their decision-making processes—at times in conjunction with the findings of science and at other times in spite of such findings.

BELIEFS AND BEHAVIOR

When Johnny says, "I believe that the ice is thick enough to skate on," he is indicating his willingness to walk, run, or skate on the sheet of ice. This is what he operationally means by his *belief. Believing* or a *belief* indicates a pattern or configuration of meanings the holder or holders of the belief are ready to use as a guide to behavior. This meaning of belief often comes as a shock to those who have never stopped to analyze the meaning of the term. If one asserts a belief that makes no difference whatever in his behavior, such a belief is merely verbal excess baggage or else a deliberate attempt to mislead or deceive others. The meaning of belief used in this volume is held by Hullfish and Smith: ". . . belief involves a willingness to act in terms of its implicit expectations."[1]

In accordance with this meaning of belief, when a teacher believes that a student can be trusted, he will allow that student to carry on significant activities unsupervised; one who believes in the legal equality of all

[1] H. Gordon Hullfish and Philip G. Smith, *Reflective Thinking: The Method of Education* (New York: Dodd, Mead and Company, 1961), p. 68.

men will in some way support measures that tend to achieve such equality, while one who believes in the inherent superiority of one racial group over all others will work in ways that will achieve and perpetuate a social system of racial dominance. A person who asserts a belief yet acts in ways inconsistent with it is confused and needs to clarify his ideas and their relationships to behavior; or, if he perpetuates the apparent inconsistency, his *behavior* is a more reliable indicator of his beliefs than are his verbal assertions.

SECULAR AND NONSECULAR SOURCES OF BELIEFS

Beliefs, as well as systems of beliefs, can be categorized as secular or nonsecular. This distinction is based upon the Latin word *seculum,* meaning "a long period of time." Whatever is secular occurs within time, is temporal, and consequently worldly. In contrast, things nonsecular exist beyond time, eternally, and thus beyond this world of temporal order. The popular distinction is between secular and religious beliefs. This distinction is accurate if, and only if, *religious* refers to some eternal, supernatural phenomenon; but, as the reader is probably aware, not all religions are so grounded.

It is important to stress that, in our country, all of the nonsecular systems of belief that play a dominant part in educational decision making are based on the Judaeo-Christian religious tradition. These religiously grounded beliefs have led to the establishment of various church-supported schools and, in some places, to church influence and control over all schools —circumstances that contradict some of our secular beliefs. This difficulty of keeping secular and nonsecular beliefs apart in practice is epitomized in the United States by the historic conflict over the "separation of church and state." While agreement upon the abstract statement of the principle of "separation" is relatively easy, application of the principle becomes amazingly complex and troublesome. The same difficulty is evident when we consider philosophy as a source of beliefs. It will become clear that in some philosophic systems the line separating the secular from the nonsecular is either blurred or does not exist.

PHILOSOPHY AS A SOURCE OF BELIEFS

In principle, philosophy is a key source of secular beliefs; for the philosophic method is one of reason, logic, and intellectual analysis. In contrast, religious beliefs are primarily articles of faith based on revelation.

"Philosophy" has been defined in innumerable ways: as "a search for wisdom," "a systematic method of criticism," "a way of making the implicit explicit," "a systematic way of thinking up new alternatives and analyzing them," "a systematic intellectual examination of ideas for meaning, consistency, and relevance to experience"; or, to paraphrase Bertrand Russell, philosophy attempts to answer ultimate questions after investigating all that makes such questions puzzling, and after realizing the vagueness and confusion that underlie an ordinary idea. All of these definitions seem to presuppose a commitment to the dictum of Socrates; namely, that "the unexamined life is not worth living."

PURPOSE OF A PHILOSOPHY OF EDUCATION

When we speak of a philosophy of education, a philosophy of law, or a philosophy of technology, we refer to philosophy *applied* to problems and concepts of education, of law, and of technology. A philosophy of education thus would constitute the application of the methods and concepts of philosophy to the solution of problems encountered by educators. This would involve, for example, study of selected works by Plato, St. Thomas Aquinas, Rousseau, Aristotle, John Dewey, Whitehead, and current writers who have attempted to clarify the meanings of concepts such as "adjustment," "the whole child," "permissiveness," "children's needs," "team teaching," "gifted," and a host of other terms used in contemporary educational discourse.

A study of educational philosophy serves three purposes: (1) the attainment of certain dispositions, labeled philosophic attitudes; (2) the acquisition of certain skills; and (3) the achievement of a philosophic synthesis that can guide our behavior. Let us look briefly at these three targets.

ATTAINMENT OF A PHILOSOPHIC ATTITUDE. The term "philosophic attitude" is popularly applied to one who has successfully anesthetized himself against problems of life and seems to go on unruffled in the midst of turmoil. More significant is the definition set forth by Smith[2] under three categories: comprehensiveness, penetration, and flexibility.

I. Comprehensiveness
  a. *He sees particulars in relation to a large field—he sees "the big picture."* This is the ability to resist "the press of particulars." By

[2] Adapted with permission from Philip G. Smith, *Philosophic Mindedness in Educational Administration* (Columbus: Ohio State University Press, 1956).

habit, or when necessary by more conscious effort, he strives to enlarge the field of his perceptions and to see the larger implications of his drives and concerns.

b. *He relates his thinking about immediate problems to more distant or long-range goals.* Involved here is a kind of intellectual and emotional stamina marshalled against "the press of the immediate" in order to make decisions in terms of relatively distant and stable objectives.

c. *He has a tolerance for theoretical considerations.* By resisting "the press of the particular and the immediate" he is able to extend his concerns to "the possible" and not remain on the level of "the actual."

d. *He has the power to generalize* (i.e., abductive generalization). By resisting "the press of the actual" he is free to create explanations which permit the extension of his understanding to an ever-increasing number of heretofore unrelated phenomena.

II. Penetration

a. *He tends to question what is generally taken for granted or thought to be self-evident.* By resisting "the press of the obvious" he calls into question the very things others do not question and thus increases his chance to move beyond the limits of prejudice, bias, and stereotypes.

b. *He formulates the fundamental ideas, questions, problems, and assumptions that, if grasped, will help resolve the situation.* Freed from the tyranny of the obvious he is enabled to consider basic ideas which may serve as keys to the solution of a wide range of problems.

c. *He demonstrates a keen sensitivity for implications and relevance.* Having penetrated to the fundamentals of the situation he "plays" with ideas and "teases out" their implications.

d. *He predicts by means of an abductive-deductive process rather than by a simple inductive process.* Having moved creatively beneath the surface of observed phenomena, he makes tentative predictions based on the implicated meanings of his abductions.

III. Flexibility

a. *He demonstrates a lack of "psychological set" in attacking problems.* He resists the inertia of the accustomed or routine ways of thinking and continually increases his repertoire of intellectual procedures.

b. *He has a tolerance for tentativeness and suspended judgment, but is willing to take action in an ambiguous situation.* Being free to deal with the unusual and having gained confidence in this process, he finds security in "the dealing" itself, not alone in the resulting products.

c. *He is able to evaluate an idea without being emotionally tied to its source and he is eager to "feed" on the ideas of others.* Feeling secure without the sanction of persons or institutions he avoids "the genetic fallacy" (even where he respects the source), and he welcomes a critical cross fertilization of ideas.

d. *He sees issues as many-sided rather than two-sided, and he develops relatively large numbers of alternative hypotheses, explanations, viewpoints, etc.* He does not confuse contraries with contradictions, and he increases his security by extending his understanding of the probable possibilities.

The characteristics described seem to be exhibited by effective thinkers in all walks of life, but are perhaps displayed most frequently and most consistently by those trained in philosophy. Therefore, the expression *philosophic attitude* is an appropriate abbreviation for this entire set of characteristics.

ACQUISITION OF PHILOSOPHIC SKILLS. One rarely thinks of philosophy as a field that includes *skills*. We associate skills with arithmetic, chemical experiments, athletics, and sewing, but not with philosophy. Nevertheless, there are vital skills to be gained from the study of philosophy—skills applicable to all the areas of life that depend upon symbols, their meanings, and their relationships. Many of these skills are involved in the daily life of the classroom. Educators constantly have to rely on definitions when they try to establish whether a statement is true or false, or whether a series of statements is consistent or inconsistent. To accomplish this purpose, they need to know what types of definitions there are, and how one tests them for adequacy; how to identify the various kinds of statements in order to distinguish synthetic propositions from analytic ones, and what method of proof is appropriate to each kind; how to determine whether or not statements are consistent with each other; how one draws an inference; and how to spot a fallacy. These are all *skills* that are necessary for the successful pursuit of any intellectual enterprise.[3]

A further important skill properly labeled philosophic is the process whereby assumptions and presuppositions are uncovered and made explicit.[4] Any serious statement can be shown to assume or presuppose some other statement. At the very least, when one makes a statement, there is an implied assumption that communication is possible and that knowledge is possible.

[3] See, for example, Max Black, *Critical Thinking* (Englewood Cliffs, N.J.: Prentice-Hall, Inc., 1946).

[4] Robert Ennis, "Assumption Finding," in B. Othaniel Smith and Robert H. Ennis, *Language and Concepts in Education* (Chicago: Rand McNally and Company, 1961).

ACHIEVEMENT OF PHILOSOPHIC SYNTHESIS. Different individuals use different "basic assumptions" or "primitive postulates" as starting points for their reasoning process. This is one point where secular and nonsecular sources of belief may be found. What one "takes for granted," what one considers to be "personally congenial" as a starting point will make a significant difference in the synthesis one reaches. Skill is required in building a synthesis, lest one put together an inconsistent set of assumptions that will lead to confusion and inconsistency in policies and programs of action.

It is generally the aim of courses in philosophy to develop in students a disposition toward philosophizing about the ongoing experiences of life. Optimally, one who possesses the philosophic attitudes and skills described above would, on the one hand, be intelligently critical in treating his various problems; on the other hand, he would develop a synthesis to guide his policies and practices. The latter is the sense in which we may speak of one's philosophy of law, of education, or of history.

A note of warning must be sounded at this point. We stated above that one who possesses the philosophic attitudes necessary for an unprejudiced appraisal of possibilities may build a philosophic synthesis—a network of consistent interrelated assumptions, arrived at after careful analysis. Such a synthesis can be achieved only through slow, careful, and at times painful effort. It is not easy to discard a previously unexamined belief or a set of beliefs long held. Yet this is precisely what might result from an honest effort at philosophizing. It is very tempting to hold on to inconsistent beliefs rather than to strive toward a consistency that might require the discarding of one or more of one's cherished assumptions. Such philosophic eclecticism must be warned against as leading to expediency in behavior, to reliance on authority, or to some other intellectually indefensible guide to behavior.

It is also unwise to regard philosophy as a categorizing of someone else's ready-made "isms," such as the well-known "Realism," "Idealism," "Experimentalism," "Existentialism," or "Scholasticism"; for these historically recognized philosophic syntheses were themselves the *results* of systematic philosophizing. One who philosophizes may arrive at one of these schools of thought; or he may construct an entirely new synthesis. Furthermore, each of these "isms" represents a range of possibilities. In this connection, it is important to heed the warning of a recognized student of philosophy, Gustave Weigel:

> It is interesting to see the reaction of not a few Catholic students to a discussion in which they are engaged. They hear some man's thought being expressed, and with joy they come to a gradual recognition. This man is a materialist! Now there is perfect serenity in the young man's soul because the thinker has been reduced to a timeless verbalism, and that was taken care of in the classroom treatment of the spirituality of the soul. The students have been trained immediately to stick any thought into pigeonholes constructed for them in college. Once the idea is in its pigeonhole, it can be ignored. It has already and forever been examined. Such students simply do not enter into the living thought of the living thinker. Rather, they substitute for it a lifeless abstraction which was included in a once-and-for-all given dictionary of definitions. In this unabridged and unrevisable dictionary there are bad words and good words. As soon as the dictionary word is applied to a phenomenon, the phenomenon is *eo ipso* judged. If the man is a materialist, he is no good and his doctrine is absurd. There is no scholarly task to be done now. It was done long ago.
>
> But, as Kant said quoting a French Abbe, there is no such thing as philosophy. There are only philosophers. Materialism does not historically show up as ever the same thing. There are Aristotelian materialism, Epicurean materialism, Stoïc materialism, Feuerbachian materialism, Marxian materialism and a Patristic materialism. These various visions cannot be reduced to a common affirmation. It is not at all explanatory to call an idea materialism. Unless you tell me whose materialism is under consideration, I simply do not know what you are talking about. The materialism of the monk Faustus of Riez in the fifth century has nothing in common with the mechanistic materialism taught by some nineteenth century thinkers. To this kind of observation, the bright student impatiently replies that everyone knows that the essence of materialism is the denial of the spiritual. But if the eager student reads the thoughts of men labeled as materialists, he will find that not one denied the existence of the spiritual. All that the bright student can answer to that is that they did not rightly use the word spiritual, which on ultimate analysis means that they did not use the dictionary he was given in his college days. By that dictionary he judges all things.[5]

The danger involved in prematurely attaching labels is not unique to the students referred to by Weigel. The tendency to oversimplify occurs in public schools as well as private ones; in secular institutions, in nonsecular ones, and in the culture at large. Stereotyping is a natural process used by men for economy in communication. It can be used and it can be misused, like any other intellectual creation of man. Dewey, whose philosophic ideas certainly differ from those of Weigel, nonetheless raises the same warning against the careless use of labels. He points up the tendency

[5] Gustave Weigel, S.J., "American Catholic Intellectualism: A Theologian's Reflections," *Review of Politics,* 19, No. 3 (July 1957), 302–303. With permission.

for philosophic "isms" to become obstacles to inquiry: "Any movement that thinks and acts in terms of an 'ism' becomes so involved in reaction against other 'isms' that it is unwittingly controlled by them. For it then forms its principles by reaction against them instead of by a comprehensive survey of actual needs, problems and possibilities."[6]

When one firmly adopts an established philosophic system as one's own and places it safely beyond criticism and examination, he violates a crucial philosophic attitude—that of flexibility. Those who have lost the attitude of flexibility, the ability to continue an open-minded criticism of their favorite "ism," are no longer students of philosophy or philosophers, but rather apostles and missionaries of some previous philosopher.

Optimally, a philosophic synthesis may become the source of the beliefs one uses to guide behavior. At the same time, the attitudes and skills acquired continue to help one in applying and constantly reshaping the synthesis in the light of new, criticized experience. The possible variations of philosophic syntheses are sufficiently complex and numerous to warrant systematic treatment in separate volumes. Our purpose here is merely to indicate the relevance of philosophy to educational decisions. To accomplish this objective, we shall be highly selective and simply contrast certain traditional and modern approaches on three educational problems: (1) What is the nature of the learner? (2) What are the purposes of education? (3) What should constitute the curriculum?

PHILOSOPHIC CONCEPTIONS OF THE LEARNER

THE TRADITIONAL VIEW

Even a cursory examination of traditional education discloses the implicit assumption that learning is a painful or distasteful process that students by nature resist. The teacher is quite justified in not trusting his students, in using threats and promises, a firm hand, or the motherly influence to control them. They must be quiet, attentive, and submissive. Under firm control they are to be exposed to the accumulated knowledge of the past. Thus exposed, the educable students will grow to like learning, while the others will find occupations that do not require a high degree of literacy. This view of the learner is inspired by certain philosophic conceptions of the nature of man, his mind, and his ideas.

[6] John Dewey, *Experience and Education* (New York: The Macmillan Company, 1938), p. vii. Material quoted here, and elsewhere in this chapter, is used by permission of Kappa Delta Pi, National Honor Society in Education, owners of the copyright.

One traditional view, based on the ideas of John Locke, asserts that man is born with a mind that is completely blank. According to this *tabula rasa,* or wax-tablet, notion of the mind, life in general writes upon this blank mind; but the school is most instrumental in transmitting ideas by carefully imprinting them upon the minds of our students.

A contrasting traditional viewpoint, the age-old Platonic notion of innate ideas, conceives of man as born with a mind that already contains ideas. The teacher's task, then, is to make these ideas explicit—i.e., to draw them out by careful questioning and thus make the student conscious of them. The most famous illustration of this process is found in Plato's *Republic,* where Socrates, through a series of careful questions, has an uneducated slave boy state the Pythagorean Theorem. (It is interesting to note, however, that Anglo-American legal systems carefully delimit the use of leading questions because of the conviction that such questions implant answers instead of drawing out what is already in the mind.)

Other traditional views are based on the assumption that man was created by a supernatural being but is spiritually handicapped at birth. The Catholic point of view assumes that each person suffers the consequences of the "original sin" and is thus *deprived.* The early Puritan view, which had a broader impact on the formation of American attitudes, was that each child is born *depraved,* or inherently bad. Although these views differ, they imply the need for strict discipline imposed by adults and enforced by the teacher.

THE MODERN VIEW

The teacher who subscribes to the modern points of view in educational philosophy does not become suspicious of students who enjoy their learning activities. He expects them to do so—not because he is a hedonist, as is often the charge, but because of the way he conceives of the nature of the learner. To him, students are curious and eager to learn about various aspects of life.

This is consistent with his assumption that man, by nature, is a curious creature who seeks satisfactions. Satisfaction is not to be confused with mere pleasure or gratification. Man can, and often does, reach satisfaction through hard work, pain, and self-sacrifice. Examples of this are all around us, in the hard work of athletes, scholars, community volunteer workers, Peace Corps members, and in most walks of life. No one who has systematically observed young children can doubt their curiosity and desire to learn. Their interests are many and varied. The modern position takes advantage of these interests and uses them for educative activities. Furthermore, it is the task of the teacher to expand the interests of the students to newer and newer fields.[7]

This view of the learner, consistent with the Darwinian hypothesis, conceives of man as the product of organic, biological evolution. He differs in degree, but not in kind, from other organisms on the phylogenetic scale. This difference in degree is a very important one. Man is continuous with nature but has evolved certain unique abilities, among them his powerful mental abilities. According to this view, the child is not born with innate ideas or with a blank tablet; he is not deprived or depraved at birth. He has, through evolution, acquired many complex abilities, which are only potentialities in the very young. These potentialities have been characterized as intellectual, physical, social, emotional, moral, and aesthetic. To what extent he develops them depends upon the quality of experiences he, as an organism, will undergo. The school is an important agency in society, but works with other social institutions to develop the various abilities of the young.

THE PURPOSES OF EDUCATION

THE TRADITIONAL VIEW

The main purpose of education, according to traditional views, is intellectual development. Historically, due largely to the influence of Athens, the training of the body was also an important task of the school. This goal was derived from the belief that body and mind, though distinct parts of man, exist in "substantial union" and that the mind can function well only if the body is cared for. Notice, however, "the body is trained, the emotions are disciplined, but the mind is educated."[8]

This primary, and often exclusive, emphasis on intellectual development is derived historically from the writings of Plato and of Aristotle. Although there are significant differences between these two ancient philosophers, they agreed on the centrality of the intellect. Aristotle makes particularly clear that man's key purpose in life is to develop his intellectual abilities. The more an individual is able to develop his intellect and spend his time in pure theoretical contemplation, the closer he resembles God. To become more and more Godlike is the highest purpose of human existence,

[7] Dewey, *Experience and Education* (see note 6).

[8] Lawrence G. Thomas et al., *Perspective on Teaching* (Englewood Cliffs, N.J.: Prentice-Hall, Inc., 1961), p. 164.

in the Aristotelian point of view. The key function of the school became that of helping man achieve his highest goal—thus, the overwhelming emphasis on intellectual development and the separation of school activities from life surrounding them.

THE MODERN VIEW

The modern philosophies of education, like the traditional ones, tend to start from the nature and purposes of man in order to decide upon the purposes of education. As indicated in our discussion of the nature of the learner, the modern views proceed from the Darwinian conception of man.[9] As such, man is observed to have various abilities and countless purposes. His abilities—or dimensions, as they are often called—have been identified as intellectual, social, physical, emotional, moral, and aesthetic. These words are attempts to describe emphases in activity. Thus, algebraic manipulations are primarily intellectual, although physical activity is involved and although such manipulations might proceed in a social setting where emotional and aesthetic factors are also present and operative.

The modern points of view in educational philosophy tend to pay serious attention to man as a complete being with various abilities. Thus, the goals of education include the development of intellectual, social, emotional, moral, aesthetic, and physical aspects of man. This is further influenced by the philosophic view that there is no single, fixed purpose toward which man strives. Rather, he creates his own purposes based upon the possibilities and limitations of his situation. Education thus has many purposes. If a single purpose needs to be stated, a high-level abstraction is offered by Dewey in his assertion that the goal of education is growth, or rather, growing.[10] It is true that this conception does not provide a fixed and final goal for education, but Dewey's followers would ask whether anybody's really does. When faced with the possibilities that one may grow in antisocial directions, Dewey replied:

> That a man may grow in efficiency as a burglar, as a gangster, or as a corrupt politician, cannot be doubted. But from the standpoint of growth as education and education as growth, the question is whether growth in this direction promotes or retards growth in general. Does this form of growth create conditions for further growth, or does it set up conditions that shut off the person who has grown in this particular

[9] For a brief but excellent summary, see John S. Brubacher, "Darwinian Evolution and Deweyan Education," *Rhode Island College Journal*, 1, No. 3 (December 1960).

[10] Dewey, *Experience and Education* (see note 6), p. 28.

direction from the occasions, stimuli, and opportunities for continuing growth in new directions?[11]

Thus, a procedural direction—not a final, fixed measuring stick—is offered to ascertain progress. School activities are to be arranged in such a way that man's varied abilities are developed. This task is much more ambitious and difficult than the narrower focus of the traditional views. Perhaps it is too difficult for one social institution. But advocates of this position urge the close cooperation of various institutions in society, since they all influence, enhance, or retard human development.

THE BASES OF THE CURRICULUM

It must be quite evident by now that the curriculum of the school is conceived differently by alternative educational philosophers. What are some of the characteristic differences?

THE TRADITIONAL VIEW

The traditional curriculum consisted of the accumulated wisdom of the past, logically organized and subdivided into manageable segments, or courses, for teaching convenience. The content of the curriculum would be the same for all students everywhere. The mastery of such a curriculum would ensure intellectual development, which is the purpose of the school. This view is widely found in our secondary schools, where the curricular content consists of "academic" or "solid" subjects and either eliminates or, at best, relegates other subjects to subordinate positions.

According to the traditional philosophy of education, the curriculum does not change with changing times; it embodies eternal truths and the wisdom of the ages. Hutchins represents this position well:

> The function of a citizen . . . may vary from society to society. . . . But the function of a man, as a man, is the same in every age and in every society, since it results from his nature as a man. The aim of an educational system is the same in every age and in every society where such a system can exist: it is to improve man as man.[12]

The curriculum is constructed and prescribed by adults, without regard for the interests of the individual student. With the authority of the

[11] *Experience and Education,* pp. 28–29.

[12] Robert Maynard Hutchins, *The Conflict in Education* (New York: Harper & Brothers, 1953), p. 68. With permission.

teacher behind each subject, the children must learn each separate segment and be able to demonstrate their knowledge in written or oral form. The entire process is subject-centered and teacher-directed.

THE MODERN VIEW

Just as the purposes of education have to do with the whole person, according to modern educational philosophy, so the curriculum is concerned with the "whole child."[13] It is concerned not only with the information he gathers in the various lessons, but also with the attitudes he develops and his moral growth.

The possession of information, in this curriculum, becomes secondary to the process of finding and using the information in the intelligent analysis and solution of problems. The curriculum can even be described as a continuous sequence of experiences wherein problems are raised, clarified, and explored; where solutions are tried out and generalizations are reached on the basis of the students' attempts to solve problems. The accumulated information of the past is used as a resource for understanding and dealing with the present. In the words of Dewey:

> But the achievements of the past provide the only means at command for understanding the present. . . .
>
> In other words, the sound principle that the objectives of learning are in the future and its immediate materials are in present experience can be carried into effect only in the degree that present experience is stretched, as it were, backward. It can expand into the future only as it is also enlarged to take in the past.[14]

This theory, which is predominantly that of John Dewey and his followers, conceives of the curriculum as necessarily related to experience and to the interest of the learner. Unlike the traditional curriculum, it varies in time and place. It relies heavily on the general logic of the scientific method—both in the learning process and in the evaluation of learning. It is more concerned with the process of *intelligent inquiry* and *creativity* than with the passing on of the information and wisdom of the past. This point of view, identified in current writings as the Experimentalist position, has made more impact on the elementary schools than on the secondary level.

[13] As Professor Lawrence Cremin warned, however, it is improper to assume that, if the schools are concerned with the education of the "whole child," they are to take care of the "whole education of the child."

[14] John Dewey, *Experience and Education* (see note 6), p. 93.

THE NEED FOR A COMTEMPORARY THEORY OF DEMOCRATIC EDUCATION

From the writings of Experimentalist philosophers, it quickly appears that they conceive of a close and necessary connection between their theories and a democratic social order. There are no fixed and final goals in Experimentalism, except procedural ones expressed by the term "growth" and the commitment to the development of creative, inquiring persons. When pushed to the limit, some Experimentalists admit to holding certain beliefs or making assumptions that function as near-absolutes, as long-range guides to theory and behavior. Examples of such firm beliefs would be a commitment to the scientific method, which Experimentalists equate with the method of intelligence, and an abiding respect for human beings. These commitments are expressed differently by the several theorists. They will deny the absolute or fixed nature of these beliefs and claim to be ready to alter them in light of new developments and changing conditions. Whether this alteration will ever occur is questionable, since the above two commitments are also used as criteria for evaluation of new possibilities.[15]

In their commitment to an open-ended universe wherein the sequence of growth leading to further growth fades into infinity, the Experimentalists see their connection to democracy. According to their most prolific writer, John Dewey, "A democracy is more than a form of government; it is primarily a mode of associated living, a conjoint communicated experience."[16] Individual-social growth results from the quality of shared experience. Education is a significant aspect of this total process, not merely a preparation for it. Thus, there is an inextricable connection between education, growth, and democracy. For purposes of analysis we may focus on one concept or the other, but this is only an artificial separation of interrelated parts of the totality of experience. It is artificial but not in a pejorative sense, just as chemical analysis of kitchen salt is an artificial but useful analysis of related parts of a whole.

The connection between the Experimentalist's point of view and

[15] Experimentalists would disclaim that these are absolutes or fixed beliefs, for they are only procedural goals that lead to further means and ends. Thus they speak of "ends-in-view" which, upon being reached, become means to new ends. This is often referred to as their principle of "ends-means continuum." Among others, the following authors would fall under the Experimentalist label: J. Dewey, G. Hullfish, J. Childs, G. Axtelle, and L. G. Thomas.

[16] John Dewey, *Democracy and Education* (New York: The Macmillan Company, 1916), p. 101.

democracy is analyzed more thoroughly in many volumes.[17] It is important to note here that Dewey's definition of democracy, generally accepted by Experimentalists, is more inclusive than most other definitions.

Many proponents of traditional philosophies also claim a firm allegiance to democracy. As we read Robert M. Hutchins, an articulate spokesman for traditional philosophy, we must recognize a vigorous proponent of the democratic credo. We find similar commitments to democracy on the part of Father John Courtney Murray and Herman H. Horne, neither of whom bear the Experimentalist label.

The traditional approach to democratic education is also well represented by the Western European democracies—the Scandinavian countries, and others—who have not adopted progressive education to any significant extent. To this the Experimentalist might reply that, while his philosophy necessarily implies a democratic way of life, democracy as such has room for a wide variety of philosophies and educational theories. A diagrammatic representation of this relationship might look like this:

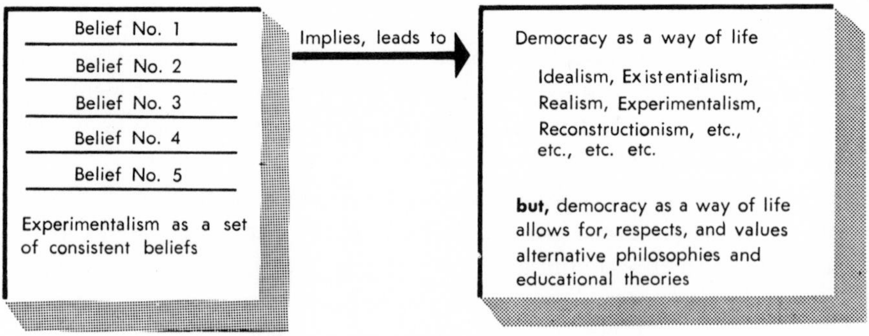

The foregoing is sufficient to illustrate the point the several philosophies and educational theories claim to be consistent with democracy. This makes apparent the need to clarify the meaning of the term. What does *democracy* mean? Does the word have but one acceptable meaning, or a range of possible ones? An educator who wishes to prepare students for a democratic way of life, or who wants to know whether or not a philosophy or a theory is consistent with democracy must first clarify his theory of

[17] See, for example, Boyd H. Bode, *Progressive Education at the Crossroads* (New York: Newson and Company, 1938); Kenneth D. Benne, *A Conception of Authority* (New York: Bureau of Publications, Teachers College, Columbia University, 1943); John Dewey, *Democracy and Education* (note 16).

democracy. As a start on this demanding task, in the next section we shall briefly compare and contrast democratic and nondemocratic ideologies.

IMPACT OF IDEOLOGIES ON EDUCATION

According to a study conducted under the auspices of UNESCO, almost every nation in the world today claims to be a democracy. The claim is made by people of such divergent ways of life and government as Canada, Yugoslavia, Hungary, Sweden, China, the Union of South Africa, the Soviet Union, the United States of America, and a long list of others. Merely to assert that "we" are democratic and "you" are not is no solution, for any group may make the assertion. It is more appropriate to set forth the assumptions and commitments of the different ideologies, including those of democracy, whereupon the way of life of any human group may be evaluated in light of the specified intellectual criteria.

A thorough treatment of competing ideologies cannot be attempted here. Limitations of space confine us to a synoptic presentation of the fascist, communist, and democratic alternatives. The reader is urged to pursue systematic work in this field toward a sound understanding of political philosophies competing not only for the minds of man but for his entire self.[18]

FASCISM

This ideology is based upon two postulates or assumptions that are beyond challenge and refutation within the logic of the system. The first one declares that the highest value, and thus the goal of all human endeavor, is the well-functioning state or nation. The Italian word *fascio,* meaning "group" or "movement," is the root of the term "fascism." The second pillar supporting this ideology is the belief that there are two kinds of people in each nation: the elite and the masses. The masses are neither interested in nor capable of ruling themselves; consequently, the small group of elite, who have both the mental ability and the moral character, rule.

There is an inherent inequality among people, and it is foolish as well as disrespectful to treat people as if they were equal. The nation must select with care its leaders from among the elite, who will then use the power of the state to harness everyone's abilities for the good of the whole. Everyone has an appropriate place in a well-ordered nation. The leading

[18] For a comparative analysis of today's major ideologies, see William Ebenstein, *Today's Isms: Communism, Fascism, Capitalism, Socialism,* 3rd ed. (Englewood Cliffs, N.J.: Prentice-Hall, Inc., 1961).

elite is in the best position to know what is good for the state. The masses are made to feel that they "belong," that they too contribute in an important way. They do not make the decisions, but they contribute their skill, their muscle, their strength of character, courage, discipline and enthusiasm in the carrying out of assigned roles.

The state derives its ultimate and all-encompassing authority from the fact that it represents the will of the people and the will of God. The state may be religious in nature, and all religions are acceptable as long as they do not defy the power of the state and do not claim universal brotherhood and equality of men.[19] There is no problem as to what are the appropriate relationships between the individual and society, for the highest purpose of the individual is to find his appropriate slot in the machinery of the state.

The good of the nation is an overriding goal which sanctions any and all means necessary to reach it. All moral questions, indeed, all aspects of life, are regulated with this one criterion in mind. This is why fascism is clearly and admittedly a totalitarian ideology. No activity, no portion of life is beyond the power of the state. The state and the leaders of the state are above the law, since they created the law to achieve the purposes of the state.

Education is no exception to the foregoing. It is a very important activity which must be considered as a major tool of the (fascist) state. All children are to train their bodies, and to develop their character. The mass man receives sufficient education to have the skills, knowledge, and folklore befitting his role in society. The elite receive special education in closely controlled boarding schools. Both students and teachers are constantly screened for unquestioning loyalty to the state.

Fascism is not merely a historical artifact. It was not just the German or Italian form of government during and before World War II. It is an ideology whose intellectual roots go back to antiquity. Its best-known theorist was Giovanni Gentile,[20] although the pronouncements of Adolf Hitler and Benito Mussolini have received wider attention.[21]

[19] This is one reason why Catholics and Jews were so severely treated and systematically eliminated in fascist Germany. They were not willing to submit to state control. Furthermore, fascism can justify use of minority groups to whip up hate, prejudice, and antagonism on the part of the masses and use of these powerful emotions to manipulate the masses for the purposes of the state.

[20] See, for example, his *Reform of Education* (New York: Harcourt, Brace and World, 1922).

[21] The beginning student often identifies facism with the nazi system of Germany during the reign of Hitler. This is a fallacy. While nazism was ideologically similar

Given the appropriate social and economic conditions within a nation and sufficient insecurity from the international scene, *any nation* might turn to fascism.[22] This is more likely to occur in an industrial nation, while an underdeveloped country is more likely to succumb to the appeals of the communist ideology.[23] It is also quite clear that while fascism feeds upon frustration, insecurity and resentment, its appeals cut across all social groups and socioeconomic classes.

Within its logic there is a place for the rich and the poor; for the leader and the follower; for the skilled; for the intellectual; the artist; the poet; as well as the unskilled laborer. They are all called upon to join, to "belong" in the great and united effort to reach the goal, the fixed and final truth so clearly known to their leaders.

COMMUNISM

The appeal of communism is quite different, yet equally inclusive. The stated goal of this ideology is a stirring one reminiscent of the ancient ideals of Christianity. The goal is a way of life characterized by abundance, by brotherly love, and by universal brotherhood, as expressed in the popularly known slogan, "From each according to his ability, to each according to his need."

Just as there are different national examples of fascism all derived from one basic ideology, there are variations among the Chinese, Cuban, Russian or Yugoslav expressions of communism. Still, there is one ideology based upon the writings of Karl Marx, Friedrich Engels, and Nikolai Lenin. Here, as in fascism, we find two basic assumptions which are offered as unquestionable truths. The entire "ism" is based on these assumptions—namely, economic determinism and the dialectic interpretation of history.

The first of these principles reflects the conviction of Marx that every aspect of life is controlled by the economic arrangements in society. There are, according to him, only two classes of people, the owners and the workers. The owners are those who control the means of production,

to fascism, it incorporated certain ideas not necessarily part of the logic of fascism. The best known of these is the idea of "Herrenvolk"—i.e., Aryan supremacy—which justified the persecution not only of political dissenters but also of racial, religious and ethnic groups such as Catholics, Jews, Slavs, and others.

22 A symposium analyzing these forces is presented in Daniel Bell, ed., *The New American Right* (New York: Criterion Books, 1955).

23 See William Ebenstein, *Totalitarianism: New Perspectives* (New York: Holt, Rinehart and Winston, Inc., 1962).

and through it they manage all social life for their own advantage. An individual's beliefs, his leisure activities, the books he reads, the music he enjoys, the friends he has, and everything else about him is generally *determined* by his *economic class*. It is to the advantage of the owners to exploit the workers, and the workers attempt to protect themselves against such exploitation. Consequently, the interests of the two classes are inherently irreconcilable, and a class war persists. The state, as other institutions of society, is used by the owners to perpetuate their superior position.

In all societies, however, opposing forces are at work. These conflicting forces are the *thesis* and the *antithesis* of the current economic arrangements which lead to the new *synthesis,* the resolution of the conflict. The synthesis becomes the new thesis, wherein the "seeds of its own destruction" arise in the form of the new antithesis, resulting in a still higher synthesis. The cycle continues until the giant historical pattern leads inevitably to the final goal, the classless society. Conflict is absent there since the economic bases for conflict have been removed and there is but one class. Communism's second cornerstone is the foregoing *duel of opposites,* the historical dialectic, which is the monolithic movement of history toward the inevitable classless society.

Marx based his dialectic interpretation of history on the ideas of the German philosopher Hegel. Hegel applied the forces of dialectic to the movement of ideas and spiritual development, starting from the assumption that reality is ultimately made up of ideas. Marx reversed this position, asserted a materialistic starting point for all of reality, and applied the Hegelian dialectic to it. This is why the communist ideology is often referred to as dialectic materialism.

According to Marx, since the eventual outcome is clear and beyond dispute, man can only hasten it or slow it down. The goal is fixed and any means necessary or useful in bringing it closer to realization is legitimate and moral. Men may disagree concerning the most appropriate means to use at any particular time. This is exemplified by the disagreement between Russia and China as to the best means to use against capitalistic nations. The end, however, is agreed upon and is changeless. If individuals or even large groups and nations must be eliminated along the way, this is unfortunate, tragic, and highly regrettable. But what must be done must be done; and the sooner it is done, the less harm will be incurred in the long run.

Force will probably be needed to wrest control from the ruling class, the owners, although in some situations the transfer of power might occur through parliamentary processes. Once the power is in the hands of the workers, the state will be used to develop the classless society. Eventually the state will "wither away" as an instrument of power and will be only an administrative instrument, coordinating the activities of the people.

It is clear that communism and fascism are equally totalitarian in practice, although not in theory. Though the state is to wither away according to communist ideology, there are no examples of this having ever occurred. Looking at the various current examples of communism, there are no grounds for predicting that such a state of affairs will occur. Communists point to the argument that this will develop only when competing economic systems disappear from the world and hence hostile social systems will not force communist nations to perpetuate a warlike posture. Once the threat of "encircling" capitalism is gone, the power of the state will not be necessary and will disappear.

Critics will offer, among other points, the argument that the stated goal of classless society toward which all of history inevitably moves is but a metaphysical assumption.[24] In the meantime, there are essential similarities between communism and fascism. They are both totalitarian in that no aspect of life is protected from governmental scrutiny and control. Education, along with other social institutions, is closely controlled and used for the purposes determined by the ruling elite.

It is true that communism does not posit a ruling elite and asserts the ultimate equality of all people. However, in practice an elite rules. This is rationalized by the claim that due to the economic arrangements in society most people do not understand the impersonal forces of history which are moving us toward the classless society. Furthermore, most people are incapable of ruling themselves. In the long run, once the economic bases of life have been rearranged and all the means of production are socially owned, no elite will be needed. In the interim it is the role of the select few, the party, to guide the process of inevitable evolution, to hasten it and to help the masses develop their competence.

Education has an important role in this process. The limitless faith of communists in education is evidenced by the great national efforts found in iron-curtain countries to make high-quality education available to more and more people in the population. The 1961 Education Act of Hungary, revising the entire range of educational institutions of the country, is an example in point. It sets forth the social ideal and its implementation,

[24] See, for example, Bertrand Russell and John Dewey, "Why I Am Not a Communist," *Modern Monthly,* April 1934.

whereby almost cradle-to-grave schooling will be available at public expense to all who would benefit by it.[25] It is also worthy of note that the law specifically requires that students as well as teachers will be constantly screened for allegiance to communism. Schools must work together with other agencies of society to build a culture that is homogeneous in ideology.[26] In these respects, as well as in some others, communism and fascism are functionally the same. The difference is found in the stated goals of the ideologies and consequently in the appeal that the two systems have for different people. It is important to note once again the need for a systematic study of these ways of life, as well as those that we shall discuss under democracy. Each of these systems contains a set of nonscientific beliefs which influence decision making in many respects. Let us now look briefly at the democratic ideology.

DEMOCRACY

Two different configurations of ideas must be considered in order to understand American conceptions of democracy. The first set often appears under the titles of Individualism, Classical Liberalism, or Nineteenth-Century Liberalism. For the sake of brevity we shall use the term Individualism. The second set of ideas, which has been emerging since the Great Depression of the 1930s, finds expression under titles such as Modern Liberalism, Pragmatic Liberalism, and Modern Democracy. We will use the term democracy to denote this chronologically more recent set of ideas.

Individualism was the result of systematic protests against absolute monarchical rule and in favor of representative parliamentary government. It exalts the liberty of the individual. In fact, the central goal of this ideology is the unique individual who would be restricted by law only where absolutely necessary. His rights are inherent and inalienable. Everyone is equal before the law, and the entire scheme of government functions under a framework of law created by the citizens' elected representatives. This is unlike the fascist and communist systems, wherein the law can be manipulated by the leaders to suit their purposes.

According to individualism, man is a rational being and thus will pursue his own self-interest. What is best for society will automatically result from each individual's pursuing his own goals. Private competition within the protection of a legal system will produce the best possible

[25] *Magyar Közlöny,* No. 74, October 17, 1961 (available in the Library of Congress).

[26] *Magyar Közlöny,* pp. 27–33 passim.

results for everyone. This is the only "natural" approach to life. These ideas were clearly formulated by the "Philosophic Radicals" of England under the leadership of Jeremy Bentham.[27] The well-known economic foundations of the system were developed by Adam Smith, Ricardo, and Malthus. Accordingly, through free competition and the law of supply and demand, the "greatest good of the greatest number" will result. Planning is unnecessary, for there is a "preestablished harmony" in the universe, or, in the phrase of Adam Smith, an "invisible hand" guides each person to labor for the general welfare.

The twin emphases of individualism were liberty and equality before the law. Equality was never conceived naively to mean factual identity or sameness in either talent or environmental blessings. It was conceived in the sense that there will be legal protection of the opportunity to compete, to associate freely, to try out one's ideas in the open marketplace, and to rise or fall in the social system.

Education was looked upon as very important in the individual's preparation for economic and social life. It was the means of gaining the basic skills for equal competition. Individualism, by and large, recommended public support of a minimal educational program for all. However, extreme representatives, like Herbert Spencer, carried the idea of laissez faire in economics and politics to its logical conclusions and opposed public support of schools.

Modern conceptions of democracy clearly carry the imprint of individualism. Most of the freedoms enjoyed in the latter half of the twentieth century first developed during the nineteenth-century heyday of individualism. The democratic ideology, while drawing upon the contributions of individualism, has developed some new and unique themes in accord with our highly specialized industrial society, in light of modern international developments, and on the basis of the growing contributions of the social sciences.

Democracy, as was noted above, values the root theme of individualism—namely, the respect and value placed upon each human being. This ideology, however, does not isolate man or set him against the group. Interdependence is a recognized fact of modern life which, like any other fact, has to be accepted in creating a life that is conducive to the full development of all members of the community. As Ebenstein puts it: "In practice, a society is democratic to the extent that it approximates the goal of

[27] See Elie Halevy, *The Growth of Philosophic Radicalism* (New York: Augustus M. Kelley, 1949).

democracy—maximum opportunities for personal self-development and individual liberty—and practices the means of democracy—rational discussion and free consent—*in the widest variety of human relations*" (italics ours).[28]

In the realm of economics, democracy is more complex than either fascism or communism. Communism demands a collective ownership of all of the means of production and allows private ownership of nonproductive property only. Fascism allows for public as well as private ownership as long as all economic arrangements serve the purposes of the state. The goals of the nation are paramount, and any aspect of the economy may be altered at the discretion of the ruling elite. By contrast, democracy respects a wide variety of economic arrangements. Pluralism is valued here as in social, religious, educational, political, and other aspects of life. Private ownership exists side by side with publicly owned and operated systems such as the well known Tennessee Valley Authority; consumers' cooperatives lure the public along with corporations, trusts, and various types of partnerships.

The laissez-faire doctrine of individualism has been displaced by a complex amalgam of economic entities and arrangements, all of them subject to control by law. Property rights are as carefully guarded as other rights of man; they are not left to the control of some mystical "invisible hand" nor to the arbitrary actions of an all-powerful elite. The importance of economics is clearly recognized. This is why democracy constantly protects the economic interests of individuals and groups but also reserves the right to protect others from the undesirable use of economic power. There is no clear, final guideline here, and situational decisions must be constantly made in light of the facts of the particular case and the competing interests involved.

It became quite apparent through the years that individual competition and the "invisible-hand" doctrine will not suffice for twentieth-century living. While the *totally planned*—and thus rigidly controlled—society of the totalitarian systems must be avoided, continuous *planning* is necessary. This process is widespread in both private and governmental organizations. Public affairs are conducted with increased reliance on scientific knowledge and expert advice. Lawyers, economists, educators, physicians, and numerous other specialists are used by private and public decision-making groups. This points up the increasing role of cooperation

[28] William Ebenstein, *Totalitarianism: New Perspectives* (New York: Holt, Rinehart and Winston, Inc., 1962), p. 5. With permission.

in our interdependent life as well as the increase in rationality in the solution of problems.

Whereas both fascism and communism are likely to use coercion and brute force, democracy makes a commitment to the peaceful solution of problems through reason and open persuasion. For this purpose, democracy relies on science as a very important method of learning about man, society, and the problems of man. In both fascism and communism, science must work within the fixed limits of the ideology; consequently, the rigorous criteria of the scientific method cannot shed light on certain important aspects of life. No such official limitation is placed on the empirical method in a democracy. This is why, in principle, all the beliefs of this way of life are open for analysis, examination and alteration.

Democracy, above all, implies freedom and diversity in a pluralistic order. It values individual variation and voluntary association. It encourages a wide variety of beliefs—religious, moral, and aesthetic, as well as various styles of life. Dissent and minority opinions are not only tolerated, but respected and valued. The American Civil Liberties Union exists in the same community as does the John Birch Society. The Black Muslim group might meet just a few blocks away from the D.A.R. In the words of the famous Lord Acton: "The most certain test by which we judge whether a country is really free is the amount of security enjoyed by minorities."

Another positive yardstick is whether there are ample channels of interaction within groups as well as among groups. In this complex, interdependent world, the channels of communication must be many and varied, if one is to have an effective way to influence others, to lend one's voice to the process of decision making. Thus it can be said that another way to measure the degree of democracy achieved is by the quality and variety of channels of interaction available within a group as well as between groups.[29]

Were we to offer a set of ideals characterizing democracy, the following aspects would be the most important:

1. The individual deserves respect and should be valued.
2. Man should rely on reason and the methods of science in the solution of his problems.
3. All ideas should be open to scrutiny and intelligent criticism.
4. Man can, and should, govern himself.
5. Society must guard freedom under law created and alterable by man.

29 Based on lectures of Professor Lawrence G. Thomas, Stanford University, Stanford, California.

6. Pluralism must be respected in values, whether religious, aesthetic, moral, economic, or other.
7. The resources of society should be available for the development of all men regardless of race, religion, or ethnic origin.

Education bears a heavier burden in a democracy than in any of its competing ideologies. A highly pluralistic society that encourages the individual to choose among many alternatives in all phases of life needs an intelligent, well-educated citizenry. Popular, representative government presupposes high-quality popular education. This was realized quite early in our history by several of our leading statesmen, who repeatedly urged a sound general education for *all* the voting public (see Chapters 2 and 11).

Each of the ideologies we discussed values education, but each does so differently and for its unique reasons. Although the technical aspects of education will roughly be the same under the various "isms," the more important aspects will not. For instance, the teaching of chemistry or of multiplication of fractions is likely to be the same, though the educator is guided by differing ideologies. On the other hand, decisions regarding who shall be educated, for what purposes, and by whom will be influenced by the divergent considerations inherent in fascism, communism, and democracy.[30]

It is crucial that educators understand these ideologies. Even in the absence of explicit understanding, men's decisions are influenced by some of the basic ideas underlying these various ways of life. One can but hope that, upon careful examination and evaluation, the American educator will choose the democratic alternative. If he has made this conscious choice, he should understand his point of view so well that his daily decisions will reflect the ideals toward which he strives. For the ideals of democracy, if they are to endure, must function in educational decisions whether at the meeting of the school board, the P.T.A., the principal's office, or in the daily interactions and transactions that constitute the teaching and the learning processes.

SUMMARY

In this chapter, we undertook a very ambitious task. Pursuing the theme of the entire volume, that educators are constantly involved in the making of decisions, we attempted to indicate the place of nonscientific

[30] For one example of these differences, see Louis Fischer, "Social Philosophies and the Concept of Giftedness," *The Gifted Child Quarterly* (Autumn 1961), pp. 93–99.

beliefs in this process. Such beliefs and systems of beliefs can be categorized as secular or nonsecular, depending on whether they start from naturalistic or supernaturalistic basic assumptions.

We demonstrated that philosophy and social philosophy are key secular sources of nonscientific beliefs used in the conduct of human affairs, including educational affairs. In addition, we briefly illustrated the relevance of philosophy to educational theory by contrasting a "Traditional" and a "Modern" point of view. We repeatedly emphasized our conviction that *philosophizing* is the goal sought, not merely the acceptance of someone else's ready-made philosophic system. One's personal set of philosophic beliefs is likely to be of more value if it is the product of proper use of philosophic skills and of possession of philosophic attitudes when grappling with educational problems.

We are also convinced that a clear understanding of the major social philosophies or ideologies is necessary for an intelligent commitment to democracy. An ideology, carefully constructed and well understood, provides a set of beliefs to guide behavior in a general sense. Such a set of beliefs is a necessity if one is to avoid expediency, blind acceptance of authority, or imitation of others who may be acting blindly also. It must be clearly understood that no definitive statement of the content of educational philosophy or of the major ideologies was attempted here; such an effort would require several volumes. Our purpose was to develop an understanding of the thesis that such knowledge is relevant and that philosophic beliefs are necessarily involved in the decisions made by educators.

SELECTED BIBLIOGRAPHY

A. Educational Philosophy

Bode, Boyd. *Progressive Education at the Crossroads.* New York: Newson, 1938.

Brameld, Theodore. *Patterns of Educational Philosophy.* Yonkers, N.Y.: World Book Co., 1950.

__________. *Towards a Reconstructed Philosophy of Education.* New York: Henry Holt and Co., Inc., 1956.

Broudy, Harry. *Building a Philosophy of Education.* Englewood Cliffs, N.J.: Prentice-Hall, Inc., 1954.

Brubacher, John S. *Modern Philosophies of Education,* 3rd ed. New York: McGraw-Hill Book Co., 1962.

Burns, Hobert W., and Brauner, Charles J., eds. *Philosophy of Education: Essays and Commentaries.* New York: The Ronald Press, 1962.

Butler, J. Donald. *Four Philosophies and Their Practice in Education and Religion,* rev. ed. New York: Harper and Brothers, 1957.

Childs, John L. *American Pragmatism and Education.* New York: Henry Holt and Co., Inc., 1956.

Dewey, John. *Democracy and Education,* New York: The Macmillan Company, 1916.

__________. *Experience and Education.* New York: The Macmillan Co., 1938.

Hullfish, Gordon H., and Philip G. Smith. *Reflective Thinking: The Method of Education.* New York: Dodd, Mead and Company, 1961.

Hutchins, R. M. *The Conflict in Education in a Democratic Society.* New York: Harper and Brothers, 1953.

Morris, Van Cleve. *Philosophy and the American School.* Boston: Houghton Mifflin Co., 1961.

Redden, John D., and Francis A. Ryan. *A Catholic Philosophy of Education.* Milwaukee: The Bruce Publishing Company, 1955.

Scheffler, Israel. *Philosophy and Education: Modern Readings.* Boston: Allyn and Bacon, Inc., 1958.

Smith, B. Othaniel, and Robert H. Ennis. *Language and Concepts in Education.* Chicago: Rand McNally and Company, 1961.

Ulich, Robert. *Philosophy of Education.* New York: American Book Co., 1961.

B. Social Philosophy

Becker, Carl L. *The Declaration of Independence* (1922). New York: Knopf, 1951.

Bell, Daniel, ed. *The New American Right.* New York: Criterion Books, 1955.

Bode, Boyd H. *Democracy as a Way of Life.* New York: Macmillan, 1937.

Chandler, Albert R. *The Clash of Political Ideals,* 3rd ed. New York: Appleton-Century-Crofts, Inc., 1957.

Cohen, Carl. *Communism, Fascism and Democracy.* New York: Random House, 1963.

Counts, George S. *The Challenge of Soviet Education.* New York: McGraw-Hill, 1957.

Dewey, John. *Democracy and Education* (1916), rev. ed. New York: Macmillan, 1931.

__________. *The Public and Its Problems.* New York: Holt, 1927.

Ebenstein, William. *Totalitarianism: New Perspective.* New York: Holt, Rinehart and Winston, Inc., 1962.

Educational Policies Commission. *Purposes of Education in American Democracy.* Washington, D.C.: National Education Association and American Association of School Administrators, 1938.

Gabriel, Ralph Henry. *The Course of American Democratic Thought,* 2nd ed. New York: The Ronald Press, 1956.

Hayek, Friedrich A. *The Road to Serfdom.* Chicago: University of Chicago Press, 1955.

Hook, Sidney. *From Hegel to Marx.* New York: Reynal and Hitchcock, 1936.

__________. *Marx and the Marxists: The Ambiguous Legacy.* Princeton: Van Nostrand, 1955.

Hunt, R. N. Carew. *The Theory and Practice of Communism,* 5th rev. ed. New York: The Macmillan Company, 1957.

Lerner, Daniel, et al. *The Nazi Elite.* Stanford, Calif.: Stanford University Press, 1951.

Lippmann, Walter. *Essays in the Public Philosophy.* Boston: Little Brown, 1955.

Mosca, Gaetano. *The Ruling Class* (1923). New York: McGraw-Hill, 1939.

Mussolini, Benito. *The Doctrine of Fascism.* Florence, 1936.

Spitz, David. *Patterns of Anti-Democratic Thought.* New York: Macmillan, 1949.

PART II

AMERICAN SOCIETY AND EDUCATION

CHAPTER 6

THE AMERICAN MASS SOCIETY AND EDUCATION

An Ecuadorean businessman once approached a large New York department-store chain with some quaint Indian rope sandals for sale. The response was immediate and positive: the store was prepared to buy five million pairs at once. The seller was aghast—he wasn't sure he could provide even twenty thousand in a year.

"Sorry," said the store's buyer. "If you can't give us five million, we can't handle them. It's a matter of *mass* merchandising."

EVOLUTION OF AMERICAN MASS SOCIETY

We often hear of such terms as mass merchandising, mass production, mass communications, mass education, even mass society. They at once imply *great volume,* but they also carry nuances of standardization, efficiency, and for some, perhaps, vulgarity. Regardless, they are modern terms used to refer to complicated social phenomena which have reshaped our culture, our every habit of living. Large populations need seemingly endless quantities of the components of modern living. At the same time, a great number of people means a corresponding rise of individual differences, so that needs extend to a greater *variety* of components. Specifically, a modern, urban, technologically oriented society, with a mature industrial economy and a growing population, depends upon *abundance* and *diversity.*

In contrast, our sandaled Ecuadorean visitor emerges from an essentially rural, handicraft culture where needs are more limited, and prolific industrial production would find few markets. Thus, his nation today is reminiscent of the United States in an earlier period, and confirms that, over the years, we have changed in some fundamental ways which educators need to recognize as they assess current educational problems.

In colonial times, America was largely agricultural and sparsely populated. Diversification of activity was limited, since family units and small community units were entirely engaged in the basic activities of wresting a living from the soil. Agricultural workers outnumbered all other workers nineteen to one; hence, nonagricultural activities were slow to develop. Among these were transportation and communication, whose arrested development contributed to the essential isolation of families and small community units. Contacts were intermittent between farms and villages; news traveled slowly and was inaccurate, and people lived and died within very limited geographical areas. In 1790, only four per cent of our population lived in cities.

Inventions, imported from England, made it possible to mechanize textile production, as well as distilling, canning, lumbering, ship building and tobacco manufacturing. Steam power, the marvelous discovery of Watts, and other forms of water power made industrialization a possibility. Communications improved due to increased speed of ships, new waterways, the building of railroads, and in 1844 the invention of the telegraph linking distant centers together forever. Rapid communication between raw material supply and business centers enabled business to move such resources more swiftly into the mainstreams of world trade. The pace of commerce and change quickened. Along the eastern seaboard there were the beginnings of the commerce that eventually evolved into a mighty industrial complex and a giant in international trade. Simultaneously, there were gradual improvements in the efficiency of agricultural production. Two distinct trends began to emerge: the development of cities and the decline of the rural population. The need of the new manufacturing enterprises for an adequate labor supply caused adjacent cities to grow. As such concentrations of people came into being, proximity encouraged a greater range of interpersonal contacts, with consequent increases in marriage and a rising urban birthrate. Cities grew still faster because industrial centers needed a large variety of auxiliary services for both business and the growing urban population, and these needs provided the entrepreneur with golden economic opportunities. As the cities experienced rapid growth, the increased efficiency of agriculture, due in a large degree to mechanized production, displaced workers who then came to the cities to seek their fortunes. Economic power centered in the cities as industrialization progressed. Thus opportunity went where the power, the people, and the money were.

Opportunity in an agriculturally oriented nation lies in the ownership and control of land. Opportunity in an industrialized nation lies in the cities. Lack of industrialization in some nations today, for example, in Latin

America, puts great pressure on the ownership of land. Thus the clamor for land reform. When the agricultural land owners become also the nation's industrialists, an oligarchy has been created and opportunities for others are extremely limited and their development is arrested. If such populations have rising expectations of a better life, an explosive atmosphere exists. And if, as in Latin America, there are rising expectations coupled with a rising population and a rural-to-urban shift, the situation becomes acute. It is clear that industrialization promotes urbanization, or at least a large concentration of people close to the factory complex. It is also clear that industrialization and the factory system lead to efficient mass-production methods which necessitate that the individual worker specialize in only one part or one operation in the production system. Similarly, the diverse nature of auxiliary services needed to supply various goods and services to those employed in the industrial complex sows the seeds of further specialization. In the rural, handicraft, largely agricultural society, a worker tended to be a generalist, the proverbial Jack-of-all-trades, since he was separated from the services of specialists. Thus, the shift to occupational specialization constituted a major social change and affected the patterns of the culture.

At once, occupational specialization demanded specialized training and a new kind of education. Workers were acutely aware of the fact that their success and advancement depended upon their possession of specialized knowledge and skills in the new industrial age. The industrial labor movement, therefore, strongly supported a free public education for all, or *mass* education. Political and economic equality of opportunity was perceived as directly related to educational opportunity. The American middle classes became dedicated to the proposition that education was a primary ingredient for vertical mobility.

PERSONAL ISOLATION AND SOCIOECONOMIC INTERDEPENDENCE

As occupational specialization in an increasingly urban society grew, individuals experienced mounting difficulty in interpersonal relationships. Traditional face-to-face relationships were changing to a more impersonal, detached mode of living, and individuals found they had little knowledge of their neighbors' specializations. Occupational labels, other than the traditional ones for doctors, lawyers and so forth took on the colorations of their technological specialties, until they were meaningless to all save those few who were engaged in the particular specialty or one of its intimately allied fields. Consider this list of occupations recently listed in the classified section of a metropolitan newspaper:

loftsman	senior reliability engineer
auto trimmer	solid state device scientist
skip tracer	IBM tab operator
steel rule diemaker	injection mold foreman
antenna and radomes engineer	square shear operator
Ozalid and Diazo operator	tissue technician
1401 programmer	order board clerk
roll form operator	Hone and Lappers "A" machinist

All of these various specialists could have children attending the same school, shop at the same supermarket, see the same movies, drive the same kind of car, and yet many would have absolutely no understanding of the daily work of the man next door, across the street, or down the block.

Occupational specialization produced interdependence among urban people. Instead of providing for the basic essentials of living with his own hands, the urban industrial worker accepted money in exchange for his work, which he, in turn, exchanged for the goods and services which provided him with the basic necessities of life. Thus he now *buys* life. He sends his children out to be educated just as he sends out his cleaning. As a specialist, he is dependent upon the grocer for his food, the landlord for his house, the gas and electric man for his warmth. He is surrounded by strangers, and yet he is dependent upon them. His world of exchange is increasingly impersonal, and he is fearful that he can be easily exploited and forgotten. His reaction is immediate and sometimes desperate. He wants protection. He wants passage of legislation that will insure his survival by so arranging his society that his dependency cannot be exploited. And he is willing to give up some of his independence to gain such security.

The urban specialist worker began to demand more ground rules to govern his relationships with the multitudes of people with whom he had to live and work *in close proximity*. He wanted policemen, firemen, building inspectors, teachers, and an abundance of laws that would insure his survival. The more complex his society became, the more numerous the alternatives of social relationships, the more he demanded rules to govern such interactions. The urban specialist worker accepted two conditions: (1) the necessity of getting along with his fellow urbanites; (2) the consequent increasing community regulation of his life.

Demographers contend that the social environment of most Americans (80 per cent by 1980) soon will be the city. Thus, we will continue to experience most of the conditions we have been describing, as well as the problems they engender.

In answer, Lewis Mumford states:

> . . . most of the city's internal functions and structures must be recast to promote effectively the larger purposes that shall be served: the unification of man's inner and outer life, and the progressive unification of mankind itself. . . . [The] alternative is the current mechanical grinding down of both the landscape and the human personality. . . . to save himself, [man] must turn his attention to the means of controlling, directing, organizing and subordinating to his own biological functions and cultural purposes the insensate forces that would, by their very super abundance, undermine his life.[1]

DEMOCRATIC EQUALITY AND CONFORMITY

Another force which developed concurrently with industrialization, occupational specialization, urbanization, and interdependence was the drive to achieve democratic equality. Mass education, or education for all at public expense, had done much to promote equal opportunity. Wide differences between races, religions, and socioeconomic classes have been persistently attacked, until we can point to a growing convergence on a common way of life. N. B. Ryder[2] points out that, in the events of most importance to our personal lives, we are becoming more and more alike. We tend to marry more at the same age, have children during the same early years of marriage, and even die at more similar ages. "Differences in educational level are gradually diminishing," says Ryder, as well as marked differences in personal income. "Even the sizes of our homes are becoming more alike," Ryder asserts. Our population is more homogeneous in birthplace (foreign born are declining rapidly), and the sharp differences between religions have been toned down. For example, Protestant and Catholic families are now almost exactly the same size, despite supposed religious differences over birth control. Negroes and whites, not long ago, experienced distinctly different living patterns, but now are becoming more and more alike in areas such as education, occupations, age of marriage, family size, area of residence, and health.

The urban society, based upon mass production and mass education,

[1] Lewis Mumford, *The City in History* (New York: Harcourt, Brace & World, Inc., 1961), 571. With permission.

[2] N. B. Ryder, "Variability and Convergence in the American Population," *Phi Delta Kappan*, 41, No. 9 (June 1960), 379–383.

is so organized that culture tends to be more generalized, in some ways even standardized. Many observers view these trends with alarm. A mass society is portrayed as a vicious, depersonalizing force that erodes individuality and freedom. Even the finest expressions of the culture, as represented by the arts, are being vulgarized, assert these critics, by the onslaught of mass demands and mass appetites. "No art form, no body of knowledge, no system of ethics," states Rosenburg,[3] "is strong enough to withstand vulgarization. Never before have the sacred and the profane, the genuine and the specious, the exalted and the debased, been so thoroughly mixed that they are all but indistinguishable."

The ultimate expression of such developments is W. H. Auden's poem "The Unknown Citizen."

"The Unknown Citizen"
(to JS/07/M/378
This Marble Monument
Is Erected by the State.)
He was found by the Bureau of Statistics to be
One against whom there was no official complaint,
And all the reports on his conduct agree
That, in the modern sense of an old fashioned
word, he was a saint,
For in everything he did he served the Greater
Community.
Except for the War till the day he retired
He worked in a factory and never got fired,
But satisfied his employers, Fudge Motors Inc.
Yet he wasn't a scab or odd in his views,
For his Union reports that he paid his dues,
(Our report on his Union shows it was sound)
And our Social Psychology workers found
That he was popular with his mates and liked a
drink.
The Press are convinced that he bought a paper
everyday.
And that his reactions to advertisements were
normal in every way.
Policies taken out in his name prove that he
was fully insured,
And his health-card shows he was once in hospital
but left it cured.

[3] Bernard Rosenburg, "Mass Culture in America," in Bernard Rosenburg and David Manning White, eds., *Mass Culture* (Glencoe, Ill.: The Free Press, 1957), p. 5.

Both Producers Research and High-Grade Living
    declare
He was fully sensible to the advantages of the
    Installment Plan
And had everything necessary to the Modern Man,
A phonograph, a radio, a car and a frigidaire.
Our researchers into Public Opinion are content
That he held the proper opinions for the time
    of year;
When there was peace, he was for peace; when
    there was war, he went.
He was married and added five children to the
    population,
Which our Eugenist says was the right number for
    a parent of his generation,
And our teachers report that he never interfered
    with their education.
Was he free? Was he happy? The question is absurd:
Had anything been wrong, we should certainly
    have heard.[4]

While evidence to support Auden's and Rosenburg's position is often sadly lacking except at the speculative and poetic level, their viewpoint has, ironically, become very popular. It was Riesman[5] who first called attention to a state of mind he called "other-directedness," or operating only as we perceive that others want us to act. In a highly interdependent society, such an argument struck a responsive note. Large concentrations of people living in close proximity needed to be considerate of their neighbors lest life turn into a jungle relationship. Whyte[6] followed with a study of the characteristics he saw in that limited segment of our population which is overaffiliated with corporate organizations. He was concerned with the dependent "belongingness" concept which seemed to exalt "groupism" over individualism. Many others followed, some responding to what they rejected as vulgar and distasteful on television, in the movies, or in other forms of entertainment, recreation, or crude expression. The hue and cry against conformity mounted until many bystanders began to believe that indeed, they, as individuals, had somehow lost their free-

[4] Copyright 1940 by W. H. Auden. Reprinted from *The Collected Poetry of W. H. Auden*, by permission of Random House, Inc.

[5] David Riesman et al., *The Lonely Crowd* (Garden City, N.Y.: Doubleday & Co., Inc., 1953).

[6] William H. Whyte, Jr., *The Organization Man* (Garden City, N.Y.: Doubleday & Co., Inc., 1957).

dom, were shrewdly being fed pap, and were obviously stamped out of precisely the same molds as their neighbors.

The clamor from voices augmented by academic prestige virtually drowned out those of the more temperate social analysts whose observations were less dramatic and inflammatory. The simple question these less strident observers first asked was whether the apparently increasing conformity in life style necessarily implies a corresponding increase in conformity of mind beyond that normal degree of conformity imposed upon all individuals inducted into a highly organized and interdependent society. They wanted to know whether the balance of sociological evidence was indeed so one-sided as the conformity theorists insisted. The answers they offered were neither positive nor negative.

Jean Gottmann, a Frenchman, found the populations of eastern seaboard cities "the richest, best educated, best housed, and best serviced in the world."[7] This, however, does not disprove the argument of excessive conformity, though one might reason that a well-educated people, if education is a liberalizing force, could not be excessively conforming. Curiously, most of those sounding the alarm considered themselves liberally educated and nonconforming, even though they were obviously products of the same culture they were now criticizing. The argument over conformity pivots, of course, on internal characteristics rather than external similarities, if we are talking about states of mind. Thus, the mere reporting of numbers of people engaged in a particular activity is not necessarily evaluative of their mental state. We could, for example, cite figures which show that more people are seeking first-rate theater than ever before (fifty million saw Shakespeare's *Richard III* on television); more people, including children, are reading more books than ever before; more people are listening to classical music, live or recorded, than ever before (fifteen million people per Saturday listen to the Metropolitan Opera broadcasts, and the number of privately supported symphony orchestras has increased from six in 1900 to thirty-two today). But such delightful reports of the distribution of "high" culture do not tell us *why* so many people are so engaged. Perhaps they were conforming to some pressure—thinking they "ought to."

If we analyze the value commitments of members of our society, we may come closer to the real motivations for their behavior and, therefore, closer to their actual states of mind. This kind of analysis is partic-

[7] Jean Gottmann, as quoted in B. J. Chandler, "Forces Influencing Urban Schools," in B. J. Chandler et al., eds., *Education in Urban Society* (New York: Dodd, Mead and Co., 1962), p. 4.

ularly pertinent for educators, since they have been given a primary franchise for the value transmission process. Urban educators, in particular, will need to look closely at the changing forms of urban society as they relate to values and beliefs. They must also examine the superabundance of both personal and impersonal forces and stimuli acting upon people, and how they contribute or refute the arguments over conformity.

According to Karl Deutsch,

> Any metropolis can be thought of as a huge engine of communication, a device to enlarge the range and reduce the cost of individual and social choices. In the familiar telephone switchboard, the choices consist of many different lines. Plugging in the wires to connect any two lines is an act of commitment, since it implies foregoing the making of other connections. . . . The units of commitment are not necessarily telephone calls, but more often face-to-face meetings and transactions. Every transaction thus implies a commitment.[8]

Such transactions also imply choices; the selection of one value rather than another must be made. The metropolis, because of its *excess* of available choices, forces great selectivity of value commitments. In itself, this is not necessarily undesirable. Surely a democracy advocates and needs the existence of a wide range of choices and the freedom to be selective within such an extended range. It also seems clear that, as David Riesman has said: "Men cannot live without values, without preferences and choices, without the vocabulary of motives that we partly learn and partly teach ourselves."[9] But what does such selectivity do to us as individuals and subsequently as a group? It is pedestrian to remark that every child and adult has a selective awareness of his environment. That is, each of us is aware of our environment only insofar as it projects itself into our experiences, and each of our experiences is restricted by dozens of determinants, such as age, sex, race, geography, social class, or particular situations. Thus we begin to be selective, consciously and unconsciously, in the very act of living.

As we have seen, at maturity the occupational world provides another screening of experiences. As our nation has embraced the necessity of occupational specialization, we have become more and more immersed in our particular occupational specialization, until we have become less and less aware of the nature of specialties other than our own. Theodore Cap-

[8] Karl Deutsch, "On Social Communication and the Metropolis," *Daedalus,* 90, No. 1 (Winter 1961), 99. With permission.

[9] David Riesman, *Individualism Reconsidered* (Garden City, N.Y.: Doubleday & Co., Inc., 1955), p. 1.

low, in his book *The Sociology of Work,*[10] points out that our responses to other people's specialties are usually to the "labels" adorning the other specialties, rather than to any actual knowledge of those specialties. All of this seems to imply that we perceive a somewhat unreal version of the world outside our own narrowly circumscribed job patterns, concerns, and contacts, our particular transactions.

A third phenomena which contributes to the selection of our experiences is what Robert Angell calls "the decline of the local community" and the corresponding rise of "organized interest groups."[11] The metropolis has destroyed the local community, for community—as it was traditionally defined by Kingsley Davis[12]—needed two components: territorial proximity and social completeness. As the metropolis grows, the factor of territorial proximity becomes increasingly meaningless, as in the case of say, New York, Chicago, or Los Angeles. Social completeness, that condition when the local community is the source of all of the basic functions of human living, departed when suburbia grew like a rust on the edge of the hard core of the city, sapping the heart strength, diversifying the commitment of the city workers.

Thus, as the closely compatible folk or small-town community declines and there is an increase of interdependence caused by occupational specialization, William Stanley claims "the individual voice has all but lost its effectiveness in the complex and impersonal relationships which now govern the most intimate concerns of ordinary men and women."[13] The answer, of course, has been for individuals to weld themselves into groups to express their concerns for various aspects of society. Any individual can belong to not one, but several associations or organized groups, depending upon his degree of interest, commitment, and his available time and energy. But, by necessity, each individual becomes selective in these associations. He cannot be affiliated with all of the groups which are available in the metropolis. Neither can he feast upon all of the numerous kinds of stimulation pressuring him—no one is that nimble or congenial. The rise of organized interest groups has, therefore, immeasurably increased selectivity.

Against this background of a progressively more selective existence,

[10] Minneapolis: University of Minnesota Press, 1954.

[11] Robert Angell, "The Decline of the Local Community," in W. O. Stanley et al., eds., *Social Foundations of Education* (New York: The Dryden Press, Inc., 1956), p. 89.

[12] Kingsley Davis, *Human Society* (New York: The Macmillan Co., 1948), pp. 310–312.

[13] William O. Stanley, "Organized Interests and Social Power," in *Social Foundations of Education* (see note 11), p. 94.

we now understand something of the urban life of Mr. and Mrs. City Dweller. They live in the metropolis because this is where opportunity is concentrated, particularly economic opportunity. They are pleased by the infinite number of stimuli they receive, although they quickly inform us that, with the multitude of choices available to them, they must exercise options or be overwhelmed. By now, the focus of people like the City Dwellers has become comparatively narrow. That is, they have probably based their responses upon the interests they developed in the world they have known, a world circumscribed by initial selective awareness of environment, by occupational specialization, and by association with their choices of organized interest groups. Like teachers returning to summer school, the City Dwellers will probably continue to reinforce their strengths and present interests and ignore their weaknesses or areas of ignorance. In short, they will become more, rather than less, committed to their existing selections, their values.

CULTURAL PLURALISM AND CONFLICT OF VALUES

The aforementioned becomes significant in the general transmission of values. First, let us again refer to an earlier definition of value (see Chapter 3): "A value is a conception, explicit or implicit, distinctive of an individual or characteristic of a group, of the desirable which influences the selection from available modes, means, and ends of action."[14] In short, what is desirable is a function of an individual or a group, and the selection of modes, means, and ends of action is governed by such conceptions as one holds as an individual and as a member of a particular group or groups. When his group values clash, he will again make a selection on the basis of some hierarchy of commitment to certain key values.

It is perfectly clear to any politician who can earn his keep that organized interest groups, occupational specialists, and others do *not* embrace the same set of values, and often will fight with great ferocity over fairly subtle details of public policy. To illustrate such a bitter dispute over a fairly modest point, it may be said that the conservationists in the Midwest have split into two passionately opposing groups. One group wants to protect the deer from slaughter. They erupt with all manner of emotionally charged arguments about guarding the innocent, brown-eyed,

[14] Robert Redfield, "Values," in S. Tax et al., eds., *An Appraisal of Anthropology Today* (Chicago: University of Chicago Press, 1953).

helpless creatures of the forests. The other group wants to protect the young trees, so that our forests will not disappear. They, of course, will defend a young tree against all enemies, foreign or domestic. The clash is inevitable, for deer eat young trees. If one wants to save trees, he must shoot the deer; but if he wants to save the deer, he apparently must forego young trees and reforestation. Ironically, the groups see no conflict between their opposing positions and their common endorsement of filling up wild areas with expanding real estate developments.

We have sometimes called this complex of special interests and commitments, "cultural pluralism." The sullen confirmation of its existence can be found in the bustling anterooms of the mayors of any of our leading cities. Riesman has suggested, "While agreement on fundamental values may seem essential for democratic functioning, the attempt to enforce such agreement seems to be a good way to bring on a civil war; and it is important to study those institutions in our society which allow society to function precisely in the face of profound disagreements on fundamentals."[15] He goes further to suggest that the big-city political machines, corrupt as they may be, act as brokers among competing urban values and, as such, perform such a vital function that we can well afford the cost of graft which accompanies such machines. He implies, of course, that such competing urban values have very pugnacious adherents, since he freely predicts civil war if the clashes are not arbitrated.

If we need still further evidence of competing values, let us take a glimpse at the mail of any congressman. Every conceivable conflict of interest appears, much to the consternation of the congressman who must balance one force against another. The ideological pluralism of the metropolis has run rampant. Mumford suggests an alternate term to describe the situation: "negative symbiosis," which, crudely defined, means people living together in constant clash, or mutual destruction of interests.

Certainly we can predict that the sociological conditions we have described will persist in the future. In fact, occupational specialization and urbanization are so likely to increase that the phenomena of selective perception we have discussed should quicken at an alarming rate. In short, more and more of our people will approach their lives with only a partial awareness of their total society and with only a narrow selection of value commitments. With increased value conflicts based upon increased cultural pluralism, more and more of our urban dwellers will confront the problem

[15] Riesman, *Individualism Reconsidered* (see note 9), p. 2. With permission.

of living in a kind of *self-imposed cultural isolation,* while the culture will face the problem of an increasing fragmentation of its value structure.

Two further assertions need to be made here. First, the outcry against a *loss* of values in the society seems to miss the mark: values have not been lost, but under the impact of runaway cultural pluralism, they have certainly been widely dispersed. Traditional values are still present, but they may not be advocated in their totality at any one time by any large majority of the society. Support for such values has become selective. Second, the concern for an alleged trend toward conformity, which we described previously, apparently ignores all factors of selective perception and therefore mistakes superficial similarities for ingrained conformity. The gross observation that two different people live in six-room houses, drive Ford cars, and own television sets surely does not establish even a vague similarity in their states of mind. On the contrary, the metropolis offers these people the possibility of satisfying almost any conceivable whim or fancy they may have. For example, the commercial expression of this diversity is the ability of specialty shops of even the most esoteric nature to succeed. In short, values have not been lost, but merely dispersed, and such dispersion precludes conformity.

The crushing problem imposed by the metropolis and its national corollary, a mass society, is therefore one of fragmentation rather than narrow unity. The management of such a crisis demands extensive thought and planning. Mumford, who sees the solution within the metropolis itself, states:

> The chief function of the city is to convert power into form, energy into culture, dead matter into the living symbols of art, biological reproduction into social creativity. The positive functions of the city cannot be performed without creating new institutional arrangements, capable of coping with the vast energies modern man now commands: arrangements just as bold as those that originally transformed the overgrown village and its stronghold into the nucleated, highly organized city. . . .
>
> The task of the coming city . . . is to put the highest concerns of man at the center of all his activities: to unite the scattered fragments of the human personality, turning artifically dismembered men—bureaucrats, specialists, experts, depersonalized agents—into complete human beings, repairing the damage that has been done by vocational separation, by social segregation, by the over-cultivation of a favored function, by tribalisms and nationalisms, by the absence of organic partnerships and ideal purposes. Before man can gain control over the forces that now threaten his very existence, he must resume possession of himself. This sets the chief mission for the city of the future: that of creating a visible regional

> and civic structure, designed to make man at home with his deeper self and his larger world, attached to images of human nurture and love.[16]

ROLE OF THE SCHOOL IN DEMOCRATIC MASS SOCIETY

Into the context of such aspirations, we must now project the school as a social institution concerned with values. Sociologically or anthropologically speaking, we have asserted, the school is an institution assigned the primary task of value transmission, of socialization of the young into the ways of the society. This we have conceived to be the school's historic role. In the formation of our country, the public school emerged as the great assimilator of diverse cultural groups; the school, in short, was a fundamental tool for ethnic acculturation. But, in the twentieth century, that job of ethnic acculturation and assimilation has been mostly accomplished. (We are assuming that the success of the current drive for the integration of Negroes and other minorities is only a matter of time rather than of value decision.) A much more complex and subtle kind of challenge now presents itself.

In 1932, George S. Counts raised the provocative question: Dare the schools build a new social order? At the time, new social orders were the topic of the day; but even so, there were those who felt Counts was presumptuous. They claimed that the schools had not yet fully accomplished their currently assigned tasks. Even today, there are still those who are magnificently dissatisfied; but Counts' question has currently been rephrased. Now we ask whether education can be utilized as an instrument of national goals, or dare we *use* the schools as a primary tool for building a new social order? By "new social order" here, we mean the bold new institutional arrangements necessary to accomplish the positive functions of the city which Mumford suggested.

Logically, in view of the school's fundamental task of value transmission, such a proposition has immediate merit. Logically too, the machinery of the educational system, with its broad coverage of the population from childhood to old age, is comprehensive enough for such an assignment. The organization of the educational enterprise is also geographically practical, with branches in every neighborhood and at every country crossroad. Financially, the investment has already been partially made in capital

[16] Lewis Mumford, *The City in History* (New York: Harcourt, Brace & World, Inc., 1961), pp. 571, 573. With permission.

equipment and yearly revenues. Philosophically, a social institution so dedicated to learning, to the broadening of human perspectives, stands alone as the leading candidate for such a leadership role. Mumford states:

> Not industry but *education* will be the center of . . . activities; and every process and function will be evaluated and approved just to the extent that it furthers human development, whilst the city itself provides a vivid theater for the spontaneous encounters and challenges and embraces of daily life.[17]

Yes, all of the yardsticks agree: the schools have the logic and the potential to be the bridge to, and the core of, the society of tomorrow.

It is, however, problematic whether such events shall come to pass. Two principal obstacles must be overcome. The first obstacle is the circularity of the problem. We are confronted by the paradox that the solution to the problem is blocked by the problem itself. For the first requirement for solution involves the decision to ignore the problem, to accept an at least temporary injunction against the further pursuit of excessive cultural pluralism. Since the school is a formal social institution, it may not operate without the legal, financial, and philosophical sanctions of the society. It has no existence except that which the society grants it. This is not true of the more fundamental and natural educative process. But it is altogether true of the formalized, institutionalized expression of the educative process, the school. Thus, all the pulling and tugging between organized interest groups or competing individuals that have produced the current political and social jungle of cultural pluralism come to play on the consideration of the role of the school.

Even within the educational community itself there exists almost open guerilla warfare as factions and individuals earnestly pursue their particular goals and ends. The frighteningly easy adoption of the mores of the competitive industrial world by the intellectual and educational world is a warning of eventual disaster. Professors vie with professors, school administrators compete with their kind, and teachers battle teachers, all for the usual rewards of heightened prestige, additional income, or alleged fringe benefits. The extremities of opinion, as illustrated, for example, in the views of Admiral Rickover and the Association for Supervision and Curriculum Development of the National Education Association (N.E.A.), produce fertile fields for power blocs and demagoguery to plow. Even valid

[17] Mumford, *The City in History* (see note 16), p. 573.

ideological debates are soon invaded by military pressure tactics and cheap political manuevering. To further confuse the issues, the "operators" have swarmed into the fray, bringing with them their parasitic concern for power for power's sake.

The result has been the virulent chaos we experience when value commitments and their implementations ride madly off in all directions. Thus there is the absolute necessity for restraint, for a truce while reassessment and reassignment of both institutional functions and institutional priorities take place. The talent and the will to meet this challenge remain as yet untested.

The second obstacle resides in our present educational system and is not altogether independent of the first challenge. Simply stated, this obstacle is the issue of quality in education. How *well* could the schools accomplish the task we are proposing for them? Given the appropriate sanctions, legal, financial and philosophical, could the present educational system be expected to rise to the new heights of talent, nobility of purpose, and perseverance which such a central social role implies? To answer this question positively, one must envisage a professional team of highly trained and professional educators, prepared to dedicate themselves to a gigantic enterprise. To answer the question negatively, one need only admit that many thousands of educators are undertrained and occupy positions ill-suited to their particular talents and desires. Quality in the schools is the product of (1) the degree of sustenance offered by the sponsoring society, and more importantly (2) the limitations of the professionals who now inhabit the enterprise and are likely to continue to do so for some time to come.

Thus the challenge of the metropolis as it represents modern mass society can be met only by restraint on the one hand and release on the other. Lynch and Rodwin state:

> Planning and dreaming are old pastimes. When applied to cities, plans and dreams have usually been aimed at solving problems of the present or inducing a return to some image of the past: expressways were devised to escape the traffic jam, slum clearance to solve the housing problem, while neighborhood development looks back to the small community, and Broadacre City, to the family farm. Only rarely do we find a contemporary plan that anticipates the future with pleasure. Men are attracted to the metropolis by real values—choice, freedom, privacy, opportunity, culture, entertainment. How can we ensure the realization of those ends?

> More importantly, what are the possibilities for metropolitan life that are as yet undreamed of? And what kind of power, knowledge, or guidance must be applied to achieve them?[18]

The central problem, then, of a mass society is one of balance. Can sufficient individualism be maintained to prevent excessive conformity? Can sufficient conformity be maintained to prevent anarchy?

Two social conditions exist. The first is the obvious interdependence of men in a technological society that has stressed occupational specialization as a key response to the needs of industrialization. Interdependence, in turn, demands adequate modes of social control that will assure individuals safety from exploitation and some measure of personal security. Such modes of social control need to be guaranteed. The second condition is equally obvious. All modes of social control need limitations imposed upon them, since excessive, unrestrained control systems produce conformity and social inflexibility, which, in turn, destroy both the freedom of the individual and the dynamic growth element of the society.

Much dramatic writing, we have seen, has appeared on the various views of the problem, but, thus far, no universal solutions have been adopted. The school's role in this problem area is central. The school may encourage the values of conformity or the values of independence, or both. It is impossible for the school to remain neutral, since it must embrace some set of values relating to social adjustment. As a social situation, every classroom demands some kind of social adjustment among the independent personalities of the various children and the teacher. Whatever values are chosen—consciously or unconsciously—to arbitrate the social situation inherent in the classroom will be the very values the children learn to apply to experiences encountered in subsequent social situations. If children experience in school the persistent appeal to submerge themselves in the group for the group's good and the group's goals, then it will be unnecessary to teach them similar conformist attitudes as adults. Conversely, if the school consistently reinforces only the value of absolute independence, the children will be directed to this value throughout their later years. The school cannot abdicate from this responsibility and the constant making of choices that it implies.

This does not, of course, mean that schools must embark upon

[18] Kevin Lynch and Lloyd Rodwin, "A World of Cities," *Daedalus,* 90, No. 1 (Winter 1961), 9–10. With permission.

detailed studies of the most controversial areas of the conformism vs. independence issue. Elementary school children, for example, seem hardly qualified to examine Greenberg's idea of "kitsch"[19] or the finer points of the social control mechanisms employed in the United States. *The Organization Man* is probably not appropriate content for an elementary school social studies program, just as it would be of dubious value for secondary students to attempt to explore all the meanings of Riesman's essays. But the school does take value positions, at levels appropriate to the children it seeks to instruct, and needs to recognize that these positions have definite impact upon the acculturation of these children. The school thus needs to ascertain the exact nature of this impact as it relates to the value patterns being learned by its charges and must modify its procedures wherever and whenever children are being persuaded to behave in a manner inappropriate for a democratic, open society.

MASS EDUCATION IN AMERICA

Mass education has provided American society with the level of skills upon which our economy and culture are based. Our system of education has produced a literate, economically powerful country with the highest material standard of living in the world. This claim is not exaggerated, nor does it disparage the contributions of other institutions and social forces. But as the world examines the basic needs of "underdeveloped" nations, the need for education and the skills and specialized knowledge it produces is usually a first concern.

Mass education in the United States, as we have stated, served as the great assimilator of diverse peoples from every corner of the earth. If America is a "melting pot," and if such a complex amalgamation has been mostly successful, mass education must claim a greater portion of the credit, since it is the one social institution in which all American children participate. The schools removed accents, rubbed tradition against tradition, sat enemy with enemy, until Italians and Jews and Chinese and Mexicans were all calling themselves Americans and eating peanut butter sandwiches together, as well as bagels, tacos, pizza, and lobster Cantonese.

Unfortunately, some developments after World War II have disturbed this assimilative function of the schools and have contributed much

[19] Clement Greenberg, "Avant-Guards and Kitsch" in *Mass Culture* (see note 3), p. 98.

to renewed fragmentation of our society. We speak here of the phenomenon of "de facto" segregation, or the one-class neighborhood.

Four distinct kinds of neighborhoods seem to be hardening every day. Chandler calls them the upper-class suburbs, suburban slums, city slums, and exclusive city neighborhoods:

> While the one-class neighborhood is a problem created by society and is not likely to be solved by the schools alone, education must struggle with some of the consequences of homogeneous communities. How is the school to fulfill its traditional role as a social unifier when compelled to serve one-class communities? How is the school to escape de facto contributions to social rigidity?—what curriculum changes can be made to overcome the negative social outcomes implicit in situations where student bodies are homogeneous?[20]

While we often hear of minority groups protesting "segregation" from certain residential areas, we rarely hear the few small voices protesting that their children may grow up without ever having any experiences with the diverse peoples who inhabit their city. The miseducation of homogeneous suburban neighborhoods may be as costly to national unity and purposes as the open segregation of Negroes is in the South or other sections of the country. Clearly, this is an urban problem peculiar to our urban mass society.

SUMMARY

Modern America needs an educational system that will continue to serve the needs of a booming, diverse, technologically based economy, that will promote some semblance of national unity on more than a ritualistic or symbolic level, and that will protect and nurture the basic humanity of its people. Thus, individualism may not be the real issue if—by that term—we mean simply the nurturing and augmentation of *differences*.

Some argue that the central concern should be for humanity. Under the influence of the bold and rigorous challenge of international Communism, others will argue that national unity in a time of peril is the only real issue. Still others insist that the schools should be responsible for the educational and vocational guidance of young people even after they leave school, so great is the importance of education to an increasingly technological society.

[20] B. J. Chandler, ed., *Education in Urban Society* (New York: Dodd, Mead & Co., 1962), p. 9. With permission.

Mass society means industrialization, occupational specialization, interdependence, and cultural pluralism. It raises serious questions for mass education—questions that educators need first to recognize, and then to act upon. Such recognition, followed by analysis, constitutes the dynamic and challenging aspect of education in that it distinguishes the important, even crucial, role of education in the American society of the future.

SELECTED BIBLIOGRAPHY

Chandler, B. J., et al., eds. *Education in Urban Society.* New York: Dodd, Mead & Co., 1962.

Editors of *Fortune. The Exploding Metropolis.* Garden City, N.Y.: Doubleday and Co., 1957.

Mannheim, Karl. *Ideology and Utopia.* New York: Harcourt Brace and Co., 1957.

Mills, C. Wright. *The Power Elite.* New York: Oxford University Press, 1957.

Mumford, Lewis. *The City in History.* New York: Harcourt, Brace and World, Inc., 1961.

Patterson, Franklin, ed. *Citizenship and a Free Society.* Thirtieth Yearbook of the National Council for the Social Studies. Washington, D.C.: National Education Association, 1960.

Riesman, David. *Individualism Reconsidered.* Garden City, N.Y.: Doubleday and Co., 1955.

__________. *The Lonely Crowd.* Garden City, N.Y.: Doubleday and Co., 1953.

Rosenburg, Bernard, and David Manning White, eds. *Mass Culture.* Glencoe, Ill.: The Free Press, 1957.

Rudy, Willis. *Schools in an Age of Mass Culture.* Englewood Cliffs, N.J.: Prentice-Hall, 1965.

Steichen, Edward. *The Family of Man.* New York: Museum of Modern Art, 1955.

Thayer, V. T. *The Role of the School in American Society.* New York: Dodd, Mead & Co., 1960.

Whyte, William H., Jr. *The Organization Man.* Garden City, N.Y.: Doubleday and Company, 1957.

CHAPTER 7

THE NEW LEISURE, AUTOMATION, AND EDUCATION

THE NEW LEISURE IN OUR CULTURE

In order to understand the meaning of the phrase "the new leisure,"[1] we need to take a quick glance backward, into history. Prior to the turn of the century or, more specifically, prior to widespread industrialization, only a minute portion of the population could claim any significant periods of time for leisure. This portion of the population was the statistically tiny but culturally important and powerful "upper crust." Historically, only the ruling class and the economic elite could claim time free from productive or service work. Life in the rural-agricultural or pastoral setting made time-consuming demands on men, women, and children alike. Hard work from dawn to dusk was the rule year round, punctuated by traditional holidays and celebrations. These were usually symbolic in nature and related to the monthly and yearly cycles of rural life. What little time was allowed and available for play was justified as a means to refresh the body and replenish the spirit and soul of man for further work.

Life for the masses was difficult and demanding, but it was also meaningful, composed of necessary work and recreative play. This combination seemed to be cyclical, rhythmic, and natural. Similarly, the life of the elite was accepted as natural—its privileges, including substantial time for leisure, provided by God or by the order of nature. This pattern, which endured for many centuries, was powerfully challenged and upset within a few short decades by the forces of technology and industrialization.

As indicated in Chapter 4, within a brief period in history America

[1] The term "leisure" as used in this work refers to periods of available time when individuals or groups are not encumbered by the necessary demands of physical and economic existence. This usage is widely accepted; for example, in the Lundberg study, leisure is defined as "the time we are free from the more obvious and formal duties which a paid job or other obligatory occupation imposes upon us" (George A. Lundberg, Mirra Komarovsky, and Mary A. McInerny, *Leisure: A Suburban Study* [New York: Columbia University Press, 1934], p. 2).

was transformed from a rural-agricultural nation to an urban-industrial one. One important by-product of industrialization, mass production, social legislation, and the rise of unionism has been the gradual shrinking of the work day and the work week. In the middle of the nineteenth century, for example, the average work week was more than 70 hours; by the middle of the twentieth century, it was nearly 40. Current developments in automation point toward a 32-hour work week for industrial workers within the near future.

The "New Leisure," then, refers to the substantial periods of free time available to large groups of people who in the past had little, if any, time unencumbered by the necessary tasks of life. It must be emphasized, however, that the popular heralding of the "New Leisure" as the "Age of Leisure" *for all* is highly misleading.

LEISURE AND THE PROFESSIONAL

A careful analysis of the cultural scene will disclose a differential distribution of the "New Leisure." While some occupational groups (mainly the industrial, clerical, and service workers) have gained significantly in the amount of time they can devote to their chosen activities, scientists, top-level management, and professional workers have not. The "explosion of knowledge"—with new information, theories, and studies flooding forth at an unprecedented pace—makes new and unrelenting demands upon their time. Highly conscientious professional workers have difficulty avoiding a seven-day work week to accomplish their tasks or keep up with relevant professional publications. Competent educators fall into this group. They find themselves working longer hours than ever before and waiting for the benefits of the "New Leisure" to accrue to them also.

Whether or not professional, scientific, and managerial workers, including teachers, will be able to claim substantial portions of the "New Leisure" is highly problematic. It will probably depend on how creative they are in dealing with the social forces which make such unprecedented demands upon their time.

GROUPS BENEFITING FROM THE "NEW LEISURE"

As mentioned, certain identifiable groups have available to them more time for leisure than ever before in history. Among these groups are the following.

1. *Certain groups in the labor force.* For many members of the labor force increased leisure time has become available chiefly as a result of in-

dustrialization, together with legal and contractual limitations on their working hours.

2. *Certain groups of women.* This category includes women who are not employed and who do not have large families. In spite of the increased percentage of women in the labor force, as documented in Chapter 4, we still have a substantial number of women with large amounts of leisure time at their disposal. The concentration is particularly heavy in the 40-50-60-year age brackets. With the decrease in the size of the American family, many mothers find their children "on their own" and quite independent while the mothers are still young and vigorous. The scores of mechanical devices, prepared foods, and other products of modern technology often remove the challenge from homemaking as well as the satisfactions historically found there. A great many of these women, though well educated, are not prepared for any occupation that would hold their interest or match their status aspirations. Occupations for which they are technically qualified carry lower prestige; consequently, they tend to reject them. The resulting leisure time is consumed in a wide variety of ways—from returning to school for further education to bridge clubs; from lessons in art, music, or tennis to daily tea or coffee klatches; from church volunteer work in churches and charitable organizations to participation in political groups and organized letter-writing campaigns on behalf of various causes. Some find satisfaction in these and other activities, while others look for help on the psychiatric couch, in group therapy, or in the host of "faith-healing" cults which exist in and around our metropolitan centers.

These women's groups are sufficiently great in number and in influence to be reckoned with as a social force on the current scene in America. Often they are highly influential in the development of educational policies and practices. In recent elections, various candidates for political office have been aware of this phenomenon and have carefully used the leisure time of these women for their purposes.

3. *Children and unemployed youth.* Leisure for these groups has increased substantially, chiefly because of two factors: (1) social legislation reducing, and almost eliminating, child labor; (2) the shift to the urban-industrial culture, which eliminates most of the tasks children could do and often had to do on the farm. As a matter of fact, the typical urban or suburban family has difficulty in finding interesting and significant chores for children and youth. The difficulties involved in teaching the value of work and of responsibility have been aggravated through cultural change.

We have extended the school year from the brief three-month period in Colonial America to a nine-month period in the latter half of the twentieth century. A further extension might occur if adequate solutions can be found to the shortage of qualified educators as well as of buildings, equipment, and teaching materials for a year-round program. Even with the extension of the school year as well as the years of schooling, children and youth have gained in the amount of leisure available to them. (An exception must be noted for many talented youngsters between the ages of 12 and 17 who, due to a panicky reaction to Sputnik I and the space race, have become special targets of cultural pressures for an undefined "excellence." Many of these children suffer physical and emotional problems as a result of overwhelming demands from the schools for high quality work in great quantities.)

Traditionally, we have thought of children as incomplete adults, even as defective adults. Due to various historical forces, we have come to respect the integrity of childhood or, for that matter, of any period in life. The play of children, or the use of leisure by children, has come to be respected and valued in its own right, as well as for what it might contribute to the long-range development of each individual. Thus, childhood and adolescence may be viewed as both ends and means. They are *ends in themselves,* to be enjoyed and used, but they are *also means to the future.* As such, they must be planned and lived with both perspectives in mind.

The number of youth leaving school yet not qualified for productive employment is alarmingly high. It has been estimated that nearly 800,000 roam the streets of our large cities. Their numbers will rise to one and one-half million before 1970.[2] The number fluctuates because of migration and intermittent employment, but the problem is sufficiently disturbing to demand the attention of civic groups as well as of influential citizens throughout the nation.

4. *The retired person.* The leisure we force on the aged by compulsory retirement raises equally significant problems. In recent years, conferences have been held on the various aspects of this problem, entire communities have sprung up to meet the special needs of this age group, and scores of articles and books discuss the leisure and other problems of elderly people.[3] The significance of this problem will be underscored by a

[2] See *The Challenge of Jobless Youth,* President's Committee on Youth Employment, April 1963.

[3] For a brief sampling, see R. W. Kleemeier, ed., *Aging and Leisure* (New York: Oxford University Press, 1961); L. C. Michelson, "The New Leisure Class," *American Journal of Sociology,* 59 (1954), 371–378; and C. Tibbetts and Wilma Donahue, eds., *Aging in Today's Society* (Englewood Cliffs, N.J.: Prentice-Hall, Inc., 1960).

quick glance at our population charts. Currently America has its largest population concentration in the first two decades of life, but there is also a very large number at, and above, the sixth decade.

The power of the elderly group will manifest itself more and more through the exercise of their political voice. For example, if a school board must cut back certain programs because of an inadequate budget, will it curtail the adult programs frequented by retired citizens, or the day schools? There are indications that elderly citizens may defeat at the polls candidates who would cut back evening-school activities. Our youth has no similar power to protect itself at the polls.

5. *The unemployed and the disemployed.* The final large group with leisure time at its disposal consists of the unemployed (those who are able and willing to work but unable to find jobs) and the disemployed (those displaced from their jobs because of technological developments). In either event, idleness results, similar to the involuntary leisure of the unemployed youth and the retired person who did not choose to retire.

As with many other problems of our culture, *mass unemployment* is a relatively new phenomenon, resulting from many factors. Dominant among these we find industrialization, the rural-urban shift of our population, and the obsolescence of industries and of personal skills. The various remedial programs sponsored or proposed by the federal government are based on the recognition that an "unemployed pool" consisting of from one to six million workers is to be expected in a rapidly changing economy as massive and as complex as that of the United States in the second half of the twentieth century.

IMPACT OF AUTOMATION ON EMPLOYMENT AND LEISURE

Will the distribution of the "new leisure" be significantly altered by the long-heralded forces of "automation"? "Our entire economy is balanced precariously on the brink of automation," warn some armchair analysts, while many others nod in unison, predicting mass "disemployment" as the machines "take over." "The inevitable result," the prediction goes, "will be mass leisure with millions roaming the streets." More sober students of the changing social scene predict less dramatic results for automation and make more conservative estimates of its impact on leisure.

Those who have studied the development and the potential of automation tend to divide into two camps. The more conservative group believes that the number of jobs and amount of leisure available to the general population will not be significantly affected by automation. The second group believes that automation will have widespread effects on employment and leisure. Among the first, conservative group is John Diebold,[4] who made the term "automation" popular. He predicts that although some jobs will be eliminated, new ones will be created. There will be more need for highly skilled technical workers in production and maintenance work and in office work, while the need for semiskilled and unskilled workers will diminish. Macmillan, in pointing up the limits of automation, makes similar predictions:

> Nevertheless, in spite of the risks involved, the economic advantages to be gained from automation are so great that there will surely be a vast extension of its use. As we have seen, the first industries in which it has been applied are those making relatively long runs of a product that changes little and for which there is an assured and even expanding market—canned goods, motor cars and plastics, for instance. Other articles which may well be made and assembled automatically in the near future are ball bearings, typewriters, cameras, radio and television sets, clocks, ovens and refrigerators, bricks, fertilizers, soaps and textiles.[5]

Anderson, analyzing the relationship between work and leisure,[6] adopts the same point of view:

> When we ask again how much of all work will come under the sway of automation, we find that it is not likely to be great. Even today no more than 20 to 25 percent of all work in the industrial urban community is really industrial. Perhaps not more than half of that will submit to full automation. The various jobs in the public service, and the number increases, would hardly be included. The same holds for most private services, which also become numerous; places for eating, drinking, sleeping, and places where people go for entertainment. Stores and service shops are outside the realm of automation (with minor exceptions), so also the different professions, so also most forms of transport. The automatic factory would block off only a small part of the entire labour market (p. 239).

[4] See *Automation, the Advent of the Automatic Factory* (New York: Van Nostrand, 1952).

[5] Robert H. Macmillan, *Automation, Friend or Foe?* (New York: Cambridge University Press, 1956), p. 85. With permission.

[6] Nel Anderson, *Work and Leisure* (London: Routledge and Kegan Paul, 1961). With permission.

If the analysis of the foregoing writers is correct (and they are by no means alone in their view[7]), the extension of leisure resulting from automation would, by and large, accrue again to the industrial workers, who have already derived most benefit from the "new leisure."

The second group seems to take a bolder approach to the potential of automation. They agree that the stage of automation developed thus far lends itself chiefly to industrial operations, but they conclude that new and as yet unpredicted applications of automation are likely to appear. Even Diebold, who adopted a quite conservative point of view in 1952, sounded a note of great urgency some ten years later when he spoke of the "automation race" with Russia.[8] Much automation has already been achieved in storage and retrieval of information, in control of inventories, and in record keeping and clerical operations in banks and other commercial establishments. Promising explorations are being carried on concerning the use of automation in library services, legal research, and even some aspects of medical diagnosis. Ruttenberg predicts:

> Radical technological change, change that goes to the root of our economic and social processes, has already begun to sweep through America. . . . This change in America's industrial system has already spread to the office worker, has already affected middle management, has become part of our government operations and, indeed, has found its way into the teaching profession. There is literally no place in American life that will not feel the effects of automation in the 1960's, because a revolution in our economic and social life has been under way for a decade.[9]

In the opinion of this group of authors, among others, automation is a Pandora's Box: its impact on leisure is as yet unknown, but its potential is unlimited. As a result of man's creative use of his intelligence, most, if not all, occupations may be altered by automation. Some occupations will be changed directly; others indirectly, through the availability of a pool of able persons and skilled persons who have been displaced from their previous positions or who have received special training for certain automated processes.

[7] See, for example, James E. Russell, "An Educational Policy Planner," in Luther H. Evans and George E. Arnstein, eds., *Automation and the Challenge to Education.* Symposium sponsored by the NEA, January 1962.

[8] John Diebold, "Urgent Need: All-Out Automation," *Nation's Business,* July 1961.

[9] Stanley H. Ruttenberg. "Educational Implications of Automation as Seen by a Trade Union Official," in Luther H. Evans and George E. Arnstein, eds., *Automation* (see note 7), p. 86. With permission. The same conviction is expressed by Ida R. Hoos, *Automation in the Office* (Washington, D.C.: Public Affairs Press, 1961).

In the light of the foregoing, traditional procedures and personnel utilization in professional work must be re-examined without blind allegiance to old forms. Lawyers and even physicians have already accomplished much through various kinds of group practice, through the utilization of technical and subprofessional personnel, and lately through the use of machines for the storage and retrieval of information.[10] The promise of the computer intrigues imaginative workers in law, medicine, and engineering alike. Already, changes are occurring in decision making in these fields and others—changes based upon the creative use of computers.[11] We have scarcely begun to nibble at this problem, and so far no one knows what could be accomplished if the full range of human intelligence were brought to bear upon it. Educators, too, must avail themselves of the inherent benefits of automation.

Only the passage of time can tell which of the two groups of forecasters predicted the effects of automation accurately. Social trends are complex and difficult to apprehend and project. Often we read our own wishes into the "trends" of the times. To approach the problem of automation rationally, one must keep an eye on social developments and a sensitive but well-trained finger on the pulse of the economy. Thus grounded, predictions are more likely to be correct, as well as correctable in light of changing conditions. Predictions concerning the amount of leisure likely to result from automation, and for *which* occupational groups, will also have to wait for a more reliable isolation and projection of social trends.

THE IMPACT OF AUTOMATION ON EDUCATION

Automation is relevant to education in two areas. The first broad area is in the culture surrounding our schools; the second is within the schools and the instructional program itself.

AUTOMATION IN THE GENERAL CULTURE

Automation accentuates and aggravates some of the consequences of industrialization. Among others, it makes the tasks of the consumer at once more difficult and more delightful. Mass production brought a wide range of possibilities to the consumer. When we look at all the choices he

[10] Lee B. Lusted, M.D., "The Proper Province of Automatic Data Processing in Medicine," *Annals of Internal Medicine,* 57, No. 5 (November 1962).

[11] For a fascinating exploration of the potential of computers, see Thomas A. Cowan, "Decision Theory in Law, Science, and Technology," *Science,* 140 (June 7, 1963), 1065–1075.

has for his meals, for his means of transportation, clothing, reading materials, recreational activities, to mention but a few, we may wonder how the consumer survives from year to year in a fair state of mental health. Not only is his range of choices greater than ever before in the history of man, but there are greater pressures upon him to choose *this* rather than *that* commodity. A walk through a large department store or several hours of continuous watching of randomly selected television programs will send the careful observer reeling. Most people protect themselves by "shutting out" the millions of products competing for their favor (and money) and selectively perceive a few items, arrangements, or ideas. The "products pushers" know this all too well and develop highly ingenious means of penetrating this protective armor of selective perception. How often do we not find that the quality of advertising far surpasses the quality of the product or of the program!

All this points up the need for careful and systematic consumer education—the development of an intelligent citizenry who will use its critical powers against those who would turn people into hypnotized children or Pavlovian dogs conditioned and thus predictably responsive to clever slogans, shapely girls, and status symbols. The schools, by developing general critical ability, can contribute to this goal.

AUTOMATION IN THE SCHOOLS

Occupational competence has long been a goal of public education in America. This goal, probably more than any other, has been challenged by rapid changes in industrialization and automation.

The history of industrialization shows that, almost invariably, technological developments have brought about an increase in the demand for professional, managerial, and technical workers as well as for skilled labor.

> In manufacturing, for example, the ratio of professional and related workers to total employment increased sevenfold from 1910 to 1957. And in the ten-year period from 1947 to 1957, 90 per cent of the total increase in manufacturing employment was accounted for by nonproductive workers.[12]

At present, it is generally recognized that we do not have an adequate supply of professional and technical personnel to meet current and growing needs.

[12] Murray Wernick, Speech before the American Statistical Society, March 4, 1958, as cited in Samuel E. Hill and Frederick Harbison, *Manpower and Innovation in American Industry* (Princeton, N.J.: Princeton University Press, 1959), p. 4.

> Even in the midst of high over-all unemployment, there has been a shortage of scientists and engineers, of managers and competent administrators, of trained researchers, teachers, skilled craftsmen, and technicians in virtually every field. This shortage may have already been a limiting factor on economic growth. And all the statistics point to even further shortages in the immediate future.
>
> This problem poses a great challenge to the American educational system in the next two decades. Without any desire to strike an alarmist pose, I must say that I believe that our national survival, both as a country and as a viable economic society, will necessitate a closer tuning of the educational effort to the changing needs of the country.
>
> Up to now the time lag between needs of society and its educational fulfillment has been too long. The stepped-up educational requirements for new workers entering the labor market have not been met. Vocational and technical training have been inadequate. Counseling and vocational guidance have often been worse than inadequate. Retraining facilities have been generally lacking.[13]

SPECIALIZATION VS. GENERAL EDUCATION. It is quite clear that our schools should not prepare students for specific or narrow occupational specialties. The logic of our times requires that we prepare students for the occupational world first of all by a careful grounding in skills and abilities that are applicable to a wide range of actual and potential occupations. Training for "a job" would be suicidal, for "the job" probably will no longer exist on the day after graduation. The more thoroughly the student is prepared "across the board," the more adaptable he will be to the possibilities that exist when he enters the world of work. Such a broad preparation will, moreover, make it easier to retrain him on the job as the need arises.[14]

In view of the foregoing, we seem to have reached a paradox: On the one hand, we live in an age of increasing specialization but, on the other, our analysis leads us to recommend a rigorous general education for all. This paradox, is, however, only apparent, for specialization will have to be superimposed on the general education of man. It is also becoming increasingly clear that the schools, if they are to continue vocational training, must cooperate closely with industry and with government. Only through such collaboration can we determine future occupational require-

[13] Frank H. Cassell, "Educational Implications of Automation as Seen by a Business Executive," in Luther H. Evans and George E. Arnstein, eds., *Automation and the Challenge to Education,* January 1962, p. 79. With permission.

[14] A similar position is expressed by Harry S. Broudy et al. in *Democracy and Excellence in American Secondary Education* (Chicago: Rand McNally and Company, 1964).

ments and attempt to prepare students with marketable skills and abilities. Another alternative, often suggested but so far rejected by our society, is that schools withdraw completely from vocational education and let commerce and industry provide the training to meet their own manpower needs. This proposal will be repeated in the years ahead. In the judgment of the authors, however, it will be rejected again, and efforts to achieve continuous solution of the problem will tend in the direction of closer cooperation among three major agencies in our society: business and industry, government, and our schools.

AUTOMATED INSTRUCTION. Automated instruction has been popularized under the label "teaching machines," but a more accurate label is that of programmed instruction. We shall treat this development only briefly, since its thorough analysis belongs more properly within the province of educational psychology. Its relevance is noted here as a significant cultural development, one aspect of automation. Our chief concern is how programmed instruction might affect the leisure time available to educators.

At the most naive level, some people ask: "Will teaching machines replace teachers?" To this Dr. William Van Til remarked in a speech: "Any teacher who could be replaced by a machine, should be." No serious student of education suggests such substitution. The early claims on behalf of teaching machines were greatly overstated, particularly by the commercial interests who invaded the field and prematurely mass-produced their gimmicks and gadgets.

A leading figure in automated teaching, Dr. Wilbur Schramm of Stanford University, is realistically cautious about the current achievements of programmed instruction but confident of its potential.[15] In his words:

> The argument that programmed instruction will replace the teacher is a kind of sensational and uninformed journalism which is unworthy of attention. Along with textbooks, teaching films and slides, instructional television, workbooks, chalkboards, and many other such things, programmed instruction is one of an arsenal of teaching devices at the command of the teacher to help him do his job better (p. 4).

Schramm underscores the need for substantial and bold new research in programming and for testing the effectiveness of programmed materials.

[15] Wilbur Schramm, *Programmed Instruction Today and Tomorrow* (New York: Fund for the Advancement of Education, 1962).

Warning of premature standardization, gimmickry, and undue commercialization, he sums up the state of the art as follows:

> Although the research gives us little reason to be satisfied with the theories and the standards of today's programming, and every reason to believe that it will be possible some day to make programs vastly more effective than today's programs, nevertheless programmed instruction shows signs of hardening, partly under commercial pressure, into a fixed and mechanical technology, with theories and procedures taken for granted.
>
> Although programmed instruction has within it the potential to turn the attention of education and educational research more intensively and productively than ever before to the process by which humans learn, there is very little sign that it is being used productively to test theories of human learning or theories of cognitive process, or to enlighten the teacher concerning the process by which she teaches.
>
> Although programmed instruction is essentially a revolutionary device, in that it has the potential to help free man from some of his bondage—the waste of human resources where there are no teachers or where people cannot go to school; the waste of time and talent where all students are locked into the same pace, and all teachers into the same routine, the tyranny of tradition which permits the study of a certain topic to begin only at a certain age, and expects a student to accomplish only so much as a questionable test of his ability says he can do; and the inadequacy of outmoded and inadequate curricula—despite this, programmed instruction is very slow to rise to such a revolutionary potential (pp. 37, 38).

Notice again Schramm's emphasis, and properly so, on further research and testing when he speculates about the potential of programmed instruction and points to its future possibilities.

> More of the effort at making programs must be placed on the growing edge of the art, rather than the safe and conservative commercial "center."
>
> More research must be directed toward the larger implications and theoretical problems of programmed instruction; in order to accomplish this, long-term commitment of top-level researchers will be required.
>
> The schools must make more imaginative applications of programmed instruction, accompanied by developmental research and testing.
>
> Teachers must be trained to use programmed methods expertly; and the possibilities of making and using programs should be explored as one introduction to the human learning process in teacher training.
>
> Other channels of teaching—such as television, textbooks, films and

other audio-visual means, workbooks, class teaching, and group study—must be examined to see where they can beneficially apply some of the principles of programmed instruction.

The skills and understandings of programmed instruction must be shared with the developing nations, and used where possible to speed economic and social development.

Adequate channels of information must be established among the many and diverse people interested in the development of programmed instruction (pp. 39, 40).

Although successful programming may well alter the activities of educators, it will probably not increase their leisure significantly. Teachers and educators in general will have to face the coming decades with the same heavy demands on their time that are likely to face other professional workers.

CURRENT USES OF LEISURE

So far, our knowledge about the uses of leisure is limited. The systematic study of the phenomenon began only around the middle of the twentieth century.[16] In addition to the independent studies by sociologists, we also saw the rise of university centers for the study of "free time" or leisure. The best known among these is the Center for the Study of Leisure at the University of Chicago.

The use of leisure is influenced by many factors. The most obvious among these are climate and geography, religion, education, population density and mobility, and governmental support. Of equal importance, though not so obvious, are socioeconomic factors, the influence of the mass media, and the complex ways in which "wants" are created in men.

The foregoing factors must be studied in their interrelatedness if one is to understand the great increase in the available leisure activities. Such a study is particularly difficult in a dynamic culture such as the United States, with its social mobility, its orientation toward achievement, and its mass production that brings within the purchasing power of all workers many products and activities which, in years past, were available only to the few. Characteristically, the American people and economy will not stand still long enough for a thorough study of "current uses of leisure." Never-

[16] There are, however, sources for earlier comments related to the topic. A comprehensive bibliography on leisure is presented by Eric Larrabee and Rolf Meyersohn, eds., *Mass Leisure* (Glencoe, Ill.: The Free Press, 1958).

theless, we can still look at the changing patterns and highlight the discernible features of the uses of leisure.

In recent years, two approaches have been used to study the use of leisure. The first one involved intensive study of one community, or of parts of a community. Examples of this would be the Swados study of Akron, Ohio,[17] the Webber study of leisure pursuits of the retired in Florida,[18] or the Swenson study of university students.[19]

The second method is a more general one, relying upon statistical information from governmental, commercial, and industrial sources. Various departments of the federal and state governments, chambers of commerce, banking associations, econometrics associations, and scores of other sources are pouring forth an endless stream of statistical information from which inferences may be drawn concerning popular uses of leisure.

Both of these methods are useful, if their findings are treated with care and intelligence. For example, the responses of the workers from the rubber plants of Akron, as described in the Swados study, will give us a more appropriate basis for predicting the behavior of steel workers in Gary, Indiana, or Weirton, West Virginia, than that of electronic workers in Palo Alto, California or of the cotton workers in the southern part of the country. Similarly, the fact that close to 20,000,000 Americans purchased fishing licenses in 1960 might be a significant bit of information, but also a highly ambiguous one. The same can be said of the fantastic rise in the number of paperback books sold or of the fact that approximately 10,000,000 recreational boats float on the waters of the United States.

The most we can say about the case-study approach is that, up to now, it has merely contributed methods for studying particular problems one might face in a particular community but does not give us general knowledge of the leisure-time activities of the entire population. This is not to belittle the importance of methodology in intellectual analysis, but merely reemphasises that the systematic, scientific analysis of leisure is yet to come. The same conclusion applies to the second method, which provides simple statistical descriptions for the economist, businessman, and, perhaps, government official concerned with long-range planning and regional developments.

[17] Harvey Swados, "Less Work—Less Leisure," *Nation* (February 22, 1958), pp. 153–158.

[18] Irving L. Webber, "The Organized Social Life of the Retired: Two Florida Communities," *American Journal of Sociology,* 59 (1959), 340–346.

[19] Jean Swensen and Jessie Rhulman, "Leisure Activities of a University Sophomore Class," *Educational and Psychological Measurement,* 12 (1952), 452–466.

All the currently available information indicates that leisure is "big business." It is booming and promises unimagined possibilities. Market analyses estimate that over $40,000,000,000 per year, or about 15 per cent of total consumer expenditure, is spent for leisure activities. Exact figures are difficult to come by due to variations in the definition of "leisure" and the ambiguous classification of certain expenditures such as "do-it-yourself" projects, automobile expenses, or even expenses connected with continuing education.

The major categories of leisure activities include vacations, travel, reading, further education, radio and television, movies, do-it-yourself projects, gardening, hobbies, fads, music (including concerts, opera, and records), theater, dance, sports, camping, boating, hunting, and fishing. Undoubtedly, some of these categories overlap, and others could be added; they are useful, however, to point up the magnitude of the enterprise, its complexity, and its promise for the future.

Zelomek discerns three major trends in the leisure market:

> First is the switch from spectator and group to active individual sports and, in general, the growing relative importance of all forms of active recreation. Second is the filtering down from upper to lower income brackets of recreational activities which were once in the luxury class. Third is the influence of suburban living and the emphasis on family activities.[20]

LEISURE AS A SOCIAL PROBLEM AND A SOCIAL ASSET

With the "new leisure" upon us and with the promise of more to come, this new social phenomenon has been heralded as a welcome asset by some, including Bertrand Russell,[21] and as our greatest problem and liability by others, including Arthur Schlesinger, Jr.:

> The most dangerous threat hanging over American society is the threat of leisure . . . and those who have the least preparation for leisure will have the most of it.[22]

[20] A. Wilbert Zelomek, *A Changing America: At Work and Play* (New York: John Wiley and Sons, Inc., 1959), p. 90. With permission.

[21] See his *In Praise of Idleness and Other Essays* (London: George Allen and Unwin, Ltd., 1935).

[22] Quoted by Harvey Swados (see note 17); see also Robert MacIver, *The Pursuit of Happiness* (New York: Simon and Schuster, Inc., 1955), especially Chapter 6, "The Great Emptiness."

This bipolarity of "viewing with alarm" on the one hand and "welcoming with open arms" on the other is indicative of several aspects of the problem. First, it is evidence of how little precise and rigorous knowledge we have of current practices and trends in the uses of leisure. This points up the need for formulation of a theoretical framework relating leisure and work as well as the various kinds of leisure activities to each other. Such a theory of leisure would provide a useful basis for a more careful analytic and empirical study of the social functions, uses, and potentialities of leisure.

Second, the bipolarity is indicative of the extent to which we have continued with our traditional orientation toward work or shaken free of it. The "work-ethic" derived from the Puritan influence in America is deeply rooted here. "The Devil finds work for idle hands," "idleness is wickedness," "into busy lives Satan will not enter," are characteristic expressions of this faith. We find modern manifestations as well as clear continuation of this traditional commitment to the value of work and its corollary, the fear of idleness. Even today, many parents are concerned lest their children have too much free time, for "they'll get into trouble" or "think of bad things to do." These same parents tend to feel guilty if they themselves read for "pleasure" instead of reading "to improve the mind." Engaging in play or sport is justified as being good for the body and not merely as a pleasant or exciting pastime. (As Ogden Nash phrased it, "We are suffering from hardening of the oughteries.")

Historically, the function of play or of leisure was to recreate the spirit, the will, and the body for productive work. Only recently have we considered even the possibility of justifying leisure on the basis of its own value and its own integrity, independent of work.

A third reason for the dichotomy between considering leisure an asset and viewing it with alarm centers on the type of recipient of the increased leisure. Although the long-range consequences of automation are not yet predictable, it is clear that in the near future it will be the man of low skill, the industrial and low-level clerical worker who will gain the most leisure time. Writers in the field tend to agree that these are the people least prepared for significant or constructive use of this new "gift." According to MacIver, leisure "is a marvelous liberation for those who learn to use it; and there are many ways. It is the great emptiness for those who don't."[23] He continues, analyzing the "new, unopulent leisure class" in pessimistic terms:

[23] Robert MacIver, *Pursuit of Happiness* (see note 22), p. 49. With permission.

> They have no training for leisure. They have, most of them, no strong interests or devotions. The habits of their work time convey no meaning to the time of liberation. Most of them live in cities, in drab and narrow confines within which they revolve in casual little circles. They see nothing ahead but the coming of old age. They want to retain the feel of life. Time is theirs, but they cannot redeem it.
>
> So they too betake themselves, in their various ways, to some form of excitation. Having no recourse in themselves, they must get out of themselves. They take the easy ways out because they see no alternative. They have never learned to climb the paths leading to the pleasures that wait in the realm of ideas, in the growing revelation of the nature of things, in the treasuries of the arts, and in the rich lore of the libraries. They must seek, instead, the quick transport, the dream, the adventure, in the tavern or where the gamblers meet.
>
> They would cover the emptiness they cannot fill. They make a goal of what is a diversion. The healthy being craves an occasional wildness, a jolt from normality, a sharpening of the edge of appetite, his own little festival of the Saturnalia, a brief excursion from his way of life. But for these others the diversion becomes the way of life and diverts no more. For them the filled glass is not the cheerful accompaniment of pleasant reunions, but a deceitful medicine for the ennui of living. For them the gambling venture is no mere holiday flutter, but a never-satisfied urge that forever defeats itself (pp. 52–53).

We do have a significant portion of our population whose work is routine, monotonous, and fragmented due to specialization and mass production, lacking in artistry, wholeness, and thus personal satisfaction. We tend to *earn a living* rather than *make a living,* and consequently have eliminated most of the creative elements of work which a preindustrial economy provided. This is why large numbers of workers, not prepared for creative or reflective use of leisure, spend their newly found time and money on brief delusions of escape, excitement and temporary "blasts, fads and jags." This illustrates the problematic aspects of the "new leisure."

The coin of leisure also has its other side. Just because large groups of people are ill-prepared to use their time and money in constructive and creative ways, we must not assume that this incapacity is "natural." The opposite assumption points to the fantastic, though as yet untapped, possibilities inherent in the modern era. Are the obstacles and challenges involved in preparing large segments of the population for "worthy use of leisure" any greater than those involved in achieving general literacy, industrializing a new continent, or exploring space? In 1918, the Educational Policies Commission listed the "worthy use of leisure" as one of the goals of American education. Since then, as well as prior to that date, tremendous numbers of people have been prepared, with various degrees of success, to use their leisure well. The optimistic view suggests the need for careful and systematic extension of education for leisure to *all* Americans.

Objective analysis suggests that the substantial increase in leisure by itself will neither doom our industrial society automatically to "emptiness" nor lead it to "great heights." Man will have to be the architect of his own future, realizing that he has created a powerful new medium with which he must work. Except for the possible destruction by a nuclear holocaust, industrialization will proceed world wide, with a stepped-up pace. Even more leisure will result from increased productivity. Modern man must realize that his newly created leisure will be either an overwhelming problem or a powerful resource.

EDUCATION AND THE "WORTHY" USE OF LEISURE

As we noted earlier, a national commission composed of educators and laymen, the Educational Policies Commission, recommended as early as 1918 that one important goal of education in America be the "worthy use of leisure." This recommendation was reaffirmed in 1938 and again, indirectly, in a 1961 publication.[24]

Statements of educational goals, however, are not self-executing. It is quite easy to find scores of statements approving this educational aim, yet difficult, if not impossible, to recognize programs of action aimed at realization of that goal. This is not unlike other areas of social life where shortcomings are easily identified and problems highlighted, yet solutions or even remedial efforts are wanting.

For example, it is fascinating to examine the readings in *Mass Leisure,* by Larrabee and Meyersohn.[25] The many dimensions of leisure are explored by capable authors, some of whom are optimistic, some pessimistic, and some quite objective, descriptive, and analytic. Yet nowhere in this volume of nearly 400 pages is the relationship between education and leisure explored. The book abounds in warnings on the lack of preparation for leisure, and underscores the great emptiness that is likely to afflict its recipients. But the intellectual critics and analysts stopped there, short of

[24] *The Central Purpose of American Education* (Washington, D.C.: Educational Policies Commission, N.E.A., January 1961), p. 6.

[25] See note 16.

the task. Where are the constructive suggestions? Must analysis lead to paralysis? To doom? It seems that the constructive suggestions come only from the recreational workers and the rare educator.

Surveying the literature in this field, Fitzgerald points up the paucity of research in education for leisure.[26] He notes that research thus far has concentrated on the availability, use, and consequences of outdoor recreational activities. He lists the following seven areas of much-needed research:

> (a) Relationships between the school program of education for leisure and the participation offerings of community agencies outside the school. (b) The place of the classroom teacher and specific parts of the curriculum in education for leisure. (c) The relationship between student organizations and education for leisure. (d) The relationship of extra-curriculum activities to education for leisure. (e) The relationship of teacher preparation to education for leisure. (f) The relationship of the teacher's personal pattern of recreation interests and skills to education for leisure. (g) Methods in developing coordination between the home and the school in education for leisure (p. 297).

In effect, by negative implication, Fitzgerald's recommendations for research point up how little we know about the actual connection between leisure and education. We do, however, have some crude, unsystematized information that is relevant. For instance, we know that college graduates read more, travel more, and also show greater interest in participant sports than those without higher education; that Southerners tend to have fewer ideas about what to do with possible extra days off from work, have fewer hobbies, and have less interest in travel, sports, and do-it-yourself projects;[27] that more and more business executives are continuing their education during their leisure hours, and that large corporations as well as large unions have been spending millions of dollars on education; and that both executives and union members are pursuing studies in fields not directly related to their occupations.[28] Generalizations like these, though supported by fact, do not shed sufficient light on the relevance of education for leisure.

The lack of a clear conception of, or agreement on, what is "worthy use of leisure" has been an important reason for the inadequate attempts to

[26] Gerald B. Fitzgerald, "Education for Leisure," *Review of Educational Research*, 20, No. 4 (October 1950), 294–298. With permission.

[27] See David Riesman, "Leisure and Work in Post-industrial Society," in *Mass Leisure* (see note 16), p. 369.

[28] See A. Wilbert Zelomek, *A Changing America* (note 20), p. 85.

connect education and leisure. "Worthy" obviously implies a value judgment, and in our pluralistic culture we have been afraid to specify what uses of leisure are valuable and which are not. Yet need we be so timid? We constantly make value judgments in the processes of education. The entire curriculum really consists of a set of value judgments, of experiences considered to be valuable, or "worthy" of attention and study.

The societal reluctance to face questions of value probably derives from the fear of imposing one's values upon others. Americans have long resisted the idea of indoctrinating all people with a fixed set of values. The phrase "worthy use of leisure" implies that certain kinds of activities ought to be carried on by all. It seems to recommend the "classics" in books, music, and so forth but to deride popular sports, folk songs, and do-it-yourself projects. While this fear may be justified, it does not necessarily follow from the expression itself. A fixed value system with a permanent hierarchic arrangement of values would be inappropriate to a pluralistic, democratic social order. This does not mean, however, that no guidelines on the worthwhile use of leisure can be established.

Neumeyer, for example, offers us a guide without specifying what particular activities one should choose:

> A desirable leisure pursuit should be permanently interesting, differ as far as possible from the activities which the necessities of life impose upon us, have its origin and fulfillment in the personality of the individual himself, and be compatible with, if not conductive to, the enrichment of life.[29]

In the final analysis, if we reject as inappropriate a fixed and permanent value hierarchy which specifies for man what activities he ought to pursue in his leisure time, we are left with two alternatives. One of these swings to the other extreme—namely, that any activity one may choose, as long as it is legal, is valuable. This choice the authors reject as one of expediency, which is intellectually indefensible. It identifies preference with value, which is improper in light of the analysis presented in Chapter 3. The final alternative, to which the authors subscribe, does not point to a fixed set of values nor does it leave choice to the other extreme of complete subjectivity.

The educator's approach calls for situational decisions in light of certain criteria. Whether or not a particular leisure activity could be con-

[29] Martin H. Neumeyer and Esther S. Neumeyer, *Leisure and Recreation—A Study of Leisure and Recreation in Their Sociological Aspects,* 3rd ed. Copyright © 1958. The Ronald Press Company. P. 178.

sidered "worthwhile" would depend on its consequences for the individual involved and for society—namely whether it would promote individual and social growth. Does the activity introduce one to new experiences and hitherto unknown qualities of living? Concurrently, will these experiences lead to his further development, or at least not have negative effects for him? If no new dimensions of life are involved, does the activity heighten or deepen one's understanding, appreciation, or enjoyment of some already existing aspect of his life? While the focus in each of these questions is on the individual, the social consequences also need to be weighed: at best they should be constructive; at least, they should not be negative.

Thus, "worthy use of leisure" has two significant aspects: it helps the individual grow in depth and variety of his understanding and enjoyment of life's many qualities; concurrently it will upgrade both the general quality of a culture and the quality of democratic participation by its citizenry.

As the reader will recall, "leisure" signifies the free time available to men apart from the pursuit of life's necessities. In a sense, *free choices* are made during *free time*. Consequently, in a society with substantial amounts of free time available to large groups of people, the quality of the culture of these large segments of the population will be shaped by what they choose to do with their leisure. Similarly, democracy in operation can be said to be a leisure-time activity. Neither participation in democratic political behavior nor the necessary reading and other inquiry related to such participation in an intelligent way can be coerced. People either choose to use their leisure for such ends or they do not. Industrialization, which led to the present availability of substantial leisure for the "common man," made possible grass-roots participation in democracy. The quality of popular democracy—indeed, its very existence—is contingent on how the new leisure, the "gift of the machine," will be used.

The foregoing discussion of what constitutes "worthy" uses of leisure points up the relevance of education. It becomes apparent that, while no special courses need be constructed to teach the appropriate uses of leisure, each course or area of study is relevant. One important result of any phase of school work could be that it might motivate the students to choose their leisure activities freely in ways relevant to that subject. We speak of "carry-over" sports, meaning activities in physical education which the student will continue when his formal education terminates. Why not "carry over" interest in reading, music, chemistry, political activity, history, French? The long-range impact on the student might even be considered the most important educational goal of each school experience. Are we not attempting to influence future interests and basic dispositions? Although the difficulties in long-range evaluation are many, it is pertinent to suggest that schools do follow-up studies to ascertain the connection, if any, between what they teach and the leisure pursuits of their graduates.

Jung's study of the leisure activities of upper-grade children in a metropolitan setting[30] is an example of the kind of information educators need on a more extensive scale to guide them in their decisions. Some of his conclusions, of interest to educators, are presented in Table 7–1.

TABLE 7–1. Summary of ethnic and socioeconomic differences of 574 children for various activities.

Activity	Ethnic or Socioeconomic Differences
Outdoor play	Negro children most involved; Oriental children least involved.
Roller skating	Much greater participation by Negro children.
Bicycle riding	Much greater participation by Negro children.
Indoor play	Oriental children led in participation in table games.
Reading	Oriental children led in most reading activities by a significant degree. White children led Negro children for most activities. Middle-status children generally exceeded lower-status children in reading activities.
Radio and phonograph Listening	No significant differences.
Television	High level of participation for all. No significant differences noted.
Hobbies	Little mentioned in diaries. Middle-status children led in activities. Oriental children participated more than other groups.
Preference for mass media	White and Negro children preferred motion pictures; Oriental children, television.
Motion pictures	No pattern of differences in frequency of attendance.
Church activities	Negro children, greatest participation; Oriental children, least participation.
Music activities	No pattern of differences.
Organizations	High membership rates for middle-status children. Boy and Girl Scouts most popular activity.
Homework	Oriental children, most involved; Negro children, least involved.
Home chores	Oriental children had the least home chores. Negro girls led in house cleaning and washing clothes.
Paid jobs	White and Negro children exceeded Oriental children to a significant degree.
Play with parents	Oriental children played with parents to a much smaller extent than white or Negro children.

[30] Raymond K. Jung, "Leisure Activities of Children of Different Socio-Economic Status and from Different Ethnic Groups," unpublished doctoral dissertation, University of California, 1964.

LEISURE AND EDUCATIONAL DECISIONS

The explorations of Jung, and of others who have gathered information about the leisure pursuits of our children and youth, are relevant to educational decisions. Considering the amount of time our school-age population spends in front of television, for example, would it not be reasonable to propose that the curriculum should attempt to prepare them for a more critical, intelligent approach to choice and viewing of programs? For a more critical viewing and evaluation of the relentless stream of high-pressure selling which is beamed into nearly every home? Why not have television in classrooms? Do we not have it in almost every hotel or motel room throughout the country? Can we, in the long run, afford not to prepare our citizenry for intelligent television viewing?

While existing studies are seriously limited in scope and depth, they indicate the tremendous possibilities for future research in this aspect of our national life, and the relevance of knowledge about current uses of leisure for educational decisions.

It is unfortunate that, historically, only physical education, reading, and perhaps music and art have been considered systematically for their relevance to leisure. This view is needlessly restrictive. With the exception of very narrow, technical vocational courses (which have a questionable place in the curriculum outside the vocational school), each subject studied has a potential claim on the students' leisure. The realization of this opportunity to shape his students' interests is a challenge to good teachers.

Teachers are not the only persons involved in influencing the present and future leisure of students. Decisions on what cocurricular (or extra-curricular) activities should be pursued, which activities should be supported, sponsored, or denied by the school often call for close cooperation between educators and laymen. Should "drag-racing" go on after school, but under school supervision? Should there be a Students-for-U.N. club? How about clubs for surfers, Greek letter fraternities, "hipsters," pompom queens, and others?

When a bond issue is lost, what parts of the total program should be trimmed or completely eliminated? Are there adequate facilities in the community for a variety of leisure activities? Are there parks, theaters, museums, forums for debates, discussions or presentations, and the endless varieties of cultural activities possible in modern life? At present, most of these decisions are made by the power and social machinery in the respective communities. The school board, superintendent, and central office personnel also have a voice in these broad decisions, as do Parent-Teacher Associations (P.T.A.s). The voice of the classroom teacher, however, does not make itself heard. He tends to act in these matters as a private citizen, except for his work through P.T.A.s and his professional organizations.

The teacher's more acknowledged contribution takes place in the classroom, in his work with individual students: first, by helping them develop standards for the use of their leisure time; and secondly, by developing in them favorable attitudes and a long-range interest in the teacher's subject. Clearly, decisions in these areas are quite different, but they are significant.

SUMMARY

In this chapter we discussed the relationship between leisure and education. Ours is the first century in the evolution of human society wherein a substantial amount of free time is available to large groups of people. This is the "New Leisure" made possible by industrialization and destined to be extended by developments in automation. The free time thus created is not equally distributed throughout the population; it favors the semiskilled, the unskilled, and the low-level service and clerical workers. Some time in the future, the fruits of automation may offer more leisure to professional workers, although this is unlikely during the next two decades.

This differential distribution of leisure has brought forth cries of fear as well as of promise. On the one hand, concern is expressed over the dangers inherent in too much free time in the hands of the unprepared masses. On the other, optimism is voiced regarding the new heights in culture and in democratic living made possible through intelligent use of our new leisure. The relevance of education in this context is clear. Whether our increasing free time becomes a significant problem or will be used to achieve a new height in the quality of living will be influenced largely by the social uses of the potential of public education.

SELECTED BIBLIOGRAPHY

Anderson, Nels. *Work and Leisure.* London: Routledge and Kegan Paul, 1961.

Brightbill, Charles K. *Man and Leisure.* Englewood Cliffs, N.J.: Prentice-Hall, Inc., 1961.

De Grazia, Sebastian. *Of Time, Work, and Leisure.* New York: Twentieth Century Fund, 1962.

Dewhurst, James F., et al. *America's Needs and Resources: A New Survey.* New York: Twentieth Century Fund, 1955.

__________. *Europe's Needs and Resources: Trends and Prospects in Eighteen Countries.* New York: Twentieth Century Fund, 1961.

Evans, Luther H., and George E. Arnstein, eds. *Automation and the Challenge to Education.* Symposium sponsored by the NEA, January 1962.

Hill, Samuel E., and Frederick Harbison. *Manpower and Innovation in American Industry.* Princeton, N.J.: Princeton University Press, 1959.

Jewish Theological Seminary of America. *The New Leisure.* Report of the Conference on the New Leisure, March 14–15, 1956, New York: The Seminary, 1956.

Kaplan, Max. *Leisure in America: A Social Inquiry.* New York: Wiley, 1960.

Kleemeier, Robert W. *Aging and Leisure: A Research Perspective into the Meaningful Use of Time.* New York: Oxford University Press, 1961.

Larrabee, Eric, and Rolf Meyersohn, eds. *Mass Leisure.* Glencoe, Ill.: The Free Press, 1958.

Lerner, Daniel. *The Passing of Traditional Society.* Glencoe, Ill.: The Free Press, 1958.

Macmillan, Robert H. *Automation: Friend or Foe?* Cambridge: Cambridge University Press, 1956, p. 85.

Michael, Donald N. *Cybernation: The Silent Conquest.* Santa Barbara, Calif.: Center for the Study of Democratic Institutions, 1962.

Neumeyer, Martin H., and Esther S. Neumeyer. *Leisure and Recreation,* 3rd ed. New York: The Ronald Press Company, 1958.

Riesman, David. *Individualism Reconsidered.* Glencoe, Ill.: The Free Press, 1954.

__________. "Leisure and Work in Post-Industrial Society," in Warren W. Kallenbach and Harold M. Hodges, Jr., eds., *Education and Society.* Columbus, Ohio: Charles E. Merrill Books, Inc., 1963.

Smigel, Erwin O. *Work and Leisure: A Contemporary Social Problem.* New Haven: College and University Press, 1963.

Watson, Goodwin, ed. "No Room at the Bottom: Automation and the Reluctant Learner," *Project on the Educational Implications of Automation.* NEA, 1963.

Wiener, Norbert. "Some Moral and Technical Consequences of Automation," *Science,* 131 (May 6, 1960), 1356.

CHAPTER 8

EDUCATION AND RELIGION

Among the many and complex decisions that educators must face from time to time, perhaps the most troublesome relate directly or indirectly to the role of religion in the public schools. This statement should come as no surprise to anyone who understands the history of church-state relations in the United States of America. In some modern states the government gives open cooperation and even support to a particular church. In others there exists open and official hostility toward organized religion, and the official ideology is clearly atheistic. In our democracy, the situation is more complex. Consequently, it must be subjected to close scrutiny if we are to understand the problem of religion in our schools.

RELIGION IN OUR DEMOCRACY

Perhaps in no area of American life can we find cultural pluralism (discussed in Chapter 6) as rampant, yet as well organized, as in religion. Although popular discussion is generally focused upon the Protestant, Catholic, and Jewish religions, there are well over 250 different organized religious sects in our country. Very few of these groups function in isolation from others. The overwhelming majority is composed of members who freely interact with members of other sects in the countless routines of daily life, in business and industry, in the arts, in sports, in the military, and in education. Members of the various religious groups segregate themselves voluntarily into their separate facilities when they consider it relevant for their respective religious purposes.

This kind of mutual tolerance and respect clearly is an American achievement. In Europe during the sixteenth and seventeenth centuries, the state generally supported a single established church. Where disagreements existed, they had to do with the question of *which church* was to be preferred over the others and not whether *any religion* should be the official one. An individual's freedom of conscience was largely prohibited, so that many of the earliest settlers came to our shores to avoid religious intolerance and persecution. However, in their new homes in America, these same colonists transplanted the dominant European pattern of state-church relations. They were convinced, as the people of Europe were, that the welfare of society required that certain religious beliefs be established, supported, and enforced by the power of the state, so as to constitute an "established" church. Several of the colonies, among them Massachusetts, Connecticut, Maryland, Virginia, New Hampshire, and North and South Carolina, adopted the pattern of the single established church. This had two consequences:

1. The state gave positive support to religion by levying taxes and using public funds and public property for the benefit of the established church.
2. The state enforced by law the exclusive rights of the preferred church to conduct public worship and compelled all persons to attend these church services no matter what their own religious beliefs. Conversely, the state used its coercive power to deny equal rights of worship to the unorthodox and in some cases even denied civil rights of suffrage and office holding in the state to the religiously unorthodox. Not only were dissenters often denied political rights, but they also were subject to civil trial and punishment by the state for heresy, blasphemy, and idolatry, for holding private religious opinions or engaging in public worship contrary to law, and in some cases even for criticizing the established ministers.[1]

Along with the principle of the "single establishment," a second and equally authentic tradition was visible in America from the very beginning. This was the tradition of freedom of conscience, which eventually culminated in the doctrine of the separation of church and state. The best-known advocates of these competing views were John Cotton and Roger Williams. Cotton argued for the establishment:

> It is better that the commonwealth be fashioned to the setting forth of God's house, which is his church: than to accommodate the church frame to the civil state. Democracy, I do not conceive that ever God did ordayne as a fit government eyther for church or commonwealth. If the people be governors, who shall be governed? As for monarchy, and aristocracy, they are both of them clearly approoved, and directed in scripture,

[1] R. Freeman Butts and Lawrence A. Cremin, *A History of Education in American Culture* (New York: Holt, Rinehart and Winston, Inc., Copyright 1953), pp. 19–20. With permission.

> yet so as referreth the soveraigntie to himselfe, and setteth up Theocracy in both, as the best forme of government in the commonwealth, as well as in the church.[2]

Williams spoke out boldly for freedom of conscience:

> It is the will and command of God, that . . . a permission of the most Paganish, Jewish, Turkish or Antichristian consciences and worships, bee granted to all men in all Nations and Countries and they are only to bee fought against with that Sword which is only (in Soule matters) able to conquer, to wit, the Sword of God's Spirit, the Word of God.[3]

As the years went by, the voices in behalf of religious freedom gathered strength in all the colonies. By the time of the Revolution, the "single establishment" was weakened in every colony; and experiments were conducted with "multiple establishments." In effect this meant some state support, legal and financial, to all churches (with "all" often meaning all Christian Protestant churches or, at best, all Christian churches). Under the principle of "multiple establishment," one could choose the religion he wanted to support, but he still *had* to choose one.

Gradually, the struggle for religious freedom was extended to state after state and resulted in periodic revisions of state constitutions. Roger Williams's view seemed to have prevailed over that of John Cotton and was supported and extended by the framers of our federal Constitution and its amendments in denying the legality of the "established" church, be it single or multiple. The First Amendment provides that "Congress shall make no laws respecting an establishment of religion, or prohibiting the free exercise thereof. . . ." The individual states have similar constitutional provisions relating to religious freedom. Even if they did not, the Supreme Court long ago ruled that the First Amendment applies to state legislatures as well as to the Congress.

Written documents, however, do not interpret themselves. Their meanings must be probed, and their relevance to the changing social scene must be periodically established. In the American political system, the Supreme Court was given the task of deciding the appropriate meaning of this crucial amendment. The rulings of the Court reflect the position that the government of the United States of America is not Christian,

[2] Quoted in Vernon Louis Parrington, *Main Currents in American Thought* (New York: Harcourt, Brace, & World, Inc., 1927), p. 31.

[3] Quoted in Butts and Cremin, *A History of Education* (see note 1), p. 71.

Jewish, Moslem, or Mohammedan; it is not atheistic, agnostic, or Unitarian. The government is the agent of a highly pluralistic culture, which is committed to respecting the rights of all the people, whether they hold any religious beliefs, many beliefs, or none at all.

The principle that there must be a "wall of separation between church and state" is nowhere stated explicitly in the Federal Constitution or its amendments. The principle originated in a phrase used by Thomas Jefferson in a letter to a religious group and amounted to his own interpretation of the First Amendment. Later, in 1879, this phrase was written into the law of the land when the Supreme Court of the United States quoted it as expressing the scope and effect of the First Amendment.[4] Since then, it has stood the test of time and been the guiding principle in subsequent legal challenges.

How is religious instruction and practice in the schools related to the foregoing? It has been a generally accepted ruling of the Court that the public schools are agencies of the state, so that whatever prohibitions apply to state officials concerning freedom of religion apply also to the public schools. Thus, through the interpretation of the First Amendment of the Federal Constitution, it has been concluded that *sectarian* religious instruction must be excluded from the public school curriculum. In 1853, for instance, a Catholic child was punished by a Protestant teacher for refusing to read and memorize certain verses from the Protestant Bible. The state superintendent in turn disciplined the teacher and informed her as follows:

> The position was early, distinctly, and almost universally taken by our statesmen, legislators, and prominent friends of education—men of the warmest religious zeal and belonging to every sect—that religious education must be banished from the common schools and consigned to the family and church. . . . Accordingly, the instruction in our schools has been limited to that ordinarily included under the head of intellectual culture, and to the propagation of those principles of morality in which all sects, and good men belonging to no sect, can equally agree.[5]

However, there is still considerable disagreement about the place of religion in the schools. These disagreements abound, and we can look to the Supreme Court for many more years to keep handing down decisions, with lively dissenting opinions, before all the problems are resolved.

[4] *Reynolds* v. *United States,* 98 U.S., 145, 164 (1879).

[5] Quoted in V. T. Thayer, *The Attack upon the American Secular School* (Boston: Beacon, 1951), p. 16.

ATTITUDES TOWARD SEPARATION OF SCHOOL AND STATE

We still have in most of our communities sincere and well-meaning citizens who want all students to study religion along with other school subjects. Often, they insist that a particular religion—such as Christianity or, still more specifically, one particular brand of Christianity—be studied. Those who succumb to this temptation usually want the students indoctrinated with a particular point of view, rather than exposed to a critical intellectual examination. Nevertheless, such indoctrination is not likely to occur in a religiously mixed community. It may—and often does—occur in a religiously homogeneous community. For instance, in certain Protestant communities in this country, school-board members often are all members of the same church. They tend to hire Protestant school administrators and teachers. There are no planned, conscious efforts to exclude others; but informally, in the processes of selection and employment, no Catholics, Jews, or agnostics are hired. In such communities, teachers tend to teach in the Sunday school, cooperate closely with the local minister, and organize definitely religious Easter and Christmas programs. Under these circumstances, Bible reading and prayers commonly find their way into the school, and the occasional Catholic, Jewish, or atheist child participates quietly in order not to be embarrassed, or moves out of town. Historically, in America, this pattern has occurred more often in predominantly Protestant towns or villages; however, it can also occur where the population subscribes overwhelmingly to another religion. The famous McCollum case in Illinois arose from a predominantly Catholic community.

PROTESTANT POSITIONS

Concerning the role of religion in the public schools, we find among Protestant theologians, even on the faculty of the same theological seminary, profound cleavages of thought. Henry P. Van Dusen, president of the famous Union Theological Seminary in New York, urges the three major faiths in America "to join forces in a united philosophy of religiously oriented learning," and asserts "that teaching which does not recognize God as the ultimate ground of truth is false teaching."[6] On the same faculty with Van Dusen, the very influential Reinhold Niebuhr disagrees. Niebuhr,

[6] Henry P. Van Dusen, *God in Education* (New York: Scribner's, 1951), p. 70.

along with his brother, Richard, subscribes to religious pluralism, and claims no role for religion in the public schools.

Although the Protestant clergy is divided on the question of religion in the schools, it is safe to assert that most of them support the secular public schools, although some would welcome into the schools a certain amount of instruction teaching about religion and its place in America. The following clear statement by the Presbyterian Church is indicative of the Protestant position:

> The Presbyterian Church in the United States of America for many years has expressed consistently its faith in the public schools of America. This persistent reaffirmation is congenial with the basic principles of its Protestant heritage. The Church's zeal for public education grows out of its concern for persons and out of its conviction that the basic values of a free people can best be maintained through a continuing allegiance to a free public school system.[7]

CATHOLIC POSITIONS

Significant disagreements on the role of religion in the schools are also found among Catholic scholars, theologians, and laymen. The dominant voice within the Catholic Church disapproves of the principle of separation of church and state. This voice is well represented by Dean Crowley of Fordham University. He points up the early encyclicals of Pope Pius IX and Pope Leo XIII, whose instructions were repeated in 1929 by Pope Pius XI in his *Encyclical on Education:*

> The school, if not a temple, is a den. A school from which religion is excluded is contrary to the fundamental principles of education. Such a school in time is bound to become irreligious. The only school that is fit for the Catholic students is a school controlled by the Church, in which religion is the foundation and crown of the youths' entire training, not only in the elementary grades, but in the high school and college as well.
>
> Numerous pastoral letters of the American hierarchy have dealt with the subject of education, and the decrees of the Third Plenary Council of Baltimore (1884) proclaim in forceful language that the parent must send his child to the Catholic school. . . . Thus the Catholic Church has been obliged, for the sake of principle, to establish a separate system of schools.[8]

[7] *Minutes of the General Assembly of the Presbyterian Church in the United States of America,* Fifth Series, Vol. 6, 1957, p. 94.

[8] Quoted in Henry Ehlers and Gordon Lee, *Crucial Issues in Education,* 2nd ed. (New York: Holt, Rinehart and Winston, Inc., 1959), pp. 145–146. With permission.

Consistent with the words of the encyclicals, the growth in enrollment of Catholic parochial schools in America has been impressive. Exact and up-to-date figures are difficult to obtain, but reliable estimates can be had from the Census data and from the publications of the various dioceses.

> In dozens of towns and suburban communities, the parochial school now enrolls 40, 50, and even, in some cases, 60 per cent of the school population. One-half the children of Green Bay, Wisconsin, and 52 per cent of the Manchester, New Hampshire, children are in Catholic schools. The Catholic school systems in many of the largest cities of the United States enroll one quarter or more of the total school population. Here are a few of the percentages: Chicago, 34; Philadelphia, 39; Detroit, 23. The figure for Hartford is 24 per cent; for Cincinnati, 28; for Boston, 30; for Milwaukee and New Orleans, 33; for Buffalo, 40; for Pittsburgh, 42.
>
> At the beginning of the century, there were 854,523 students enrolled in Catholic primary and secondary schools in the United States. This represented 5.2 per cent of the entire elementary and secondary school population of the nation. Today, the number has grown to over five million, or about 14 per cent of the total enrollment. The trend shows no sign of abating. It seems to be limited only by available resources. Very many, perhaps most, of the other five million Catholic school children that are now in public schools would not be there if there were enough desks and schools to accommodate these children within the Catholic system.[9]

One may question McCluskey's conclusion, for many prominent Catholics firmly believe in the separation of church and state—in both education and other matters. Among their ranks we find the well-known scholar and philosopher Lord Acton, the late President John F. Kennedy, the author-educator Jacques Maritain, and theologians John Courtney Murray and Victor White. Father White, a British Dominican priest, takes a strong stand against the "sacral state," an arrangement wherein all social institutions are subordinate to the church. White claims that such an arrangement violates true Catholic faith:

> . . . the sacral state has its attractions, and the medieval ideal of synthesis of church and state is so impressive that we have been slow to see that it was an anomaly rather than a norm. But its departure should be a matter of rejoicing. . . . A pluralistic society is one in which a Christian must be a Christian indeed; in which even the theologian can

[9] Neil G. McCluskey, S. J. "Public Funds for Parochial Schools? Yes!" *Teachers College Record* (New York: Bureau of Publications, Teachers College, Columbia University), 62, No. 1 (October 1960), 2. With permission.

> breathe more freely. . . . For toleration brings intercommunication; wider and deeper knowledge of the variety of the needs of the human soul, and of the mysterious and manifold ways of God with man.[10]

It is quite clear that the Catholic position cannot be stated in a monolithic, homogeneous voice. Intellectual leaders in the Catholic community find that there is room for honest differences of opinion and commitment on the church-state question. Probably, most of the clergy follow the view of the encyclicals and denounce separation. At the same time, no reliable conclusions can be offered concerning the position of Catholic laymen in America. There is strong evidence for the support of the parochial schools, but there is also impressive evidence for the support of the public schools. Before one hazards a prediction concerning the future direction of the Catholic position, he should consider the following statement:

> It may be that under certain circumstances, such as the exceptional good will of the political powers, the Church deems it preferable to acquiesce to a factual separation of Church and State, but in no case will she ever admit that Church and State should be kept separate. Their separation remains an evil even while, for reasons of expediency, it is being tolerated. The same remark applies to the school problem.[11]

JEWISH POSITIONS

The dominant view in the Jewish community of America clearly supports the public schools and respects the wall of separation between church and state. A minority is in favor of a separate parochial-school system, which includes instruction in the sacred books of the Jewish faith. However, even the proponents of Jewish parochial schools are firm and clear in their support of the doctrine of separation. A professional educator from the Jewish Theological Seminary of America sums up this position as follows:

> It is, however, true that the vast masses of the Jewish people in this country are loyal both in principle and in practice to the public school. Throughout its long history the synagogue never viewed itself as having exclusive, or even primary, authority over the child's education. That authority always rested among Jews with the parents. Nor did the Jewish

[10] Quoted in Ehlers and Lee (see note 8), pp. 148–149. With permission.

[11] Etienne Gilson, ed., *The Church Speaks to the Modern World: The Social Teachings of Leo XIII* (Garden City, N.Y.: Doubleday, Image D7), p. 17. Copyright 1954 by Doubleday & Company, Inc. Reprinted by permission of the publisher.

religious school ever view it as its peculiar province to instruct a child in *all* the knowledge that he needs for his human welfare. Vocational training or secular knowledge was never under exclusively religious sponsorship among Jews. The American Jewish religious day school which teaches French, Latin, geometry, and the sciences, along with Talmud, Bible, and the prayerbook, is by and large a distinctly American product. Such schools existed among Jews in Eastern Europe before the First World War only in very limited number and because of the very special political and social conditions under which these Jews lived at that time. The schools did not grow out of any theological or religious convictions on the relationship that should exist between the synagogue and the school.[12]

The same sentiments are stated by Rabbi Arthur Gilbert:

Religious education and training are the exclusive responsibility of the home, church and synagogue . . .

It is not the function of the public school to resolve the controversy among moral philosophers over the relative merits of sanctions . . .

The teacher may not use his position in the school to become a missionary for his own religious beliefs. . . .[13]

By and large, Jews in America want the home and the various "Sunday School" arrangements to provide religious education for the youth of the country. While Jewish parochial schools are found in some communities, the overwhelming majority of Jews attend and support our secular public schools.

THE "OFFICIAL" POSITION

From the foregoing it should be clear that there is evidence of some disagreement within each of the major faiths in our country concerning the appropriate relationship between religion and education. The dominant position among the Protestant and Jewish clergies supports the principle of separation, while the dominant voice among the Catholic clergy opposes it. The current "official" position of the country prescribes the separation of church and state and thereby prohibits religious instruction in the public schools which are an arm of the state. Whether or not the

[12] Simon Greenberg, "A Jewish Educator's View," in F. Ernest Johnson, ed., *American Education and Religion* (New York: Harper & Brothers, 1952), pp. 48–49. With permission.

[13] Rabbi Arthur Gilbert, "Should There Be Religion in the Schools?" *National Jewish Monthly,* published by B'nai B'rith, December 1956 and January 1957. With permission.

application of separation to the public schools will continue in the future is an intriguing topic for speculation. The answer will be given only by social and philosophic developments as they will be reflected in the legal changes of the decades ahead.

LEGAL TESTS OF "SEPARATION" IN THE SCHOOLS

What does the legal doctrine of separation mean for the public schools, and how does it relate to private schools?

THE WALL OF SEPARATION AND THE PUBLIC SCHOOLS

The body of American constitutional law contains three groups of cases that explored the principle of separation in the public schools. The first group of decisions is represented by the "health and vaccination cases"; the second, by the "flag-salute cases"; and the third, by the "Bible-reading cases."

Regarding "health and vaccinations," religious groups have protested that their beliefs are violated by certain medical requirements of the schools. However, the Court permits the state to require that students be vaccinated against smallpox as a condition of school attendance. Compulsory chest X rays, anti-polio vaccinations, and physical examinations as admission prerequisites have also been upheld to protect the health and welfare of the community.

The "flag-salute cases" were more controversial. Members of certain religious sects, such as the Jehovah's Witnesses, believe that saluting a flag constitutes a violation of their religious convictions. In the first case that went up to the Supreme Court on this issue, the Gobitis case,[14] the Court did not recognize this religious belief as worthy of protection in our schools. When the same issue reached the Court a second time, in the Barnette case,[15] however, the Gobitis decision was reversed. This reversal, in effect, protects a public school student's right not to salute the flag, if such would violate his religious beliefs. In writing the majority opinion of the Court on this case, Justice Jackson gave his memorable interpretation of the First Amendment:

[14] *Minerville School District* v. *Gobitis,* 310 U.S., 586, 60 S. Ct. 1011 (1940).

[15] *West Virginia State Board of Education* v. *Barnette,* 310 U.S. 624, 63 S. Ct. 1178 (1943).

> If there is any fixed star in our constitutional constellation, it is that no official, high or petty, can prescribe what shall be orthodox in politics, nationalism, religion, or other matters of opinion or force citizens to confess by word or act their faith therein. If there are any circumstances which permit an exception, they do not now occur to us.

The "Bible-reading cases" are more complex than either of the foregoing. The law is anything but settled in this area; moreover, the designation of these cases is misleading. They include not only readings from the Bible but also prayers in schools, the singing of hymns, observance of religious holidays, and a host of other practices. Before the legal limitations of the First Amendment can be made as clear and definite as schoolmen would like them to be, the Supreme Court will have to render a legal definition of "religion" and will have to specify whether the Amendment excludes *all* religion and religious practices from the public schools or only *sectarian* practices.

The practice of daily reading from the Bible has a long and troublesome history in American public education. Horace Mann, an outstanding figure in the development of the secular public schools, considered Bible reading to be an essential part of the school program. A recent survey by R. H. Dierenfeld, reported by the Public Affairs Press, showed that thirteen states of the Union required Bible reading by law, twelve permitted it as a result of judicial decisions, and another thirteen condoned it "under the general terms of the law or by reason of silence." Only eleven states prohibited Bible reading. Of the total number of American school districts, a majority actually practices Bible reading in the public schools.[16]

Through the years the Courts have rendered what appeared to be conflicting decisions on Bible-reading cases. These judgments often were not really in conflict, but merely appeared so to the laymen who understand neither the many technicalities judges must consider nor the distinctions that are significant in law but not in lay "common sense." On June 25, 1962, the Supreme Court handed down a decision that caused a storm throughout the nation.[17] In a 6 to 1 vote, the Court ruled unconstitutional a nondenominational prayer composed by the New York Board of Regents and recited in New York's public schools at the start of each school day. The short prayer read as follows: "Almighty God, we acknowledge our depend-

[16] Reported in the *New York Times Western Edition,* June 18, 1963, p. 7.
[17] *Engel* v. *Vitale,* 370 U.S. 421, 82 S. Ct. 1261 (1962).

ence upon Thee, and we beg Thy blessings upon us, our parents, our teachers, and our country."

In fact, students were not compelled to recite the prayer; they could remain silent or be excused from the room. Nevertheless, the majority opinion, written by Justice Black, held that the official support of the prayer reading by the school authorities tended to be coercive. The prayer was "wholly inconsistent with the establishment clause" of the First Amendment. This situation was also unique in that it was the New York Board of Regents, an official body and thus an arm of the state government, that had *composed* the prayer. Would the Court have ruled otherwise, if the prayer had not constituted officially composed material? To illustrate the conflict and confusion concerning the legality of Bible reading and prayers in public schools, we need cite but two cases.

In the Schempp case, a Pennsylvania statute requiring Bible reading followed by a mass recitation of the Lord's Prayer was declared unconstitutional by a U.S. District Court in 1959.[18] A similar practice, but without the prayer recitation, was declared acceptable in Florida two years later in the Chamberlain case.[19] The Florida case is significant, because it dealt with a whole range of practices which the plaintiff considered to be objectionable introduction of religion into the public schools. The decision has been appealed to the Florida Supreme Court and will probably find its way to the highest court of the land.

This is precisely what happened in the Schempp case. The school district appealed the adverse decision of the District Court to the United States Supreme Court. The highest tribunal of the land rendered its historic decision on July 17, 1963.[20] In an 8:1 decision, it upheld the lower court and ruled unconstitutional Bible reading and the recitation of the Lord's Prayer as part of the regular program of exercises in the public schools. Justice Clark, delivering the opinion of the Court, emphasized the importance of religion in the history and traditions of the United States but underscored the neutrality of the government in matters of religion.

[18] *Schempp* v. *School District of Abington Township, Pennsylvania,* 177 F. Supp. 398, U.S. District Court E.D. Pa. (Sept. 16, 1959); as amended September 22, 1959.

[19] *Chamberlain* v. *Dade County Board of Instruction,* The Circuit Court of the Eleventh Judicial Circuit in and for Dade County, Florida—in Chancery—59C 1928 (1961).

[20] *School District of Abington Township, Pennsylvania, et al.* v. *Schempp et al.* 374 U.S. 203, 83 S. Ct. 1560 (1963). The same citation applies to the Murray case. The Schempp case—together with its companion, the Murray case—is presented in *The New York Times Western Edition,* Tuesday, June 18, 1963, pp. 6–7.

"In the relationship between man and religion, the state is firmly committed to a position of neutrality." The Court thus reaffirmed the principle of church-state separation. Observers, as well as newspapers, were quick to point up the fact that the majority opinion contained the voices of Justice Clark, a Protestant; Justice Brennan, a Roman Catholic; and Justice Goldberg, a Jewish member of the Court.

The Court clearly expressed its respect for religion and for various religious beliefs. In a direct statement that should be of interest to educators in the process of curriculum construction, the Court said: "In addition, it might well be said that one's education is not complete without a study of comparative religion or the history of religion and its relationship to the advancement of civilization. It certainly may be said that the Bible is worthy of study for its literary and historic qualities."

In its opinion the Court also made it clear that opposition or hostility toward religion would also be a violation of the First Amendment. ". . . the state may not establish a 'religion of secularism' in the sense of affirmatively opposing or showing hostility to religion, thus 'preferring those who believe in no religion over those who do believe.' "

The language of the Court is sufficiently clear at present to guide schoolmen. Bible reading as a ritual, or routine exercise, is to be discontinued, and so is the recitation of prayers. This ruling holds, even though any or all students may withdraw from the exercise. Nevertheless, the further meaning of "neutrality" awaits judicial interpretation. We may raise certain questions which are as yet unanswered by the Court, and for which the principle of "neutrality" offers no clear guidance. May there be prayers said at public school ceremonies or assemblies? May school publications carry religious symbols? Do Christmas and Hanukkah programs violate the "neutrality" principle? May kindergarten and primary grade teachers teach "little prayers" to children, to be said before their daily nourishment? There are other, similar questions, which will find their way to the Court in the years ahead.

THE WALL OF SEPARATION AND THE PAROCHIAL SCHOOLS

In the American culture, education is the responsibility of each state. This has been the accepted interpretation of the Tenth Amendment to the Constitution, which reserves to the several states and to the people those powers not delegated to the federal government nor denied by it to the states. There is much variation among our fifty states in the provisions made for the education of the populace. But one provision they do have in common, among others, is that every state must provide a system of publicly financed schools for its residents.[21] Must parents then send their children to these schools? In 1925 the Supreme Court unanimously answered "no."

In the famous Oregon case,[22] the Court invalidated the Oregon Compulsory Attendance Act, which required children to attend public school through the eighth grade. Parents have a right to send their children to competent private schools, if they so choose. In the words of the Court:

> The familiar statement that education is a public function means no more than that it is a function that the State may undertake, because it vitally interests and concerns the State that children shall be furnished the means of education and not left to grow up in ignorance. The fundamental theory of liberty under which all governments in this Union repose excludes any general power of the State to standardize its children by forcing them to accept instruction from public teachers only. The child is not the mere creature of the State; those who nurture him and direct his destiny have the right, coupled with the high duty, to recognize and prepare him for additional obligations.

Private schools, parochial and secular, existed in the United States long before establishment of public school systems. Their existence is protected by law, although it is clear that the state has the right under its police power to inspect and regulate *all* schools, private and public, secular and parochial. Just as it was necessary to maintain the wall of separation in the public schools, so history has shown that the First Amendment is relevant to private parochial schools as well.

The situations relevant to this problem fall into three categories. The first group may be labeled the "released-time" controversies; the second, "auxiliary services"; a third, the "general-support" issue.

"RELEASED TIME." This problem area relates to both the public schools and parochial education. "Released time" refers to the arrangement whereby children are given religious instruction on school time by special teachers of the denomination of the parents' choice. For several decades, children have been excused from part of the public school program to re-

[21] This provision itself has been challenged in Prince Edwards County, Virginia, where, as a consequence of social conflict over legal orders to integrate the schools, all public schools were closed for several years.

[22] *Pierce* v. *Society of the Sisters of the Holy Name of Jesus and Mary,* 268 U.S. 510, 45 S. Ct. 571 (1925).

ceive religious instruction. Nonparticipants were given work during such periods, and the schools provided some minor administrative assistance to make the program possible. Two famous cases guide us in decisions concerning "released-time" programs.

The McCollum case[23] held that it is unconstitutional to conduct such a program on public school property. Such a program, according to the court, constituted a "utilization of the tax-established and tax-supported public school system to aid religious groups to spread their faith." The McCollum case was followed shortly by the Zorach decision,[24] which, in a 6:3 vote, upheld the legality of released-time programs where the religious instruction occurred off the school grounds.

It is interesting to look at two excerpts from the majority opinion written by Justice Douglas in the Zorach case:

> This "released-time" program involves neither religious instruction in public school classrooms nor the expenditure of public funds. All costs, including the application blanks, are paid by the religious organizations. The case is therefore unlike McCollum v. Board of Education . . . which involved a "released-time" program from Illinois. In that case the classrooms were turned over to religious instructors. We accordingly held that the program violated the First Amendment which . . . prohibits the states from establishing religion or prohibiting its free exercise.

He further states that:

> Government may not finance religious groups nor undertake religious instruction, nor blend secular and sectarian education nor use secular institutions to force one or some religion on any person. But we find no constitutional requirement which makes it necessary for government to be hostile to religion and to throw its weight against efforts to widen the effective scope of religious influence. The government must be neutral when it comes to competition between sects. It may not thrust any sect on any person. It may not make a religious observance compulsory. It may not coerce anyone to attend church, to observe a religious holiday, or to take religious instruction. But it can close its doors to suspend its operations as to those who want to repair to their religious sanctuary for worship or instruction. No more than that is undertaken here. . . .

In view of the serious split in the Court's opinion, the dissenting words of Justice Black warrant attention:

[23] *People of the State of Illinois ex rel. McCollum* v. *Board of Education of School District Number 71,* 333 U.S. 203, 608 S. Ct. 461 (1948).

[24] *Zorach* v. *Clauson,* 343 U.S. 306 (1952).

> . . . the sole question is whether New York can use its compulsory education laws to help religious sects get attendants presumably too unenthusiastic to go unless moved to do so by the pressure of this state machinery. That this is the plan, purpose, design and consequence of the New York program cannot be denied. The state thus makes religious sects beneficiaries of its power to compel children to attend secular schools . . . eight Justices of this Court invalidated the released-time system in McCollum on the premise that a state can no more "aid all religions" than it can aid one. . . . It is this neutrality the Court abandons today when it treats New York's coercive system as a program which *merely* encourages religious instruction or cooperates with religious authorities. . . .
>
> State help to religion injects political and party prejudices into a holy field. It too often substitutes force for prayer, hate for love, and persecution for persuasion. Government should not be allowed, under cover of the soft euphemism of "cooperation," to steal into the sacred area of religious choice.

The results of these two decisions would indicate that as long as participation in released-time religious instruction is voluntary, as long as it is not held on school grounds, and as long as no administrative assistance is rendered by the school, it does not violate the First Amendment. However, in spite of the clear implications of the McCollum and Zorach decisions, many public school classrooms are still being used during school hours for released-time religious instruction.[25] The consequences flowing from the released-time religious instruction programs have been so numerous and unanticipated, that the results have been judged far less than satisfactory. By and large, they have satisfied neither the supporters of the experiments nor those who have opposed them. The complications have been so numerous for teachers, administrators, school boards, parents, and children alike, that the programs have often been discontinued.

We call attention to one of these complications because of its frequency of occurrence. It is a very rare classroom where all students participate in the program of released-time religious education. In most cases, less than half of the students do. The teacher faces a most difficult decision when some of his students leave while the others remain in the classroom. Should he continue with significant learning experiences for those remaining? If he does, the "released" students will suffer, and their parents will complain. Should he mark time and perform merely a custodial service for

[25] See a comment by Erwin L. Sharer in *Religious Education* (January-February 1953), p. 42.

those who stay? This, too, is objectionable for obvious reasons. In addition to that of wasting time, the charge has also been raised that religious control enters the secular school, because the absence of some students for purposes of religious instruction also influences the educational content offered to the remaining students. Many teachers, some sympathetic to religious instruction and others not, have found themselves tempted to alter their teaching in order to respectively help or hinder attendance in the "released-time" programs. These, as well as other, difficulties have lead to some attempts to change released-time into *dismissed-time* programs by shortening the school day. The popularity with which this variation will be received is questionable, in light of the mounting pressures on the schools to transmit more and more of man's rapidly accumulating store of knowledge.

The latest development is the *shared-time* program. One example of this is found in the Detroit area. Approximately 200 seventh and eighth graders of the St. Norbert parish school attend the Cherry Hill Junior-Senior High School (public) half of each day for science, mathematics, art, music, shop, and homemaking courses. They study language arts and religion at their parochial school. In this way the parochial school can function without the added economic strain of having to provide more classrooms and more teachers to handle the entire program.

The legality of this arrangement has not yet been tested, but its educational value has been questioned by various writers, among them a devout Catholic author, Mary Perkins Ryan.[26] In her volume, which is in deep sympathy with the goals of her church, she seriously questions and doubts the soundness of parochial schools in the American culture.

AUXILIARY SERVICES. Under this heading we find cases involving a variety of state laws providing textbooks, transportation, medical services, and other so-called "auxiliary services" for children attending private parochial schools. Again, there are two landmark cases relevant for our consideration. The first one, the Cochran case,[27] gave birth to the child-benefit theory. The case tested the constitutionality of a Louisiana statute which provided free textbooks to *all* school children within the state. The Supreme Court upheld the statute as not a violation of the Constitution, because

[26] *Are Parochial Schools the Answer?* (New York: Holt, Rinehart and Winston, 1963), p. 160.

[27] *Cochran et al.* v. *Louisiana State Board of Education et al.,* 281 U.S. 370, 50 S. Ct. 334 (1930).

the individual children, not the religious institution they attend, benefit from the public support. Thus the child-benefit theory was born. This rationale formed the basis of the other famous decision relating to auxiliary services, the Everson case.[28]

In the Everson case, the Court, in a 5:4 decision, upheld the constitutionality of a New Jersey statute authorizing payment by local school districts of transportation costs of children attending *all* nonprofit schools. The law specifically designated parents of children in Catholic parochial schools as qualifying for reimbursement.

All of the justices on the Court agreed that the Constitution rules out any financial aid to religion. However, the Court split almost down the middle in deciding whether the aid offered parents by the New Jersey statute was "aid to religion." While reiterating the principle that the state must be neutral in its relations with groups of religious believers and nonbelievers, Justice Black relied on the child-benefit theory to conclude that no money was contributed to the schools by the state.

The dissent was vigorous in its assertions that the majority opinion negated the principle of separation of church and state. Justice Rutledge, in his dissenting opinion, specifically rejected the child-benefit theory. He claimed that full support of religious schools, or of all schools, could be justified by it.

Justice Jackson was equally strong in his dissent as he said:

> I should be surprised if any Catholic would deny that the parochial school is a vital, if not the most vital, part of the Roman Catholic Church. . . . Catholic education is the rock on which the whole structure rests, and to render tax aid to its Church school is indistinguishable to me from rendering the same aid to the Church itself.

It is the opinion of the authors that the law is highly unsettled on the question of auxiliary services and benefits to children. In the years to come we will hear more on this aspect of the wall of separation. As a matter of fact, the very close (5 to 4) decision in the Everson case is a reliable indication that the Supreme Court will be called upon to draw a more precise, clear guideline for our states to follow. We shall see, indeed, that the most recent developments on the question of federal aid to education are closely related to the foregoing cases, and particularly to the "child benefit" theory.

[28] *Everson* v. *Board of Education of the Township of Ewing, et al.,* 330 U.S. 1, 67 S. Ct. 504 (1947).

GENERAL SUPPORT. Under the heading of "general support" there are as yet no court cases, only voluminous debates and arguments. This is due to the fact that until 1965 no laws, federal or state, provided for general, across-the-board support for church-related schools. President Johnson signed a general-support bill into law in April 1965. The law, while not specifically designed to aid parochial schools, makes such aid technically possible. Serious students of constitutional law await the legal challenges which will most likely follow. Legal attacks, of course, cannot be made until funds or other aids are actually rendered to parochial schools. The conclusion has been widely acceptd that such aid would be a clear violation of the First and Fourteenth Amendments to the Constitution. President Kennedy, who himself was a practicing Catholic, supported this conclusion, as evidenced by his 1961 message to Congress on education. In recommending federal assistance for classroom construction and teachers' salaries for public schools, the President said:

> In accordance with the clear prohibition of the Constitution, no elementary or secondary school funds are allocated for constructing church schools or paying church school teachers' salaries; and thus non-public school children are rightfully not counted in determining the funds each state will receive for its public schools.[29]

The largest organized group in America taking exception to this interpretation of the Constitution is found among those of Catholic faith. Most Catholics consider it their religious duty to support parochial schools and to send their children there. We noted several outstanding dissenters to this view, but the articulate dissent is a small minority. The Roman Catholic parent bears a double financial burden—the taxes for the support of public schools (a burden imposed by law) and the cost of supporting the parochial school (a burden imposed by his religion and his conscience).

It is vigorously argued that the parents' right to choose the appropriate education for their children is vitiated by the requirement of double payment. Cardinal McIntyre, of Los Angeles, claims this to be a "discrimination that is unjust,"[30] Blum calls it an effective denial of academic freedom,[31] and Father McCluskey asserts that it is a denial of re-

[29] *Congressional Record,* 87th Congress, First Session, 107, No. 29 (February 20, 1961), 2285.

[30] Richard Frohnen, "McIntyre Home, Battles Kennedy's School Plan," *Los Angeles Times,* Part I, p. 24, March 24, 1961.

[31] Virgil C. Blum, S. J. "Academic Freedom and Tax Support for Independent Education," *Phi Delta Kappan,* 40, No. 9 (June 1959).

ligious freedom and, "My second reason for suggesting appropriate public recognition and support for church-related schools is that only in this way can the nation's youthful talent be fully realized."[32]

Opposition to general support for parochial schools is based on two premises. The first one, the Constitutional prohibition, has been already mentioned and discussed. The meaning and extent of this limitation is a matter for the courts to decide. The Constitution can, of course, be amended, and there are forces at work today attempting to remove or alter its provisions for separation of church and state. If enough citizens become convinced of the undesirability of the wall separating church and state, the Constitution may be appropriately amended. One can only speculate about the future possibility of such action and of the consequences that would follow.

The second premise upon which opposition to public support of religious schools is based is simply stated by R. Freeman Butts:

> I believe that a genuinely free public education is the very foundation and chief regenerative agency of a free society. It is not simply another welfare benefit for individuals like unemployment insurance, old age pensions, or poor relief. I believe, therefore, that we should not change radically the present balance between private and public education. Private schools should be encouraged, and parents who so desire should be free to send their children to them; but not with public subsidy for religious purposes. We should go no further in public support of private or parochial schools.[33]

It has been generally accepted in American history that the quality of our democracy is directly related to the availability of high-quality, publicly supported education for all youth. Effective participation in political activity, economic activity, the arts, and so forth all presuppose sound education. This is why Gardner Murphy spoke of education as the "servant of all our purposes." Father McCluskey recognizes this key role of education, but not of *public* education, when he says:

> The expansion of any rival independent system is, in some measure, made at the expense of the public schools. It can be granted that this situation somewhat affects the good of the present structure of public education. The well-being of American society, however, is neither identical

[32] Neil McCluskey, S. J. "Public Funds for Parochial Schools? Yes!" (see note 9), p. 5. With permission.

[33] R. Freeman Butts. "Public Funds for Parochial Schools? No!" *Teachers College Record,* 62, No. 1 (October 1960), 62. With permission.

> nor coextensive with the good of the public schools. The common good of American society has been nobly served by the public schools, yes; but it would be a case of wagging the puppy by the tail to insist that society conform forever to a rigid pattern of public education. We must not forget that service to society is the function of all public institutions, including every type of school."[34]

McCluskey's reasoning—along with that of Father Blum, Cardinals Spellman, McIntyre, and others—is based upon the child-benefit theory which first appeared in the Everson case. Opponents agree with Justice Rutledge in his dissent that the logic of this theory could enable full public support for all schools, religious and otherwise. It is further argued that if tax monies were turned over to each parent to use in the school of his choice, there would be a proliferation of parochial schools as well as of private schools along racial, ethnic, and social class lines. (This arrangement would be similar, in effect, to the historic "multiple establishment.") This would weaken, or even destroy, the public schools of America and thus the very fabric of our society, which relies heavily upon the common experiences our public schools provide for the children of our highly pluralistic population.

This point of view was expressed by President Woodrow Wilson:

> You know that the great melting-pot of America, the place where we are all made Americans of, is the public school, where men of every race and of every origin and of every station in life, send their children *or ought to send their children,* and where, being mixed together, the youngsters are all infused with the American spirit and developed into American men and American women.[35]

Justice Frankfurter also strongly underscored this view in the McCollum decision:

> Separation means separation, not something less. Jeffersons's metaphor in describing the relation between Church and State speaks of a "wall of separation," not of a fine line easily overstepped. The public school is at once the symbol of our democracy and the most pervasive means for promoting our common destiny. In no activity of the state is it more vital to keep out divisive forces than in its schools, to avoid confusing, not to say fusing, what the Constitution sought to keep strictly

[34] Neil McCluskey, S. J. "Public Funds for Parochial Schools? Yes!" (see note 9), p. 7. With permission.

[35] Woodrow Wilson, *The New Freedom* (London: Chapman Hall, Ltd., 1913), p. 95.

apart. "The great American principle of eternal separation"—Elihu Root's phrase bears repetition—is one of the vital reliances of our Constitutional system for assuring unities among our people stronger than our diversities. . . .

Additional support for this view came from Maurice Thomas, in his 1953 Horace Mann lecture:

> America has fought the battle of segregation in terms of education only for the rich and well-born through the establishment of free public schools. We are continuing also the fight against segregation on the basis of color. We do not allow segregation as to ethnic groups in our schools. I look with strong disfavor upon segregating children in terms of religion.
>
> The American people must face up to this problem and they will have to find a more satisfactory solution. That solution must be a return to the support of and faith in our free public school system. It is difficult, indeed—if not impossible—to secure adequate financial support for our public schools in certain sections of the United States. Many people who do not have children in school, and groups who send their children elsewhere, are not willing to be taxed for the support of an institution which they do not use. It thus becomes apparent that this discussion is vital if we are going to support our American school system. The system cannot continue if it is not well supported, and I believe that any forces, groups, or organizations that make it difficult, if not impossible, to provide an adequate base for an expanding, improving school system in America are doing a disservice to democracy.[36]

Many other individuals and groups have gone on record vigorously opposing any further expansion of public aid to religious schools. Among them we find R. Freeman Butts; V. T. Thayer; James B. Conant; and Presbyterian, Jewish, Unitarian, and many other religious groups with the clear exception of the Roman Catholic church.

The dilemma is a serious one. In his dissenting opinion in the Everson case, Justice Rutledge described the problem of the parents succinctly:

> No one conscious of religious values can be unsympathetic toward the burden which our constitutional separation puts on parents who desire religious instruction mixed with secular for their children. . . . Of course discrimination in the legal sense does not exist. The child attending the religious school has the same right as any other to attend the public school. But he foregoes exercising it because the same guaranty which assures this

[36] As quoted by Thomas in "Voluntary Religious Isolation—Another School Segregation Story," *Phi Delta Kappan,* 40, No. 9 (June 1959), 358. With permission.

> freedom forbids the public school or any agency of the state to give or aid him in securing the religious instruction he seeks.[37]

No one can predict the future course of developments in America on the church-state issue. To paraphrase Max Lerner, the future represents possibilities. We will make our own future. In the meantime, however, it is still important to ask about the place of values in the public school curriculum. If church and state must be separated by a wall "high and impregnable," is there no place for religion, morality, and values in the secular schools?

RELIGION AND MORALITY IN THE SECULAR SCHOOLS

Justice Clark stated in the Schempp case that one's education is not complete without an intellectual analysis of the place of religion in society. Writers in the field agree, regardless of their own religious commitments, that students ought to study *about* religion, as an academic subject, in the same way that they study about other significant developments in the history of civilizations. These statements carefully distinguish between teaching "religion" and teaching "about" religion.

The following propositions, issued by the Commission on Religion and Education, represent the sentiments that urge teaching "about" religion without ignoring the issue of morality:

> 1. The problem is to find a way in public education to give due recognition to the place of religion in the culture and in the convictions of our people while at the same time safeguarding the separation of church and state.
>
> 2. The separation of American public education from church control was not intended to exclude all study of religion from the school program.
>
> 3. Teaching a common core of religious beliefs in the public schools is not a satisfactory solution.
>
> 4. Teaching "moral and spiritual values" cannot be regarded as an adequate substitute for an appropriate consideration of religion in the school program.
>
> 5. Teaching which opposes or denies religion is as much a violation of religious liberty as teaching which advocates or supports any particular religious belief.

[37] Mr. Justice Rutledge, Dissenting, *Everson* v. *Board of Education* (see note 28).

6. Introducing factual study of religion will not commit the public schools to any particular religious belief.

7. The role of the school in the study of religion is distinct from, though complementary to, the role of the church.

8. The public school should stimulate the young toward a vigorous, personal reaction to the challenge of religion.

9. The public school should assist youth to have an intelligent understanding of the historical and contemporary role of religion in human affairs . . .[38]

The Educational Policies Commission of the National Education Association supported the same position in a 1951 publication entitled *Moral and Spiritual Values in the Public Schools:*[39]

> The public schools can teach objectively *about* religion without advocating or teaching any religious creed. To omit from the classroom all references to religion and the institutions of religion is to neglect an important part of American life. Knowledge about religion is essential for a full understanding of our culture, literature, art, history, and current affairs. That religious beliefs are controversial is not an adequate reason for excluding teaching about religion from the public schools.

These recommendations present genuine difficulties, not the least of which is the possibility that poorly trained, overzealous, or unsympathetic teachers might use such instruction "on the one hand as a Trojan horse for the introduction of sectarian teaching, and on the other hand, to sanction an objectivity which concentrates so exclusively upon bare facts that it fails to stimulate young people to come to terms with the issues of life."[40] These objections, however, do not deal with the principle involved but with the means whereby the objective is to be achieved. Just as we want competent teachers to conduct classes in algebra, history, or French, so we would need to prepare competent teachers to teach about religion.

Nonetheless, due to the sensitive issues posed by instruction in this area, it is well to heed Thayer's warning:

> Not all advocates of the study of religion and the "erasing of religious illiteracy" are as scrupulously concerned to respect the sensibili-

[38] *The Function of the Public Schools in Dealing with Religion: A Report on the Exploratory Study Made by the Committee on Religion and Education* (Washington, D.C.: American Council on Education, 1953), pp. 1–7. Used by permission.

[39] Washington, D.C.: National Education Association, 1951, pp. 77–78. With permission.

[40] V. T. Thayer, *The Role of the School in American Society* (New York: Dodd, Mead & Company, Inc., 1960), p. 409. With permission.

> ties of minorities or to realize the obligations of a teacher to his students in an area where honest men differ fundamentally. Indeed, they are convinced that "objectivity" is undermining both religion and the democracy which they believe derives its life blood from religion. The spirit of nonsectarianism, they contend, has overshot its mark and has led to a "religious vacuum" in public education which militates against religion. This vacuum they propose to fill by a "factual study of religion" which differs little, if at all, from that proposed by the advocates of a "common core" of religious instruction. Certainly, the "facts" presented constitute a none too critical description of the orthodox faiths and their organizational expressions in contemporary life and exclude an equally sympathetic presentation of the views of numerous groups which have abandoned orthodoxy together with the grounds for this deviation. In short, the purpose is less the pursuit of truth in a highly confused and complex area of living and more the "saving of souls" as one segment of the community conceives salvation (p. 410).

There has been a long-standing fear shared by many religious people that a secular school cannot teach morality or moral values. This fear is justified if, and only if, one assumes that values must originate from a divine, supernatural source. While this is the assumption held by most religious people, it does not follow logically that the public school cannot teach moral and spiritual values. Neither does it follow that agreement is impossible among people who start from differing theological or metaphysical assumptions. Four different individuals may agree that stealing is undesirable, though one starts from theistic, one from deistic, one from atheistic, and the fourth from agnostic assumptions.

It has been said that brotherly love was practiced among Egyptians long before the birth of Christ. It does exist among theistic Protestants, Catholics, and Jews; or among Moslems, atheistic Russians, and various other groups throughout the world. While faith may claim a monopoly on values for one religion or another, neither logic nor the principles of democracy would support this claim. Sidney Hook expresses this position in the following words:

> The underlying premises, whether theological, metaphysical, or naturalistic, from which different groups justify their common democratic beliefs and practices must not be subject to integration. It is enough, so to speak, that human beings live in accordance with democratic laws; it is foolish intolerance to make only one justification of the laws legal.[41]

[41] Sidney Hook, "The Dilemma of T. S. Eliot," *Nation,* 160 (January 20, 1945), 70.

The same position is expressed by Jacques Maritain, a leading Catholic philosopher:

> The only solution is of the pluralistic type. Men belonging to most different philosophical or religious creeds and families could and should cooperate in the common task and for the common welfare of the earthly community, provided they similarly assent to the basic tenets of a society of free men . . .
>
> Thus it is that men possessing quite different, even opposite, metaphysical or religious outlooks—materialists, idealists, agnostics, Christians and Jews, Moslems and Buddhists—can converge, not by virtue of any identity of doctrine, but by virtue of an analogical similitude in practical principles, toward the same practical conclusions, and can share in the same practical democratic philosophy, provided that they similarly revere, perhaps for quite diverse reasons, truth and intelligence, human dignity, freedom, brotherly love, and the absolute value of moral good.[42]

One development that has muddied the waters on the American scene has been the growing reference to secularism as a religion. One argument asserts that, since secularism is the "religion of the non-believer" and since the current recommendations are for a secular approach to values, we now have the religion of the non-believer entering the public school. Thus there is a new violation of the wall of separation.[43] This interpretation of religion is inconsistent with Western intellectual history. Whether or not it will be recognized by our courts as a legitimate interpretation is a secret of the future.

Meanwhile, there is substantial agreement that many values are broadly held and sufficiently independent of sectarian roots to have a place in our public schools. Some of the values which may thus be taught are kindness, respect for human beings, temperance, loyalty to democracy, honesty, and prudence. An exhaustive list of such values would be difficult to agree upon. Due to their generality and high level of abstraction, different persons would list them differently.[44]

V. T. Thayer, who has worked and written in this field for many

[42] Jacques Maritain, "The Foundations of Democracy," *Nation,* 160 (April 21, 1945), 440–441. With permission.

[43] This line of argument is ably developed by William B. Ball, "Of Schema, Hotheads, Theology, and Smoke," *Teachers College Record* (New York: Teachers College, Columbia University), 64, No. 5 (February 1963).

[44] See, for example, *The Public Schools and Spiritual Values,* Seventh Yearbook, John Dewey Society (New York: Harper, 1944) and compare with the National Education Association statement of 1951.

years, sums up an appropriate position for the nonsectarian public schools when he asserts that:

> Values . . . are the monopoly of no one segment of our society, nor does their validity derive from any one religious faith or philosophic school. They are common values because all recognize them as common essentials of communication and interrelationship. . . . Precisely because the public school is the representative of all the people, it is sacredly obligated to educate for the common values in ways that are exclusively public and nonsectarian.[45]

SUMMARY

In this chapter we have briefly presented the key principles, issues, and legal cases relating to the very complex and emotionally charged problem of the relationship between religion and education in the American social order. Since the broader cultural setting influences educational decisions, educators must look beyond the schools to deal intelligently with the problems they encounter. Consequently, intelligent educational decisions relating to the role of religion in the public schools can be made only if the church-state relations in the culture at large are well understood. In our country, we must understand the limitations imposed by the First and Fourteenth Amendments to our Constitution as interpreted by our courts. We have, therefore, presented those legal cases that are relevant to the question whether, and how, religion should be taught in our public schools. It must be understood that both public and parochial schools function within the framework of one and the same law.

Discussion of the key interpretations of the doctrine of separation led to the conclusion that, while sectarian religious practices may not be conducted in the public schools, teaching about religion, as an academic subject is certainly consistent with our constitutional democracy. The chapter ended with a brief discussion of the place of moral and spiritual values in the secular schools. Our conclusion was that many moral values can be agreed upon by religious and nonreligious people, and should be taught in a nonsectarian program, even though we may respectfully disagree concerning the ultimate or metaphysical justification of such values.

[45] V. T. Thayer, "Education in Moral and Spiritual Values," *Hawaii Educational Review,* 37 (March 1949), 205.

SELECTED BIBLIOGRAPHY

Boles, Donald E. *The Bible, Religion and the Public Schools.* Ames, Iowa: Iowa State University Press, 1963.

Brown, Robert McAffee, and Gustave Weigel, S. J. *An American Dialogue.* New York: Doubleday, 1960.

Butts, R. Freeman. *The American Tradition in Religion and Education.* Boston: Beacon Press, 1950.

__________. "The Relation between Religion and Education," *Progressive Education,* 33 (September 1956), 140–142.

Childs, John L. *Education and Morals.* New York: Appleton-Century-Crofts, Inc., 1950.

Conant, James B. *Education and Liberty.* Cambridge, Mass.: Harvard University Press, 1953, pp. 77–87, 150–152.

Dewey, John. *A Common Faith.* New Haven: Yale University Press, 1934.

Educational Policies Commission. *Moral and Spiritual Values in the Public Schools.* Washington, D.C.: National Education Association, 1951.

Ehlers, Henry, and Gordon Lee. *Crucial Issues in Education,* 2nd ed. New York: Holt, Rinehart, and Winston, 1959.

Johnson, F. Ernest, ed. *American Education and Religion.* New York: Harper & Brothers, 1952. (A series of addresses representing alternative positions regarding the proper place of religion in education.)

Miller, Alexander. *Faith and Learning.* New York: Associated Press, 1960.

Religion and the Schools. New York: The Fund for the Republic, 1959. (A forthright statement of the Protestant, Catholic, Jewish, and nonreligious positions.)

Religion in the Public Schools. Washington, D.C.: American Association of School Administrators, 1964.

Religious Education. (A periodical which is probably the best single source of information relevant to the issue of religion and education.)

Ryan, Mary Perkins. *Are Parochial Schools the Answer?* New York: Holt, Rinehart and Winston, 1963.

Thayer, V. T. *Religion in Public Education.* New York: Viking Press, 1947.

__________. *The Attack upon the American Secular School.* Boston: Beacon Press, 1951.

Van Dusen, Henry P. *God in Education.* New York: Scribner's, 1951.

CHAPTER 9

EDUCATION AND THE CULTURE OF DEPRIVATION

Asked to summarize American civilization in one word, Professor Max Lerner replied: "Access." He explained:

> We have a Declaration of Independence which says that all men are born free and equal. I hope they are born free and will remain free; I know they are not born equal. They are born very unequal, as every parent, teacher, employer, and army commander knows. They are born with very unequal potentials. But as I understand the essence of the revolutionary tradition of America, it is that there should be equal access to equal opportunity so that every one of those youngsters born with unequal abilities shall be able to develop his unequal abilities to the full.[1]

It is generally recognized that the key means whereby access to a nation's cultural opportunities is achieved is the process of education. We have long admitted that the primary route to opportunity for our children, born with unequal abilities, is education, and have reinforced this admission with the further commitment that such education must be, in Tumin's words, "equal, equally good and equally enduring."[2] Thus, any child in America who is denied equal access to equal opportunity to develop his particular abilities to the full has been euphemistically described as educationally, economically, socially, or culturally deprived, neglected, unappreciated, underprivileged, or disadvantaged.

Actually, what is being described is a particularly diverse subculture in the United States—a subculture whose chief characteristic is deprivation. We are therefore talking about a "culture of deprivation" somewhat comparable to the "culture of poverty" described by Oscar Lewis in his studies

[1] Max Lerner, in Paul R. Hanna, ed. *Education: An Instrument of National Goals* (New York: McGraw-Hill Book Co., 1962), p. 111.

[2] Melvin Tumin, "The Process of Integration," in G. J. Klopf and I. A. Laster, eds., *Integrating the Urban School* (New York: Bureau of Publications, Teachers College, Columbia University, 1963), p. 13.

of Mexico.[3] The culture of deprivation implies that there exists a set of economic, social, and psychological variables that intervene in the lives of people and cause them to become deprived of equal access to equal opportunity. As a result of these interventions, such people exhibit different patterns of behavior in their response to the world—patterns that are different from those of the mainstream of American culture.

The culture of deprivation may contain many valuable and viable behavior patterns and values. Because it is "different," it should not necessarily be condemned as "inferior." But the continued use of euphemisms to describe the phenomenon contributes little to an understanding of the problems evoked by the culture of deprivation. For example, some groups react violently to the term "culturally deprived" since they see in such a juxtaposition of terms a veiled deprecatory implication. It is true that inherent in the term "culturally deprived" are all the potential uses and misuses of a single symbol when it represents a complex set of phenomena. To avoid the most obvious misconceptions, it does not mean deprived of *any* culture, for in the affairs of man, this is impossible. Neither does it imply the ascendancy or superiority of one culture or subculture over another. Finally, it does not imply any single causation of deprivation.

However, it may be more acceptable to simply refer to "deprived" children who are, because of their deprivation, members of a distinct subculture.

Implicit in our discussion of the relationship of education and this culture of deprivation is the notion that American democratic culture has an ideal, a goal, a dream to fulfill; and that some children, because of a variety of complex reasons, are being denied access to their rightful share of that destiny, and that the dream, therefore, is as yet unfulfilled. Since the process of education is so intimately and irrevocably a part of this problem, it is our contention that educators share a large responsibility for clearing away the major obstacles facing these children. By their decisions, educators may reconcile the present glaring cultural disparities or they may widen the schisms and extend the contradictions.

WHO ARE THE DEPRIVED?

Traditionally, we have tended to restrict our considerations of deprivation to children in the lower socioeconomic classes or to children of

[3] Oscar Lewis, *Five Families* (New York: John Wiley & Sons, 1962) and *The Children of Sanchez* (New York: Random House, Vintage edition, 1963).

distinct racial minorities who, historically, have been the victims of prejudice. As such, we have tended to view Negroes as the most deprived, and indeed, this may be an entirely accurate assessment. But we must look too at Mexican-Americans, Puerto Ricans, various Oriental groups, members of religious minorities when their religious affiliation causes deprivation, and even suburban white Protestant middle-class children, if those affiliations tend to cause lack of access to equal, equally good, and equally enduring education.

There is no way to estimate the magnitude of the culture of deprivation in precise numbers. While we can estimate that there are approximately 16 to 18 million Negroes of all ages living in the United States, as well as 3.5 to 4 million children of Spanish-speaking subcultures, we cannot assert that *all* such peoples are deprived or even estimate the degree of deprivation of those who are. We can simply frame the problem with the assertion that there are millions of children who, because of their identification with a marked racial, ethnic, or socioeconomic group, are probably deprived. Reissman estimates the numbers to be *one in every three* urban American children,[4] but his definition of "deprivation" does not include those children, who, while possessing the material benefits of American culture, are isolated from its diversity.[5] The deprived might, therefore, be the Negroes whom Conant discusses in his *Slums and Suburbs,*[6] the Puerto Ricans of the New York City study,[7] the migrants of Thomas's study,[8] the Indians whom Zintz and others studied,[9] the lower-lower class children of Warner's Yankee City studies,[10] and a host of other children who have been blocked off from their right to equal access.

Whatever the group, or whatever the individual, the deprived child exhibits at least *one* of the following symptoms:

1. He lacks the social experiences which our present school cur-

[4] Frank Reissman, *The Culturally Deprived Child* (New York: Harper & Brothers, 1961), p. 1.

[5] A colleague tells of introducing the child of a movie star to the simple pleasures of finding a dandelion. A white suburban mother complains to authorities that her child has no opportunities to meet Negro children.

[6] James B. Conant, *Slums and Suburbs* (New York: McGraw-Hill Book Co., Inc., 1961).

[7] *The Puerto Rican Study,* New York City Board of Education, New York, 1958.

[8] D. R. Thomas, *Determining an Effective Educational Program for Children of Migratory Workers in Wisconsin,* University of Wisconsin, 1961.

[9] Miles Zintz, *The Indian Research Study,* University of New Mexico, 1960.

[10] W. Lloyd Warner et al., *Yankee City Studies* (New Haven: Yale University Press, 1941, 1942).

ricula assume to be common to all students; that is, his experiences in the society are marked by sharp differences from the "normal" or "regular" pattern assumed by the middle-class-oriented school.

2. He has experienced deprivation in his sensory and perceptual experiences to such a degree that his development may have been retarded.

3. He has experienced deprivation in the area of symbolic experiences, so that his language functioning is impaired and his conceptual development inhibited. Children whose native language and subculture differ from American English and American culture may be deprived in this way.

4. He has motivational orientations that are inappropriate to present school achievement or success standards.

5. He has been exposed to values and expectations that tend to generate conflict between himself and the schools as presently constituted.

While the above list of symptoms is by no means exhaustive, it comprises the major handicaps plaguing the deprived child. Dealing with such deprivation offers a considerable challenge to American educators, for at its base, it represents an extension of the drive for equal rights, privileges, and opportunities for all currently confronting the nation. In Tumin's words, this drive

> . . . is so relatively new—at least in any form of concrete practice—and it so upsets existing sets of special privileges, and entails so much fumbling and experimenting, without any certain guarantees of success, that it is no wonder that so many of us find it difficult to rise to the conception of what is entailed for us, what we must be willing to do if it is to work, what traditional values must be displaced, what new forms of social relationships are demanded. . . .[11]

THE CAUSES OF DEPRIVATION

The relationships between society and education are intricate. Their many dimensions become apparent when the culture of deprivation constitutes at once a major educational challenge and a significant social problem. The social origins of the educational problem are further revealed when we seek the principal factors that foster deprivation: (1) segregation, (2) economic disadvantage, (3) language and bicultural barriers, (4) religious difference, and (5) geographic isolation.

[11] Melvin Tumin, "The Process of Integration" (see note 2), p. 14.

SEGREGATION

Segregation, or the placing apart of one group from others or the rest, can be found in the United States in two forms: (1) by law (*de jure*) and (2) by reality (*de facto,* meaning "in fact").

Until May 17, 1954, when the United States Supreme Court—in *Brown et al.* v. *Board of Education of Topeka, Kansas et al.* (347 U.S. 483 [1953])—declared public school segregation unconstitutional, legal segregation was mandatory in many states: Alabama, Arkansas, Delaware, Florida, Georgia, Kentucky, Louisiana, Maryland, Mississippi, Missouri, North Carolina, Oklahoma, South Carolina, Tennessee, Texas, Virginia, West Virginia, and the District of Columbia. Segregation was legally optional in Arizona, Kansas, New Mexico, and Wyoming; and in California, the School Code permitted segregation of Indian children or children of Chinese, Japanese, or Mongolian descent. *De facto* segregation also affects Mexican-American children in California, Arizona, Colorado, New Mexico, and Texas; and Oriental children have been isolated in California, Oregon, and Washington. The general practice that children attend the closest neighborhood school, in fact, segregates many other children into distinct socioeconomic groupings. Highly mobile children, such as the children of migratory workers, often cannot attend schools outside their native state because of residence requirements in the various states through which they pass. The first legal challenge to segregation in schools came in 1849, when a Negro named Benjamin Roberts challenged the city of Boston. Charles Sumner, his attorney, denounced the argument that separate facilities for Negroes could be equal, for they imposed the stigma of caste and violated the principle of equality for all human beings "before God and the law." Roberts, however, lost his case before the Massachusetts Supreme Court. In 1856, in the famous Dred Scott case (19 Howard 393 [1856]), the U.S. Supreme Court argued that the wording of the Declaration of Independence revealed that slaves and their descendants were never acknowledged as a part of the people, and therefore did not have equal claim upon the constitutional guarantees given the people. This decision was principally aimed at Negroes, although the Court's decision apparently influenced decisions on subsequent cases involving other racial groups. Later, in the historic case *Plessy* v. *Ferguson* (163 U.S. 537 [1895]), involving the right of the state of Louisiana to provide for separate railway carriages for the white and colored races, the doctrine of "separate but equal" was upheld. The Court argued at the time:

> We consider the underlying fallacy of the plaintiff's argument to consist in the assumption that the enforced separation of the two races stamps the colored race with a badge of inferiority. If this be so, it is not by reason of anything found in the act, but solely because the colored race chooses to put that construction upon it.

The Plessy-Ferguson decision went without modification until 1927, when the U.S. Supreme Court ruled that children of Chinese ancestry can be required to attend segregated schools and that such a requirement does not violate the Fourteenth Amendment of the Constitution (*Gong Lum* v. *Rice,* 275 U.S. 78 [1927]). In 1938, in *Missouri ex rel Garnes* v. *Canada* (305 U.S. 337 [1938]), the Court required the state of Missouri to furnish the Negro plaintiff with equal facilities within its borders for the study of law. This meant the erection of a separate but equal law school, an expensive proposition. In 1945, in California, a Mexican-American named Mendez challenged the Orange County schools' segregation practices, and the U.S. District Court ruled that segregation violates the Fourteenth Amendment. Judge Paul J. McCormick held that separate facilities *deprive* Mexican-American children "of a common cultural attitude . . . which is imperative for the perpetuation of American institutions and ideals." Mendez was upheld by the Ninth Circuit Court on April 14, 1947 (D.C. Cal., 64 F. Supp. 55, 161 F. 2d 774).

In 1948, however, in *Sipuel* v. *Board of Regents* (332 U.S. 631 [1948]), in Oklahoma, the U.S. Supreme Court returned to the "separate but equal" doctrine. But two years later, in two crucial cases—*Sweatt* v. *Painter* (330 U.S. 629 [1950]) and *McLaurin* v. *Oklahoma State Regents* (330 U.S. 637 [1950])—the Court ruled that the plaintiffs' rights were violated by the specially devised systems of intramural segregation that kept McLaurin apart from his fellow students while he was in the same classes, and by the unequal facilities offered Sweatt by the University of Texas.

Finally came the momentous decision of 1954, in which Chief Justice Earl Warren, speaking for the unanimous court, stated:

> Does segregation of children in public schools solely on the basis of race, even though the physical facilities and other tangible factors may be equal, *deprive* the children of the minority groups of equal educational opportunities? We believe that it does. . . . to separate [children] from others of similar age and qualifications solely because of their race generates a feeling of inferiority as to their status in the community that may affect their hearts and minds in a way unlikely ever to be undone. . . . Segregation of white and colored children in public schools has a detri-

> mental effect upon colored children. The impact is greater when it has the sanction of the law; for the policy of separating the races is usually interpreted as denoting the inferiority of the Negro group. A sense of inferiority affects the motivation of a child to learn. Segregation with the sanction of law, therefore, has a tendency to retard the educational and mental development of Negro children and to *deprive* them of some of the benefits they would receive in a racially integrated school system. . . . We conclude that in the field of public education the doctrine of separate but equal has no place. Separate educational facilities are inherently unequal. . . . Such segregation is a denial of the equal protection of the laws.

Resistance to this precedent-shattering decision was immediate, angry, and militant in those states where the traditions of segregation had been woven into the fabric of social living for over a hundred years. Understanding of this resistance is essential to its eventual elimination. Within the structure of our legal system, however, unyielding resistance could not be condoned, nor could compromises be negotiated. The Supreme Court therefore ruled that desegregation should proceed with all due "deliberate speed." Thus, the ten most segregated states—Alabama, Arkansas, Florida, Georgia, Louisiana, Mississippi, North Carolina, South Carolina, Tennessee, and Virginia—were faced with problems of major social and educational change.

Other states, too, faced changes in varying degrees as their laws permitted *de jure* segregation. All states were confronted with the necessity of dealing with well-established *de facto* segregation, which often was extremely difficult to erase because it was so deeply embedded in residential patterns and yet violated no laws.[12] The momentum of the drive for equality for all brought many communities to the brink of civil strife; in some areas, violence did break out, setting neighbor against neighbor, black against white, educator against educator. Indeed, the violence of the reaction to the Supreme Court's decision is a dark chapter in our history and as yet unfinished.

On the one hand, Negro leaders issued their battle cry of "all, here, now" and proceeded to implement their challenge with demonstrations, boycotts, and lawsuits. On the other hand, staunch segregationists responded

[12] The U.S. Supreme Court, in its 1964 Gary, Indiana, decision, reaffirmed the legality of unintentional *de facto* segregation by upholding the legality of the concept of the neighborhood school. The value question concerning neighborhood schools has not yet been answered.

with open defiance of federal court orders, lengthy legal maneuvers, police brutality, closing of schools, bombings of Negro churches, assassinations, and even an open appeal to anarchy (as when Governor Wallace of Alabama stated that Supreme Court decisions apply only to the specific case involved in the specific decision).

International attention was focused on the confrontation of federal troops and Governor Faubus in Little Rock, Arkansas, and on similar confrontations between federal forces and Governor Barnett at Oxford, Mississippi, and Governor Wallace at Tuscaloosa, Alabama. Perhaps the most dramatic event to mar the image of a democratic America occurred in Birmingham, Alabama, in May and June of 1963, when white police officials countered Negro demonstrations with fire hoses and snarling dogs. The devastating impact of pictures of Negroes being attacked by dogs and inundated by powerful fire hoses set off an even greater push for equal rights for Negroes in all aspects of social life. In 1964, Congress finally passed the most comprehensive civil-rights bill since Reconstruction days, and the first attempted prosecutions under its provisions came in the Georgia murder of educator Lemuel Penn and the murders of three civil-rights workers at Philadelphia, Mississippi.

Southerners frantically proclaimed their defenses. Thomas R. Waring, a South Carolina editor, stated that Southerners had valid reasons for continuing segregation.[13] He cited what he believed to be five major differences between Negroes and whites: health standards, home environment (poverty, etc.), marital standards, crime, and a wide disparity in intellectual development. In his supporting arguments, Waring openly admitted that he lacked the statistics to prove his points, but argued for the strong *belief* among Southerners that such differences are inherent in the two races. Behind such arguments echoed the specter of intermarriage, and this specter aroused high emotions among men who believed, with a circuit court judge in Mississippi, that "the loveliest and purest of God's creatures, the nearest thing to an angelic being that treads the terrestrial ball is a well-bred, cultured Southern white woman or her blue-eyed, golden-haired little girl."[14]

In New Orleans, during the integration of the William Franz elementary school, five- and six-year-old Negro children were screamed at by

[13] Thomas R. Waring, "The Southern Case against Desegregation," *Harper's Magazine,* January 1956, pp. 39–45.

[14] John B. Martin, "The Deep South Says 'Never,'" *Saturday Evening Post,* June 15, 1957, pp. 23 ff.

white mothers of their prospective classmates. Inez Robb, a national columnist, was so outraged that she asked: "From under what rocks do these termagants—violent, vicious, and ignorant—crawl by day to commit physical and verbal assault on any and all who meet with their displeasure? What kind of harpies are these, scarves over their pincurls and slacks straining over their fat behinds, whose ghoulish pleasure it is to threaten five and six year old children? to maul old men? to spit and strike ministers of the gospel?"

The high degree of emotionalism which has permeated the segregation issue from the moment of the Supreme Court's decision has brought about a virtual stalemate. Progress toward integration has proceeded at an incredibly slow pace; if that pace continues, desegregation will not be complete for thousands of years. A brief glance at the statistics for June 1962, eight years after the decision, which James Graham Cook reports, substantiates this point:[15]

	No. of Negroes Enrolled in Public Grade Schools	No. of Negroes in Schools with Whites	Per cent
Alabama	276,029	0	00.
Arkansas	108,841	151	00.139
Florida	242,097	648	00.268
Georgia	303,005	8	00.003
Louisiana	295,000	12	00.004
Mississippi	286,800	0	00.
North Carolina	332,962	203	00.061
South Carolina	265,076	0	00.
Tennessee	155,500	1,167	00.75
Virginia	216,860	536	00.247
Totals	2,482,170	2,725	Average 00.1

Progress in border states has been similar, and the moves toward the elimination of *de facto* segregation in the East, West, and North have met relatively little success.

The drive against *de facto* segregation has brought about a tragic dilemma for some educators. Neighborhood school-attendance policies are easily defended, particularly for elementary schools, on such obvious grounds as safety and proximity to the home for young children. Where

[15] James Graham Cook, *The Segregationists* (New York: Appleton-Century-Crofts, 1962), p. 1.

school-attendance boundaries have been clearly gerrymandered to facilitate segregation, opponents have the possibility of recourse in the courts. But school officials have little power to control the sale and distribution of housing, and militant Negro demonstrations against *de facto* segregation *not* caused by deliberate gerrymandering have put some of these school officials in a tragic dilemma. Sympathetic to the Negro and his strivings, these school officials are sometimes made to appear hostile and uncooperative because they cannot, for a variety of valid reasons, not the least of which is inadequate funds, rearrange school attendance patterns.

Resistance to the *de facto* segregation of schools has usually been less violent than resistance in other social areas, but perhaps more determined and certainly more effective, since progress here has been extremely slow. But segregated schooling is only one form of segregation; other forms —segregated housing, transportation, employment, even inequality in the courts—must be removed before the problem of school segregation can be completely solved. The peaceful road to such reform is slow and arduous, but progress is being made where Negro and white leaders have been willing to face the realities and negotiate in good faith.

For educators, the decision to support total integration and all its implications has clear roots in the scientific study of children and in the value commitment associated with professional service to children in our American democracy. The National Education Association (NEA) Code of Ethics states the position unequivocably in its First Principle:

> 1. The teacher will deal justly and impartially with students regardless of their physical, mental, emotional, political, economic, social, racial, or religious characteristics.
>
> 2. The teacher will recognize the differences among students and seek to meet their individual needs.

The fact that educators have been slow to accept and act upon this commitment may reflect as much on the diversity of views in the teaching ranks and the depth of the problem as it does on the professional commitment of such personnel. The inability of the NEA to pass a resolution in support of the Supreme Court for many years is further testimony on the complexity of the problem of trying to get masses of people to face the realities of social change. But the NEA resolution finally did pass, and the commitment is beginning to manifest itself.

Some Southern white leaders, too, have begun to face the reality of desegregation, and we now hear Editor Ralph McGill, of the Atlanta *Constitution,* saying:

> Since 1945 there had been yearly reminders that the United States could no longer ignore its own principles, its fourteenth constitutional amendment, and the demands of civilization and morality. The decision (Supreme Court on schools) was, all in one, fulcrum and lever. Customs, traditions and political structure began to find themselves moved out of the way. In all America no one was so lucky as the Southerner who was a part of this social revolution, of this determination to reaffirm the principles of what we have called the American dream.[16]

ECONOMIC DISADVANTAGE

In the minds of many Americans, poverty no longer exists in the United States. Galbraith asserted that we are escaping "from the obsolete and contrived preoccupations associated with the assumption of poverty" as we recognize that we are, in his terms, "an affluent society."[17] But Michael Harrington reports that, as of 1963, 25 per cent of the nation (about 50,000,000 people) is still ill-housed, ill-clothed, and ill-fed.[18] Perhaps the average middle-class teacher has had no direct experience with the real world of poverty, and therefore has little ability to understand its impact. Research workers are only beginning to explore and document the far-reaching influences of poverty on children's physical, intellectual, social, and emotional development. But the educators of today must face the consequences of such economic disadvantage.

For example, the average *gross* income for agricultural migrant workers is less than $900 a year. With both parents working, there is still only $1,800 gross per year. Migrant workers often complete a year's work with the same amount or less than they started with at the season's beginning. Children as young as six have been pressed into service as pickers to raise the family's income.

As Galbraith reminds us:

> There is no firm definition of this phenomenon (poverty) and again, save as a tactic for countering the intellectual obstructionist, no precise definition is needed—people are poverty-stricken when their income,

[16] Ralph McGill, "The South Has Many Faces," *Atlantic Monthly,* April 1963.

[17] John Kenneth Galbraith, *The Affluent Society* (Boston: Houghton Mifflin Co., 1958), p. 3.

[18] Michael Harrington, *The Other America* (New York: Macmillan Co., 1963), p. 1.

> even if adequate for survival, falls markedly behind that of the community. Then they cannot have what the larger community regards as the minimum necessary for decency; and they cannot wholly escape, therefore, the judgment of the larger community that they are indecent. They are degraded for, in the literal sense, they live outside the grades or categories which the community regards as acceptable.[19]

The characteristic concerns, therefore, of economically disadvantaged families are the isolation and rejection from the larger community, the grinding economic insecurity and consequently heightened importance of the breadwinner's job, and the undesirable area of residence. While the middle and upper classes have the luxury of centering much attention upon their children, the lower-class family must be adult-centered or, more appropriately, breadwinner-centered. Middle-class people, in particular, seem to have great difficulty in accepting this focus on the adult rather than the children, since their own cultural pattern is so deeply committed to the child-centered home. Middle-class-oriented teachers often condemn lower-class parents for what appears to be a crass disregard for the educational welfare of their children. As Galbraith has intimated above, such judgments slip easily into moral judgments on the relative "decency" of such lower-class people.

Preoccupied with his economic problems, with his discouragement, with his lack of skill to improve his lot, the economically disadvantaged parent has neither the resources nor concerns to pursue "cultural" activities. He reads very little; he has no vital concern for the larger problems of his community, his nation, or the world. In fact, his feeling of alienation causes him to express hostility toward, or rejection of, the society around him. Mexican-Americans who live in the Rio Grande Valley, for example, have been American citizens since 1848, but still refer to Anglo people as "los americanos" and "white" people, and to themselves as something different from these categories. Basically, the disadvantaged parent is seeking security rather than risk; he often has deep inferiority feelings about himself, and is consequently defensive and suspicious of people he views as "successful" or "superior." He holds on to what little he has with great tenacity—his traditions, his religion, even his meager work skills. Cotton pickers in Arizona rejected the possibility of employment in lettuce fields

[19] Galbraith (see note 17). President Johnson's "War on Poverty" stipulated as a definition of "poor" any family whose gross annual income was below $3,000 in 1964. In that year an estimated 35,000,000 Americans fell into this definition of the "poor."

because they "knew" cotton and were afraid to try a new experience. Their continual unemployment was tragic, but unresolvable. They could not gain from welfare benefits, since they were nonresidents; hence, the oft-repeated charges of "indigence," "laziness," "irresponsibility," even "mentally retarded," the accusations that they were looking for a "free handout," were untrue.

The debilitating effect of such economic disadvantages on children is clear. "A comparison of four slum areas in the city of Chicago with four good areas in the same city revealed twenty times as much juvenile delinquency, twelve times as much mortality from tuberculosis, four times as much mortality from pneumonia, three times as much truancy, and more than twice as much infant mortality. . . ."[20]

Many economically disadvantaged children are hostile, unhealthy, and estranged. They have none of the common artifacts of the dominant culture available to them—books, magazines, records, art, etc. They do not go to plays, concerts, or museums, or on vacation trips. Their diet is narrow, monotonous, and often insufficient. They have not had their "shots," or their eyes examined, their teeth straightened, or their minds stimulated by the many experiences which are as common as bedtime stories to the middle- or upper-class child. Consequently, an economically disadvantaged child does poorly in school, for the world of the school is predominantly middle class, with its assumption that verbal intelligence—based upon middle-class concepts, experiences, and vocabulary—is the only measure of capacity. Since education is a primary path of access to equal opportunity, the economically disadvantaged child is *deprived* by his life experiences of the probability of succeeding. Education offers no more access to this child than does his economic status; thus the vicious circle continues.

Since compulsory-attendance laws apply to children in all states of the Union, the schools have a unique opportunity to become acquainted with cultural deprivation due to economic disadvantage. In Chapter 4 we noted the increasing concern with this problem,[21] and gave examples of how schools in many areas are attempting to deal with it. But, as in other matters, the school cannot organize the society to suit its educational com-

[20] *Mid-century White House Conference on Children and Youth,* in Stanley et al., p. 183.

[21] See also the state of California's Compensatory Education Act of 1963, which allocated some $645,000 to special programs for culturally disadvantaged children and youth. Extension of this act into a multimillion-dollar program is being sought by State Senator J. Eugene McAteer of San Francisco in 1965.

mitments or purposes, since the school is part of the social context. The decisions of educators to attack the educational problems caused by economic disadvantage carry with them the parallel commitment to recognize the social roots of the problems and offer leadership in their solution as well.

LANGUAGE BARRIER AND BICULTURAL BACKGROUND

When a child comes from a family whose language is other than English, or whose basic culture is other than American, he faces immediate problems in his educational experience. We are speaking here of the "some twenty-two million children in the United States for whom English is a second language,"[22] and we are pointing to their need to achieve better decoding, encoding, and association processes in language development. If such a child is to have equal access to American culture, he must overcome these problems.

Every culture develops a language of its own to meet its specific needs, so that language is a function of culture. Consequently, the language developed to suit the demands of a specific culture may prove to be an inadequate instrument in a very different culture. For example, the Navajo language, which is adapted to the needs of the traditional Navajo culture, is totally unsuited to competition-dominated American life: since this concept is alien to the Navajo people, they have no word for "competition." Conversely, our own language would be inadequate to meet the needs of the Eskimo people, who have developed some forty-odd terms for snow because this variety satisfies a fundamental need of that culture.

Thus the problem of deprivation due to the barrier of language is also a problem of cultural differences. Cora Dubois has stated the problems of teaching the bicultural learner as follows:

> Whereas the educator's problem with the monocultural learner is to stage cross-cultural experiences, his problem with the bi-cultural learner is to help his pupil discover the differing systems of rewards and the variant roles provided by secondary group relationships in different cultures, and to help him reach a viable adjustment in the face of choice. Here the role of the educator-teacher as a warm supportive figure seems to emerge with even more saliency than in the case of the monocultural

[22] Ruth Strang, "The Linguistically Handicapped Child: Learning English as a Second Language—a Theoretical Model," *Exceptional Children,* 30 (1963), 14–16. This estimate may be quite high.

> learner. Educators and teachers must in their persons, provide support to the bi-cultural learner that the monocultural learner derives from a society milieu whose system of rewards and roles are relatively apparent to him. The bi-cultural learner must be assisted to select social roles that promise rewards commensurate with his capacities as a learner. Variant social roles and their attendant rewards will need to be stressed in the education of the bi-cultural learner. But at the same time, in the achievement of these social roles and rewards, he must not have to suppress or reject the alternative cultural resources acquired through his bi-cultural experience. Probably one of the greatest barriers to the development of intercultural understanding among the foreign-born or second-generation students in the United States has been the rigorous insistence in American schools, until recently, on the exclusive quality of American values. When these were reinforced by the relatively accessible rewards and variant roles offered by American society, the alienation of our foreign-born from their own cultural origin and their rejection of it was assured. We appear to have built national solidarity at the expense of intercultural understanding.[23]

Unfortunately, the bicultural learning problem has not yet been solved. For example, thousands of Spanish-speaking children of Mexican culture attend American schools in Texas, New Mexico, Colorado, Arizona, and California; French-speaking children with Canadian backgrounds inhabit schools in New York; and children from German and Polish homes go to schools in Wisconsin and Michigan; many have remained almost wholly unassimilated into the mainstream of American culture. Throughout the nation, thousands of children of diverse Indian tribes face the crucial problems of learning both a new culture and a new language—and their mother tongue may have nothing in common with any modern, popular language.

Under present typical school conditions, the child whose native tongue is not English faces a number of difficult tasks. Although such children must first learn to understand and speak the English language, they quickly discover that their teacher has no knowledge of their native tongue. They also find that their language books, written to teach English to children whose mother tongue is English, naturally stress the kinds of language problems that are common to these children. Little attention is given to problems such as mastering English-language sounds—problems common to non-English-speaking children. In other words, no special

[23] Cora Dubois, "Learning Intercultural Understanding" in George Spindler, ed., *Education and Anthropology* (Stanford, Calif.: Stanford University Press, 1955), pp. 101–102. With permission.

effort is made to deal with the specific linguistic problems confronting the student who is learning English as a *second* language. Since American schools base much of their evaluation of success on verbal achievement in English, the child whose original language is not English is at a distinct disadvantage. He may, in fact, find that his intelligence is seriously questioned when he fails to perform adequately on an intelligence test based upon the understanding and manipulation of English.

There are inherent differences between English and other languages that are likely to cause distortions of juncture, syntax, and emphasis. Attempts by the non-English-speaking child at word attack may be severely inhibited by his difficulties in enunciation and his lack of general English language experience. When confronted with a new word, he cannot draw upon a word family as a clue; he cannot readily construct plurals if he has had limited experience with alternative forms. Even the content of the stories he is asked to read as a part of learning in school may contain many cultural artifacts with which he has no familiarity. He exists at a great experiential distance from, and cannot identify with, the "Dick and Jane" model of the common primary level reader.

As the non-English-speaking child enters the American school, he finds himself at immediate odds with the very cultural premises upon which the school rests. He is likely to find a sincere middle-class teacher who does not know the foreign child's language or culture, who is not trained in either crosscultural studies or linguistics, and who is not aware of either her own biases or those embedded in the materials she uses in her program of instruction. She may, in some geographical areas, even have a distinct regional accent that only serves to confuse the non-English-speaking student further. For instance, when a Spanish-speaking pupil says "ca-ro-té" instead of "carrot," he is told he is wrong, but his teacher's pronunciation of "daoug" for "dog" may be considered perfectly acceptable.

In an illustrative example of the complexity of the problem, the administrator of a school district in a southwestern state hired an Indian girl to teach in the local school, which had enrolled some Indian children from the X tribe nearby. Unfortunately, he did not realize, or had neglected to ascertain, that his Indian teacher was from the Y tribe, whose language and culture had absolutely nothing in common with the X tribe. In the same school, 47 per cent of the children were from Spanish-speaking homes but none of the adults on the staff spoke a word of Spanish.

In California, a Spanish-speaking boy of eleven, who competently cared for his four younger brothers and sisters, delivered a paper route, and cooked the suppers, was tested by the school and assigned an IQ of 36—commonly considered low enough for institutionalization. It was not until *later* that the administrators of the test discovered that the boy could not read, write, or speak English.[24]

Such incidents, while extreme, serve to illustrate and dramatize the problems confronting both the bicultural learner and his teachers. The current distance from a solution of these problems may be considered the index of the bicultural learner's *degree* of *deprivation.* It is Spindler's contention[25] that teachers in America need a kind of "cultural therapy," beginning with what he calls "cultural shock" treatments in the form of value-projective techniques which enable the prospective teacher to understand, first, his own matrix of values, and then, perhaps, the matrix of values associated with other groups with whom he may come into contact in his teaching experience. To this we must add some special work in linguistics, and, if possible, some additional preparation in the field of teaching English as a foreign language.

RELIGIOUS DIFFERENCES AND DEPRIVATION

Equal access to the culture implies an open society, where free inquiry, tentative individual judgments, and the cross-fertilization of ideas are significant characteristics of the educational system. If this is true, then the question must be raised about the millions of children who attend non-public schools, usually religious, where these requirements may be lacking. Does a child who attends a religious school have equal access to all of the culture? Of course, parents who choose to place their children in private schools do so for some identifiable reason. If the private school has a strong religious position, then presumably the children who attend are there to learn that particular religious point of view. And if the school's religious point of view permeates all of the areas of the curriculum, then the characteristics of free inquiry, tentative judgments, and the cross-fertilization of ideas are not likely to be present. Under such circumstances, it is reasonable to ask whether these children really have the opportunity of equal *access* to the total culture.

[24] It might be interesting to note that similar mistakes are not made when the eleven year old is a recent immigrant from Denmark, Germany, or other European nations. Is it reasonable to infer that a negative stereotype operates in our schools against certain ethnic or subcultural groups?

[25] George Spindler, *The Transmission of American Culture* (Cambridge, Mass.: Harvard University Press, 1959), pp. 45–47.

There should be no implication here that every child must *accept* the total culture. We are not here concerned with what part of the culture the student chooses to accept or reject. We are concerned with his opportunity to make his own choices for himself and not have significant ideas and concepts of his culture withheld from his scrutiny because of the deliberate bias or deficiencies of his education.

Where religious prejudice exists, public and private schools have been known to employ differential admittance procedures, as well as outright discriminatory practices against the minority religious groups. The most common form of such implementation of religious prejudice is the "quota" system employed to limit the number of students of a particular religious faith who may be admitted to, say, a medical school, or a law school. Wherever such practices are employed, the excluded student, if he is in all other ways qualified, has suffered a form of deprivation insofar as he has been denied equal access to equal opportunity.

Religious discrimination occurs when a religiously homogeneous community rejects children of other faiths, or is, at best, careless about protecting their rights. Thus, tightly knit denominational enclaves may deprive not only their own children of access to equal opportunity in the broad culture but also deny equal opportunity to those children in the community who do not share the dominant set of beliefs and, consequently, are subjects of community abuse and scorn. California, for example, has faced this problem with public schools in communities vigorously affiliated to the Mennonite sect. Similar problems in Utah, Arizona, Nevada, and Idaho exist where some communities are almost entirely Mormon in religious affiliation. In one overwhelmingly Catholic community in Illinois, court action was necessary to stop nuns in habit from teaching in the public schools. Conflicts have also occurred between public school officials and adherents of the Amish sects in Pennsylvania.

In all cases where a religious group has held itself aloof from the mainstream of American culture, the question of the deprivation of its children becomes relevant. We stress once again that such children are not required to *accept* the values and behavior patterns of the dominant culture, but schools need to at least offer the child an exposure to, or the opportunity to know, the total culture, and on the bases of such knowledge, allow him to accept or reject that culture.

It may also be relevant to add that, as the United States assumes the role of world leader, access to knowledge about all world religions, explored without prejudice, may become prerequisite to any definition of adequate education.

GEOGRAPHICAL ISOLATION

During the first six years of the 1950s, almost 85 per cent of the nation's population explosion occurred in the urban areas. Demographers predict that by 1975 the growth in urban areas will be 70 per cent over that of 1950. In short, the mainstream of American culture, the matrix of social and economic opportunities, will be centered in the urban areas. By contrast, the rural population faces the loss to urban culture and economic power of not only its traditions and its people but also its resources. Rural education, caught in the same decline, has had to face unprecedented hardships. It has become more and more difficult to recruit teachers, and with declining farm income, it has become more and more difficult to pay adequate salaries to those teachers who are recruited. The consequences in many rural states have been quite severe. Often the teachers left to manage the ramshackle little country schoolhouses are those least qualified. In fact, the lowest standards for teachers in America exist in those midwestern states which have significant rural populations and developed systems of rural education. Modern equipment, particularly in science, is virtually unknown in these schools. Modern mathematics is a strange new tale, and structural linguistics a secret code. The explosion of knowledge has been muffled; the distribution of culture often stopped at the last crossroad. Whatever the nostalgia, many rural children of an urban today find little opportunity along the dusty country roads of a rural yesterday.

More desperate than that of the settled rural population is the plight of the agricultural migrant worker and his children. Dr. Hector Garcia describes the migrant child's future as follows:

> The children of migrant parents are born in a world completely of their own. An anemic mother, and possibly a tubercular father—a life that will take him into his world where he may possibly die within a year, either of diarrhea, tuberculosis, or malnutrition. His infancy would be a very close association with his brothers and sisters. Their home would be a one or two room shack, with no inside running water, and no flush toilet facilities. If he lives to be of school age, he could possibly go to many schools on different occasions at different places, but will never average more than three years of schooling in his lifetime—his future life will be one of wandering, poverty, and more sickness.[26]

[26] Hector Garcia, *Report on Farm Labor* (Washington, D.C.: The National Committee on Farm Labor, 1959), pp. 5–6.

Thomas, in his testimony before the United States Senate Subcommittee on Migratory Labor, described the educational scene of the migrant child as follows:

> Look beyond the screen of statistics at the child behind in school, in poor health, housed in a coop, whose father works for 131 days a year for 50 cents per hour. That child hasn't much of a chance to develop his talents, to be useful to himself or to his country. This is the ugliest kind of human waste.
>
> Educationally, the children of migrant workers are, indeed a pathetic lot. Buffeted about from place to place, their lives in a constant flux, it is hardly expected that they would be anything else. Congress, unfailingly spending money ($6,500,000 in 1958) to look after the welfare of our migratory birds, has done relatively little (virtually nothing of a direct nature) to look after the welfare of our migratory children. Only sparse and intermittent Federal, State, and local efforts are being made to correct this last main source of illiteracy in America.
>
> Take the case of the children of Texas-Mexican migrant workers. Taking leave from their home base between early March and late May, in order to accompany their parents on their trek north, these children may not return to school again until October or November. There is more truth than fiction in the chance remark that "you can't educate a procession." As the migrants move from crop to crop, their unannounced arrival and departure too often go unnoticed. But, in spite of this educational "short-change," one superintendent remarked, when asked whether missing three months of school would set the child back permanently, "No sir, if the child had the ability, the background, he might be able to make his grade anyway." This ostrich-like posture has been used many times to cover an ugly situation.
>
> School officials in communities where migrant labor is used extensively have a legitimate argument when they say that their schools are already overcrowded, and that local tax rolls cannot bear the further expenditure of taking in non-resident migrant children.
>
> "School officials may also argue that the tradition of local support and control of the school is too strong to allow for the intrusion of such measures as State and interstate educational programs for migrant children. In a nation that prides itself on its institutional flexibility, this stubborn adherence to an unworkable practice when dealing with migrants seems utter folly. Because the migrant problem transcends local and State lines, it has been repeatedly recommended that interstate and Federal action strongly supplement local action.[27]

Opposition to possible solutions of the educational problems of chil-

[27] Donald R. Thomas, Testimony, Hearings before the Subcommittee on Migratory Labor of the Committee on Labor and Public Welfare, United States Senate, 86th Congress, Madison, Wisconsin, Sept. 28, 1959. See pp. 313–334 of the *Proceedings*.

dren of migratory workers has traditionally come from farmer and grower associations. Just as their powerful lobbies in the Congress have prevented agricultural workers from enjoying the benefits of minimum age laws, workman's compensation, minimum wage laws, social security, and National Labor Relations Board recognition, so have these groups tended to frustrate efforts to relieve the educational hardships of the children of such workers.

Several temporary programs, usually financed by research funds, have formulated promising guidelines for remedial school programs, but frequently, when the research grant funds are depleted, the programs die, and the knowledge gained is lost in the dusty files of school district and college research offices. When a new wave of interest swells, old formulas are brought out, occasional new grants are made and—for a time—some children benefit. But the present existence of over a quarter of a million migrant children who have received little or no adequate and sustained schooling testifies to the erosions of time and the persistent history of neglect.

MULTIPLE DEPRIVATION AMONG NEGROES AND MEXICANS

In the United States, two groups stand out as victims of multiple deprivation: (1) the Negro and (2) the Mexican-Americans of the Southwest. In both cases, the combination of economic deprivation and membership in a victimized racial and ethnic group is evident. In both groups, these conditions are discouragingly persistent. What has happened to individuals in these groups as a result of such grinding, unceasing deprivation is a tragic story. The bitter hatred of the Black Muslim sect, the hopeless withdrawal of the Mexican field worker, are social costs which the United States may be ill-equipped to pay. A prominent Black Muslim leader told the authors that he had never met an honest white man, and earnestly believed he never would. As we have said, many Mexican-Americans of the Southwest, citizens of the United States since 1848, still refer to all their fellow citizens as "los Americanos"—a symptom of their total lack of identification with *their own nation.* The Muslims go further and reject their country, demanding instead a separate black nation in United States territory, for "certainly we have paid for such land with our lives and labor," as one of their leaders said.

More moderate leaders of these two groups are still militant about correcting the long-standing abuses which have maintained the deprivation. Strife and violence are now significant and desperate responses, particularly among Negroes. The sleeping political giant of the Spanish-speaking people in Texas, New Mexico, Arizona, and California, also stirs, particularly as they see the Negro's progress. But the solution to deprivation cannot be achieved by strife and agitation alone. The attainment of rights is hollow if there are insufficient skills to exercise such rights. In a modern technological society, equal access to all the cultural opportunities cannot be obtained without education—or the skills and training necessary for social, economic, and political viability. Thus education is the key, and the schools have the unique opportunity of playing a central role in the solution of this urgent problem.

FORMAL EDUCATION'S CONTRIBUTION TO DEPRIVATION

It is impossible to ignore the fact that schools have, in some cases, contributed to the perpetuation of deprivation. Since the school is a fundamental social institution, it follows that where society is deficient, the schools are likely to reflect such deficiencies. There is little doubt that in some schools there is open and *intentional* discrimination; deliberately segregated schools, either *de facto* or *de jure,* fall into this category. The contribution to deprivation of these schools is clear and their choice of values evident.

In some instances, schools practice discrimination that is unintentional or at least indirect. In the first case it may be open discrimination—not because the educators want it, but because the community's values are such that educators cannot fruitfully challenge the community's feelings and beliefs.

In the second case it may take the form of assigning the least qualified teachers to classrooms inhabited by deprived children, in which case the problem simply spirals. If the prestige system within a school district fosters the notion that assignment to a deprived class is a punishment, rather than a reward for good teaching, then deprivation is reinforced rather than diminished. The shortage of teachers should never be manipulated to hurt the already injured. Not long ago it was said that 450 classrooms in a large midwestern city did not have a permanently assigned teacher, but were "living from substitute to substitute." The greater proportion of these unstable classrooms were in areas inhabited by easily identifiable deprived children.

The schools also contribute to deprivation when they design curricula which are ill-suited to the needs, abilities, and interests of deprived children. One of the tragedies of recent agitation to make public schools "strictly academic" is the impact such programs have on deprived children. The ostrich-like assumption of some of the middle-class academic spokesmen for such programs is that all children are like their own children, and if not, there is little hope for them. One cynical advocate of "basic education" remarked that it was foolish to spend $5,000 on a "5¢ child."

The cost factor in remedying the plight of the deprived may, indeed, be significant.[28] But schools which use the specter of special costs for special programs to avoid engaging in meaningful programs for these children are rationalizing their responsibility. It is clear that economic efficiency is not served by doing a poor educational job, just as it is clear that, having discovered marked inefficiency in the educational procedures, a school may be forced to expend extra monies to adjust the program to more efficient procedures. It is a fundamental fact that schools are organized to educate children, not save money. Efficiency is always relative to some organizing criteria; hence, efficiency in education must be defined in terms of educational success.[29]

The economic argument is but one of a series of rationalizations which have been developed to defend schools from the deserved charge of intrenched neglect of deprived children. There is little doubt that deprived children represent one of the most complex and difficult educational problems any school may ever face. The task, for example, of moving economically impoverished, Poche-speaking[30] children from limited oral experiences to competent English-language performance in speech, reading, and writing, is a horrendous one. It is, of course, easier not to deal with such a task by the simple mechanisms of ignoring the problem, or pretending it does not exist, or rationalizing that nothing can be done about it anyway. "It's bigger than all of us" is a favorite response in some schools. "I wouldn't even know where to start" is another artful dodge. But again, the decisions return to basic value assumptions. If educators dare to pro-

[28] President Johnson, in 1965, obtained from Congress over one billion dollars, most of which would go to schools in deprived areas.

[29] See P. C. Sexton, *Education and Income* (New York: Viking Press, 1961).

[30] "Poche" is a term for a border Spanish which is neither Spanish nor English, but rather a hybrid of the two. It is commonly spoken in Texas, New Mexico, Arizona, and California. In some areas, it also contains some Indian languages such as Papago, Pima, or Apache.

claim their status as "professional," they must immediately abandon their easy rationalizations for neglect. Cancer, polio, and a myriad of other diseases are dreadful problems, but the search for their cures has never been abandoned, and success has sometimes come after years of research and hard work.

Another obstacle to the solution of the problem of deprivation is related to the social system of the school. The line-staff organization of schools tends to produce a status-prestige system and bureaucracy which relies heavily upon the degree of authority one may employ. The main source of the teacher's prestige lies in her authority over her class, for she has little prestige beyond that level. The school principal's prestige to a large degree depends on his authority over the teachers in his school, and again, such prestige diminishes at the edge of the school grounds. The superintendent, in turn, holds prestige as the authority second only to the board of trustees. Such a system tends to maximize the insecurity of each level of authority and minimize its prestige.

To admit that the problem of educating deprived children is unsolved tends to be perceived at all levels as an admission of personal failure. It arouses the administrator's occupational fear of "trouble" and implies that the teacher is undeserving of her status as a successful teacher. The teacher cannot readily admit to her children that she does not know how to help them, does not understand them, cannot communicate with them in their language or on their terms. Therefore she demands that they operate on her terms by virtue of her authority and prestige, and the problem persists. The administrator, more often concerned with pleasing the community power structure (or what he imagines will please that group) tends to develop a fear of having any major problem exposed "naked" to that power group, since he feels his continued employment is dependent upon his running a "tight ship" free from any "controversy."[31] In the long run, it is this unfortunate aspect of the social system of the school which may prove as difficult to overcome as the direct problem of the deprived children.

Another fundamental situation which perpetuates the problems of the deprived is the common organization of schools into questionable

[31] *School* administration in some districts has tended to become predominantly *business* administration, with little recognition of educational problems and little desire to solve such problems, when recognized, if the solutions sought tend to disrupt "administrative" procedures and business efficiency. In brief, maintenance of the bureaucratic structure supersedes education as the *raison d'être* of the school district.

compartments called "grades." All children who start first grade at approximately the same age (because their birthdays fell on, or before, a certain arbitrary deadline) are obviously not equal in social, emotional, physical, and intellectual development. They do, in fact, represent a broad range of abilities, talents, and experiences. If the curriculum is graded, and if success is measured in terms of achieving the standard of the average student before passing to the next grade, then it is a matter of simple arithmetic to conclude that 50 per cent of the children will fail. Since deprived children are obviously bunched on the lower end of such an achievement curve, they are virtually doomed to failure before they start. It is difficult to see why schools persist in imposing the age-grade system of organization on *any* children in view of the ample evidence of individual differences, but it is even more difficult to rationalize this system when dealing with the deprived. Educational decisions based upon scientific evidence as well as value commitments to democracy and fair play should long ago have eliminated this organizational scheme.[32]

Finally, many of the problems of the deprived are beyond the present competence of practicing teachers and administrators. It has been known for many years that present teacher-education programs fail to provide teachers with adequate knowledge of children of lower socioeconomic status, children of distinct ethnic minorities whose languages and cultures are specifically different, and children with significant educational problems. Teacher-education programs have traditionally focused upon teaching the normal, "average" child a body of knowledge deemed significant by middle-class, ethnically unidentifiable patrons. Such preparation has achieved a significant measure of success. But when dealing with the special problems of the deprived, a teacher needs additional help and training. She must understand, and be able to work with, children whose behavior and past experiences are sometimes drastically different from her own values and experiences. Such teachers need specific technical knowledge, skills, and attitudes in order to deal effectively with non-English-speaking children, migrant children, children with deviant behavior resulting from deprivation, and a host of other special cases. Additional work in anthropology, sociology, psychology, and applied linguistics are all pertinent to teacher training. First-hand experience with related community

[32] For a thorough discussion of this problem, see John Goodlad and Robert Anderson, *The Non-Graded Elementary School,* rev. ed. (New York: Harcourt, Brace and World, 1963).

agencies and some knowledge of research tools and experimental procedures would also be prerequisite.

The slogan "Anyone can teach in a middle-class school, but it takes real skill to teach deprived children," while it must not be taken literally, may offer a challenge that will attract that special kind of teacher who possesses both the skills and the commitment to do an effective job with these children. Neither the bureaucratic structure nor the inadequacies of administrators should impair the effectiveness of such a teacher.

Public schools have a social responsibility to provide appropriate educational equality for all American children. Many American educators have already accepted this charge as their ethical responsibility, and have made appropriate decisions to implement this accepted responsibility. Such a commitment is, perhaps, a way to recapture, in Max Lerner's words, the spirit of the authentic American revolution, our most prized possession.

SUMMARY

Many American children are deprived of access to equal opportunity to develop their unequal abilities to the full. Particularly, they are deprived of access to equally good and enduring education, the primary route to full opportunity. Such children are said to have come from a culture of deprivation. The manifestations of such deprivation are varied and complex, as are its causes.

Factors such as segregation, economic disadvantage, language and bicultural barriers, religious differences, and geographic isolation are significant causes of deprivation. Certain school practices and procedures also contribute to the perpetuation of deprivation.

Educators on all levels face a major challenge to their professional competence and commitment when they confront deprived children. This is but one vital aspect of the pressure of major social change which seeks to realize the spirit of the American democratic experiment.

SELECTED BIBLIOGRAPHY

Conant, J. B. *Slums and Suburbs.* New York: McGraw-Hill, 1959.

Davis, Allison. *Social Class Influences upon Learning.* Cambridge, Mass.: Harvard University Press, 1948.

Harrington, Michael. *The Other America.* New York: The Macmillan Co., 1963.

Klopf, G. J., and I. A. Laster, eds. *Integrating the Urban School.* New York: Bureau of Publications, Teachers College, Columbia University, 1963.

Passo, A. H., ed. *Education in Depressed Areas.* New York: Bureau of Publications, Teachers College, Columbia University, 1963.

The Puerto Rican Study, 1953–57. New York: Board of Education of New York City, 1958.

Reissman, Frank. *The Culturally Deprived Child.* New York: Harper & Brothers, 1961.

Sexton, P. C. *Education and Income.* New York: Viking Press, 1961.

Spindler, George D., ed. *Education and Culture.* New York: Holt, Rinehart and Winston, 1963.

Tireman, L. S. *Teaching Spanish-Speaking Children.* Albuquerque, New Mexico: University of New Mexico Press, 1951.

Warner, W. L., R. J. Havighurst, and M. B. Loeb, *Who Shall Be Educated?* New York: Harper & Brothers, 1944.

CHAPTER 10

EDUCATION AND THE GIFTED CHILD

In the sixth decade of the twentieth century, when two educators meet in an informal setting, the conversation soon turns to education of the gifted child. Every school and every school district has its own "solution" to the development of talent. At times these are merely new words to describe old programs; at times they are expedient arrangements to placate some powerful voice in the community; and occasionally they represent serious efforts based on careful study of past efforts and current possibilities.

CURRENT CONCERN FOR THE GIFTED STUDENT

To have a significant future, a professional activity must draw upon the past. Activity which is ahistorical is doomed to repeat the mistakes of the past. Key figures in history realized this continuity of human endeavor as they tended to minimize their own accomplishments by saying, in effect, that "I could reach high, for I stood on the shoulders of giants who preceded me." New activities and developments in the field of formal education tend to ignore or minimize the lessons of history. Time and again an idea is heralded as a new and bold innovation which should be adopted, or at least tried out, by anyone who is "modern" and in tune with the "trend" of the times. Many, if not most, of these "innovations" have been tried out as bold new ideas more than once. More careful use of history would save repeating past errors and would also make it possible for educators to "stand on the shoulders of giants." (Perhaps less confusion would occur if history were taught as a rich resource for dealing with present problems rather than as "history for the sake of history.")

The current concern for doing something *special* for gifted students exhibits this ahistorical quality. Most educators, as well as school boards, make their decisions without careful scrutiny of the past and proceed to modify their local programs periodically on a trial-and-error-basis. Yet for centuries man has attempted to specify what constitutes appropriate educational diet for the most able students. In the Western tradition, one of the earliest writers on the subject was Plato; on the early American scene, the writings of Jefferson are relevant to this topic.

In his most famous work, *The Republic,* Plato urged a long period of special education for the ablest, who would eventually become the philosopher-kings and manage the affairs of the state. Plato suggested a careful screening of all children at an early age, so that talent would be developed wherever it might be found. Somewhat similar ideas were expressed by Thomas Jefferson in his effort to develop the educational system of his home state, Virginia. Writing to John Adams in 1813, he described his efforts to revamp the laws of Virginia:

> These laws, drawn by myself, laid the axe to the root of pseudo-aristocracy. And had another, which I proposed, been adopted by the legislature, our work would have been complete. It was a bill for the more general diffusion of learning. This proposed to divide every county into wards of five or six miles square, like your townships, to establish in each ward a free school for reading, writing and common arithmetic, to provide for the annual selection of the best subjects (that is, pupils) from these schools, who might receive at the public expense a higher degree of education at a district school and from these district schools to select a certain number of the most promising subjects, to be completed at a university where all the useful sciences should be taught. Worth and genius would thus have been sought out from every condition of life, and completely prepared by education for defeating the competition of wealth and birth for public trusts.[1]

The twin concerns of Jefferson, "the more general diffusion of learning" and the special education of students of "worth and genius" are the two over-all objectives of American public education. History provides ample evidence that since the time of Plato, human interest in the education of the most able has always been with us. As with other interests and movements in history, the intensity of the concern varied from high to low as other movements competed for the center of the stage.[2]

[1] Quoted in Roy J. Honeywell, *The Educational Work of Thomas Jefferson* (Cambridge, Mass.: Harvard University Press, 1931), pp. 8–9. With permission.

[2] For a brief but sound sketch of historic developments, see Abraham J. Tannenbaum, "History of Interest in the Gifted," in Nelson Henry, ed. *Education for the Gifted.* Fifty-seventh Yearbook of the National Society for the Study of Education, Part III (Chicago: University of Chicago Press, 1958).

This chapter highlights some of the important problems that educators must consider in making decisions about programs for gifted children. Although many important contributions in this area can be gleaned from psychology and from the systematic study of curriculum and methodology,[3] the scope of our work does not include these areas of professional knowledge. Instead, we focus briefly upon the important social and philosophic considerations that must enter the decision-making process—since psychological, curricular, and methodological considerations take on meaning only when viewed from historical, social, and philosophic perspectives.

REASONS FOR CURRENT CONCERN

TECHNOLOGICAL CHANGE AND INTERNATIONAL COMPETITION. Rapid progress in science, technology, and related fields has produced a general shortage of bright and well-educated candidates to fill the growing needs of our expanding economy. Coupled with this, we find the pressures generated by international competition. The race for the exploration of outer space, for instance, requires more than money; it requires large numbers of intelligent and highly trained personnel.

Many of the developing nations of the world, in their desire to achieve economic well-being, are determined to industrialize. They can industrialize most rapidly by borrowing men, equipment, and know-how from technologically advanced societies. Democratic and totalitarian nations find themselves competing for the sympathy and support of these preindustrial countries. In this process, thousands of able and highly trained workers in all fields of specialization are "loaned" to developing countries. This practice has increased the pressures for the thorough education of our ablest students.

When we behold the current rate of change and make educational decisions in light of them, it is well to recall Snow's warning:

> The rate of change has increased so much that imagination can't keep up. There is bound to be more social change, affecting more people, in the next decade than in any before. There is bound to be more change again, in the 1970's.[4]

The schools, as "residual legatees" of American society, inherit all those tasks which are not specifically bestowed upon other agencies. When

[3] See, for instance, Louis A. Fliegler, *Curriculum Planning for the Gifted* (Englewood Cliffs, N.J.: Prentice-Hall, Inc., 1961).

[4] Charles P. Snow, *The Two Cultures and the Scientific Revolution* (Cambridge, England: Cambridge University Press, 1959), p. 40.

the Soviet Union orbited Sputnik I, a general cultural hysteria focused upon the schools. The proponents of a "get tough with the kids" policy never stopped to consider that merely getting tough is not sufficient. Nor did they consider the fact that:

> The Soviet scientists who have succeeded in placing a satellite in an orbit are in few cases products of the Soviet school system now operating. Many of them, in fact, received their education elsewhere than in the Soviet Union.
>
> Citizens ought not to overestimate the speed with which an educational program, even at the college and university level, will change scientific or intellectual achievement. Education is a long-term investment, the profits of which are many years in the making."[5]

The urgency to improve programs for the gifted, evidenced during the past decade, resulted primarily from the twin forces of international competition and the spiraling demands of a scientific-technological society.[6]

INSISTENCE OF EDUCATORS. Another force, not as powerful as technological change and international competition, but more consistent and systematic, has been the professional educators' steady request for curriculum revision. These educators, who have time and again urged special and qualitatively different education for the gifted, have received strong support from psychological research. It has taken much effort to dispel popular antagonism toward the highly able. The historic belief that only a thin line separates genius from madness, or that nature balances one's high abilities with insanity or immorality, gave way but slowly to twentieth-century empirical findings. The works of Terman[7] and his collaborators stand unimpeached in their conclusion that individuals in the top 1 per cent mental-ability range also possess superior physical, social, moral, and emotional traits.

It is easy merely to urge curriculum revision, to call for the development of talented youth and to warn against the "wastage of the gifted," but difficult to launch constructive programs. Once educators understand

[5] Educational Policies Commission, *The Contemporary Challenge to American Education* (Washington, D.C.: National Education Association, 1958), pp. 20–21.

[6] This trend is reflected in titles of books; note, for example, one by Burton R. Clark: *Educating the Expert Society* (San Francisco: Chandler Publishing Company, 1962).

[7] Lewis M. Terman, *Genetic Studies of Genius,* Vol. II (Stanford, Calif.: Stanford University Press, 1926).

the reasons for the current concerns, they must pause long enough to clarify the problem before tentative solutions might be tendered for consideration. The initial question which inevitably arises is: "Who are the gifted?"

DEFINITIONS OF "GIFTED"

The meaning of "gifted" is not a simple matter of semantics, to be eliminated by a stipulated definition. Alternative definitions of "giftedness" point to different consequences. The way we define the term carries with it certain implicit assumptions about values; that we value certain abilities over and above others. We shall look at some of these value positions in the following section of this chapter. At this point let us indicate simply that the many discussions concerning the meaning of "giftedness" are summarized by two positions.

The earlier position is expressed in Lewis M. Terman's monumental *Genetic Studies of Genius*. Terman considered the term "gifted" to designate persons of school age who fall within the top 1 per cent of general intellectual ability, as measured by the Stanford-Binet Intelligence Scale or comparable instrument.[8] This position is supported by some current writers.[9] The broader definition, one that is more generally found in our schools, is expressed by Paul Witty: "That our definition of giftedness be expanded and that we consider any child gifted whose performance, in a potentially valuable line of human activity, is consistently remarkable."[10]

The Educational Policies Commission uses the IQ measure as the central criterion and proposes to differentiate between the highly gifted and the moderately gifted students. The Commission writes:

> In this statement, the term "highly gifted" is used to designate those who are in the top one per cent of the total population with respect to intellectual capacity (that is, roughly, individuals with an I.Q. above 137). Similarly, the term "moderately gifted" will apply to individuals

[8] Lewis M. Terman et al., *Mental and Physical Traits of a Thousand Gifted Children* (Stanford, Calif.: Stanford University Press, 1926), p. 43.

[9] See, for example, Virgil S. Ward, *Educating the Gifted: An Axiomatic Approach* (Columbus, Ohio: Charles E. Merrill Books, Inc., 1961).

[10] Paul Witty, "Who Are the Gifted?" in Nelson B. Henry, ed., *Education for the Gifted.* Fifty-seventh Yearbook of the National Society for the Study of Education, Part II (Chicago: University of Chicago Press, 1958), p. 62.

> who fall within the top ten per cent below the top one per cent (that is, between 120 and 137 I.Q.).[11]

A similar distinction is implied in the work of James B. Conant, who reserves the term "gifted" for the top 2 or 3 per cent of the general population, while referring to the top 15 to 20 per cent as "academically talented."[12]

It is not necessary for the purposes of our chapter to choose among these alternative conceptions of giftedness. However, before any group of decision makers can proceed intelligently with educational decisions, they must reach agreement about the meaning they will attach to the term. This is the analytic, philosophic phase of decision making—a phase that is too often inadequately treated.

The probable consequences of alternative definitions of giftedness need to be explored at this stage of the process. There is an ever increasing body of research available that should be brought to bear on this task. To paraphrase Terman and Oden, we now have the basic facts that provide a necessary prologue to further advances in the education of the gifted.

While sound evidence is removing the mystery and superstition surrounding the physical and mental characteristics of gifted children, our value conflicts on the subject remain. As noted in chapter 1 of our book, scientific findings may be necessary but insufficient for decision making. This is certainly the case with the education of the gifted. We may know the objective characteristics of gifted children (what they *are capable of* doing) and still not know what they *should* do, what they *should* become, and what their role in society should be. We shall explore the major value problems in the pages that follow.

VALUE PROBLEMS IN CONSTRUCTING PROGRAMS FOR THE GIFTED

The value problem that first comes to the surface in any discussion of giftedness is implicit in the definition. If one chooses Terman's conception and attaches the label "gifted" to the intellectually superior, top 1 per cent of the student group, one is bound to infer that nonintellectual

[11] Educational Policies Commission, *Education of the Gifted* (Washington, D.C.: National Education Association, 1950), p. 43.

[12] National Education Association, *The Identification and Education of the Academically Talented Student in the American Secondary School* (Washington, D.C.: National Education Association, 1958), p. 16.

abilities are less valuable. This conflict of values can be avoided by use of Witty's more general formulation. It is sufficiently broad to include in giftedness both high academic potential and talent in the arts (painting, sculpture, music, dance, dramatics, creative writing, poetry), athletics, and even social competence.

Proponents of the Terman definition tend to assert that the American schools have historically provided for those who have special talent in music and athletics. Evidence for this claim is offered by statistics about athletic facilities, interscholastic athletics, and school bands. While this might be the case, it does not justify the exclusion of art, dramatics, other types of music or other activities listed above. At this point in the discussion of programs for the gifted, the question of the budget generally enters. In effect, the argument usually is that there is not enough money in the school budget to make provisions for those with high ability in all these areas. Consequently, it is urged that special treatment be reserved for the students with the highest IQ for "they will be the leaders of tomorrow." In effect, this is asserting a specific value position, for tomorrow there will be "leaders" in all of these activities; the question still remains unresolved as to which one, or ones, the public should support.

A similar conflict arises over the question of appropriate class sizes, or the so-called ratio of students to teachers. Many communities maintain that the public should support an 18 to 1 students-teacher ratio for the gifted against one of 35 to 1 for the "average" students. Interestingly enough, most teachers would agree that the 18 to 1 ratio would also be an excellent one for the average student. But, since the budget cannot bear such a ratio, and since there are not enough qualified teachers to meet these demands, the optimal ratio is reserved for the gifted. This arrangement is justified by the claim that society will benefit in the long run, for these are the people who will occupy leadership positions and will use their abilities for the good of society. The Terman studies are generally cited to bolster this position. Ward, for example, after citing key passages from Terman and Oden's *The Gifted Child Grows Up,* enthusiastically states:

> When the magnitude of such contributions is considered, and it is recalled that the contributors are among only one thousand of the intellectually superior persons as identified at ten and eleven years of age, of one state in the United States, the question of devising an educational scheme commensurate in design with the extreme capacities thus represented must be accepted as of tremendous social consequence.[13]

[13] Virgil S. Ward, *Educating the Gifted: An Axiomatic Approach* (Columbus, Ohio: Charles E. Merrill Books, Inc., 1961), p. 21.

The parents of the child with an "average" IQ, however, cannot help but wonder about the educational consequences for their child if he were exposed to an 18 to 1 student-teacher ratio year after year. These parents are concerned with the benefits that would accrue to their child, and to society, from such an arrangement. It is relevant to mention here that in a great many school districts such ratios, and better, have been provided for the education of the blind, the deaf, the mentally retarded, as well as for others with special needs. The proponents of special programs for the gifted urge that all of the arguments in favor of better student-teacher ratios for the handicapped apply perforce to the gifted. It is our contention that these debates cannot be settled rationally in the absence of further empirical studies. Although we now have a significant body of information on the characteristics of gifted children, we lack equally valid and reliable knowledge on the pedagogic aspects of the problem.

As we noted in our first chapter, many value problems can be treated with more light and less heat if relevant evidence is available. For example, educators should have factual information on whether class size makes a more significant difference when teaching children with IQ's ranging from 125 to 135 than when teaching the 115 to 125 group. How about the 165 to 175 group? Might a well-stocked library and occasional lectures by experts in the community do equally well for the top 1 per cent, once they have mastered the basic skills needed for independent work? Or at least for part of their curriculum? How can team teaching assist us in varying the instruction given to large and small groups? What would happen to social learning under these circumstances? Do we care? Would the consequences be the same in programs which separate the gifted from their age mates? These and many other problems need to be investigated before we can speak with authority about educational programs for the gifted.

Similar value problems arise in issues concerning better equipment for the gifted, better-qualified teachers, more time off for teachers to prepare their lessons, and a host of related matters.

Without doubt, a significant body of research literature is available concerning the education of the gifted. It is no longer defensible to avoid all action, or special programs for the gifted, under the guise that not enough is known about them. As Newland boldly writes:

> . . . the results of the largest single study of any type of exceptional children have been available for use in the identification of the gifted, in

> delineating quite objectively their needs, and in suggesting kinds of educational adjustment for them (Terman et al., 1925; Terman et al., 1947). The largest single follow-up study of any kind of exceptional children was done on bright children admitted prior to the conventional school-entering age, restudied in high school, and further studied at college entrance (Hobson, 1948). Major studies of the Cleveland major work class program have been made (Sumption, 1941), and a ten-year follow-up study has been made of a single special school program for the gifted (Hildreth, 1952). Major objective evaluations of educational and social outcomes of college acceleration programs have been studied for seven years (Pressey, 1949). Three systematic statewide studies of educational mortality among high school potential college material were made nearly 20 years ago. . . . Surely the extent and the nature of the need for some special provisions for the gifted, and information on the various possible provisions for the gifted are "on the record" for him who would but read.[14]

While Newland is quite right in his assertion, it is still correct to call attention to the need for research on the value problems raised by class sizes, special equipment, special arrangements for teachers, and the practice of separating the gifted students from others.

DEMOCRACY, NATIONAL GOALS, AND GIFTED STUDENTS

More serious value problems arise when we consider the over-all purposes of educating all of our youth. Assuming that the problems involved in the definition and identification of giftedness are satisfactorily resolved, we are still faced with the further problem of how to deal with this group of students. For what purposes do we educate our most able youth? Are the goals of their education the same as for the nongifted? Is society exploiting the gifted student? If curricular goals for the gifted did not differ significantly from goals for the "average" student, would we have reason for our current concern? Would there be any need for books on a curriculum for the gifted? The answer, then, must be that the objectives, the goals of education for the gifted and the nongifted, differ. This is the conclusion offered by Lucito, among others. He bases his position on the belief that the gifted will play certain unique roles in society, which he describes as follows:

[14] T. E. Newland, "Something Can Be Done for the Gifted," *Cook County Education Digest,* 20 (1957), 3–4.

> First, the gifted can be expected to be the major contributors to knowledge by offering innovations, evaluating them, and solving complex problems. Second, they can be expected to be the major participants in complex, practical decision-making.[15]

The difficulties implicit in this justification of special programs become apparent when one considers the relationship between giftedness and creativity. While it is clear from the Terman studies that a high proportion of the gifted become innovators, research workers, and leaders in various social roles, it is also quite evident that there is no direct correlation between high intelligence and creativity. The works of Getzels and Jackson[16] on one hand and Torrance[17] on the other, indicate that there are students of high IQ with low creative potential and students with IQ scores below the gifted range who are highly creative. Lucito, while recognizing this fact,[18] does not take sufficient account of it in his curricular suggestions.

However, Lucito is not alone in attempting to justify curricular planning for the gifted by reference to their future roles in society. Indeed, this is the rationale offered by writers in general. The lay public, including government officials, business leaders, the military, as well as the spokesmen for industry, all tend to refer to the needs of the nation, the needs of society, "the needs of tomorrow," or the personnel needed to carry out our national goals. As Vice Admiral Hyman G. Rickover phrases it: "The issue really is, are we doing all we should to provide the people for the kind of society we will have in the next decade?"[19] The value problem implicit in all of these expressions is seldom made clear. Implicit in all these statements is the assumption that gifted children should be educated in order to serve the needs of society. There are those who would push this still further and would consciously use gifted individuals as means to advance societal goals.

It is tempting in times of international tension, competition, and insecurity to become rather careless with the rights of individuals. Talented students can be forced, persuaded, or seduced through special incentives

[15] Leonard J. Lucito, "Gifted Children," in Lloyd M. Dunn, ed., *Exceptional Children in the Schools* (New York: Holt, Rinehart and Winston, Inc., 1963), p. 206.

[16] J. W. Getzels and P. W. Jackson, *Creativity and Intelligence* (New York: Wiley, 1962).

[17] E. P. Torrance, *Guiding Creative Talent* (Englewood Cliffs, N.J.: Prentice-Hall, 1962).

[18] Lucito (see note 15), p. 185.

[19] Quoted in the *Los Angeles Times,* Monday, April 22, 1963, Part I, p. 20.

to specialize in occupations most needed by the nation. This is a generally accepted policy in the Soviet Union and her satellite nations. As we saw from the analysis of social ideologies in Chapter 5, both Fascist and Communist states manage the lives of their inhabitants as dictated by the needs of the nation. By contrast, a society which is attempting to move closer and closer to the democratic ideal is supposed to be careful in defining the desired relationship between the individual and society. Some of our authors who write about the gifted, unlike the laymen who speak on the topic, seem to realize the complexity of the problem and tend to speak with caution. The usual pronouncement is to the effect that the best education for the gifted will result in the most benefit to society. When formulated this way, the emphasis is appropriately on the individual. In practice, however, the emphasis is somehow reversed. When society has certain needs, whether for scientists, mathematicians, language specialists, or pilots, powerful incentives appear that attract the gifted as a huge magnet attracts metal filings.

This value problem is illustrated in the case of Allan, a high school student in one of our metropolitan centers. Allan is a very bright fourteen-year-old boy. His father is a moderately successful physician, his mother a college-educated housewife active on behalf of various civic and charitable causes. Allan has been interested in most subjects in school and done excellent work in all of them. His specific interests and talents have polarized on creative writing—particularly poetry, and mathematics. He has exhausted his school's offerings in both of these areas and spends his leisure hours writing poetry or on independent exploration of higher mathematics. It is true that with his school record and his general abilities, Allan would have access to many institutions of higher learning and to many scholarships. He would, however, face many more temptations of substantial support and better scholarships in both public and private institutions if he pursued his talents in mathematics rather than in poetry. "In midcentury America the nation needs top talent in the sciences and mathematics in order to keep ahead of Russia and to keep up with the needs of science and technology," so the argument goes.

While this line of reasoning cannot be readily dismissed (because we do have to consider the very real needs of the nation), we must also guard the individual. He must not become a mere cog in the giant societal machine. The trend of the 1950s lost sight of this, and the various scholarship programs of the federal government as well as of business and industry were designed almost exclusively in terms of a narrow conception of the "manpower needs" of the nation. The decade of the 1960s has slowed down this trend, and some broadening has occurred in the various programs which support the higher education of able youth.

In a democracy, the relationship of the individual to society is very complex. The individual is not merely a means for social ends; nor is he always the end, independent of the needs of others. The gifted student must not become a tool to be used by society; yet he is part of society and his talents and abilities do further social goals. In the complex, interactive process in which both the individual and society are involved, both are shaped by the process and in turn alter it. There is a constant and continuing need to re-examine this relationship in order to avoid the excesses of the totalitarian state on the one hand or the damage that occurs from uncontrolled rugged individualism on the other.[20]

Application of the ideas of Plato on education of the gifted to the American culture leads to another value conflict. It is quite clear that if we are concerned with individuals, if we wish to respect them, we should try to prevent the fantastic waste of talent that is going on all around us. For years now, repeated studies have shown that many of our brightest students drop out before high school graduation. Of the top 30 per cent of high school students, only about 60 per cent enter college; and of these, only about 40 per cent earn a bachelor's degree.[21] We have to face the question of how to encourage all people to develop the ability they have.

Historically, Americans have rejected Plato's solution of carefully selecting the top few and giving them advanced education in order to become the rulers of the state. We have even rejected the ideas of Jefferson, who recommended a periodic siphoning off of the top 10 per cent for increasingly advanced education. Americans have looked with disfavor and suspicion at various European patterns of education, which tended to promote elite-mass separation. The cultural value of equality has played an important role in the development of our public schools, which were to ensure that people learned to respect and value each other regardless of their parents' status and accidents of birth. The cultural drive for equality has led many parents to insist that their children were "just average kinds" though, in fact, the children were highly gifted.

[20] For a powerful novel depicting a complex interplay of these forces competing for one brilliant child, see John Hersey, *The Child Buyer* (New York: Alfred A. Knopf, 1960).

[21] D. Wolfe, "Diversity of Talent," *American Psychologist*, 15 (1960), 535–545.

Only in recent years has there emerged popular recognition that what our Founding Fathers were concerned with was legal equality, not identity of talent. In the field of education, as in other fields, there is a gradual abandoning of the notion that equal treatment means identical treatment. Instead, equal treatment is now taken to mean equitable treatment, or, as Coombs and Komisar[22] phrased it, fitting treatment. It is quite clear that a school program which is equitable for a normal child will not be equitable or fitting for one who is blind, or deaf. Would not the same reasoning hold for the mentally retarded child and perforce for the gifted? The logic of this argument is generally admitted. This does not, however, alleviate our fear of a ruling elite, the fear that an all-powerful intellectual elite might arise that would have the power to rule and make decisions, while being out of contact with the bulk of the population on whose behalf they are making decisions.

This fear has been expressed time and again by educators and others. James B. Conant, an influential writer on education, has analyzed the grounds upon which these fears are based.[23] Because he shares this concern, and because he is committed to the democratic ideology, Conant supports a system of schooling which attempts to provide equitable educational treatment yet avoids the rise of an elite, out of touch with the common man. He recommends that we continue the comprehensive high school, an American contribution to educational thought, wherein students from various backgrounds follow curricula that match their individual abilities and goals. It is of interest that England is beginning to move in the direction of the comprehensive high school, and that other countries are exploring its possibilities.[24]

To what extent, then, is it possible to provide a fitting education for the gifted in a democratic society? Is it possible to accomplish this without creating a social distance that sets them apart and alienates them from society? Is not the problem of a fitting, or equitable, education for the gifted really but one aspect of the more general problem—that of providing an excellent and equitable treatment for all of our students? Theoretically,

[22] Jerrold R. Coombs and B. Paul Komisar, "The Equality Principle in Education," *Proceedings of the 19th Annual Meeting of the Philosophy of Education Society,* 1963, pp. 112–120.

[23] James B. Conant, *Education and Liberty* (New York: Vintage Books, Caravelle Edition, 1953).

[24] This is a fascinating phenomenon, occurring as it does at a time when American educators are studying European schools in order to improve our own.

we strive for the best education for each student. As a matter of practical fact, however, we have shortchanged gifted children in some of our schools and have let them flourish at the expense of the less gifted in other schools. We cannot balance out human suffering or waste of talent by pointing to different schools or communities which have favored one group or another. Our educational decisions must be such as to provide fitting opportunities for children of varied talents to develop whatever abilities they have. This conclusion is often derided as sentimental or romantic, but the writers submit that it is practical, it is possible, and it is the only one consistent with the ideals of democracy.

SUMMARY

In this chapter we briefly analyzed the current concern for the gifted student; some of the difficult value questions which surround the education of the gifted; and the relevance of democratic ideals to schooling our ablest youth. It was indicated that the current high level of interest in the gifted student has been brought about by the expanding needs of a scientific, technological civilization; by the international competition in space and for the support of the developing nations, and by the persistent work of professional educators. Some of the value problems in this area have resulted from prejudice and ignorance, some from the shortage of funds and qualified personnel, and some from serious fears concerning democratic ideals.

It was concluded that the gifted child, as other children, must be provided educational opportunities befitting his abilities and his interests, and that he should not be made merely an instrument for societal needs. Educational decisions must not be made in favor of one group of children at the expense of others. At our advanced stage of cultural development, we should be ready to meet our democratic ideal: an excellent education for children of all abilities.

SELECTED BIBLIOGRAPHY

California State Department of Education. *Educational Programs for Gifted Pupils.* Sacramento, Calif.: California State Department of Education, 1961.

Educational Policies Commission. *Education of the Gifted.* Washington, D.C.: National Education Association, 1950.

Fliegler, Louis A. *Curriculum Planning for the Gifted.* Englewood Cliffs, N.J.: Prentice-Hall, Inc., 1961.

Freehill, M. F. *Gifted Children.* New York: MacMillan, 1961.

Getzels, J. W., and P. W. Jackson. *Creativity and Intelligence—Explorations with Gifted Students.* New York: John Wiley & Sons, 1962.

Gowan, J. C. *An Annotated Bibliography on the Academically Talented Student.* Washington, D.C.: National Education Association, 1961.

———, and George D. Demos. *The Education and Guidance of the Ablest.* Springfield, Ill.: C. C. Thomas Co., 1964.

Henry, Nelson B., ed. *Education for the Gifted.* Fifty-seventh Yearbook of the National Society for the Study of Education, Part II. Chicago: University of Chicago Press, 1958.

Passow, A. Harry, et al. *Planning for Talented Youth: Considerations for Public Schools.* New York: Bureau of Publications, Teachers College, Columbia University, 1955.

Terman, L. M., et al. *Genetic Studies of Genius.* Stanford, Calif.: Stanford University Press, 1925–59. 5 vols.

Torrance, E. P. *Guiding Creative Talent.* Englewood Cliffs, N.J.: Prentice-Hall, 1962.

Ward, Virgil S. *Educating the Gifted: An Axiomatic Approach.* Columbus, Ohio: Charles E. Merrill Books, Inc., 1961.

CHAPTER 11

EXPANDED FEDERAL AID TO EDUCATION

An increasing population, new demands for more education for more people to meet the needs of a technological, space age, and renewed vigor in the drive for equal educational opportunity have confronted public education with a severe financial crisis. Traditional sources of the bulk of school revenues, such as the local property tax and state aid, have been both increasingly unable and reluctant to meet these rising demands. In the search for additional sources of funds it was natural for educators to focus more of their attention on the federal government, which collects the largest share of the tax dollar. Such attention is not new, nor is the federal government's participation in school financing, but it has provoked much debate—partly consistent with historical events, and partly grounded in contemporary controversies and problems.

The participation of the federal government in education is presumed by some to be barred by the apparently conscious omission of education from the Constitution. This omission is claimed to be a conscious decision, not an oversight, because many of the authors of the Constitution were men of abounding faith in education and, like Thomas Jefferson, considered it prerequisite to the successful functioning of a democracy. Further, the Congress *did* pass the Survey Ordinance of 1785, just nine years after the Declaration of Independence, in which all public lands west of the original thirteen colonies were to assign one lot in every township for schools. It is not difficult to see why the Constitution had to leave education as primarily a state function in the Constitution, if one considers the diverse interests and philosophies of the original states (newly emerged from a background of established religions that had dominated education) and the general weakness of the central government. The universalization of education, which came with rapid mass transportation and communication and other technical and social changes, was not foreseen in colonial times.

The federal government, however, has always had an influence on education. In the mid-nineteenth century, when Horace Mann and Henry Barnard were campaigning at both the state and the national level for a comprehensive public, tax-supported, school system, Congress stepped in and, with the Morrell Act of 1862, set aside public land in every state for at least one college. Such colleges are now referred to as the "land-grant" colleges, and each wears this appellation with pride and a sense of tradition. This congressional action came ten years before the celebrated Kalamazoo Case of 1872, which was considered to be the crucial victory for free, tax-supported public elementary and secondary schools.

Nevertheless, local control and support of public education grew as the basic tradition in American education. Individual states made their decisions on such matters as the curriculum, tax support, and teacher standards independently of one another and of the federal government. Such decisions usually reflected the needs of the particular state, its economic resources, and the degree and kind of its commitment to education, as well as to particular forms of schooling. Rural states naturally created systems that differed sharply from those of the predominantly urban seaboard states. Rural states similarly conceived of education's purposes and programs in distinctly different ways than urban, industrial states. For the most part, however, the financial support of public schools assumed a common pattern. School revenues were based primarily on taxes levied on real property; thus, a school district's wealth was dependent upon the real estate values within its borders. Since there were, and still are, significant differences in such property values from one area to another, there developed significant differences in the abilities of local communities to support their schools.

STATE-AID PROGRAMS

The citizens of several states who were concerned about the varying quality of public education due to the differences in ability to finance schools, soon hit upon a type of tax program that seemed to solve part of the problem. The state government would collect taxes from a variety of sources according to their ability to pay, and then give individual school districts a direct and equal subsidy. Such equalization programs operated on the theory that rich districts needed to help poor districts, if the entire state's educational program was to flourish. The equalization programs specifically outlawed the possibility of any individual school district cutting local taxes to the point where it would live solely off state aid. All districts had to make a sincere effort to support their schools locally, via the property tax, to the best of their ability.

Some states found that important activities they wished their schools to engage in sometimes were beyond the capacity of a local district to finance—even with state-equalization aid. Special programs for special children, training requiring special equipment, programs needing uniformity throughout the state—all challenged the state's role. Local districts demanded help, and state legislatures quickly authorized the state education departments to finance and participate in these special programs. But again, the ability to engage in any educational activity depended upon the willingness and the economic resources of the local communities. In many cases, their willingness outstripped their economic resources, so that concerned educators and lay citizens had to cast about for new sources of revenue.

THE GROWING NEED FOR FEDERAL FINANCING

The Smith-Hughes Act of 1917 responded to the problem of financing vocational training, which had been too expensive an activity for some states and communities to provide. Here the federal government intervened financially to achieve a goal local and state resources could not achieve on their own. Because it dealt with such a specific kind of education intended to achieve such specific objectives, the Congress included many control features: standards for the program, eligibility, disbursement procedures, etc. At the time, such controls were conceived of as logical safeguards against irresponsible or fraudulent use of such funds.

After World War II, the federal government again became active in education with the massive scholarship program for veterans dubbed the "G.I. Bill of Rights." The G.I. bill money pumped millions of needed dollars into the treasuries of colleges, universities, and trade schools. Few controls were attached to these scholarship funds, and the fees the various institutions charged were rarely challenged. Cases of fraudulent claims by both veterans and "schools" they attended were, on the whole, few.

This lack of control was also a feature of another federal activity soon to be legislated by Congress. Many school districts found themselves adjacent to federal installations such as army camps or tax-exempt defense plants. Personnel attached to such installations resided in the district and sent their children to local schools, but the number of children often far exceeded the district's tax base to provide for them. Congress, therefore, sought to relieve such instances of financial strain by granting federal aid funds "in lieu" of the local taxes that would have supported a particular school program if federal installations were taxable. School districts that qualified—i.e., those having a certain percentage of the enrolled children who were the progeny of federal employees—simply had to take a federal employee census and then submit the number of children of such employees to the federal government in order to get per capita cash payments. This "federal impact" program has continued; many local school districts are still dependent upon it.

The federal government also participates in public education through the provisions of the National Defense Education Act of 1958. This Act provided more than a billion dollars primarily to aid students through scholarships and to aid schools and colleges that create certain special programs or engage in certain kinds of research. The control features, such as the oath required of recipients of any of the funds, created some heated opposition, but most educational institutions and school systems overlooked the inconvenience of the controls in order to benefit from the funds, which in many cases were desperately needed or desired in order to increase the competence and service of the schools. Special activities supported by the U.S. Office of Education and the National Science Foundation are other examples of current indirect Federal participation in school finance.

GENERAL FEDERAL AID

As school populations skyrocketed in the post–World War II world, and as other new demands were made on the schools, the pressure on local financing of schools became increasingly intolerable. Local tax sources, primarily the property owners, found their tax bills mounting at alarming rates. More and more governmental services were demanded—increased old-age benefits, unemployment insurance, and other social-welfare benefits, and the property owner found himself always high on the list of resources. State governments, too, found that school-support programs were increasingly difficult to manage, and the discrepancies between states began to be noticed as the population became increasingly mobile. Since the federal government was collecting about three-fourths of every tax dollar, it seemed once more appropriate to seek relief from the source that appeared to have the most funds. Blanket federal-aid-to-education bills began to appear in the hoppers of the Congress. Most of these bills attempted to establish the principle of equalization among school districts. Control features were kept at a minimum or specifically excluded. But controversy arose on a variety of issues, and magnificent debates were held at every country crossroad as well as in the committee rooms of the Congress. Almost everyone but a small minority agreed that education needed additional funds, but there was much disagreement about who should receive the aid and whether the federal government should continue to be involved.

THE FINANCIAL NEEDS OF SCHOOLS

The needs of education in the next decade seem to be staggering by almost any estimate. The White House Conference in 1956 stated: ". . . it seems obvious that within the next decade, the dollars spent on education in this nation should be approximately doubled."[1]

A committee of sixteen prominent citizens studied the problem under the auspices of the Rockefeller Brothers Fund. The committee concluded:

> Even allowing for considerably greater efficiency in the use of educational funds, it is likely that ten years hence our schools and colleges will require at least double their present level of financial support to handle our growing student population. In other words, by 1967, the entire educational effort is likely to call for expenditures on the order of $30 billion, measured at today's prices.[2]

The Committee for Economic Development estimated that "if resources per pupil were held constant, the cost of public schools, with prices in the private economy stable, would rise 31 per cent from 1958–59 to 1964–65 (and) from 1958–59 to 1969–70 the increase would be 47 per cent."[3]

The National Education Association estimated a cost of $33.6 billion in 1969–70 as compared with $12.3 billion in 1959–60.[4] This estimate does not envision any extravagances; it merely assumes only adequate

[1] Committee for the White House Conference, *A Report to the President* (Washington, D.C.: Government Printing Office, 1956), pp. 6–7.

[2] Rockefeller Brothers Fund, *The Pursuit of Excellence* (Garden City, N.Y.: Doubleday and Company, 1958), p. 34.

[3] Committee for Economic Development, *Paying for Better Schools* (New York: The Committee, 1959), p. 20.

[4] National Education Association, *Financing the Public Schools, 1960–70* (Washington, D.C.: 1962), p. 133.

staffing and adequate salaries. It is clear that the doubling of school expenditures in a period of ten years would place severe pressure on the present tax sources used by our schools. The national economy, however, is well able to handle such a burden, and some experts see no alternative but to expend such funds if our economy is to remain healthy and growing. A technological society, it is argued, cannot long survive without increased education to provide the skills and competencies necessary for the dynamic growth of such a society.

Speaking in purely economic terms, the National Committee for Support of the Public Schools, states:

> One need not credit a high percentage of the income of our affluent society to the effects of education to rate this public service as a productive investment. The gross national product of the United States, according to the latest available estimate for the middle of 1962, had reached $552 billion. In the light of recent economic research, it would seem a low estimate to credit ten per cent of this figure, or $52 billion, to the economic effects of education. Less than one-half of this figure, or $25 billion, is being expended this year by educational institutions, from kindergarten through university, both public and private. . . . for current expenses and for school building construction and other capital outlays.[5]

The adequacy of financing of public education is not a matter of ability but rather one of choice. We have the economic resources, but some practices distort the tax picture and may make it seem that adequate resources are not available. For example, we have mentioned that the principal tax source for schools is the local property tax. But *unequal* assessments of the value of property can distribute such a tax burden in an inequitable manner. A political structure that allows excessive exemptions or write-offs, or favors one group of property owners over another, tends to defeat the long-range or broader goals of the society by distorting the *actual* tax base. Resistance to school taxes might decrease if *all* taxpayers felt that *everyone* was paying on an equitable basis. Still, for some states and for some areas within certain states, even with extensive revision of local tax laws, there would be insufficient funds to meet our educational challenge.

The broader tax base of general state revenues has been the answer for some states, as we have indicated. But "states differ markedly in tax-

[5] National Committee for Support of the Public Schools, *Changing Demands on Education and Their Fiscal Implications* (Washington, D.C., 1963), p. 93.

able capacity."[6] A range of average expenditure per pupil of from $220 per pupil to $615 per pupil testifies to such differences, and since these figures are averages, the real range is much lower and much higher in terms of some schools. Such needs and such differences imply the necessary consideration of new tax sources.

INADEQUACY OF FEDERAL PARTICIPATION

The picture presented by Figure 11–1 clearly indicates that local and state collections of taxes are far overshadowed by federal tax collections:

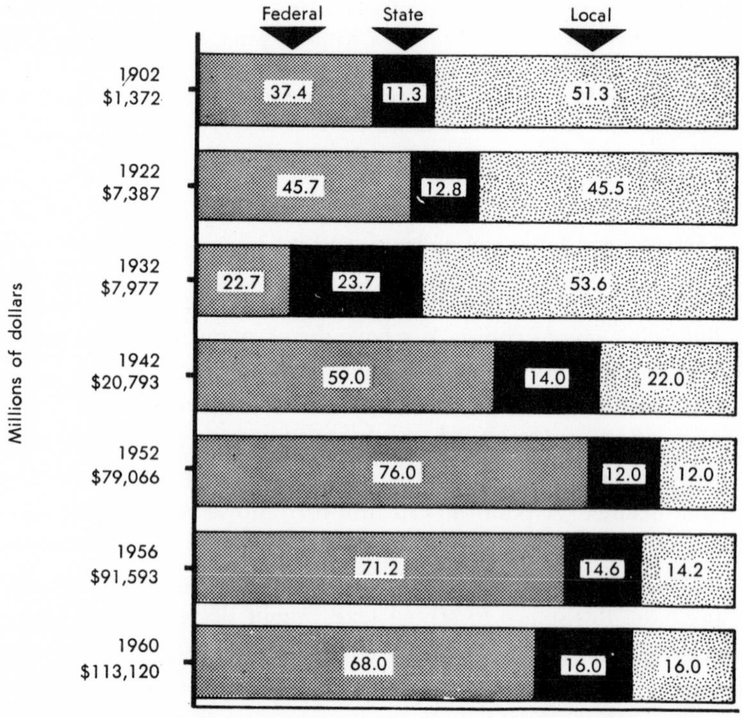

FIGURE 11–1. Total Tax Revenues and Per Cent Collected by Local, State and Federal Government, 1902–60 (as presented in *Changing Demands on Education and Their Fiscal Implications*, p. 98).

SOURCES: For tax revenue 1902–1959, United States Department of Commerce, Bureau of the Census, Washington, D.C., 1960. For tax revenue 1960, United States Department of Commerce, Bureau of the Census, 1962.

[6] National Committee, p. 97.

Of these huge percentages of federal tax collections, only 4.6 per cent of total school revenues in 1955–56 came from federal sources, and this declined to 3.7 per cent in 1961–62. Therefore, from a purely economic standpoint, the low level of federal participation in school financing demands explanation. Such demands have been made and pursued to the point that bills have been constantly introduced into the Congress to expand this limited federal participation. Thus the issue has been joined.

OPPONENTS OF FEDERAL AID

Certainly the most consistent opponents of expanded federal aid to education have been the so-called "economy-minded" group, the *economic* conservatives. Led by the United States Chamber of Commerce and certain conservative congressmen and senators, this group has opposed every federal aid bill to appear before Congress except for a brief retreat into neutrality in the spring of 1945 because of the teacher shortage that had developed in the later years of the war and the immediate postwar years. The basic position of the Chamber of Commerce has been that public education, as a state function, should be financed by state and local resources. The chamber's chief allies in the struggle against expanded federal aid have been the Southern States Industrial Council, the Investment Bankers Association, the National Association of Manufacturers, the American Farm Bureau, the National Grange, and various other business and industrial groups.

Since these groups oppose expanded federal aid for economic reasons, the nature of their objections must be ascertained. Briefly, their general position is that the federal government can ill afford to continue to expand its responsibilities and, consequently, its expenditures. The argument runs that the national debt is staggering, and that already the prior claims of national defense and other strictly federal functions are excessive and beyond the capacity of the federal government to maintain without deficit financing and a consequent growth in the debt. State governments, on the other hand, are alleged to be solvent and operating within their incomes and able to vary their methods of taxation with greater freedom than can the federal government. The balanced budget, "living within your income," and other appeals of this kind are evoked by economic conservatives.

Militant supporters of expanded federal aid to education point out, however, that the economic conservatives have a consistent record of opposing increased expenditures for education at both the *state* and *local* levels too. They argue that the "economy-minded" groups are not opposed to federal aid, but to *any* aid, since aid requires the expenditure of funds. It must be noted that these economy-minded groups often have a legitimate self-interest they feel must be served: usually, they represent the largest property owners and the largest incomes; hence, they are the largest contributors to school revenues through taxation. It has long been the practice of large tax-paying units to have their representatives elected or appointed to any and all tax-fixing bodies such as school boards and city, county, and state tax boards. The expected function of such representatives is to put a brake on taxation wherever it is deemed feasible, so that the tax-paying unit they represent will not suffer any more than necessary. Naturally, too, there are different interpretations by various groups as to what are the limits of "necessary" expenditures and, therefore, "necessary" taxes.

The economic argument ultimately rests upon an examination of the nation's capacity to support education. Per capita income in the United States ranges from $1,173 in Mississippi to $3,013 in Delaware, and this represents a percentage increase over 1950 of 26 per cent in Montana and of 68 per cent in Alabama.[7] This figure points to the reality of an expanding economy and therefore expanding income, but the differentials between low-income states and high-income states are immense. Even though studies indicate that poorer states are improving their position more rapidly than the richer ones, the range remains persistent and significant. Ultimately, the capacity to support education rests upon income levels, and income levels are becoming increasingly correlated with educational attainment levels and the economic impact of educated skills and competencies. There seems little argument in any quarter that the more highly educated a population, the more likely that its economy will grow. Thus, the argument over economy in educational expenditures appears to rest on differences of opinion on the *timing* of investment. The economic conservative is committed to the slow, pay-as-you-go-and-are-able philosophy, while others endorse a plunge-now-to-reap-greater-benefits-later position.

The second major rallying point for opponents to expanded federal aid to education is the issue of federal control. This particular issue is interlaced with so many paradoxical positions that both proponents and opponents, at times, seem to lose their grasp on the central issue itself. For example, many measures that have passed the Congress and been enacted into law provide for some form of control, if only in the matter of

[7] *Survey of Current Business,* August 1961.

eligibility for funds. In contrast, proposed measures containing no controls have consistently been defeated, and often because of the issue of the threat of federal control. A pro-federal-aid congressional candidate once debated his opponent, an anti-federal-aid candidate. The anti-federal-aid spokesman decried the regimentation and overcentralization of education that would be inevitable if federal aid were granted.[8] The pro-federal-aid candidate responded with the declaration that the current proposal before Congress specifically forbade federal intervention in state and local educational affairs and that the measure was simply a distribution of funds, the use of which was to be determined by state and local authorities. The anti-aid man shot back the accusation that, if the federal government was going to expend funds without having control over their use, such action could only be labeled the worst possible "fiscal irresponsibility."

There has been a tradition in the United States of suspicion of too much power invested in the federal government. This suspiciousness rests on the fear of a loss of individual liberty and a desirable measure of local autonomy in the affairs of government. Despite the recognized need to expand and improve our educational system, and despite the obvious necessity for increased federal participation in the fiscal support of education, the specter of control with a resultant loss of liberty seems to insinuate itself into most public discussions of expanded federal aid. There are, however, questions about this issue that are rarely posed and more rarely answered. For example, what liberties have been or would be lost? And what liberties are being lost *now* because education is starving for funds? Fundamentally, the question that must be asked, if it is agreed that federal aid would necessarily impose some controls, is this: are all controls necessarily bad? Certainly, it may be argued that the controls imposed by the Pure Food and Drug Act, the Federal Deposit Insurance Corporation, the Securities-Exchange Commission, the Federal Communications Commission, and many other regulatory agencies or acts have not been seriously challenged because their *functions* are recognized as useful and essential. The principal objections to the "G.I. Bill" to aid education were directed at the *lack* of certain kinds of control features in the bill and its consequent misuse to support "diploma mills" and other abuses.

It may be argued, therefore, that stating the issue as control vs. no

[8] This has been the persistent hue and cry of the so-called "far-rightist" groups who see such federal participation as "creeping socialism" at best, or "communistic" at worst.

control is a distorting oversimplification of the problem. The need for controls depends upon what task is attempted. If a specific task suggesting the need for controls is undertaken, then a further decision on the degree and kind of controls is necessary. If expanded federal aid to education is conceived of as simply a transfusion of funds from the federal government into the bloodstream of state educational programs, then few, if any, controls seem necessary. If, on the other hand, expanded federal aid is also conceived of as an opportunity to raise the standards of the nation's educational enterprise, certain kinds and degrees of control might be appropriate.[9] It is the task chosen for achievement that dictates the form of federal participation.

If the maintenance of a high measure of local fiscal autonomy in education is perceived as more important than building an adequate number of schools, staffed by adequately paid qualified teachers, then the federal government's role will be clearly as nonparticipant. If on the other hand, the opposite value choice is made, then the role of the federal government changes to that of participant, and decisions must be made on the extent and form of that participation. Argued on this basis, it is not inconsistent for opponents of expanded federal aid to education to be *for* federal reclamation projects in the various states, or agricultural regulations, or a host of other federal interventions that tend to diminish local autonomy. But if these opponents of expanded federal aid to education argue against such aid on the *general* principle of the dangers to liberty of federal intervention in local affairs, then they must logically oppose other forms of such intervention in other areas of economic and social life.

Suspicion of the federal government may or may not be appropriate, but the control issue is not served by the injection of such extraneous issues as debates over "progressive education" or "Communist infiltration" of schools. Whatever controls the federal government might be ordered and empowered by Congress to impose, issues of curriculum are constitutionally reserved to the states, and therefore debates over federal control of teachers, textbooks, or curriculum are essentially irrelevant.

The opposition to expanded federal aid to education on the grounds cited would appear to be easily dismissed, except for the fact that powerful political groups still use such arguments and, therefore, *must* be listened

[9] President Johnson's "Elementary and Secondary Education Bill of 1965" intends to accomplish some specific tasks; thus, it has certain controls implicit in it, because it defines who is eligible and to what specific uses the money is to be put.

to. The most consistent spokesman for such arguments has been that women's patriotic organization, the Daughters of the American Revolution. They have been joined by the National Economic Council, the Church League of America, the Friends of the Public Schools, the Ladies of the Grand Army of the Republic, the Wheel of Progress, the Society for Constitutional Security, the Spengler Unit of the American Legion Auxiliary, and the Nineteenth Women's Patriotic Conference on Defense.[10] In addition to these groups, powerful conservative senators and congressmen such as former Senator Barry Goldwater of Arizona used their political acumen to oppose federal aid on these grounds. Mister Goldwater, however, did propose what he called "federal" aid to education, by enactment of a system of federal income-tax exemptions. Unfortunately, his plan contained no provisions *guaranteeing* that the exempted funds would be channeled into the local schools.

Congressman Wingate Lucas of Texas directly confronted then-Commissioner of Education Earl McGrath with the control issue in the 1950 House Subcommittee hearings:

> *Mr. Lucas:* There is no intention on the part of the Office of Education or yourself, Dr. McGrath, to direct the local school districts or the state educational authorities as to what is best within the state, is there?
>
> *Dr. McGrath:* No sir, I have repeatedly testified before this and other committees to that effect, but I am glad you give me an opportunity to repeat this statement that the Commissioner of Education, nor any of his staff, has any desire or intention to interfere with the internal operation of education in the 48 states, nor to impose any standards or programs or teaching methods or techniques or books on those states.[11]

Despite such lucid reassurances, opponents of expanded federal aid to education continue to insist that federal aid must necessarily result in federal control, and that their opposition must, therefore, be steadfast.

Two other issues have figured prominently in the defeat of all bills advocating expanded federal aid. One is the perennial quarrel over whether such aid should be extended to parochial schools, and the other is the opposition of some to any aid to schools practicing the segregation of races. Since both issues carry heavy increments of emotion, not to men-

[10] Frank Munger, and Richard Fenno, *National Politics and Federal Aid to Education* (Syracuse: Syracuse University Press, 1962), p. 31.

[11] House Committee on Education and Labor, *Federal Aid to School Construction,* 81st Congress, 2nd Session, 1950, p. 169.

tion serious constitutional questions, it may be that they have been the most publicized issues in the controversy. The public press often has attributed defeats of federal aid bills to the opposition of "Catholics" or "segregationists," but these are difficult assertions to prove, for congressmen rarely have directly connected their votes to these reasons, except in the case of southern opposition to the Powell Amendment.

The Powell Amendment, added to the 1956 bill on federal aid, called for withholding of aid to segregated schools. Proposed by Negro Congressman Adam Clayton Powell of New York, but opposed by Negro Congressman William Dawson of Chicago, the Amendment is generally given credit for the defeat of the federal-aid proposal that year, for it unified segregationist southern congressmen, who, combined with economic conservatives and anti-federal-control forces, were able to kill the measure. Negro leadership has not always been united, as the above-mentioned split would indicate, and the National Association for the Advancement of Colored People (NAACP) has often found itself at odds with factions in its own ranks as well as with the powerful supporters of expanded federal aid such as the NEA and the Council of Chief State School Officers (CSSO). In the 1955 Senate hearings, the NEA and CSSO spokesmen criticized what they deemed an "intransigent" attitude on the part of NAACP; the NAACP spokesman retorted to such criticism sharply with such words as "cruel," "reprehensible," "dishonest," and "vicious" to describe the testimony of the educators.[12]

The basic arguments of the Negro leaders rest on two premises: (1) equal educational opportunity can be achieved by expanded federal aid only in poor states (often containing large percentages of Negroes); and (2) no such aid should be given to any school district practicing segregation in defiance of the United States Supreme Court ban on such segregation.

While most supporters of expanded federal aid tend to agree with the Negro position in principle, they are equally concerned that, in view of the present distribution of voting strength in the Congress (a significant and consistent southern segregationist bloc), it is impractical to pin all hopes for expanded federal aid on compliance with the Negro position. Tragically, too, the Negro position has been used cynically by forces opposing federal aid for other reasons to arouse the almost automatic opposi-

[12] Munger and Fenno (see note 10), p. 72.

tion of segregationist congressmen, and thus to achieve voting strength they themselves did not formerly possess. The rising militancy of Negro organizations throughout the nation and the political strength such militancy may engender could, in future years, override such tactics, and the support of expanded federal aid by Negro groups could become constructive rather than the "kiss of death."

The position of the Catholic hierarchy has usually been to oppose expanded federal aid. This position stems from the church's traditional opposition to increased central government control over education in any country. The church argues that since centralized state control has always worked to the detriment of the parochial system, it must be opposed whenever it threatens.

It is ironic that the Catholic hierarchy has this almost instinctive distrust of the power of federal control, since one of the burning issues in the Kennedy-Nixon presidential campaign was the instinctive distrust of some Protestants of the power implications if the federal government were headed by a Roman Catholic. It is also ironic that such opposition is not directed against centralized educational power as such, but rather against *secular* or state-centralized educational power: the concentration of educational power in the hands of a few is, after all, a common phenomenon—for example, in numerous Latin American nations; but there it is the church that happens to possess the power. The position of the church is usually presented by Monsignor Frederick Hockwalt of the National Catholic Welfare Conference; he has consistently opposed expanded federal aid on the grounds stated.

However, as supporters of expanded federal aid have been able to offer reassurances that federal control features have been specifically eliminated and forbidden, the position of the church has been modified: it still opposes federal aid; but, if federal funds are made available, the church wants equal treatment for secular and parochial schools. The argument for aid to parochial schools, in spite of the generally well-known principle of separation of church and state, is simply to appeal to the "general welfare" provisions of the Preamble to the Constitution. The church argues that, since the educational aid is to the child, not to the organization, it is proper and constitutional in that it "promotes the general welfare." Nevertheless, although use of tax funds to aid in the transportation of parochial school children has been deemed constitutional, the legal problem is not at all clear or ultimately resolved. (For a discussion of this problem, see Chapter 8.)

There are some congressmen who believe that aid to parochial schools is unconstitutional; they consider it, therefore, imperative to vote against *any* federal aid measures that include aid to parochial schools. Thus, it is likely that political maneuvers will again be used to kill a federal aid measure: conservative groups can vote *for* an amendment to include parochial schools, and then reverse their vote and, in combination with anti-parochial school people, defeat the *entire* measure. The history of votes on expanded federal aid reveals a series of such maneuvers, whereby amendments are supported in order to gradually accumulate enough opposition so that a vote switch can kill the *total* bill. If such tactics seem cynical and unprincipled, then many of the votes of Congress on a wide variety of measures are similarly cynical and unprincipled, for such voting practices are part of the rough and tumble in-fighting of most congressional battles.

SUPPORT OF FEDERAL AID

Support for expanded federal aid to education is, of course, led by various professional education groups, the most significant of which is the National Education Association (NEA). Support for federal participation in education has been the NEA's policy almost since its creation in 1857 and has been absolutely unswerving, if not always effective. As chief proponent of expanded federal aid, the NEA has also been the chief target of opponents to such aid, and its responses to such attacks have not always made it an effective fighter for its goals. The NEA is an unwieldly amalgamation of various occupational specialities associated with education. As such, it sometimes finds its subgroups at odds with one another; at other times, a sizable proportion of its membership is totally disinterested in the association's national policies and the political impact it achieves.

The chief ally of the NEA on the issue of expanded federal aid has been its rival, the American Federation of Teachers (AF of T), and the AF of T's fraternal brothers—the body of organized labor. The emphasis of the AF of T and its parent AFL-CIO has, however, been consistent with trade union principles and consequently concentrated on aid to improve teachers' salaries and general working conditions. Organized labor also has favored federal aid to parochial schools.

Support for expanded federal aid has also come from powerful women's groups such as the National Congress of Parent-Teacher Associations, the General Federation of Women's Clubs, the American Association of University Women, and the League of Women Voters.

FEDERAL AID AS A VALUE PROBLEM

Ultimately the issue of expanded federal aid reduces itself to a value choice to be made by the American public directly or indirectly. That education needs a massive infusion of funds to meet the challenges and necessities of the future is generally agreed on; hence it is the source of funds that becomes crucial. But the value issue is raised again when the consistent response of the Congress is to find some reason not to grant federal funds, the only real source of finances that remains, even while proclaiming the need for such funds. In short, the choices are clear. Which is most dear to society—education or the various reasons given not to expend funds; i.e., aid to segregated schools and to parochial schools, alleged federal control, economic conservatism, etc., etc.? Only when some priority of values has been established can the decision be made on the basis of a clear-cut choice.

Present estimates of the situation suggest that federal aid to education will continue, but in the same manner as in the past—that is, piecemeal and dedicated to some particular program but never general or across the board. While such an approach may, in the long run, accomplish the purpose of supplying education with its needed revenues, some will again point out that specific measures almost always contain control provisions. Thus, the only issue upon which both proponents and opponents tend to agree—opposition to federal control—will come about because of the inability of these groups to agree on *general uncontrolled* aid. Regardless, the overwhelming need for education in a growing economy in a technological age argues that the necessary financial support eventually will be obtained either within present patterns, or in new institutional relationships to be created at the local, state, and federal levels.

SUMMARY

The federal government has always participated in school finances, even though education is a state function. The states, having experienced increased difficulty in financing schools equally and adequately, face new challenges today as predictions of need forecast heavy new expenditures.

Opposition to expanded federal aid to education has centered on economic arguments (too much expense), fear of federal control, aid to parochial schools, and aid to segregated schools. Such opposition has usually been able to defeat general federal aid bills presented to the Congress.

Support of expanded federal aid to education has been led by professional educators, organized labor, powerful women's organizations, and liberal elements in Congress. Thus far, these supporters have been unable to muster enough strength to pass federal aid bills in Congress except to support some specific program or other.

Predictions are that a general federal aid bill may be many years away, but the outlook for passage of bills to support specific programs is optimistic. The American public has not yet clearly indicated its value choices in public school financing.

SELECTED BIBLIOGRAPHY

Mort, Paul R., and Walter C. Reusser. *Public School Finance,* 2nd ed. New York: McGraw-Hill Book Company, 1951.

Munger, Frank, and Richard Fenno. *National Politics and Federal Aid to Education.* Syracuse, N.Y.: Syracuse University Press, 1962.

National Committee for Support of the Public Schools. *Changing Demands on Education and Their Fiscal Implications.* Washington, D.C., 1963.

National Education Association. *Financing the Public Schools, 1960–70.* Washington, D.C., 1962.

Rockefeller Brothers Fund. *The Pursuit of Excellence.* Garden City, N.Y.: Doubleday and Company, 1958.

Sufrin, Sidney C. *Issues in Federal Aid to Education.* Syracuse, N.Y.: Syracuse University Press, 1962.

CHAPTER 12

CONTROVERSIAL ISSUES IN THE CLASSROOM

Perhaps by now the reader will have gained the impression that American education is a patchwork of paradox, a web of interlocking debates among diverse social forces. There is, perhaps, no better focus for this prevalence of discord than in the interesting problem of teaching "controversial issues." For nowhere in education do we find a greater impact of the inevitable relativity of individual perception and the corresponding necessity for clear thought. Just as children do not have duplicate dreams, neither do they learn in absolute unison. When, as adults, they face the world and its complexities, they come to all issues with perceptions skewed by their infinitely different kinds of experiences. Thus rational thought, the most difficult of human endeavors, is absolutely necessary if resolution, progress, and freedom are to survive.

A controversial issue is one that invites disagreement. In a pluralistic culture encouraging freedom of thought, open debate, and diversity of opinion, the number of issues that are controversial is far greater than would be found in a closed, controlled, and regimented society. For the logical opposite of controversy is agreement; if such agreement is coerced, we have regimentation at worst and conformity at best. Often in the past, the answer to all questions of controversy has been an almost religious faith that the "facts" involved are absolute and that, if one sticks to those "facts," there can be no legitimate debate. Presumably too, in the teaching of such issues, someone—preferably the teacher—is in possession of all of the pertinent "facts" and can point out the differences between "fact" and "fancy."

In chemistry, how many basic elements are there? The answer, not many years ago, would have been a resounding "92," with full assurance that the speaker possessed the "fact." Why was the Civil War fought? Now the "facts" take on shades of local perception. Is the earth flat? Surely this was once a controversial issue. Should there be federal aid to education? Should Communists be allowed to teach in the public schools? Does academic freedom mean being forced to hire professors to teach your children doctrines in which you do not believe? Shall evolution be taught in schools? Are the United Nations, sex, religion, socialized medicine, or sanitation legitimate areas of study for children in public schools? Almost anything which comes into our lives, gets us interested and active and forces us to take a position contrary to someone else's, constitutes a controversial issue.

INEVITABILITY OF CONTROVERSY IN THE CLASSROOM

It is impossible to eliminate controversy from life; and it is illogical to attempt to eliminate it from the schools, which have the primary mission of cultural transmission or induction into life. Earl Kelley suggests that, if the schools were to deal only with "settled" issues, the curriculum would be sparse indeed, and most assuredly would contain nothing of current flavor.[1] Dealing with controversy or "unsettled" questions would seem to be necessary in a scientific age and in an open and free democratic society. Acceptance rather than investigation, meeting only settled issues rather than unsettling old canons, would not seem to be the way of the twentieth-century scientific man. P. W. Bridgman, a Nobel prize-winning physicist, describes scientific procedure as follows:

> . . . the most vital feature of the scientist's procedure has been merely to do his utmost with his mind, no holds barred. This means in particular that no special privileges are accorded to authority or to tradition, that personal prejudices and predilections are carefully guarded against, that one makes continued check to assure oneself that one is not making mistakes, and that any line of inquiry will be followed that appears at all promising.[2]

In short, the scientific approach must, of necessity, view answers as tentative, incomplete, and subject to a hundred visions and revisions. Such an approach inherently opposes orthodoxy and the established order, and thus inevitably promotes both discovery and controversy.

[1] Earl C. Kelley, "The Teaching of Controversial Issues," *Review of General Semantics*, 19, No. 2 (July 1962), 134–135.

[2] P. W. Bridgman, *Reflections of a Physicist* (New York: Philosophical Library, 1950), p. 370.

THE AMERICAN LEANING TOWARD ORTHODOXY

American education, taken in historical perspective, has not dealt with controversy easily. Almost at the outset, the clamor was for strict orthodoxy. In a later chapter, we will describe some of the colonial demands for orthodoxy of teachers. Enforcement of this orthodoxy was extended to the entire population, as testified to by the Salem witch trials and the pronouncements of John Cotton in his tract *Spiritual Milk for American Babes Drawn Out of the Breasts of Both Testaments for Their Souls' Nourishment,* in which he stated that *all children* must learn that they were conceived in sin, born in iniquity, and that they were corrupt in nature and doomed to death and damnation.[3] Early American educators did not dare to raise the question of open inquiry, nor did their students, if in fact such a question ever occurred to most of them. Orthodoxy was so complete that one cannot even imagine a Scopes trial kind of controversy arising in that pious day and age.

While American education in the eighteenth and nineteenth centuries reveals a distinctive lack of controversy in teaching, it must be said that the mere establishment of free public education was sufficiently controversial to claim the total attention of educators. Horace Mann, in the attempt to establish a nonsectarian curriculum for public schools, was "accused of conducting 'godless' immoral schools which bred delinquency and vice."[4] The opponents of tax-supported schools accused educators, who were generally selected because of their absolutely orthodox political, social, and religious beliefs, of a myriad of dire crimes against the very orthodoxy these educators had so eagerly embraced. Thus, the idea that early American schools might have initiated controversy by audaciously seeking to teach about unorthodox subjects seems both wistful and inaccurate.

It was not until the twentieth century that American public education took tentative steps out of conformity and began to raise questions and to deal with unsettled questions of any serious import. Even then these probes were timid and easily defeated by militant groups who objected to open inquiry as a proper method of education. Perhaps this tradition in some way accounts for the fact that, contrary to the role played by educa-

[3] R. Freeman Butts and Lawrence A. Cremin, *A History of Education in American Culture* (New York: Holt, Rinehart and Winston, Inc., Copyright 1953), p. 67. With permission.

[4] Butts and Cremin, *A History of Education,* p. 273.

tional institutions in other countries, the American school has never been a center for political, social, and religious agitation. American students have rarely exerted any significant influence on community life, except perhaps as they engage in athletic or in "hi-jinks" activities.[5]

Within the general mythology of American education there exists the impression, particularly among college personnel, that significant deviations from orthodoxy are the rule rather than the exception. The disparities between this claim and empirical evidence seem sufficient to all but obliterate such assertions. Educators, being in effect public servants, are peculiarly vulnerable to attacks on their behavior. Consequently, they can rarely afford to test the culture's willingness to accept them in the dual roles of critical evaluators of current ideas and institutions on the one hand, and teachers of the uninformed and as yet undisciplined young on the other. Always acutely aware of the implications of having the younger generation taught to question, to be unrestricted by tradition or authority in their search for new truths, the American public has steadfastly imposed significant pressures upon educators to "keep them in line." But, much of the research on the cultural orientation of teachers indicates that they have not chafed under these restrictions. For example, one study reported that some 67 per cent of a national sample of teachers indicated that they felt it *improper* for teachers to engage openly in political activity.[6] Some teachers even feel that it is "controversial" for them to support their own school bond elections and, *ipso facto,* that being "controversial" is being "bad" or "unprofessional."

THE ISSUE OF INDOCTRINATION VS. FREEDOM

The fundamental problem faced by our schools is to delineate clearly their role in a democratic, pluralistic society. As a basic institution of the society, the schools have the defined task of perpetuating the culture by transmitting it to the new generation. This implies the systematic teach-

[5] The exception to this pattern has been the recent activities urging equal civil rights for Negroes, in many cases spearheaded by student groups. A corollary to this activity has been the increasing number of students who have volunteerd to tutor disadvantaged children. The Berkeley, California, student uprisings in 1964 received national attention, partly because it was so unusual for college students to be so militant.

[6] National Education Association, "The Status of the American Public School Teacher," *NEA Research Bulletin,* 35, No. 1 (1957).

ing of selected parts of the culture deemed important to the survival of that culture. This also implies transmission of the underlying value system characteristic of the culture. At a glance, this process seems to be frank indoctrination into a set system of values and symbols. We teach kindergarten and first grade children to salute the flag and recite the "Pledge of Allegiance" long before either act has any real meaning to them. Children are asked to accept the authority of the teacher on all matters without question in their early school years, until such behavior becomes almost automatic and these same children continue to refuse to ask questions or even discuss any issues with their teachers in later years, when such questioning and such discussion is considered a necessary adjunct to the learning process.

In other words, our society wants the right of open inquiry maintained, but only after certain prerequisites to cultural survival have been learned by indoctrination. There are some things we, as a culture, simply do not want to discuss. This gives a peculiarly difficult assignment to the schools: The pluralistic society wants its right to be pluralistic maintained, with a full measure of individual freedom, but it does not want the status quo too badly shaken, and it also does not want its education to be so bland that children learn little of anything. Sometimes it appears that we want children to develop the individualistic courage and spirit of the rugged pioneers, but to do so without leaving home.

The line between indoctrination and freedom has always been vague and ill-defined, and American society at large—frantically pursuing its various self-interests—has done little to help the schools achieve clarity of purpose on these matters. For example, consider the following statement issued by the California State Board of Education (a lay group) in January 1963, and distributed to all that state's school superintendents, some of whom have had to endure wild onslaughts from every pressure group imaginable:

> An important purpose of the education in this nation is to help children learn to think critically, and to be able to analyze the written word before accepting it as truth. This ability is essential in a democracy in which citizens must participate in the making of decisions. It is essential in a nation of free people in which citizens are expected to deal intelligently with controversy and to recognize propaganda.
>
> The ability to deal with controversy will not be developed by avoiding controversy. The ability to recognize propaganda will not develop through exposure only to that doctrine with which all people agree. Freedom is not promoted by censorship. To eliminate from our schools all

> discussion and materials with which any group or individual disagrees will result only in a weakening of our school system, and an erosion of the very foundations of our nation's freedom.
>
> We are aware of the strong pressures to which various school boards have been subjected by various groups who seek to impose their views; we commend those boards that, in the absence of sound evidence, have declined to be swayed; who have recognized that opinion is not necessarily fact; that an unsubstantiated allegation is not acceptable evidence; and who have continued in use educational material that they deem to have value.

While the opening paragraphs of this statement appear to be a ringing declaration of educational courage, the ultimate responsibility of choice is left to the local school district. Thus specific controversies are left unjudged, and state support is deferred. The local district remains as vulnerable as ever, except as the highly abstract notions on the importance of learning to think critically are endorsed. The kinds of pressure mounted on local school boards are often beyond the capabilities of either the board or the superintendent or—in some cases, individual teachers—to resist. National pressure groups can pour endless resources into a local struggle and soon overwhelm the local authorities. Since the barroom-brawl tactics of such groups usually are not available to public servants (if, indeed, such officials cared to use such methods), the struggle is one-sided unless powerful allies rally to support the school's need to maintain open inquiry, regardless of what toes may be stepped upon.

Again, the choices appear to be essentially value choices. What kind of education do we want for our children—orthodoxy or open inquiry? If we choose orthodoxy, what will become of democracy? If we choose open inquiry, can we protect the schools and the educators from the inevitable attacks which will come from those who perceive their values, or way of life, threatened by such inquiry?

THE ISSUE OF LOYALTY VS. NONCONFORMITY

Specifically, the issues that appear to generate the most heat are those that seem to involve questions of loyalty to present institutions. This has become increasingly true since the end of World War II, because the threat of communism to the United States poses many difficult questions. Communism, as an ideology alien to almost all American social institutions, as a nationalistic military threat, and as a major competitor for the minds of uncommitted men in newly emerging nations, constitutes one of the gravest threats to the perpetuation of American society our nation has ever confronted. Coupled with the fear of nuclear war, the tensions and fears have sometimes mounted to almost hysterical levels.

The sensitive arena of the schools has felt the impact; almost every day in some community or state, proposals intended to insure the *absolute* undying loyalty of children and teachers to their country are advanced. Often such proposals are highly restrictive in form and suspicious and accusative in tone and may, in some cases, actually tend to destroy the very liberties they seek to protect. Resistance to such unreasonable or self-defeating proposals is often greeted with charges of disloyalty, as if disagreement perforce proved the existence of the perceived threat. The free and easy use of the label "Communist," "traitor," or even "dupe" has made the task of maintaining democratic institutions even more difficult, particularly for public officials (including educators) whose continued service is at public will. The consistent reaction of the majority of such officials has been to protect themselves in enveloping cloaks of orthodoxy.

A state senator charges that sex education in schools is Communistic; the educators respond by removing *all* legitimate health education materials that may touch upon sex from the schools. A social studies text series critically evaluates some aspects of the business community, and suddenly finds itself labeled "red" and removed from circulation. Even innocent stories about the intermarriage of black and white rabbits are banned in one southern state as subversive because of the implied racial propaganda. Robin Hood suddenly is discovered to be at least a Communist, if not a breeder of juvenile delinquency. Even "progressive" education is twisted about until its deficiencies are rationalized as a "subversive" plot to undermine the nation. Columbia University's Teachers College is often a primary target, since it is "well-known as a hotbed of British Fabianism" according to an organization known as The American Flag Committee. This group also is aroused by the use of UNESCO materials in American schools, since it feels that UNESCO is out to "teach disloyalty to children," "poison the minds of teachers," "suppress the truth," "discard logical teaching methods," and "corrupt the morals of children."[7]

THE DOCTRINE OF "CLEAR AND PRESENT DANGER"

There is little doubt that the intensity of feelings about the international Communist conspiracy, the tension over the threat of nuclear war,

[7] *Congressional Record.* Speech of Representative John T. Wood, 82nd Congress, October 18, 1951.

and the myriad of other problems worrying the American public have produced a volatile social situation in which tempers flare, reason departs, and the schools, which almost always reflect with barometric accuracy the pressure level of any social controversy, are suffocated by public attention. Legally, the doctrine of "clear and present danger" has been the guide for our courts on matters of censorship of political and social dissenters. Justice Oliver Wendell Holmes stated (in *Abrams et al.* v. *United States,* 250 U.S. 616 [1918]):

> Persecution for the expression of opinion seems to me perfectly logical. If you have no doubt of your premises or your power and want a certain result with all your heart, you naturally express your wishes in law and sweep away all opposition. To allow opposition by speech seems to indicate that you think the speech impotent, as when a man says that he has squared a circle, or that you do not care whole-heartedly for the result, or that you doubt either your power or your premises. But when men have realized that time has upset many fighting faiths, they may come to believe even more than they believe the very foundations of their own conduct that the ultimate good desired is better reached by free trade in ideas—that the best test of truth is the power of the thought to get itself accepted in the competition of the market, and that truth is the only ground upon which their wishes safely can be carried out. That, at any rate, is the theory of our constitution. It is an experiment, as all life is an experiment. Every year, if not every day, we have to wager our salvation upon some prophesy based upon imperfect knowledge. While that experiment is part of our system, I think that we should be eternally vigilant against attempts to check the expression of opinions that we loathe and believe to be fraught with death, unless they so imminently threaten immediate interference with the lawful and pressing purposes of the law that an immediate check is required to save the country. . . .

Few, if any, of the controversies that concern our public schools seem to qualify as "clear and present dangers," except in the minds of those whose dramatic exuberance and abounding hysteria has gone unchecked. If one can believe, as Senator Thomas Kuchel of California has claimed some of his constituents do, that Chinese Communist troops in powder-blue uniforms are poised on the Mexican border, or that United Nations "cannibal" troops, with rings in their noses, are training in Georgia to take over the United States, then it is apparently equally possible to believe that the reading of Robin Hood or of the Dictionary of American Slang is a prelude to revolution, or total moral decay, or both and, therefore, constitutes a "clear and present danger."

CONFORMIST PRESSURES ON EDUCATORS

It is perhaps more realistic to deal with the issue of loyalty on the less extreme levels of operation in local school districts. Although the charges may not be as strident and implausible, the pressures on educators not to "offend" any segment of the community or become "controversial" are clear and present realities, as most school people will readily testify anonymously. One California school district has recommended the following summary guide to teachers:

> The best protection against criticism in teaching controversial issues is the *liking* and *respect* of students for their teacher. Next most important is vigilance to observe possible misinterpretations, misunderstandings, or hurt feelings in the class and taking steps to rectify the situation.

The plaintive, almost terror-stricken defensive tone of this statement may cause the reader to wince, but it accurately communicates a common response of vulnerable educators to the ordeal they face when dealing with "controversial" issues. The second line of defense for schools has been to have a "declared policy" on the teaching of controversial issues that constitutes a statement of ground rules for teachers. Consider the following:

> POLICY ON THE STUDY OF CURRENT PUBLIC PROBLEMS
>
> It shall be the policy of the Los Angeles City Schools to foster the study of vital present-day public problems in the classroom. This policy is in keeping with our point of view toward meeting our pupils' needs for effective living in American democracy.
>
> The study of current problems is always *based on the foundation of positive instruction toward a belief in the ideals and processes of American democracy,* and on the understanding of totalitarian ideals and methods which are contrary to American democracy. Proposed solutions of public problems are tested in the light of democratic procedures: concern for the worth of the individual and for the common welfare; recognition of fair play; and emphasis on peaceful, constitutional methods of progress.
>
> Furthermore, vital problems are discussed and studied in terms suited to the degree of maturity of the learners and their capacity for understanding concepts and values. Instruction for developing objective judgment begins at the elementary level, but many issues are not included in the elementary curriculum because they cannot be understood at that level. It is the policy of the Los Angeles City Schools to provide teachers with *approved courses of study and authorized materials of instruction*

> *which serve as guides to the selection of problems for discussion at appropriate grade levels.*
>
> It shall be the policy of the Los Angeles City Schools to provide pupils with an opportunity to study current issues in an *atmosphere as free as practicable from partisanship or emotional approach.* We recognize the professional responsibility of teachers to distinguish between teaching and advocating, to refrain from using classroom prestige to promote partisan or sectarian viewpoints. Rather, the teacher keeps himself well informed, aids pupils in the search for facts, and helps them to learn to think clearly in arriving at tentative conclusions about these facts.
>
> We have a responsibility to teach pupils to be concerned about finding possible answers to problems pertaining to their respective age levels; to teach them to be willing to take a stand on questions which citizens must decide and yet to maintain an attitude of openmindedness toward new facts which may lead to new conclusions. *We teach our pupils to respect the rights of others to be different in their opinions.* We believe that *accurate information and effective thinking will discourage the uncritical acceptance of unsound proposals for solving public problems, and will focus the experience of history upon current problems.* However, it is recommended that the discussion of highly controversial issues of a local nature be deferred until sufficient facts and perspective can be secured to base discussion upon reason rather than upon undue emotion.[8]

If an individual teacher carefully follows such a policy, her tenure is secure and her reputation clear. But, in the same process orthodoxy has been established and freedom compromised, for *official* and *approved* courses of study rarely include materials that could become obvious targets for the many pressure groups patrolling the corridors.[9] In short, the teacher is being asked, or rather ordered, in the words of still another district's policy statement, "to demonstrate continual respect for the prevailing viewpoint of the community, the mores of our nation including representative democracy." In a pluralistic culture, this would, indeed, be a remarkable acrobatic feat. Thus, the danger of conformity decried by writers such as Riesman and Whyte actually appears to be most formidable when pressure groups of widely diverse interests all converge upon public education, in the name of loyalty or morality, and insist upon the advocacy of their causes, or the elimination of their particular targets of hate. When public school officials, from school boards to teachers, cower before such pressure, then

[8] Curriculum Division, Los Angeles City Schools, November 1951.

[9] It must be recalled that, in this school district, pressure groups once had all use of UNESCO materials banned.

conformity—or at least a well-blanched version of education—becomes a real possibility.

LEARNING THEORY AND CONTROVERSIAL ISSUES

A common objective of public education, particularly since the Experimentalist school of thought came into influence, has been the development of the ability to think critically. This has recently been linked with the value of promoting creativity. When a modern educator speaks of the ability to think critically, he is actually speaking of the skills of thinking philosophically, scientifically, or both. The justification for such an educational objective rests upon more than simple preference or belief. It is derivative of certain principles of learning empirically detected by research psychologists and educators.

That learners seem to learn more effectively in genuine problem-solving situations has long been an assertion of psychologists. In fact, the generalization can be made, and is by some psychologists, that all learning is essentially problem solving. The learner needs, for a wide variety of reasons, to solve some situation in his life, whether it be a formal lesson or a complex personal problem. Such a need creates a tension within him, which moves him to seek a solution. Thereupon he attempts to formulate a possible course of action (hypothesis), which he then tests by trial (experimentation) and thus either solves the problem or fails. If he does not succeed, he may set up a second, third, or even several alternative hypotheses, until he finally achieves a solution satisfying *his* need. The skill with which he attacks the problem, reviews the evidence, reasons the hypothesis, and systematically checks his experiments may be called the skill of *critical thinking*. That is, critical thinking involves the careful review of evidence with judgment suspended until the process is completed, the employment of logic to discover relationships and sequences, and the attitude of objectivity that tends to produce a more reliable and valid solution.

If problem-solving behavior is central to modern learning theory, and if the skills of critical thinking are prerequisite to adequate problem solving, then the question of whether or not critical thinking skills should be stressed in the schools seems settled. Some problems, however, are not amenable to application of critical thinking skills without potential threat to the status quo. If the learner has been made aware of the problem-solving process and trained in the utilization of critical thinking skills, he cannot easily dismiss such processes simply because his investigations and logic seem to challenge present practices in the community. In other words, the choice of whether or not effective learning is to take place through use of the skills of critical thinking has to be made early in the learner's career. If most concerned people endorse the development of the ability to think critically as an important objective of education, the consequences of such behavior should be known and accepted.

Critical thinking necessarily implies divergent thinking as the learner explores the variety of alternatives for action he perceives. If a society objects to such divergence and would rather achieve convergence of thought, then critical thinking, and certainly creative thought, have no place in the schools. Once a society starts to forbid divergence in the schools, the existence of divergent and individual thought in the whole of that society is endangered, for the rising generation—the leaders of tomorrow—will have been taught that conformity is the greater value, if not the *only* value permitted to exist.

The current advocacy of the promotion of creativity also carries with it known risks as well as hoped-for rewards. Ghiselin points out:

> Because every creative act overpasses the established order in some way and in some degree, it is likely at first to appear eccentric to most men. An inventor ordinarily must begin in isolation and draw the group to himself only as it is discovered, sometimes very slowly, that he has invented some part of what they are in need of. At the beginning of his struggle for realization his originality may achieve no more striking manifestation than an extreme dissatisfaction with established order.[10]

While risk to the established order is inherent in the release of creativity, tremendous gains can also be derived from it. A society that fears the risks will become stagnant and perish, while one encouraging creativity may make great strides forward as a result of finding new and better ways of achieving its goals and those of its individual members. The absolute power of the present must be overcome if the future is to be obtained, for the constant and convergent repetition of the present cannot produce a new life or a new time.

The teaching of controversial issues in the schools constitutes an excellent opportunity for the teaching of the skills of critical thinking and

[10] Bernard Ghiselin, ed., *The Creative Process.* Mentor Books, by arrangement with University of California Press, Berkeley, California, 1952, p. 13.

the release of the dynamic forces of creativity. Viewed in this way, controversial issues become opportunities rather than threats. But such an attitude is not easily obtained in the face of hysterical pressures and powerful politics. But then, freedom has never been maintained at bargain prices, and the issue of whether or not critical thinking and creativity shall be permitted in the public schools boils down to the basic question of freedom.

APPROPRIATENESS OF PRESENTING CONTROVERSY TO CHILDREN

Up to this point, because the questions and problems discussed thus far seem to have far greater significance and thus priority, we have deliberately refrained from asking whether the study of controversial issues is appropriate subject matter for impressionable young children. The very question of appropriateness seems almost irrelevant if we harken back to Kelley's assertion that to avoid controversy is, in essence, to avoid life.

The real question of appropriateness is one involving the organization and arrangement of curricular experiences. Presumably, competent scholars and curriculum workers have devised procedures for judging the appropriate place for a particular subject area or a specific kind of problem. That is to say, curriculum designers are supposed to be sufficiently cognizant of the developmental patterns of the male and female child in all areas of emotional, social, physical, and intellectual growth to enable them to hypothesize with very little risk that a certain issue would be most appropriately handled at a particular level of development and schooling. Professionally trained teachers should be able to demonstrate similar skills in judgment.

A confident public would have little difficulty turning the problem of appropriateness over to the educators whose trained critical judgment would select opportune times for the introduction of particularly important, even though vexing, controversial issues. The flexibility needed by educators would be granted, and Havighurst's "teachable moments"[11] would be safeguarded. Without such public confidence, educators can quickly find themselves on the defensive trying to justify the introduction of an issue at one time rather than at another, or even *at all*. Equally as important as public confidence: educators themselves must employ the

[11] Robert J. Havighurst, *Developmental Tasks and Education,* 2nd ed. (New York: Longmans, Green & Co., 1952).

skills of critical thinking as they provide children with the intellectual tools necessary to profit from experience with controversial issues. Such profit is obviously not obtained if the learner merely rearranges his prejudices or multiplies his misconceptions. Educators must adopt the appropriate critical attitudes of suspended judgment and objective investigation of all known factors; this implies constant scholarship.

THE GOALS OF EDUCATION REEXAMINED

The primary goal of American education is to perpetuate the best of American culture and the values that undergird it. Perhaps the most unique feature of our culture is its total commitment to individual freedom as expressed in the moving spirit of the American revolution. The dedication of American society to the enhancement of individual freedom, even at the cost of chaos at times, is a well-known historical fact. That American education, through its free public schools, has played a major role in the development and maintenance of such freedom is already clearly documented.

Fundamental to the commitment to freedom is the belief that such freedom must inevitably produce the best possible living for everyone, and there would appear to be ample proof in the American experiment that such a belief is justifiable. Thus Kelley can say:

> Freedom begets creativity, and creativity, the devising of something new, is the growing edge of learning and of life. . . . All human progress depends upon the creation of the new as the free human contrives toward a better life.[12]

Such creativity necessarily is predicated upon freedom of the mind to roam the pathways of scholarship and experience. Any imposition of controls on the human mind in some part compromises freedom and the mind's creativity. Any refusal to allow the open discussion and investigation of ideas is an imposed control; it is also a confession of fear that the undesirable idea, in free and open competition with other ideas, will emerge victorious. Kelley states:

> Freedom promotes courage, which is so essential in the establishment and maintenance of the life good to live. Up to the present time in

[12] Kelley (see note 1), pp. 145–146.

> our development, there have always been those who would enslave others. To retain one's freedom, one must be willing to take risks, and when he sees that what happens to others also happens to him, then the courageous one will dare to take risks in behalf of others. Enslavement begets fear, so that the enslaved one becomes less and less able to muster the courage needed to struggle for freedom.[13]

It is clear that the solution to the teaching of controversial issues involves a recommitment to the fundamental values and goals of American education. It also involves the injection of large quantities of courage, so that both the teacher and the learner may be forever free. In times of rapid social change and upheaval, under the tensions and fears of external threats, such commitment and courage are not easy to achieve. Yet, the alternatives are still so repugnant, that any real choice is thereby eliminated. The greatest danger to freedom is not frontal assault but *erosion;* consequently, the role of education in a free American society must always be to take all steps to prevent such erosion. Dealing with real problems in life, examining unsettled issues with vigor and discipline, and freeing the mind so that its unique creativity can be released are surely the most important of these steps.

How teachers should approach the problem of teaching controversial issues is well stated by Kelley:

> The questioning of the advisability of teaching current, and hence controversial, issues is based on a concept of the denial of freedom. When the teacher abandons the idea that he alone is going to choose what is to be learned, the problem disappears. The learning which ensues when learners are consulted is mostly controversial in some degree, because it is largely current. Settled matters are studied as they are apropos to current issues. The teacher then becomes the facilitator of learning and a defender of freedom. This is a fine role for anyone teaching in a democracy.[14]

Such a conclusion appears to be neither "idealistic" in the cloudy sense nor "theoretical" in the impractical sense—that is, unless the underlying values of the American experiment are also impractical and wildly idealistic. While such a solution to the pressing problems of teaching controversial issues does not point out exactly how the individual educator should handle his particular problem at a specific time, in a specific place, it offers him an overarching principle to which he can safely adhere in the

[13] Kelley, p. 146.
[14] Kelley, p. 147.

authentic tradition of his nation. In the perspective of history, such a tradition offers much reassurance.

SUMMARY

A controversial issue is one that contains elements upon which there is lack of agreement. Within a culturally pluralistic society, there is an almost infinite number of controversial issues. As a basic social institution, education must face the inevitability of dealing with controversial issues at all times.

Attempts have been made throughout history to force education to adhere to political, social, or religious orthodoxy, but human events have always made such orthodoxy questionable. The pursuit and discovery of new "truths" has also tended to break down attempts to enforce conformity. Particularly in a free, democratic society, the drift of opinion has been away from indoctrination and toward freedom of inquiry.

Much pressure has been exerted on our schools to prevent them from dealing with controversial issues: in the name of "loyalty," many schools have been hard pressed to survive the intense and often inflammatory attacks upon freedom of inquiry. Fortunately, American legal precedent still rests upon the yardstick of "clear and present danger," and our educators, thus protected, have the opportunity to measure their courage and their convictions.

SELECTED BIBLIOGRAPHY

Ehlers, Henry, and Gordon Lee. *Crucial Issues in Education,* rev. ed. New York: Holt-Dryden, 1959.

Ghiselin, Bernard, ed. *The Creative Process.* Berkeley, Calif.: Mentor Books by arrangement with University of California Press, 1952.

Kelley, Earl. "The Teaching of Controversial Issues," *Review of General Semantics,* 19, No. 2 (July 1962).

Social Forces Influencing American Education. Chicago: National Society for the Study of Education, University of Chicago Press, 1961.

Popper, Karl. *The Open Society and Its Enemies.* Princeton: Princeton University Press, 1950.

Raywid, Mary Anne. *The Ax-Grinders.* New York: The Macmillan Co., 1962.

Wahlke, John C., ed. *Loyalty in a Democratic State.* Boston: D. C. Heath and Company, 1952.

PART III

TEACHERS AND TEACHING

CHAPTER 13

TEACHING IN THE UNITED STATES

HISTORY OF TEACHING

An analysis of teaching must involve both a history of teaching and predictions for its future. It is difficult to select a point of origin, perhaps because there are no really accurate accounts of the status of teachers as far back as paleolithic times. Only Professor Benjamin's prehistoric expert, Dr. Peddiwell, can report:

> By the beginning of the fishnet era, the profession of teaching was pretty well developed, and after the era was well underway, the status and preparation of teachers were rather adequately standardized. In the earlier days of the real-tiger era, teachers had been largely recruited from the ranks of those tribesmen who were too clumsy to grab fish, too weak to club horses, or too timid to face a saber-tooth. By the middle of the fishnet era, this situation had been vastly improved. Teachers were still selected to some extent from the more stupid and less aggressive elements of the population, but any slight disadvantage arising from that condition was more than offset by the new requirements for possession of the teacher's bone [early equivalent of a teacher's certificate, which implies a formal training program].[1]

CLASSICAL AND MEDIEVAL CONCEPTS OF TEACHING

This bit of satiric pseudo-history, however, reflects correctly the origins of the *pedagogue,* a Greek word meaning "to lead a child." In ancient Greece teaching of the young was generally assigned to slaves, a condition of no noticeable prestige. In earlier societies, teaching the *young* was considered a woman's job, or was relegated to the aged, the lame, or the socially useless. In contrast, instructors of *adults* have often acquired

[1] Harold Benjamin, *The Saber-Tooth Curriculum* (New York: McGraw-Hill Book Company, Inc., 1939), p. 48. With permission.

great reputations—witness Socrates, Plato, and Aristotle. Apparently, recognition was accorded teachers in direct ratio to the age group they taught. Echoes of this belief reverberate in many contemporary discussions of education, and our prestige system reflects an even stronger adherence to this idea than many dare verbalize. A young teacher trainee announced the other day that she was choosing to teach in the primary grades because she "wasn't smart enough" for older children. Another student attempted to convince her classmates that "a college degree and specialized teacher training are unnecessary for teachers of children under eight years of age; all that is needed is average intelligence and a love of children." The smug superiority complex of many a college professor similarly attests to this belief.

Cubberly[2] reports:

> In 1722 country school masters in Prussia were ordered selected from tailors, weavers, blacksmiths, wheelrights, and carpenters, and in 1728 they were granted the tailoring monopoly in their villages to help them live. Later Frederick the Great ordered that his crippled and superannuated soldiers should be given teaching positions in the elementary vernacular schools of Prussia.

It should be noted that in 1956 the Ford Foundation was sponsoring special programs of teacher education to press into teaching service retired personnel of the United States armed forces.

In the Middle Ages, the dominance of the church over all areas of knowledge made teaching a natural function of the priests. In one sense the problem of prestige was, therefore, solved if prestige was, indeed, a significant problem at that time. The church supported the priests, who in turn supplied the teaching function. This tradition of combining the clerical and teaching functions persisted down through time and is still present in the organization of many of today's religious groups, notably the Roman Catholics, who maintain special orders of priests and nuns dedicated solely to teaching. It is not difficult to comprehend the rationalization that teaching demands a certain sacrifice of normal social expectancies and therefore is suitable for dedicated, altruistic persons who have little regard for the material considerations or social normality.

[2] E. P. Cubberly, *The History of Education* (Boston, Houghton-Mifflin Company, 1920), p. 446.

TEACHING IN COLONIAL AMERICA

In colonial America, each person was expected to know how to read the Bible. The elimination of the priests as the sole interpreters of theology had been, after all, a cardinal idea of the Reformation. Butts and Cremin[3] report the following summary of the purpose of elementary education in colonial times:

> One of the most elaborate and thoughtful statements of an ideal elementary education according to the view of the Church of England is contained in the instructions given their school masters in 1706 by the Society for the Propagation of the Gospel in Foreign Parts. The goal of education was to teach children to believe and live as Christians. In order to achieve this goal, the children must be taught to read English so that they could read the Bible and other religious books, must learn the catechism by heart after being carefully taught its meaning, must learn the prayers appropriate to school and home, and must be taught how to worship in church and take part in the services. The teacher should also teach the children how to write and how to do arithmetic as a preparation for a useful employment. Special attention was to be given to the manners of the children in order that they be "modest, gentle, well-behaved, just and affable, and courteous to all their companions; respectful to their Superiors," especially to the ministers. They must also be taught to love truth and honesty and to avoid lying and evil speaking. Discipline should be by kind and gentle methods, and punishment given with understanding rather than brutality. Teachers should also be ready to teach Indian and Negro children as well as white children.

This was, of course, quite a different view of discipline from that of influential Calvinist Puritans:

> An authoritarian education was seen as the only possible way to implement beliefs that the child's nature was inherently evil. Since the child was prone to sin, the best way to keep him under control was to instill in him a fear of breaking God's laws and a fear of the awful and dreadful consequences of sin.[4]

Massachusetts and Connecticut even proposed the death penalty for continuously rebellious children. "Not only through catechisms, school books, and laws but also through poetry, sermons, and published advice to parents

[3] R. Freeman Butts and Lawrence A. Cremin, *A History of Education in American Culture* (New York: Holt, Rinehart and Winston, Inc., Copyright 1953), p. 120. With permission.

[4] Butts and Cremin, p. 66.

and ministers was the authoritarian Calvinist outlook on children kept in the literature of the colonial period."[5]

The growing conflict between the established religions in the colonies and the variety of splinter groups and sects spread throughout the new world. Religious freedom demanded diversity of thought and of educational systems; concurrently, there was a quickening of the movement toward a more democratic approach in all spheres of life—political, economic, and social. The growth of the middle classes challenged the dual system of education, which allocated the Latin grammar schools to the upper classes and the elementary school apprentice program to the lower classes. The middle classes, primarily made up of the merchant and trading people, were demanding a type of education that would produce young people more suited to the needs of the developing commercial life.

Now Brim[6] has stated that "the allocation of materials to institutions within a society must provide for two basic things. It must be sufficient to motivate the necessary personnel to enter the institution and to continue an adequate performance of duties, and it must provide the means necessary for the achievement of its aims." In the colonial period, teachers (those motivated to enter the institution of education) must be characterized as usually having little commitment to education per se, as being insufficient in number to meet the rising demands, and as varying considerably in their qualifications. The social prestige of teachers was distributed over the full range, although generally the distribution was badly skewed toward the lower end.

CHARACTERISTICS OF THE COLONIAL SCHOOLMASTER. The historical reputation, correct or overdrawn, of the colonial schoolmaster evolves into caricature precisely because he occupied a sensitive spot in society. Education, we have stated, involves the transmission of the deep-felt values of a human group. Those who are entrusted with this delicate operation are, therefore, operating in an area of extra sensitivity and extra emotional tension. The indiscretions of one teacher trigger an extra precautionary concern for the conduct of all others, and the majority cannot help but feel uncomfortable under such scrutiny. If this process made the colonial schoolmaster "at least as good as his contemporaries and probably better,"[7]

[5] Butts and Cremin, p. 67.

[6] O. G. Brim, Jr., *Sociology and the Field of Education* (New York: Russell Sage Foundation, 1958), p. 24. With permission.

[7] Willard S. Elsbree, *The American Teacher* (New York: American Book Co., 1939), p. 31.

it most probably was an "insipid" kind of goodness, or at least "strangeness," that could inspire the creation of an Ichabod Crane or an ineffective, frightened creature of the Caspar Milquetoast variety. Whatever the cause, the stereotype was apparently fairly negative. The point to emphasize is that persons motivated to enter teaching must have been aware of the stereotype and could see themselves in this role by choice, or otherwise were desperate enough to enter teaching in spite of the stereotype, since teaching afforded some kind of temporary relief from other pressing problems.

> Teaching, then as now, was often looked upon as a waiting station until something better came along, or as a part time job to supplement an otherwise inadequate income. Young prospective clergymen would teach school for a time while waiting for a call to a pastorate, or established clergymen whose main task was their pastorate would teach children or boys for fees to help keep the wolf from the door. Then there were always the adventurers and misfits who had tried other enterprises unsuccessfully and then turned as a last resort to teaching in order to keep body and soul together until a more remunerative business or scheme could be devised. Indentured servants sometimes could use teaching as a means of building up enough of an estate to buy their freedom.[8]

Certainly, the minimal teaching requirements helped to produce this motley crew of educators. In truth, often a person could receive an appointment as a teacher simply by proving that he was orthodox in his religion, loyal to the present government, and in possession of a moral reputation above reproach. Of course, he had to exhibit at least a rudimentary knowledge of reading, writing, and the other subjects he would be expected to teach. Thus, in some classrooms teachers were scholarly and pious churchmen, while the schoolroom down the road might be presided over by a man barely educated beyond the level of those he proposed to instruct.

Neither was there any apparent agitation among schoolmasters to change their status, since any sign of unrest or dissatisfaction could be quickly stamped out by removing the teacher's appointment. Philip Vichers Fithian, a tutor to children of a Virginia planter, reports that "it was advisable to attend church regularly on Sundays, stay close in the retirement of his rooms, pursue the scholarly life, read his books, and stay totally away from women."[9] Fithian's life would have been even more rigid had he resided in the Puritan sphere of influence. His tenure there would have been short, for it would have been difficult for him to remain above the

[8] Butts and Cremin (see note 3), p. 133. With permission.
[9] Quoted in Butts and Cremin (see note 3), p. 134. With permission.

reproach of all the zealous guardians of morality; besides, if he had been a scholar at all, he could have moved on to a station in the clergy or to some college post.

Such close public scrutiny did not prevent the colonial schoolmaster from being a busy man. Salaries were meager, sometimes paid in livestock or other goods. The proper schoolmaster then sought additional forms of income—an acceptable practice, since school teaching was not considered a very demanding job. After completing his regular duties in the classroom and accomplishing the many other assignments he might find recorded as part of his job, the schoolmaster might tend a small farm, ply another trade, or serve with some remuneration in some civic capacity. As a part of his job, he might find himself doing the custodial duties for both the school and the church, assisting the pastor in other enterprises, ringing the church bells, digging graves in the churchyard, running errands, or perhaps acting as church secretary. As an employee of the civil government, he might be required to serve, without additional compensation, as a court summons server, town clerk, public accountant, or town crier.

Such rendering of additional services became a tradition; and even today teachers find themselves expected to contribute their time and energies to community agencies such as Boy and Girl Scout groups (as well as their junior equivalents), Sunday school classes, community choral groups, and the like. It is, in other words, a clear tradition in American education that the job of teaching is not considered a normal portion of work and that teachers can, and should, supplement their incomes with second jobs ("moonlighting," as we call it today). They may also reasonably be required to do extra chores not always pertinent to teaching to aid the community enterprise. This tradition may, however, be fading in the wake of the modern urban explosion. The obvious implication of this tradition is the notion that teaching, not being a full-time job, can hardly be considered a profession.

THE "DAME SCHOOL." The tradition of the "dame school" has a firm place in the history of American schools and teaching. Although colonial Americans were committed to the idea that a woman's place was in the home, the shortage of schoolmasters, the low esteem accorded teachers of the young, and the presence of women who could read and write persuaded villagers to compromise. A woman might be allowed to take little children into her home and hear them recite their alphabets and lead them through other primary educational tasks, provided that all the while she went about her home doing her household chores. Such an arrangement could be made in some areas for widows or maiden aunts, and the town might pay them for such service out of public funds. Such pay was exceedingly small, since a woman could never receive a salary equal to that of a man. In some places, a woman might be recruited to teach the little children during the summer months while the male schoolmaster was otherwise employed, but the man took over after the harvest and with the coming of winter. Women were also assigned the education of the poor in some cases, and were often given no more than informal recognition for whatever they accomplished.

Pennsylvania was a notable exception to this pattern, since the Quakers did not discriminate against women to the same degree as did other sects. It was apparently common to find women teaching school in Pennsylvania communities, but this does not change the general picture of low status for women teachers. The concept of teaching as a part-time enterprise, combined with the idea that a woman's job is relatively unimportant, handicapped teaching from the very beginning of American education—if, indeed, we cannot push such a generalization even further back into history.

THE LANCASTERIAN TEACHING METHOD. One tax-saving innovation which influenced this early period was the Lancasterian method of teaching, for here one educated teacher, aided by a group of unpaid monitors, would lecture to a large number of students. Such a method envisioned the possibility of educating larger numbers of children of all the various social classes. In addition, the Lancasterian method offered the chance for teacher aspirants to observe a master teacher at work. Thus, "model" schools came into existence during the brief period this method was seen as useful. Education under this system, of course, had its limitations, since there was little chance that troubled students would receive assistance from such a distant master. Recent proposals to use television to project the image of the master teacher to large numbers of pupils are reminiscent, and again, the denial of individual differences among students is the basic argument against use of such techniques. Dickens' Mr. Gradgrind (in the novel *Hard Times*) seems to reflect one kind of person who might have advocated this kind of education:

> Now, what I want is Facts. Teach these boys and girls nothing but Facts. Facts alone are wanted in life. Plant nothing else, and root out everything else. You can only form the minds of reasoning animals upon Facts; nothing else will ever be of any service to them. This is the principle

> on which I bring up my own children, and this is the principle on which I bring up these children. Stick to the Facts, sir!!

NINETEENTH-CENTURY DEVELOPMENTS

EMERGENCE OF TEACHER-TRAINING INSTITUTIONS. In any case, the problem of a supply of adequate teachers, no matter what teaching method was used, became a crucial obstacle to the fulfillment of the dream of mass education. Since the New England area was so influential, the problem focused there; for these people wanted a measure of quality in teachers as well as sufficient quantity. The creation of normal schools and teachers colleges appears to indicate that teacher preparation was considered a post–high school task and one to be supported by public taxes. Certainly the teacher-training schools in Germany, particularly Prussia, were seen as models to be adapted to the American scene, for American visitors seem to have been impressed by these Prussian efforts. The first public normal school, founded in Lexington, Massachusetts, in 1839, was a monument to the efforts of educational leaders of the day, and marked a personal victory for Horace Mann, a young lawyer who, ironically, had first become prominent in the Massachusetts legislature as the result of his pleas for institutions for the insane. The Lexington school offered in its one-year program:

> (1) a review of the Common Branches—spelling, reading, writing, grammar and arithmetic; (2) advanced studies (except ancient languages) as time permitted (e.g., geometry; algebra; natural, intellectual and moral philosophy; political economy; and natural history); (3) the physical, mental and moral development of children; (4) the science and art of teaching each of the Common Branches; (5) the art of school government; and (6) practice in teaching and governing a "model" school.[10]

For 1839, this was, indeed, an ambitious program, particularly when one considers the constant struggle for funds and instructors and the almost impossible load of responsibilities carried by Cyrus Pierce, the first principal at Lexington. The Lexington school becomes almost legendary when one remembers that over a hundred years later, teacher education in many states has changed only imperceptably in conception and content. Cyrus Pierce's diaries record the exacerbating day-by-day grappling with problems—problems that only Mann's energy and Pierce's devotion could

[10] Elsbree, *The American Teacher* (see note 7), p. 148. With permission.

have surmounted. But the success of Lexington inspired others, and the movement spread. In 1850, Connecticut, under the leadership of Henry Barnard, established the New Britain Normal school, inspired by Massachusetts and by New York's Albany Normal, inaugurated in 1844.

Cyrus Pierce's diaries also point to another development. He refers frequently to his "young ladies" as having insufficient training in this or that and presenting him with many a headache in the supervision of their lives, in and out of school. Women, in other words, were beginning to move into teaching in significant numbers. In the years 1845 through 1848, the Albany Normal School reported that more than half of its graduates were women.

The prevailing feeling that school teaching involved only a minimum of qualifications, in conjunction with the ever present austerity imposed upon tax-supported institutions, made the use of women as public school teachers a natural outcome. The attempt to ensure quality, implied by the normal school movement, was not a value that would easily supersede the desire for economy or the custom of asserting the "natural superiority" of men. Urban male teachers in the period preceding the Civil War earned about three times as much as their female counterparts; in rural areas, although the margin was not so great, the same inequality was present. Teachers' "salaries were a bit above those of skilled labor, but far from the professional salaries envisioned by the reformers. For many the problem was shrugged off by pointing out that the young women who taught lived at home and, therefore, did not need as large a salary. Others regarded teachers as misfits anyway—persons who could not succeed in the business world and who therefore did not deserve better salaries."[11] Coupled with the impact of the Civil War on manpower, the "genteel respectability" of teaching as a suitable occupation for a proper young lady "in waiting" and the frugal salary structure produced such an influx of women into teaching that by 1870, over 60 per cent of America's teachers were women. The female ratio rose to a high of 85 per cent in 1920, before it settled down to the current trend of about three women for every man in the public school-teaching ranks.

Educational leaders in the formative period of American education have not received great attention in the annals of American history, yet it is almost possible to say that, in many states, the distinctive pattern of

[11] Butts and Cremin, *A History of Education in American Culture* (see note 3), p. 285. With permission.

education that today constitutes our massive public education enterprise was wrought out of the hopes, toils, and worldly goods of these few leaders *almost in spite* of the general population. Horace Mann, the lawyer from Massachusetts, later to become the influential president of Antioch College, Ohio, perhaps towers above the rest, but others too faced the endless discouragements and bitter controversies and kept on trying to increase the quality and efficiency of this massive movement.

EMERGENCE OF TEACHERS' ORGANIZATIONS. The Lyceum movement, originated by Josiah Holbrook in 1826, was organized to advance the cause of education, particularly in the public schools. It developed quickly in states like New York, Massachusetts, Rhode Island, Pennsylvania, Virginia, and Illinois and soon provoked the creation of some sort of organization of school teachers. Membership in the Lyceum was both professional and lay, and, in the case of a sister organization, the Western Literary Institute and College of Professional Teachers, a lobbyist was employed and a journal issued. "Public school teachers," states Elsbree,[12] "though active, did not play the leading roles in . . . these propaganda societies, nor was their economic, social, or professional welfare a major consideration in the work of the associations."

Finally, in 1857, the National Teachers Association was formed, presumably to represent only those engaged in the business of education. Two groups were conspicuously absent from full membership: laymen and women teachers, although two women signed the original constitution. The preponderance of women teachers was, however, finally recognized, and they gained full membership nine years later, in 1866. The business of the association was to advance the cause of teaching and popular education, but they usually kept away from such controversial issues as salaries, tenure, or thorny social problems.

In 1870, the National Teachers Association became the National Education Association (NEA), which had among its members a major share of the educational leaders of the day but, between 1870 and 1900, mustered a membership list equivalent to no more than 7 per cent of the number of practicing teachers (since the membership included administrators and other educational personnel, the percentage of teachers belonging drops still lower); in one dismal year, 1885, a roll call was answered by less than the equivalent of 1 per cent of all teachers then teaching. It can be

[12] *The American Teacher* (see note 7), p. 243. With permission.

said, however, that the organization of local, state, and national associations dedicated to the problems of education provided at least the creation of a forum for discussion and the machinery for action, thus, progress could be visualized.

EFFORTS TO PRODUCE HIGH-QUALITY TEACHING. Two perpetual obstacles confronting efforts to provide the means necessary to achieve the society's goal of high-quality mass education for its children were the issues of quality and quantity of teachers. Quality could be achieved by better preparation of teachers and better supervision of those already employed. But quantity involved attracting sufficient numbers of qualified people and holding them on the job. Thus, a vicious circle was created in the beginning and persists to a great extent today: low economic and social status for the occupation of teaching tended to drive better candidates away; lesser-quality people entered and lent weight to the argument that teachers were not good enough to deserve greater prestige and pay; continuing low pay drove better people away. Two citations seem illustrative of the financial distress of teachers of the time. Horace Mann commented in 1843 on a town in Massachusetts:

> Not long since in one of the most cultivated towns in the Commonwealth I took great pains to ascertain the wages of journeymen, shoemakers, carpenters, blacksmiths, painters, carriagemakers, wheelwrights, harnessmakers, cabinet and piano-forte makers, and some others. The result—showed that while every class of these received more, some—received 50 percent and a few 100 percent more than was paid to any of the teachers of the district schools in the same town.[13]

The 13th Annual Report of the Superintendent of Public Instruction in California stated in 1863 that the average salary of teachers was $357 a year, and commented as follows:

> Out of this annual average salary, teachers must board and clothe themselves, and pay their income tax! An average servant girl receives $300 a year and her board; and average farm hands get the same; and even an able bodied Chinaman gets $300 a year, boarding himself. The lowest monthly wages paid to any male teachers was $29, the teacher boarding himself. A missionary ought to be sent to that district at once by the State Educational Society.[14]

[13] Quoted in Elsbree (see note 7), p. 279. With permission.
[14] Quoted in Elsbree, p. 281. With permission.

In American society such salaries surely were a gauge of the status of the occupation of school teaching. But teachers were victims of still another practice that could not but discourage even the most humble and devoted pedagogue. This was the custom of having the teacher live with the various patrons of the school, each such boarding lasting for whatever period had been determined as the equal and fair share of the various patrons. The teacher thus had no life of his own, was subject to the pleasure of his current host, and had to abide whatever the level of living with which he was confronted. He or she became a fifth wheel in a family for just long enough to become acquainted and then was moved on, to begin the dreary task again. Elsbree[15] reports that in 1862 in Vermont 68 per cent of all teachers were subjected to this mode of living, while Connecticut, in 1846, claimed 84 per cent participation in this cheerless fate. Certainly, such a practice was cause enough for adventurous spirits to look away from teaching as a career, and leave it, in general, to the lacklustre individuals who provided the image of the public school teacher.

Low salaries and rotating boarding had another effect on the lives of teachers. Lack of funds restricted the potential activities of teachers in their "spare" time, but living with the parents of the school children enjoined the teacher to remain on the highest moral level at all times. Under this living, of course, there was automatic close supervision, and rules were set forth governing all forms of social life. In short, teachers lived in a grim and sparsely furnished fishbowl and were easily inspired to seek another occupation. If we recall that the average age of teachers in this period was below twenty-five, it seems reasonable to believe that such young people as could were quick to escape and that the rapid turnover of teachers was even more common then than it is today. Thus, the problem of a sufficient supply of teachers had these obstacles to overcome.

In the matter of quality, there was a concerted effort on the part of educational leaders to improve the preparation of teachers and raise the level of instruction in the schools. Teacher institutes were created for short periods to study and discuss problems of teaching with groups of classroom teachers. The demand for additional preparation of teachers eventually produced the teachers' college.

John Swett of California led a fight to change the practice of having laymen conduct certification examinations on the local level. He proposed that certification of teachers become a state function, conducted by qualified

[15] *The American Teacher*, p. 288.

professional examiners drawn from the ranks of teachers and administrators. There were faint signs that serious consideration was being given to the notion that a teacher, particularly at the secondary level, ought to have some form of liberal education. Normal schools in some states evolved into four-year institutions, and by 1920 there were 46 teachers' colleges in the land. Even universities had begun to see their role in educating future high school and college teachers; the University of Iowa established a chair in education in 1873. Training for elementary teachers was to wait until later for such attention.

In the classrooms, improvement was slow. Although attempts to elevate standards often produced opposite results, it is clear that school administration was now based on a sincere and legitimate desire to raise the level of instruction. While school supervisors and superintendents were often woefully lacking in knowledge of what they were doing, they did establish the machinery for adequate supervision. While supervisors "inspected" schools for evidence of correct room arrangement, classroom control, adherence to subject matter, and a myriad of minutiae, they also introduced new teaching materials and aids that were sorely needed. What developed was an interesting pattern of conformity on the one hand and private vision on the other. In these developmental years, teaching had no design or craftsmanship; it lacked the conceptual framework upon which is built the delicate relationship between instructor and pupil. But men like Horace Mann had hope, and they pleaded for a willingness to invest, to plunge recklessly in behalf of "our clients, the next generation."

PUBLIC SCHOOL TEACHING IN THE TWENTIETH CENTURY

The distinctive American public school teacher who poked her head into the twentieth-century schoolroom was a product of an equally distinctive American educational system. Caught in the dream of a mass-educated citizenry supporting a democratic government and a capitalist economy, American education had produced at least the reality of mass education of a sort. Compulsory attendance of all children between seven and seventeen was the rule in most states, and the increasing urbanization of what was developing as the greatest industrial nation in the world seemed to assure compliance with this ideal of mass education, for only rural America appeared to drag its feet (and in the view of some, perhaps still does).

With a growing economic prosperity and vigorous industrial development, the population soared, and the demand for teachers became overwhelming. If the demand outstripped any orderly development of programs of adequate teacher preparation, it was no more startling than other social and economic events of the time. The normal school, chief trainer of teachers, was a mushrooming institution. Teachers colleges grew in number, and even universities occasionally participated in teacher education. Certification became a state function—governed, it is true, by functionaries, but at least out of the hands of local laymen whose vested interests had long made a mockery of any theory of professional qualifications.[16] Schoolrooms were no longer isolated kingdoms, even if school districts did occasionally become the special empires of their administrative officers. Teachers found increasing amounts of materials, written for their youthful charges, that applied the best techniques and were based upon the latest research about children and learning. Textbooks and materials were developing into a billion-dollar industry and the children were reaping the benefits.

In secondary education, the concern for quality teachers was pushing requirements for certification higher and higher, and subject-matter specialists were soon developed. Selective certification codified teacher specialization, until it was necessary for a prospective teacher to select her field early in her training period—be it elementary or secondary; and, if the latter, in a particular subject-matter area. The generalist, liberally educated in many fields, was a man of the past. But each state in our blossoming union was independent in matters of education by a lack of Constitutional proviso, and what happened in Missouri rarely affected the specific pattern wrought for Virginia. Not only were practices distinctive at the level of specifics, but a teacher from New York might find herself barred from teaching in Nebraska because of the twists and turns of state certification laws.

For teachers in the field there was the constant prodding to improve. The institution of the summer school, as a special in-service training opportunity, was developed, as were the extension services of colleges and universities. A teacher could easily add to her training by attending a summer session or attending a class in her own school building at night, led by a faculty member from a nearby college or university. And, indeed, there was much to learn, for increasing numbers of people had turned their attention toward developing the methodology of teaching. Psycholo-

[16] Recently California has faced a determined effort on the part of a *lay* State Board of Education, and a *lay* State Legislature to take over completely the determination of professional qualifications for teaching, as well as the definition of all school curricula.

gists were making strides in developing greater understanding of children, and administrative specialists were pressing to ravel and unravel the mysteries of the emerging school bureaucracy and the complicated financial and legal relationships within the society. Salesmen from the book companies moved about the country like strolling players, convincing educators that precisely this set of books or this teaching aid was the solution to all of the teacher's multiple problems. Teaching, weakened to some extent by inbreeding, was nevertheless coming into its own as a recognized and necessary function in the society. But the years of struggle had left its scars.

Economically, teachers were still little better than paupers. An expanding economy that was creating staggering fortunes seemed to have little generosity and little desire to make education its partner. School boards hung back and preferred to keep taxes down to the minimum level. The "general groping for social betterment which was produced by the misery that came in the wake of the industrial revolution and the factory system"[17] apparently overlooked the schoolmarms. Even the wave of liberalism that produced Charles Beard and John Dewey failed to notice, as in Grecian days, the public school teacher of the young. Massive social reforms had little impact upon institutionalized education and its practitioners. Teachers found all the good statuses had been taken; wherever they looked they faced reserved tables. Although an element of stability had been built into their lives with the introduction of tenure laws in some states, teachers remained a relatively unstable group with large turnovers in staff—a common condition in most schools. The same kind of social taboos that had plagued them earlier emerged as part of the distinctive pattern. Socially, teachers were to remain, in a sense, second-class citizens, living under the close scrutiny of the public, often subjected to unreasonable restrictions on their private lives, and vulnerable to criticism at every turn.

The challenge to change this picture came from the Carnegie Foundation for the Advancement of Teaching in its 1957 report:[18]

> The people of the United States have a virtually unlimited faith in higher education. They know what it means for their own children, and what it means to the future of America. But they do not yet understand that this precious national resource is built squarely on the vitality of the

[17] Harry Elmer Barnes, "The Development of Sociology," in V. F. Calverton, ed., *The Making of Society* (New York: Modern Library, 1937), p. 661.

[18] 1957 Report of the Carnegie Foundation for the Advancement of Teaching, as quoted in *Reporter Magazine,* February 1958, p. 8.

> teaching profession. And they do not realize that the teaching profession is slowly withering away.

Max Ascoli, editor of *Reporter Magazine,* adds: "Future historians will marvel at the level of literacy and at the achievements of science that can be credited to our wildly pluralistic, decentralized educational system which has been operating at a discount rate, with the people paying in times of comparative prosperity less than fifty per cent for values received."[19] "What is honored in a country will be cultivated there," observed the philosopher Plato.

CONTEMPORARY TEACHER EDUCATION

A young man or woman who chooses teaching as a career enrolls in a teacher-training program at some point in his or her college career. Naively, the student may think he is enrolling in a training program to acquire such theories, skills, and abilities as will designate him a specialist, with an appropriate license that allows only such specialists to practice this "profession." Enrollment in a law school, a medical school, or a school of social welfare would produce such results. But enrollment in a teacher-training school turns out to be something quite different.

The disturbing reality of American education is that teacher-training programs (1) are seldom based upon any systematically established or tested criteria; (2) are usually without any apparent links to the aims and functions of education; (3) are open targets for any hungry crusader looking for a cause; and (4) are arenas in which some of the most virulent disagreements in education confront one another.

Within the social system of professional education, the teacher-education process and its personnel operate in relative isolation. Direct influence on such programs is usually applicable only through the screen of state government—either the legislature, the state board of education, or perhaps the trustees of the college or university. Local school boards have no direct access to teacher-education programs; neither do school administrators, PTA groups, or even professional organizations. The general public is similarly kept at a distance, because there are no readily available pressure points where influence might be applied.

Antagonists have tried to conjure this situation into a national con-

[19] Max Ascoli, Editorial, *Reporter Magazine,* February 1958. With permission.

spiracy of professional educators to (1) control education for devious ends, (2) protect flagrant incompetence, or (3) simply pork barrel for the "establishment." While such notions have received much attention in the uncritical mass media, their basis in fact is dubious. *All* college programs operate within a system, and *all* college programs of training for *any* occupation exhibit similar detachment. Public concern for the training of doctors, lawyers, ministers, social workers, agronomists, home economists, or any other college-level occupation faces the same obstacles to direct access as are present in teacher education. And attempts to change the system, such as making college curricula open to inspection and revision by public bodies, have been stoutly resisted by *all* segments of the college community under the banner of "academic freedom" or "institutional autonomy."

It is a tradition of long standing that colleges reserve to themselves the right to choose the design of any training program for any occupation. This is not to imply that colleges remain pugnaciously at odds with the rest of society, for they are usually quite sensitive and responsive to the public and professional pulse. But it does mean that the *choice,* or initiative, has tended to remain within the grasp of the colleges. Whether such autonomy continues to be justified demands further investigation by *all* concerned people in *all* relevant training programs.

We have stated that our investigations point to a lack of systematically tested criteria for programs of teacher training. Presumably, when a training program is instituted in any field, certain prescriptions must be followed. First, there must be a decision on what the final product is to be. This "objective" of the program may be to produce a person with particular skills who will perform a specified function. Second, there must be a procedure designed to accomplish the agreed-upon objective. A program is designed which, it is hypothesized, will actually produce the desired end. Third, there must be a systematic program of evaluation that attempts to check, in fact, whether or not the objective has been reached. Or, to put it in other terms, there is first a clearly defined problem, then the selection of a method of solution, and finally a verification to see whether we have produced the correct answer.

Teacher-education programs typically reveal disparities at all three points in this three-step process. First, the problem or objective is not at all clearly defined, at least in terms of its relationships to the aims and functions of education. Second, teacher-education programs usually stop at the procedure stage and entirely abandon the evaluation process. In most institutions, once teacher trainees have completed their programs and have graduated, the teacher-training institution considers its job completed and thereafter maintains little contact, except for placement services, with its graduates.[20] Once in a while, an institution will ask its graduates to comment on the training program, perhaps on which courses helped them most and which helped them least and why. But this type of procedure does not constitute legitimate evaluation, because the graduate is not answering with any awareness of the original objectives or the design of the procedures intended to accomplish the objectives. He can reply pragmatically in terms of how the program helped him fit into his present position, but this is invalid, because the criteria governing success in his present position may be, and often are, quite different from those governing his training program. Certainly, it is possible that some useful information can be gained by such inquiries, but it is equally true that if such evaluations produce valid answers to the original problem, such results are purely coincidental.

The lack of validation of the training objectives and procedures serves only to reinforce the essential isolation of teacher-education programs from the rest of the institution of education. And, as we have stated, no pressure points appear to exist at present that could disrupt this process and, thereby, force teacher education to reassess its appropriateness to the reality of the primary education community—the schools-children-parents axis.

There is, however, one period during the teacher-induction process when differences between the conceptions of the teacher-education institutions and the everyday world of schools are noticeable. This moment is when the teacher trainee becomes enmeshed in what is called the "direct experience" phase of his training. Usually this period consists of some forms of "practice" or "student" teaching, when the candidate is farmed out to a classroom of children and directed for a period of time in the practice of the acts of teaching. Obviously, if the teacher trainee has been absorbed, up to this time, in an invalid program, the student-teaching experience is likely to be fairly traumatic, a sudden dip into polar waters. Charles H. Wilson[21] states: "I would rather go through basic training again in the army than go through practice teaching."

[20] It should be noted again that this lack of systematic prescription at the various steps is not unlike what happens in law, medical, and other professional schools. Inadequacies, however, are not justified just because they occur in various walks of life.

[21] *A Teacher Is a Person* (New York: Henry Holt and Company, 1956), p. 45.

At least two factors reduce the trauma, however, and eventually become the rationalizations that bridge the chasm. The first is the development of a specialized vocabulary, typical of most specialized occupations. Such a vocabulary is usually essential to the articulation of very precise and special meanings and is entirely justifiable. In professional education, however, the tendency has been somewhat the opposite, in that the specialized vocabulary seems almost deliberately ambiguous.

> "When I use a word," Humpty Dumpty said, in a rather scornful tone, "it means just what I choose it to mean—neither more nor less."
>
> "The question is," said Alice, "whether you can make words mean so many different things."
>
> "The question is," said Humpty Dumpty, "which is to be master—that's all."

Having become the "masters" rather than the "slaves" of words, the teacher of education can give one meaning to an educational term, while the practitioner in the field gives it another. When the differences in meanings precipitate a definite discord, it is explained as a fundamental schism that inevitably exists between theory and practice. Teachers in the field can easily reject notions presented by teachers of education as mere intrusions of the "theoretical," while the educators expiate their failures to communicate by adopting the stance that most people "in the field" are fixed on the practice level and have long since lost the capacity to grasp any "theoretical" illuminations. It is a remarkable phenomena that practicing teachers can move from the work world of the school to the work world of the college, encounter numerous contradictions, and yet experience no unusual discomforts. The explanation seems to lie in the implication that teachers are apparently not deeply involved in either world, for careful intellectual scholarship would unearth contradictions close to the surface of any significant issue or problem.

THE AMERICAN CONFLICT OVER THE PURPOSES OF EDUCATION

There has been a perpetual dilemma in American culture over the aims and functions of education. A society must have a clear picture of the purposes of its educational process before decisions can be made about the kind of teachers needed and, therefore, the kind of teacher education to be given. It is clear that our American society has never proclaimed these purposes adequately or consistently. In fact, American education has tended to be an arena for constant controversy and leaves little choice to educators but to steer as neutral a course as possible, bobbing and weaving, side-stepping and ducking among the embattled patrons. Walter Lippmann[22] has said that a public philosophy (upon which a sound educational system must be based) should be in the public interest, and "the public interest may be presumed to be what men would choose if they saw clearly, thought rationally, acted disinterestedly and benevolently." A review of history does not produce evidence that any such Utopia has ever come to pass, and commentators on the current scene seem to offer little assurance of its imminent arrival. But institutionalized occupations go on; they cannot wait for the evolution of a public philosophy. It is like the Italian family in which one son was a Socialist, his brother a Communist, and the father a Monarchist. The din of argument reverberated all day, but when mother announced that dinner was served, all were of one accord. In short, the institutionalized role of cook and the basic function of eating went on.

Thus, in lieu of values insisted upon by the total society, teachers of education have inevitably accepted the responsibility to cast their own images of what teachers ought to be in the light of their own particular set of commitments. Two distinctive patterns have emerged from this process and can be readily identified as particular responses to certain behavior patterns. The two traditions shall be designated as the "liberal" and the "technical," in accordance with Borrowman's useful definitions.[23] Borrowman states: "The liberal function of education is to make certain that the individual sees every problem of living, including the professional ones, in the broadest scope possible." The technical function, on the other hand, is "The cultivation of skill in the actual performance of a previously determined task." Advocates of these two traditions naturally face some serious problems if both are to attain their objectives, because the technical function must achieve greater "liberality," while the liberal function needs to face some excruciatingly technical realities.

THE LIBERAL TRADITION

The liberal tradition grew out of the notion that education is primarily focused upon knowledge and the development of the mind. The

[22] Walter Lippmann, *The Public Philosophy* (Boston: Little, Brown and Company, 1955), p. 178.

[23] Merle L. Borrowman, *The Liberal and Technical in Teacher Education* (New York: Bureau of Publications, Teachers College, Columbia University, 1956), pp. 4–5.

orientation was largely an academic one associated with university education and the liberal arts college. Woodring[24] describes the product as follows:

> The liberally educated man is one who can make wise decisions independently. He can choose between good and bad, truth and falsehood, the beautiful and the ugly, the worthwhile and the trivial. His education will improve his ability to make ethical decisions, political decisions, decisions within the home and on the job. It will enable him to choose and to appreciate a good book, a good painting, or a good piece of music. It will free him of provincialism and prepare him to understand cultures other than his own. It will enable him to make the many decisions necessary in planning a good life and conducting it properly. This education should be common to all, and independent of vocational choice. If he is to make wise independent decisions, the individual must be able to think critically and logically. But even the clearest and most logical thinking will not lead to sound conclusions unless it proceeds from sound premises. The individual must possess a vast amount of accurate information about his world, his culture, and himself. He must have a knowledge of political, social, and economic history because sound decisions in these areas cannot be made without background information of an historical nature. He must know the sciences because many important decisions rest upon a knowledge of the world and of men and much of this information has been accumulated and verified through the scientific method. He must be familiar with great literature because literature offers another approach to knowledge of man and society and because literature deals with values and he must make value judgments. He must know philosophy because all decisions, without exception, rest upon interpretations of reality, of truth, and of value. He must know mathematics because a knowledge of quantities or their relationship is essential to choice. These bodies of knowledge and these intellectual disciplines are not the ultimate end of education, but a grasp of them is essential to that end.

Not many of us are likely to live up to Woodring's model, but, equally true, many of us may be desirous of achieving such excellence. The liberal tradition is obviously a tradition of "higher" education and academic impeccability. This places it on the highest prestige levels of the educational world. "The university professor," says Williams,[25] "sits at the apex of the vast educational pyramid in America, respected by parents, by

[24] Paul Woodring, *New Directions in Teacher Education* (New York: The Fund for the Advancement of Education, 1957), p. 8.

[25] George Williams, *Some of My Best Friends Are Professors* (New York: Abelard-Schuman, 1958), p. 35.

teachers in the public schools, by students, and by alumni." He goes on to confess that, as a university professor, "I have felt as a feudal lord must feel among the peasants; and sometimes I blush to find that, in spite of myself, I 'Assume the god/Affect to nod/ And seem to shade the spheres.' " It should be added that university professors *do not* like to think of themselves as, primarily, teachers, but as scholars and scientists. Most universities reinforce this conception by placing almost total emphasis on research and writing as the criteria for occupational success. In contrast, Dewey stated: "The mere absorption of facts and truths is so exclusively individual an affair that it tends very naturally to pass into selfishness. There is no obvious social motive for the acquirement of mere learning, there is no clear social gain in success there at."[26]

In his four years of college, an average student in a university can take only about thirty-two courses—out of as many as two thousand offered by many universities. At best, then, the student is sampling only about one sixtieth of the available liberal education. He must, therefore, be highly selective—either by his own volition or by virtue of choices forced upon him by university programs or officials. What follows then is a highly competitive race for students. When Woodring[27] speaks of "liberal arts colleges (turning) their backs on the problems of teacher education" and being "preoccupied with other things," perhaps he means that one of the most important things with which the university community is "preoccupied" is the scramble for supremacy and students. In the cafeteria-style universities of today, every professor must consider his area as the "entree" and every other area a mere "relish." When this competition is injected into a discussion of the design of a teacher-education program, the results are more than a casual comedy. One cannot help recalling that delectable scene in Charlie Chaplin's *The Great Dictator,* when Hitler and Mussolini maneuver among the chairs and tables, each seeking the highest position so that he might look down on the other.

Also incorporated in the attitudes of the university liberal arts professor is the notion that he is, in fact, a successful teacher, and that this achievement was accomplished without the benefit of so-called professional training in pedagogy. It is irrelevant to this discussion to engage in a dispute over the accuracy of this assumption. It is enough to report Williams'

[26] John Dewey, *The School and Society* (Chicago: University of Chicago Press, Phoenix Books), p. 15.

[27] *New Directions in Teacher Education* (see note 24), p. 23.

conclusion that colleges fail with the majority of their students; and this is true despite the fact that college students represent a select intellectual group in the general population. "Professors," says Williams, "are universally reluctant to assume responsibility for [the] really monstrous failures in teaching" in colleges and universities. The conviction that good teaching is not the result of "professional training" gives rise to the further notion that "professional courses of any kind [are] inconsistent with the proper aims of the liberal arts college, and that the presence of such courses in the curriculum would vitiate the liberal arts program."[28]

The point, then, is that the liberal tradition and its adherents have steadfastly detached themselves philosophically, psychologically, and sociologically from the field of everyday public school education. In fact, the liberal tradition has, in many respects, tried to detach itself from any practical involvement in teacher education, which, as we have already stated, is itself detached from the front line educational community. This latter position has become increasingly difficult to maintain in the face of the major trend toward multipurpose institutions of higher education. It is clear that more and more each year, the specialized institution (in this case, the normal school or teachers college) is destined for near extinction, as is the pure liberal arts college.

Conant reports that, "nothing revealed by a close study of institutions designated as *teachers colleges,* as compared to those designated as *liberal arts colleges,* justifies a sweeping assertion that one *type* of institution consistently gives the student a better education than the other."[29] The stubborn insistence of liberal arts advocates that their position automatically assures superiority has done little to relieve the tensions between themselves and the so-called technical educators in those fields having a technical phase in their training program.

THE TECHNICAL TRADITION

Let us return to the second tradition, the technical emphasis. Borrowman defines the technical function as "the cultivation of skill in the actual performance of a previously determined task."[30] Two parts of this definition need particular attention: the first is the emphasis on "actual experi-

[28] Williams (see note 25), p. 23.

[29] James B. Conant, *The Education of American Teachers* (New York: McGraw-Hill Book Co., 1963), p. 77.

[30] Borrowman (see note 23), pp. 4–5.

ence," and the second is the source of definitions of "previously determined skill." Let us explore the second notion first, since herein lurk the assumptions that have alienated teacher education from the field of practice.

The exceedingly low quality of the teaching present in the early elementary or "common" schools in the United States drove educational leaders to the necessity of emergency action. Recall Cyrus Pierce's complaint at Lexington, in 1839, that he had to spend much valuable time just teaching the rudimentary skills of number, reading, and writing to his young ladies. As women entered the elementary field and as their number grew in the teaching ranks, quality sank lower. One must hasten to assure the reader that there is no prejudice in this observation. We have established the socially inferior position alloted women in these earlier days, and we have alluded to the idea that inadequacy can be born of an overwhelming preoccupation with survival. The significant point is that elementary education was in a sad state, and as the crisis grew, the measures adopted to stem the tide grew proportionately desperate. American education has always seemed to need the convening of emergency meetings to deal with a rapid build-up of successive waves of crises.

Thus the "normal" school was created and its popularity spread quickly throughout the various states; but the programs of these institutions were, at best, stopgap. A young lady about to assume the management of a classroom of active youngsters "just had to have training" in at least some fundamental classroom management skills. The normal school determined which skills were needed and proceeded earnestly to try and develop these skills in future teachers. Almost any success they achieved in this process was immediately apparent in the elementary school classrooms of the day. In short, stopgap measures produced improvement—perhaps not so much because this training was inherently good, but rather because any training was oxygen to a suffocating system of education. The heady consequences of this success, which mounted over the years, can be detected in the modern educational world. Some teacher-education leaders begin with the assumption that they can construct a definition of what constitutes teacher competence. These definitions are sometimes developed by describing actual teacher performance and then drawing out the skills involved, which thereupon become the criteria for educational programs for teachers. Or a second technique is used: teachers of education first describe to one another what they think a good teacher should be able to do; next, they extract the skills involved, and finally a new teacher-education program is born.

Many critics of teacher education who offer reform solutions to the problems of teacher training are really engaging in the process just mentioned, except that they like *their* words better. Both the critics and the teachers of education may be entirely sincere, but solutions, born in desperation, rarely prove adequate in the face of the complexity of such problems in a democratic America that steadfastly fails to define aims and functions carefully.

Since the normal school, like many of its modern counterparts—the isolated teachers college or the school of education, emphasized the skills needed on the job, teacher-education programs often rely heavily upon an on-the-job training approach. We have previously referred to this as the "direct experience" phase of teacher training. Complicated by an uncritical acceptance of a catch phrase allegedly taken from John Dewey—"learn by doing," the technical function truly becomes no more than "training," which, no doubt, makes a better welder, a skillful cabinet maker, or even a proficient piano technician. The reduction of teacher education to the skill-training level obviously prevents the achievement of professionalization, but then such aspirations may seem irrelevant to practitioners who are, as we have said, preoccupied with survival. Teacher trainees, early sensing the urgency of the survival factor, seem drawn to the "direct-experience" phase of their training and frequently display impatience toward consideration of abstract material or confinement to the theoretical aspects of the teaching process. A day's observation in the field frequently sends future teachers scurrying to start their own collection of teaching devices, distinctive methods, and unusual learning games.

IMPLICATIONS FOR EDUCATORS

It does not matter which tradition, the liberal or the technical, is in the ascendency at any particular time; both are detached from the public and the schools. E. B. Tylor long ago urged that we try to get rid of those practices which have nothing to commend them but the fact that they are survivals of the past.[31] As long as teacher education is detached, it also matters little just what kind of compromise is affected between the two traditions. Bigelow[32] fears that professional education is being asked to capitulate—the technical surrendering to the liberal. Advocates of the liberal tradition, on the other hand, have issued national proclamations to the effect that they have suffered a series of defeats at the hands of the

[31] E. B. Tylor, *Primitive Culture,* as interpreted by Morton White, *Social Thought in America* (Boston: Beacon Press, 1957), p. 18.

[32] Karl W. Bigelow, "New Directions in Teacher Education Appraised," *Teachers College Record,* 59, No. 6 (March 1958), 356.

"technical educationists." Even Conant's attempt to find a middle ground has achieved only limited success in practice.[33]

The teacher, as a human being and a so-called specialist, is caught between these opposing forces and, in order to survive the conflict, may withdraw his vitally needed concern for his own future and that of his occupation. It would be tragic if such a withdrawal occurred; for teachers, since they constitute the real force of public education, could well act as a unifying force. Schools themselves could play a larger part than they now do in the preparation of future practitioners. The schools have the plants, the children, and much experience. They are closer to the real problems of education, and lack only the assistance of leaders who have had the opportunity to survey and examine the larger scene. Both liberal and technical educators could suggest long-range considerations as well as carry on increasingly sophisticated research. Dewey said: "A man is imperfectly intelligent when he forms plans apart from study of the actual conditions, including his own capacities."[34]

The essential problem is to establish direction and noncompetitive responsibility. Accomplishment of these two goals would require careful definition of the aims and functions of teaching and, therefore, teacher education, followed by allocation of appropriate responsibility. More extensive use of the public schools and their personnel in the process would serve to diminish the detachment of teacher education from the rest of the educational world. Flexibility rather than strict formulas would help recognition of the fact that the education of teachers is no less dependent upon individual differences than is the education of children. Neither is teacher education any less diverse.

The serious educational decision maker will find many competing values, little empirical evidence, and much unnecessary agitation when he considers the problems of teacher education. Decisions concerning teaching *will be made* because of the pressure of events. The challenge to educators is whether such decisions will be thoughtful and responsible, or merely repetitions of the clichés and mistakes of the past.

SUMMARY

Teaching as an occupation had extremely modest beginnings in western civilization and throughout history has made relatively small gains.

[33] Conant (see note 29).
[34] John Dewey, *Democracy and Education* (New York: The Macmillan Co. 1916).

This has been especially true of the teaching of young children, for gains in prestige and remuneration in this occupation usually have come in direct proportion to the age of the children taught. American education had particularly inauspicious beginnings and has had to struggle for its existence throughout its history. Low salaries and low-level performances were just two debilitating factors.

Constant attention by educators to the raising of standards and the improvement of occupational status has slowly elevated teaching, but public support has not always been equally dedicated to such improvement.

The education of teachers has suffered from lack of definition, superficial standards, and much criticism. Specifically, teacher education has suffered from low admission standards, lack of tested criteria, stopgap approaches, a false dichotomy between theory and practice, and a public feud between the "liberal" and the "technical" tradition. Underlying these issues are fundamental value choices that may not have been resolved sufficiently to allow educators to proceed in a clearly defined manner. Educators themselves can make a major contribution to clarifying the issues and precipitating the appropriate choices.

SELECTED BIBLIOGRAPHY

Borrowman, Merle. *The Liberal and Technical in Teacher Education.* New York: Bureau of Publications, Teachers College, Columbia University, 1956.

Butts, R. Freeman, and Lawrence A. Cremin. *A History of Education in American Culture.* New York: Henry Holt and Company, 1953.

Conant, James Bryant. *The Education of American Teachers.* New York: McGraw-Hill Book Company, 1963.

The Education of Teachers. 2nd Bowling Green Conference. Washington, D.C.: National Commission on Teacher Education and Professional Standards, 1958.

The Education of Teachers. Kansas Conference. Washington, D.C: National Commission on Teacher Education and Professional Standards, 1959.

Elsbree, Willard S. *The American Teacher.* New York: American Book Company, 1939.

Gage, N. L., ed. *Handbook of Research on Teaching.* Chicago: Rand McNally and Company, 1963.

Williams, George. *Some of My Best Friends Are Professors.* New York: Abelard-Schuman, 1958.

Woodring, Paul. *New Directions in Teacher Education.* New York: Fund for the Advancement of Education, 1957.

CHAPTER 14

TEACHERS

Almost everyone feels he knows all about teaching, but few admit much knowledge about teachers. Many people engage in teaching, both formally and informally, and surely the impact of such teaching is felt in the environment. Nevertheless, the untidy truth is that there is, and has always been, a persistent confusion about who teachers are. Grandiose generalizations, screened through the haze of nostalgia, have led many to believe in stereotypes, and the stereotype of the distinctive American teacher which has emerged is, in many way, unfortunate. Picture a woman, usually a maiden lady of undetermined age with a grim set line in her mouth and hard eyes, with hair neatly and tightly bound in a knot on her head. Despite the fact that she was usually young, public memory usually recalls her as old. Teachers are, to use an image from D. H. Lawrence, "odd wintry flowers upon the withered stem, yet new strange flowers." The alternative picture is that of an effusive, childless old woman who "just loves" every child; a "kissgranny or hugmoppet," in the words of James Thurber. In other words, the stereotype of the school teacher is pitiful and somewhat poignant. Teachers are lonely women who live in cramped apartments, with underwear and stockings drying in the bathroom. Their plan books have embroidered covers, and they are the humble devoted servants of a community; but they have to go to the next town if they have a date. Each career is a private dedication, hampered by the necessity of Boy Scoutism and church decorum. Teachers are thought of as frightened people, eating cheerless meals in respectable diners, carrying on their mission in a world in which plumbing has surpassed poetry.

As for the males who have survived in teaching, the stereotype is no more kind. The male teacher is likely to be pictured as slight, effeminate, frightened and fussy, as well as a little odd. A timid man. The teacher, in short, has emerged as a kind of cultural rag, bottle and sack man, "poking the peevish gutter" of his time.

SOCIAL-CLASS ORIGINS OF TEACHERS

Harold Laski, describing teaching as "the last refuge of the shabby genteel," perhaps caught the essence of the argument over the social origins of teachers, their motivations for entering teaching, and the resultant pattern of their lives.

To begin with, school teaching is essentially a white-collar job. It presumes that practitioners will be reasonably neat and well dressed and will deal, in general, with affairs of the mind rather than the hands. These conditions alone, in the eyes of some, raise school teaching above the pedestrian level of the telephone operator, the waitress, or the "working-class drone who dresses in overalls, carries a lunchbox, and has dirty fingernails."

If we want to establish a sound theoretical framework that shows how the teacher emerges as an occupational type, we must determine how his social origins, the society he lives in, and the teaching profession itself have shaped his values about himself, his career, and society at large. Examination of the teacher on the basis of samples from widely differing sections of our nation will reveal certain central tendencies.

According to Greenhoe,[1] reporting on a nationwide sample of over 9,000 teachers, they are "predominantly of native-white stock, invariably come from middle-class homes, are of rural or small town origin." This picture was reconfirmed in 1957 by the NEA study[2] of 5,600 teachers, in which 68.2 per cent of the sample reported family descent from farm, managerial and self-employed, and professional and semiprofessional parents.

Having determined the teacher's social origins, we still need to discover the value orientation of teachers and teacher aspirants. As we shall show later, teaching as an occupation and the aspiring teacher influence each other and are largely compatible. Since a person's value orientation is the result of an enculturation process and is pertinent to his present status in society, we must, therefore, identify the general pattern of enculturation and describe the present status of both teachers and teacher aspirants. This is, of course, no simple task. It is not easy to generalize accurately about a group of people as large as the teaching group. It is even more difficult

[1] Florence Greenhoe, *Community Contacts and Participation of Teachers* (Washington, D.C.: American Council on Public Affairs, 1941), p. 8.

[2] "The Status of the American Public School Teacher," *NEA Research Bulletin*, 35, No. 1 (February 1957), 9.

when one considers that one standard measurement, social-class ranking, has become increasingly inappropriate and ambiguous.

In an effort to decrease confusion at the outset, let us define social class not in the predominantly economic sense as Warner does, but rather as an interlocking combination of the three most apparent values lurking behind the American concept of success—namely, *economic wealth* and *prestige ranking;* and, considering the element of moral respectability in the tradition-oriented American value system, *moral respectability,* without which neither economic wealth nor prestige retain their importance. For instance, gangster Frank Costello achieved economic wealth, while actress Elizabeth Taylor has achieved much prestige, but neither has an unquestioned aura of moral respectability. Neither, therefore, enjoys a prestige that intertwines wealth and respectability. What we need is a definition of social class that combines a scale of economic wealth and a ranking of prestige with adherence to moral acceptability.

To identify teachers and teacher-aspirants as primarily middle class thus suggests their tendency toward a certain value orientation. As we indicated, two components of such a value pattern are the work-success ethic and moral respectability. The implications of these two values, when applied in a myriad of specific situations, may be said to constitute the dominant cluster of behaviors known as American middle-class culture. Consequently, the controlling group in public education seeks persons for teaching whose attitudes are clearly in sympathy with these behaviors; in turn, this process is influential in the selection and perpetuation of the value pattern itself. The teacher occupies a certain status in a stratified society. The traditional values associated with their particular stratum both affect the operation of the schools and characterize the occupation of teaching. Brookover[3] goes further when he suggests that teachers "so desire the security, status and approval which those in control are in a position to give" that many "completely internalize the desires and beliefs of the controlling group."

Seen within the confines of the value framework described, then, teachers in the public schools generally may be said to come from the lower middle class. That is to say, prospective teachers mature in the lower ranks of the middle-income range of society and move to the slightly higher occupational status of teachers. Position or status of an occupation, among

[3] Wilbur B. Brookover, *The Sociology of Education* (New York: American Book Co., 1955), p. 69.

other factors, determines an individual's prestige ranking and allocates his social privileges. The public school teacher, when compared with 95 other occupations as to relative prestige, has a rank order of 36.[4] In accounting for this rank, we must remember that an occupational label often displaces other prestige-defining factors such as religion, race, political affiliation, sex, or ancestry.

Perhaps the intensity of this internalization of the standard middle-class values, or at least the appearance of such internalization, accounts for the tendency among teachers and teacher aspirants to reject evidence or data pertinent to education that seem to run counter to their particular value patterns. For example, if one believes, as the American middle classes appear to believe almost religiously, that hard work can overcome any obstacle and that success is limited only by the amount of effort one is willing to sustain, then the "different" child, the child who does not or cannot learn, must be viewed as morally bad, indolent, lazy, and a ne'er-do-well. The child who does not see value in education—which is, according to this ethic, the road to self-improvement—must be a deviant, a misfit, and a laggard. Lack of ability is no excuse, and lack of motivation is even worse.

In the face of the obvious fact that children are different—intellectually, emotionally, physically, and socially, the convinced middle-class teacher or student teacher may continue to assume a fallacious work-success *ethic* equally applicable to all.

WHY TEACHERS BECOME TEACHERS

People seek occupational compatibility. Such compatibility certainly involves the reconciliation of value orientations. That is, one does not usually enter an occupation whose value symbols are noticeably contrary to one's own values and those espoused by the group with whom one identifies. This implied link between the value orientation of the occupation of teaching and the value orientation of prospective teachers, now requires closer examination. A teacher's values, like those of nonteachers, certainly are in consonance with the pattern of culture acquired during his individual process of maturation. Moreover, these values also have been influenced by the teacher's exposure to other value systems and by his present status in his society. Value orientations thus are the product of encultura-

[4] National Opinion Research Center, *College Study of Intergroup Relations* (Chicago: University of Chicago Press, 1947), p. 2.

tion, acculturation, and present status. This is illustrated in part by the influence of relatives on persons selecting teaching as a career.

TABLE 14–1. Percentage Distribution of Students Selecting and Not Selecting Teaching as a Vocation, Based upon Numbers Who Had Relatives with a Teaching Background.

Relative	Teacher Group Male	Teacher Group Female	Teacher Group Total	Non-Teacher Group Male	Non-Teacher Group Female	Non-Teacher Group Total
Father	19	13	16	8	10	10
Mother	14	26	21	15	16	15
Brother or Sister	6	13	10	3	2	3
Aunt or Uncle	35	58	47	36	39	37

SOURCE: Robert Richey and William Fox, *An Analysis of Various Factors Associated with the Selection of Teaching as a Vocation.* Bulletin of the School of Education, Indiana University, May 1948, p. 20.

Spindler[5] hypothesizes that "the child training of most of the people who become teachers has been more tradition . . . oriented." He characterizes such an orientation as containing the "work-success ethic and moral respectability" and suggests that "self-denial, altruism and a moralistic self-concept seem to be functional prerequisites for the historically-derived role of school teacher in American society." In other words, a common value pattern begins to emerge that produces the hazy outlines of a stereotype.

According to Thomas,[6] "perhaps it would be more appropriate to introduce the term 'occupational label' for, in a sense, it is 'labels' which have been produced by the tremendous increase in occupational specialization. It is clear that as society and its groupings have become more obscure to all but their practitioners, the average man finds himself without sufficient knowledge of other occupations, and, when called upon to respond in some way to specialties other than his own, he must of necessity respond to labels rather than content. The functions and purposes of other specialties have eluded him." His initial aspiration, then, "to his own occupation came as a result of response to a label—in other words, the behavior pattern which is represented by the label selects similar people, or similar

[5] George D. Spindler, "Education in a Transforming American Culture," *Harvard Educational Review,* 25, No. 3 (Summer 1955), 154.

[6] Donald R. Thomas, "Who Wants to Be a Teacher?" *Teachers College Record,* 60, No. 3 (December 1958), 166.

people select that behavior pattern, in sufficient numbers and with sufficient orthodoxy that the label continues to be illustrative of the occupation."

E. B. Reuter uses the term "occupational type," which he defines as "the type of personality determined by a particular occupation, either because the occupation selects the type, or because the personality is formed by the conditions of life within the occupation, or both."[7] By means of this concept, which had been used also by other investigators, Frederic Terrien decided to test the hypothesis that "an occupation can channel the behavior of its adherents into a system, and, in so channeling group behavior, determine the occupational type."[8] Specifically applying this hypothesis to teachers as an occupational group, Terrien found that:

> . . . a number of social processes operated in connection with the teaching group. Its work was well defined by the historically increasing operation of the division of labor. Persons entering the profession were confronted with a definition of the situation created partly by society through its stereotyped evaluation of the manipulators of the abstract, and partly by the in-group itself, which possessed a fairly well defined conception of self. Collective behavior was found to obtain in the group.

Terrien continues:

> These factors, plus the role of educators as agents of social control, tended to create a status for teachers quite different from that of any other group of functionaries in the society. This status, in turn, acted to bring about a marked degree of systemized behavior, and to pre-select persons for the occupation who indicated a strong degree of typing.[9]

In short, the motivation to enter teaching is not a random idea. There is a centripetal force involved, which apparently reinforces the model of the teacher by attracting like people, by drawing into its sphere the image of itself: the accumulation of impressions of people has left an image, and now new people seek to emulate that image.

We have been suggesting that people enter teaching for personality (value-oriented) reasons rather than specific external rewards. This conclusion is similar to that of Esther Lloyd-Jones and Mary V. Holman,[10]

[7] As quoted in Frederic Terrien, *The Behavior System and Occupational Type Associated with Teaching,* Ph.D. dissertation, Yale University Library, 1950, p. 161.

[8] Terrien, p. i.

[9] Terrien, p. i.

[10] Esther Lloyd-Jones and Mary V. Holman, "Why People Become Teachers," in Lindley J. Styles, ed., *The Teacher's Role in American Society* (New York: Harper & Brothers, 1957), p. 235.

after they had reviewed a wide variety of research studies approaching this question. It is obvious that our society continues to be able to recruit teachers despite low salaries, which indicates that other reasons are more powerful than the rewards to be gained. It is true that recent trends in teacher supply seem to indicate an increasing inability to recruit sufficient numbers of people to fill the demand of our public schools but, considering the actual numbers who enter teaching, the point remains valid. Personality needs seem to continue to be the most persuasive reasons for entry into this occupation.

One specific personality need directing young people to teaching is certainly that of security in a socially acceptable position. There seems to be a curious lack of adventure in the teacher candidate. As was true in times past, the "safe" moral respectability of teaching is satisfying to some and continues to recruit those who need both safety and some temporary activity to fill their days. Teaching for these people is protective coloration and a place to wait for marriage or a better job. It satisfies an urge to serve, while not seriously challenging the controlling groups in the society. It pays enough to support a quiet and respectable existence, while carrying the increments of idealism, service, and dedication.

The selection of teaching as a career often is also a truly idealistic choice; the ideals dictating this choice are internally consistent with the value orientation usually associated with the particular social stratum we have called "middle class." Colleges preparing teachers use idealism as a recruitment incentive. Byers[11] reports that 60 or 70 selected colleges stressed (1) opportunity for service, 82 per cent; (2) social significance, 63 per cent; and (3) joy of working with children, 58 per cent. If these criteria continue to be offered as the bases of choice, it is likely that (a) there will be a considerable turnover in the teaching ranks as realism sets in; (b) other occupations offering greater incentives will be chosen on the basis of realistic appraisals; and (c) teaching will, therefore, face a dwindling future.

Another factor that selects some individuals for teaching (while discouraging others) is the willingness to conform to the dominant group where controversy and conflicting pressures exist. As stated earlier, teachers internalize standard middle-class values, or *at least appear* to do so. It may be that teachers create a caricature of these values and that this *unreal*

[11] Loretta Byers, "Organization and Procedures Employed by Colleges to Recruit Candidates for Elementary-School Teaching," *Journal of Teacher Education,* December 1950, p. 295.

system is, for them, the only reality in which they can exist. If education is primarily the transmission of culture, teachers must be alert to the ingredients of that culture. If the hallmarks of a culture are contradictory, the teacher is faced with the dubious task of transmitting contradictions, or reconciling them. Her dilemma is heightened if the insistent demands made upon her by the control groups represent contradictory values. Since teachers have always been subjected to unusually close scrutiny by the community, and continued employment is often dependent upon satisfying the narrow and conflicting conceptions of observant neighbors, the teacher may be forced to live in an explosive mental world. Some who aspire to teaching do not, however, see these awkward conditions as a handicap. Consider this statement by a teacher trainee (1958):

> Also, I don't feel as if the teacher should take the role of an enthusiastic social reformer, since that is not her main job. She is a teacher, not a sociologist. In addition to this, the teacher could be a valuable contributor to local politics. But if she is too enthusiastic about that, and especially if she is enthusiastic about the political party her employers are not enthusiastic about, she is in danger of being ridiculed and losing her revered status with her pupils or of even losing her job.

Or, from a statement of another teacher trainee (1958):

> I was being interviewed by the superintendent of the school system where I will work next year and he asked if I intended to join one of their churches. When I answered that I was, he said that was fine because they like to have teachers who were church members. I am a church member and I do intend to join one of their churches, but even if I were not, I think it would still be an advisable move to make in that situation and particular city.

In short, the young teacher wants to "play it safe," regardless of his or her personal commitments.

It is also interesting to note that the future public school and college students who are not going to be teachers are, in some cases, even more conservative about the teacher's role than are students taking up teaching. In short, we must conclude that the teacher's life will have to be fairly conservative and responsive to outside pressures.

OBSTACLES TO RECRUITMENT

Several factors seem to influence recruitment of teachers today. The first is the general notion that low standards of admission and a low level of academic performance and intellectual striving prevail in teacher-training institutions. This condition is certainly associated with the history of such institutions and the tendency to value field practice (direct experience) over theoretical orientation. The teacher of teachers in the teachers college, in the past, often was not a highly trained scholar; rather, he or she was a successful practitioner, graduated from the field. Thus, students aspiring to academic "excellence" were, and still are, prone to seek careers other than teaching and to seek institutions whose academic reputation promises an education of "high" quality. Education students, therefore, often had lower test averages in national examinations than students in other professional fields that depend upon a strong academic education. As the universities moved into the field of teacher training, the picture changed, since universities rarely permit seriously diverse admission standards. Because of the history of teacher education, faculties and students of some universities are loath to fully accept their colleagues in schools of education, although at both the professional and student level these educators may be equally qualified in general education and scholarship. Educators at a university frequently feel the pressure of rejection by their peers as they attempt to span the imagined chasm between liberal and technical education in a professional field. A further deterrent to recruitment is the fact that in some professional education circles, an oversensitive and defensive attitude is adopted, which expresses itself in a kind of disparagement of mental ability as a factor in teaching success. Some teachers and administrators actually nourish anti-intellectualism by claiming that highly intelligent teachers would not be "practical." Needless to say, this strange position contributes little to the stature of teachers and teacher education.

Some young people rebel when such pressures to conform are applied; and, in order to forestall potential public interference in their lives, they quickly abandon teaching as a possible career. Some educational leaders claim that when teachers constantly complain about these kinds of conditions, as well as low salaries and poor working conditions, they discourage young people from entering teaching, and are, therefore, contributing to the shortage of teachers and the perpetuation of low standards. It does not seem likely that the recruitment picture will change, simply because the victims of the adverse conditions of teaching have ceased to register protests. This simple lesson is clear in the history of labor-management relations in industry and agriculture, and it is the *raison d'être* of organized labor. While not denying the "power of positive thinking," it seems foolhardy to be a Pollyana and ask educators to sustain a note of glib optimism in the face of the history of neglect of teachers in America from colonial times to the twentieth century. Indeed, the very emphasis of some educational organizations on a mythology of positivism can be said to be one source of the frustration that precipitated the organization of teachers into trade unions and created such mechanisms as the single-salary scale—a device that surely denies any assumption of individual professional autonomy.

If low salaries, poor working conditions, low prestige, and excessive public scrutiny are driving recruits away from teaching, it would be more appropriate for educators to change these conditions than to engage in any conspiracy of silence. Perhaps prospective teachers need to develop a kind of scar tissue to face without illusions the painful questions of their own future and of all public education.

Moreover, qualified teachers need to speak out in their own behalf when their "strictly" academic colleagues snipe and thrust at their competence. They need to raise questions about the validity of the "prestige" awarded people who criticize teachers and public education without either knowledge or experience, just for the sake of criticism—in short, the "scapegoat" needs to use its horns.

THE PROBLEM OF QUALITY AND QUANTITY IN THE TEACHER FORCE

Perhaps the central issue that has plagued teaching for all of these many years has been the value question of what constitutes teaching competence. The neophyte teacher will always want to know what is expected of her, and the oldtimer wants to know on what basis she is being rewarded or punished. The answers to these questions are not at all simple, for the field of education has failed to supply suitable solutions to the issue of teacher competence. "Teachers and teaching are parts of a complex situation involving pupils, purposes, values, activities and products and can be studied from many points of view."[12] And, states Brim: "The fact is . . . that continuing attention has been given to the problem of finding suitable criteria, that is, personal and social criteria which are related to success in the educational role. However, even though there is a vast body of research on the relation of teacher characteristics to effectiveness in

[12] Arvil S. Barr and Robert E. Jones, "Measurement and Prediction of Teaching Efficiency," *Review of Educational Research,* 28, No. 3 (June 1958), 261. With permission.

teaching, the reviews of this research show no consistent relation between any characteristics, including intelligence, and such teaching effectiveness."[13] As difficult a task as teaching of children and youth may be, the conduct of this type of formal education will remain seriously impaired until decisions on what constitutes teaching success are made and acted upon.

The lack of universal agreement on what constitutes teacher competence has actually become a major reason for many kinds of prevailing interpersonal and institutional relationships that are necessary to our understanding of teachers, teaching, and the field of education. It may even be possible to assert that the problem of defining teacher competences is, in the final analysis, the heart of the whole matter of the professionalization of teaching and teachers. While it may seem to some readers that this is an exclusively professional problem, it is in reality the very core of the problem of defining roles and statuses for educators as they perform functions in a society.

Barr states that there are at least three fundamental and common ways of talking about this problem:

"(1) in terms of character and personality traits; qualities of a person; (2) in terms of desired competencies, performances, ability to do; and (3) in terms of behavior controls; knowledges, generalized skills, attitudes, and ideals."[14] It should be noted that Barr also states that, "until more progress has been made in resolving the philosophical and scientific conflicts inherent in these several ways of talking about teaching, it seemed best not to attempt a single dimensional classification."[15]

It is obvious that the resolution of these conflicts is imperative and must not be avoided in order to serve short-term goals, for, in addition to these philosophical and scientific conflicts, definitions of teacher competence have been further marred by the persistent assumption that there is "a single optimum type of teacher, which one tries to produce through training, and to which one demands the conformity of all educational personnel."[16]

In light of the foregoing, what the neophyte teacher will face when

[13] O. G. Brim, Jr., *Sociology and the Field of Education* (New York: Russell Sage Foundation, 1958), p. 32.

[14] Arvil S. Barr, "The Measurement and Prediction of Teaching Efficiency: A Summary of Investigations," *Journal of Experimental Education,* 16, No. 4 (June, 1948), 226.

[15] Barr, p. 204.

[16] Brim (see note 13), p. 33. With permission.

she steps timidly out of her training institution into the real professional world is a diapason of strident demands.

Definitions of teaching success touch upon every area in the field of education and mushroom into every aspect of a teacher's personality and private and professional life. One cannot avoid noticing the use to which adequate role research could be put in surveying such a fundamental problem. Role conflicts, for example, can be traced—in part—to differences in value expectations demanded by different statuses. The relationship between role expectations and value orientations underscores the importance of resolving both the sociological and philosophical conflicts involved in the teacher competence issue.

The problems faced are not easily conquered by present research techniques. For example, if we discuss teacher competence in terms of teacher personality, it is extremely difficult to solve two basic issues: (1) the resolution of value conflicts over what constitutes a "good" personality, and (2) the fact that the personality variables present in any teacher-pupil interaction are so numerous that it is virtually impossible to demonstrate empirically the superiority of any single variable as the cause of a desired effect. Statistical operations are only tools and cannot reduce the conceptual complexity inherent in the analysis of personal interactions.

If we move away from personality and talk in terms of desired competence, we face the same value dilemma. In addition, we encounter (1) semantic problems in the discussions of competence, (2) ambiguity resulting from attempts to reach a level of abstraction upon which everyone can agree, or (3) confusion over whether *ability* (before the teaching-act skill) or *achievement* (after the teaching-act results) should be the starting point. Finally (4), if we choose to talk in terms of behavior controls, we are stopped short by the necessity to relate the selection and education of teachers to the practice of teaching in the field, for often there is a schism between these two areas.

For the sake of argument, however, let us (1) assume that the value questions could be resolved (it is easy for anyone to assume that his value system is a rallying point), and (2) set aside Brim's objection to the single optimum-type teacher. We would then still have to face another reality: If we were going to accept some optimum definition, we would have to assume that it was possible and realistic to expect that a preponderance of teachers (and it must be remembered that we are speaking of a *mass* occupation involving hundreds of thousands of people) could achieve such "greatness," such high levels of intelligence, dedication, energy, and creativeness as are implied in any optimum criteria. Obviously, such an assumption is alarmingly naive.

In order to solve this problem, we can productively apply the ideas that (1) society allots certain functions to institutions, and (2) materials, resources, and personnel within an institution are further allotted to appropriate roles and statuses in order to accomplish the institution's allotted functions efficiently. These ideas could nourish some redeeming solution to what might seem a hopeless dilemma. Under the allocation process, differentiated functions for teachers could be defined, and appropriate specialized roles and statuses created to which standards of minimum competence would then be assigned. In other words, teachers would *not* all be assigned equal statuses or duplicate roles, but would be assigned according to their particular areas of special qualification. Teaching may be, after all, essentially an act of individual talent. The neophyte would then be a true specialist, and one would not need to fear Robert Frost's warning:

> Before I built a wall I'd ask to know
> What I was walling in or walling out
> And to whom I was like to give offense.

At least, in this process we would not have to face the ultimate irony of, for example, demanding that *all* teachers should lead the community, or the shabby suggestion that the bonded indebtedness of a school district also imposes some personal obligation on teachers. In short, what is good teaching is also society's notion of what is good education. The neophyte teacher clearly has the right to know, at the outset of her career, her society's concept of a good education and, therefore, according to her allotted status and roles, what will be defined as success for her.

Concurrently with expectations for success, the neophyte teacher must also face her own career future. Women's career patterns (and we should think primarily in terms of women, since 75 per cent of America's elementary and secondary teachers are women) seem to fall into seven types, asserts Super: conventional, stable-working, stable-homemaking, double-track, interrupted, unstable, and multiple-trial. Women teachers today seem to fall into the double-track pattern, which means holding a job and maintaining a home simultaneously with occasional time off for childbearing, or the interrupted pattern, which means starting a job, giving it up for a time to be a full-time homemaker and then, in later life, returning to the job. Super states that "There has been until very recently little recognition of the widespread existence of the double-track and interrupted career patterns."[17] A review of the professional expectations for teachers illustrates such a tendency to overlook the fact that the typical American public school teacher is now married and has one child, thereby automatically placing her in one or the other of the two above-mentioned types of career patterns. This raises concerns about the appropriateness of the education offered such women at either the pre-service or in-service level, as well as the appropriateness of the role expectations demanded of teachers with such career patterns. The detachment of the teacher-education process has certainly tended to direct teacher educators to the operating assumption that teacher trainees are all headed for a highly motivated and stable (typically masculine middle-class, says Super) career pattern. Apparently such an assumption ignores reality and thereby helps to create the initial dilemma of the neophyte teacher. She has been educated to fit a career pattern contrary to her own, and she can expect to have her competence judged in this ill-fitting garment. Should society change the teachers or the expectations set for them? Clearly, if public education is going to persuade more married women to return to teaching to meet its growing needs, it must resolve these questions.

For example, it would be possible for teacher-training institutions to hold periodic "refresher" institutes for graduate teachers who are presently not active in the field in order to keep these trained people abreast of developments and retain their commitment to the occupation.

THE EMPLOYMENT OF TEACHERS

Despite the fact that teacher salaries have increased gradually and working conditions have made similarly slow but steady progress, the demand for new teachers still exceeds the supply. The causes for the continued imbalance are many: (1) the child population continues to increase; (2) there is greater demand for education for more students at the upper levels; (3) although salaries have increased, so has the cost of living, and, coupled with a devaluation of the dollar, the net gains are almost imperceptible; (4) the prestige of teaching, which may have risen just after the impact of the competition with Russia was felt, has probably declined again under the onslaught of criticism directed at the schools as

[17] Donald E. Super, "Education and the Nature of Occupations and Careers," *Teachers College Record,* 58, No. 6 (March 1957), 304–305.

the scapegoat for a dozen foreign and domestic crises; (5) an expanding business economy is far too formidable a competitive opponent to secure and hold competent teaching personnel in noncompetitive public employment.

So long as demand outstrips supply, and most predictions are that this condition may last for many years to come, any discussion of selection factors becomes academic rather than real. The overriding issue of simply recruiting *enough* teachers outweighs many important considerations concerned with quality. In an increasingly urban society where the personal identification of teachers and their private lives becomes less and less possible, the impersonal forces of quantity and mobility prevail, and hiring agents may spend more time persuading than screening.

Although much has been said in the public press about the need to raise the standards for teaching, in the practical infighting in legislatures, other forces have either prevailed or at least watered down significant gains. Some states still must report that most of their elementary school teachers do not have four-year degrees, while others may report the requirement of a four-year degree but make the practical admission that they are unable to enforce this standard. The two most significant reasons for this condition are (1) short supply of teachers, and (2) refusal to supply sufficient funds to offer reasonable salaries to better prepared teachers.

It cannot be claimed that the United States does not have the funds to support its growing educational needs. While it is possible to assert in some cases that there is an improper and disproportionate demand on the real property tax base, it seems apparent, when one examines the expenditures of the average American on luxuries, that the funds are available but choices are being made to spend such funds elsewhere. In 1962, the City of Los Angeles had a major school bond issue defeated despite desperately overcrowded conditions in a rapidly expanding population area. During this same period, the Santa Anita race track was reporting sums of as much as $1,800,000 being wagered *daily* on horses.

The American teacher, now older and wiser, and more committed to activities outside the classroom, such as home and family, is still an anachronism in modern society. She engages in an occupation in which there are no promotions, salaries have little relationship to merit, and prestige or its symbols is negligible. This cold reality will, perhaps, someday be faced squarely by both the public and education's practitioners. Ultimately, as we have asserted from the beginning, it is a matter of choices, some of which are made consciously and some of which are made unconsciously or by default. Meanwhile, stereotypes bloom, conflicting forces engage in debate, the teacher supply is unable to meet demands, and American public education continues to reflect the circumstances of its birth, its childhood, and its now raging adolescence.

SUMMARY

As people, American teachers exhibit a definite set of characteristics which can be defined as an occupational type. Overwhelmingly classified as a predominantly female occupation, public school teaching in America retains the image of a sharply tragic existence on idealism, confusion, and sparse recompense. The counter image of a stiffly moralistic and strictly orthodox female of unknown age offers little encouragement.

The consequences of financial starvation, a negative stereotype, and an excess of criticism are an increasing teacher shortage in a time when education is needed more than ever. The attrition rate in the ranks of young teachers is extremely high and the recruitment levels have failed to hold their own in the face of the demand.

The choice presented to the public is clear cut but has not yet been made, even though there are increasing signs that time is running out.

SELECTED BIBLIOGRAPHY

Caplow, Theodore. *The Sociology of Work.* Minneapolis: The University of Minnesota Press, 1954.

Elsbree, Willard S. *The American Teacher.* New York: American Book Company, 1939.

Foff, Arthur. "Teacher Stereotypes in the American Novel." Unpublished Ed.D. dissertation, Stanford University, 1953.

Journal of Educational Sociology, Vol. 29, September 1955.

Lieberman, Myron. *The Future of Public Education.* Chicago: The University of Chicago Press, 1960.

"The Status of the American Public-School Teacher," *National Education Association Research Bulletin,* 35, No. 1, February 1957.

Stiles, Lindley, ed. *The Teacher's Role in American Society.* New York: Harper & Brothers, 1957.

Terrien, Frederic. "The Behavior System and Occupational Type Associated with Teaching." Unpublished Ph.D. dissertation, Yale University, 1950.

Waller, Willard. *The Sociology of Teaching.* New York: John Wiley and Sons, 1932.

CHAPTER 15

PROFESSIONALISM IN EDUCATION

One persistent but so far illusory goal of American educators is to have society recognize their occupation as a profession. Despite the notion in some quarters that, in the long run, possession of this talisman may be irrelevant, educators have pursued the goal of professionalization with increasing vigor and commitment. There are some educators who have declared the struggle over and are content to claim possession of the prize by virtue of self-recognition. But others, fearing that society has not yet conferred such distinction upon the occupation, insist that there are some specific criteria that must be met before the application can be approved. Still another group considers the whole aspiration as superfluous and diversionary. A brief examination of the issues involved may clarify the problem for those who are still uncommitted.

THE CRITERIA OF PROFESSIONALISM

Two theoretical criteria seem to be most significant as qualifications for the appellation "profession." The first is given in Whitehead's definition of a profession as "an avocation whose activities are subjected to theoretical analysis and are modified by theoretical conclusions derived from that analysis."[1] The second qualification, in the words of Thomas and Kinney, is that a profession is an occupation whose "members are expected to give priority to the interests of society over those of themselves or their clients."[2] Both of these criteria need clarification if they are to be operational, for they contain nuances of meaning that invite controversial inter-

[1] A. N. Whitehead, *Adventures of Ideas* (New York: The Macmillan Co., 1933), p. 72.

[2] Lucien C. Kinney and Lawrence G. Thomas, *Toward Professional Maturity in Education* (San Francisco: California Teachers Association, 1953), p. 3.

pretations. Lieberman,[3] drawing on authoritative sources, insists upon four more pertinent operational criteria:

1. A long period of specialized training.
2. A broad range of autonomy for both the individual practitioners and for the occupational group as a whole.
3. An acceptance by the practitioners of broad personal responsibility for judgments made and acts performed within the scope of professional autonomy.
4. A comprehensive self-governing organization of practitioners.

OBSTACLES TO PROFESSIONALIZATION

At first glance, educators would appear to meet—at least superficially—some of these criteria. Conflicts arise, however, when we attempt to define "educator." Who is an educator? Surely, teachers must be educators, but are all people who wear the label "teacher" really teachers, or are some of them "teachers" and the others "professional teachers"? If professional teaching follows Whitehead's definition, do manual arts instructors, coaches, or Arthur Murray's employees qualify? And to step into an even more controversial area, are school administrators, *as they function as administrators,* professional within Whitehead's definition? What we are saying is that the question of professionalism has to face the prior problem of function with as much objectivity as possible. There is little evidence to date that the problem has been faced.

The question of professionalism also raises the problem of defining competence in order to distinguish one who is qualified from one who is not. As we have already stated in previous chapters, the question of what constitutes competence in education, even at the level of licensure, is by no means a settled issue. In fact, it remains one of the most perplexing problems of education as an occupation.

A third concern that appears prerequisite to any consideration of professionalism is an assessment of the social structure supporting the occupation. In the United States, most educators are public employees; that is, they are employed by agencies of government such as school districts, county or state educational agencies, or state colleges and universities. As such, edu-

[3] Myron Lieberman, *Education as a Profession* (Englewood Cliffs, N.J.: Prentice-Hall, Inc., 1956), pp. 3–5.

cators are immediately subject to the many restrictions our society imposes on public employees and are, therefore, at the outset, limited in the amount and kind of autonomy they may claim. In addition, public employees are limited in the rewards available for their services, because the institutions employing them depend upon public support. Moreover, the history of teaching and of teachers in the United States shows that, in addition, their personal and professional autonomy has been restricted by a series of informal—but highly persuasive—moral regulations considered by various segments of the society as essential to the occupation.

A fourth concern, which perhaps is relevant only if the other problems are solved, focuses upon the organizational problems of educators. Teaching, says Caplow,[4] is characterized by an intermittent employment pattern, because it is a predominantly female occupation, subject to the social and natural laws governing marriage and pregnancy. Predominantly female occupations are difficult to organize for effective maintenance of self-government and high standards. Thus, the instability of education as an occupation immeasurably damages its efforts to create a unified cohesive organization.

Finally, education has another characteristic that seems to work against its achievement of professional status. Education, with its tremendous variety of jobs, is a *mass* occupation. Because it has literally millions of practitioners, it has extreme difficulty in restricting entrance to only those who meet "professional" standards. While American society has accepted the idea that it does not want to be serviced by less than highly trained medical or legal practitioners, it has not made a similar commitment to superior educational services. Neither has the American public decided to reward the practitioners of education sufficiently to assure recruitment of only the most highly qualified in massive numbers.

We have been suggesting, then, that educators are presently aspiring toward a goal, but that achievement of this goal, as presently defined, is still some distance away because there are still entirely too many unresolved problems.

Fischer,[5] for example, has raised the question of whether teachers are "professional" practitioners. To answer this query, he raised these additional questions: Upon what fields of science is education based, and are

[4] Theodore Caplow, *The Sociology of Work* (Minneapolis: University of Minnesota Press, 1954), pp. 245–246.

[5] Louis Fischer, "A Profession without Members?" *Journal of Teacher Education,* 12, No. 2 (June 1961), 139–142.

the practitioners of teaching familiar with the relevant contributions these sciences offer to teaching? Surely if teaching is to be professional, according to Whitehead's criteria, these questions are relevant. In a study involving over 300 graduate students of education in four institutions, Fischer proceeded to inquire into these educators' knowledge of the basic theoretical foundations of educational practice. His results indicated an almost total absence of such knowledge. Thus, if his sample was representative, he had to conclude that teachers are not professional practitioners, as judged by his criteria.

Membership in the educational organization making the most extensive claims for professionalism, the National Education Association (NEA), has rarely exceeded 50–55 per cent of those eligible. This leads to the conclusion that there is, at *present,* no comprehensive, self-governing organization of practitioners—one of the hallmarks of a profession. The American Federation of Teachers (AF of T), at present, can make even less claim to comprehensive membership.

Illustration upon illustration could be compiled to substantiate the obvious conclusion that practitioners in the field of education have not yet achieved their goal of professionalization. This conclusion in no way detracts from the notion of claiming professional status for education in the *ideal.* The authors share the impatience of those who object to educational leaders declaring education a profession by personal or organizational edict. At the same time, they also reject the notion that professionalization is irrelevant to the practice of education.

PROFESSIONALISM AND THE FUNCTIONS OF EDUCATION

Education, conceived of as a process of selective transmission of culture, is entirely amenable to use of scientific techniques. Teaching can be defined as the competent diagnosis of a complex learning situation followed by acts of hypothesizing and verification. As such, teaching may be conceived of as the application of the relevant primary scientific disciplines.

Teaching may also be conceived of as an art, or as an act expressing individual talent. Most art forms involve communication between people, which is a social act. Since effective teaching depends heavily upon the art of communication, it may be considered an art form. The teacher can be both the artist and the actor; he creates and is both the form and the content. His experience is his technique, and his technique is at once his experience. But practiced solely as an art, unrelated to science, teaching becomes less amenable to the measures which would establish professionalization.

Perceived simply as a technical craft, teaching relinquishes all claim to professional status, for the successful practice of a craft does not depend upon theoretical analysis and does not entail promotion of society's interests over those of the practitioner. While some occupations, by their nature, occupy a middle ground between a profession and a craft (airline pilots, for example), teaching, conceived *ideally,* should not share this ambiguous status.

Thus, teaching may be practiced in different ways and, in actuality, is. Be that as it may, most practitioners aspire to the ideal of professionalism—in the opinion of the authors, the most desirable alternative. Since the path ahead is lengthy and arduous, we hope educators will not succumb like the wayfarer in Crane's poem:

> The wayfarer,
> Perceiving the pathway to truth
> Was struck with astonishment,
> It was thickly grown with weeds.
> "Ha," he said,
> "I see no one has passed here
> In a long time."
> Later he saw that each weed
> Was a singular knife.
> "Well," he mumbled at last,
> "Doubtless there are other roads."[6]

ROADS TO PROFESSIONALIZATION

One of the successful roads to professionalization has always been control of access to the occupation. This is not simply a matter of restricting supply in order to create artificial scarcity and thereby extract higher rewards for scarce services. Controlling access to a true profession involves control over the setting of entrance standards to insure high performance by those who are admitted. If the standards of a profession are sufficiently high, they may inadvertently create a shortage of qualified personnel, but the main intention is to ensure quality performance. This point is particularly significant for the professionalization of teachers, because the demand for educational services has always so greatly outstripped the supply, that

[6] Stephen Crane, *The Collected Poems of Stephen Crane* (New York: Alfred A. Knopf, Inc., 1930).

the imposition of *any* standards acts as a further deterrent to adequate recruitment and, consequently, is difficult to sell to the general public.

CERTIFICATION

Standards for admission to an occupation are usually maintained through two interrelated processes known as *certification* and *accreditation*. Certification is an alternate term for licensure. As we have stated in previous chapters, licensure of educational personnel aims at restricting access to those who possess a certain type of training and can demonstrate certain understandings, skills, and abilities. This presents two problems.

First, as already mentioned, is the problem of adequately defining competence in teaching and other educational tasks, if licensure is to be meaningful to society and practitioners alike. This problem has not yet been solved. But, although certification of teachers and other educational personnel is now an established practice, it often is virtually meaningless as a means of setting high uniform standards and achieving professionalization.

The second problem of certification stems from the decentralized organization of American education as a state function. Consequently, there are 50 different sets of certification requirements of widely varying standards. For example, the certification requirements for elementary teaching range from as few as 30 hours of post–high school education to five years of college work—almost the equivalent of a master's degree. A teacher licensed in one state may find it impossible to obtain a license in another. In extreme cases, experienced classroom teachers from a state with low certification requirements may be required to begin again as college freshmen and complete a four- or five-year program of training before being allowed to teach in states having high certification requirements. States with high requirements, if faced with any serious shortage of teachers, find their requirements assaulted by a variety of groups who feel that it is more important to have enough teachers, than to have high-quality teachers. Frequently the arguments of these groups lead to a discussion and appraisal of the necessity of training at all and the kind and quality of that training.

The problem of certification also overlaps with that of justifying the stipulated requirements and guaranteeing that training programs will produce, with some degree of uniformity, educators with the necessary qualifications. This latter problem is essentially that of *accreditation*.

ACCREDITATION

Accreditation is a procedure that evaluates the quality of training in a particular institution in terms of a standard of performance laid down for a particular occupational field by either an outside agency or an institution of more advanced training in that field. Accreditation of a high school rests on the presumption that its program is of such quality that a certain percentage of its graduates will succeed in college. Similarly, college programs are accredited if their graduates can be expected to perform adequately in the fields for which they were trained.

Since states differing in their certification requirements obviously have different standards for what constitutes adequate training, interstate accreditation faces many obstacles. For example, many states do not require applicants for certification to have completed a *formal* training program in a single institution; "equivalent" training is acceptable, or in other words, training obtained in bits and pieces from a variety of institutions over an extended period of time. Conversely, part time study in a single institution's specially designed accredited program may not meet the implied standards of the accreditation agency. In California, only 25 to 30 per cent of the teachers who are certified each year completed their training in a single California institution's designed and accredited program, or conversely, 70 to 75 per cent of these teachers obtain licenses by submitting training records garnered from a variety of institutions in or out of the state. The problem relevant to accreditation procedures is that such an applicant may never have met any institution's requirements for full-fledged candidacy, according to California's definition, but instead was enrolled as a special student or obtained equivalent course credits for work done in extension services operating outside the implied standard for accreditation. In still other states it is entirely possible for a teacher aspirant to qualify for a license on the basis of extension courses, without ever having set foot on a college campus.

Yet without accreditation agencies, states would have no way of judging the value of any one institution's training program. The scandal of post–World War II "diploma mills" is well known, and society's indifference to accreditation problems produced a number of people who obtained master's, even doctor's, degrees in such complex disciplines as psychology and psychiatry by correspondence courses given by nonaccredited "schools."

Still another problem stems from the fact that in some states the certification agency and the state university apply different standards of accreditation. For example, an applicant for a teacher's license in a rural area of such a state may obtain his license on the basis of his training in a county-supported two-year normal school. Should he later wish to teach in an urban area requiring of teachers a bachelor's degree, he will find his normal-school credits unacceptable at the state university; and he must, therefore, start his training all over again.

On July 1, 1954, the accreditation of teacher education was invested in a group called The National Council for the Accreditation of Teacher Education (NCATE). This Council was to be composed of six representatives of teacher-training institutions, six representatives of state departments of education, six members of the National Education Association's Commission on Teacher Education and Professional Standards, and representatives from the National School Boards Association. Although NCATE had no legal status, it was expected that each institution involved in teacher education would (1) voluntarily submit to NCATE's inspections and accreditation recommendations and (2) accept NCATE's rulings on all other institutions. NCATE, in turn, gave temporary blanket accreditation to all institutions then members of the American Association of Colleges for Teacher Education (AACTE).

NCATE released the following summary of the situation as it existed in September of 1954:

> A. 1209 colleges and universities are approved for teacher education by the 48 state departments of education (and the District of Columbia).
>
> B. 885 of these are accredited for general excellence as institutions but not specifically for teacher education by their appropriate regional associations.
>
> C. 284 of the 1209 are specifically accredited for teacher education by NCATE.
>
> D. 14 of these 284 are not accredited by the regional association.
>
> E. 270 of the 1209 are accredited by both NCATE and the appropriate regional associations.
>
> F. 310 of the 1209 have no accreditation except by their own state departments of education.
>
> G. 615 of the 1209 have general regional accreditation, but are not accredited for teacher education by NCATE.[7]

[7] The National Council for Accreditation of Teacher Education, *A Statement of Purposes, Policies, and Procedures* (Washington, D.C.: National Council, 1954), p. 6.

As can be readily seen, NCATE started with less than 25 per cent of the teacher-education institutions in the fold and in the cases of 14 was in disagreement with regional associations. But the problems of regional differences in standards and persuading the regional associations to yield power to the national council, were just the beginning of NCATE's troubles. Some basic definitions and policies had been curiously overlooked in the creation of NCATE.

Teacher education, ideally conceived, is a happy combination of both liberal and technical education. NCATE, however, in essence represented only the technical educators, or those who strongly identified with the NEA. For those embracing the cause of liberal education for teachers and shunning any association with "professional educators," NCATE represented a challenge. They demanded representation, not directly, but through appeals to the public via the mass media. Some NEA-oriented educators are immediately opposed to what they feel could be domination by the liberal arts advocates, since in most multipurpose colleges professional educators are greatly outnumbered. Thus, the basic questions of professionalization were raised once more: Who is a teacher? Can one speak of a teaching profession, when people who teach, such as university professors, do not wish to be classified as teachers, or at least not to be so classified if it means intimate association with other teachers who hold less prestigious positions in the eyes of the public? Can an organization effectively represent an occupation, if its leadership considers one segment of the practitioners outcasts, betrayers, and the "enemy"?

If the occupation called teaching is thus divided, who then shall do the accrediting? The suggestion that accreditation should be a governmental function has met with stiff opposition from almost all quarters; undeniably, such governmental intervention also raises legal questions of jurisdiction. If there cannot be a national accreditation agency acceptable to all, what alternatives are left? Clearly, American state and regional differences are so provincial that our system of education suffers from the resultant patchwork approach. Whereas the legal and medical professions, also organized on a local basis, have contrived agreement to invest the power of accreditation in their respective national professional associations, there is little willingness among the disputing factions in education to yield to such a solution. Present power and present rights are difficult to abandon, despite the obvious necessity to achieve some workable compromise. Liberal-arts adherents are reluctant to relinquish their present power in the colleges by losing themselves in a vast organization like the NEA. States-rights advocates share the aversion to national jurisdiction. The NEA, on the other hand, argues that it cannot abdicate from its concern for the affairs of public education, which—it claims with some justification—the liberal arts people do not and, more importantly, will not share, unless their views are accepted as supreme. Other nationally oriented educators decry the waste and lack of realism of the separatist state or isolationist position.

This struggle is, of course, debilitating to the entire educational enterprise. In some states, the impatient public has, therefore, seized the initiative through their elected legislatures and set patterns of certification and accreditation. Such patterns are often virtually impossible to implement or are the result of listening to the loudest or most prestige-laden spokesman of one faction or the other; they thus tend to be a retreat from any meaningful progress toward the intended goals of both accreditation and certification. The resolution of this dilemma is sure to carry high priority in the immediate future.

THE LACK OF GROUP AUTONOMY AND UNITY

The problems and struggles over certification and accreditation amply illustrate the lack of unity in education. Practicing educators identify with some of the several organizations and reject identification with others. Numerically, the National Education Association (NEA) is the largest group; its membership includes the various kinds of practicing educators, as well as some people who are merely interested in education. Recently the American Federation of Teachers (AF of T) has experienced a rapid growth in membership, although it specifically excludes administrative educators. Among college personnel, the American Association of University Professors (AAUP) holds a dominant position. In a number of situations and on some issues, these three groups find themselves in absolute opposition to one another. Thus, education has no single voice similar to the American Medical Association or the American Bar Association. Since many of the purposes of NEA, AF of T, and the AAUP are different, it is possible for some educators to belong to all three without perceiving any apparent contradictions in such multiple membership. Progress toward the professionalization of education naturally is impaired by this lack of organizational unity.

THE NONREPRESENTATIVE CHARACTER OF THE NEA

For educators primarily concerned with the elementary and secondary schools of the nation, the NEA speaks with greatest authority, although it is under increasing attack, is diminishing in its impact, and faces the stiff competition of a burgeoning AF of T. To resolve the functional differences among educators, the NEA is divided into departments and other subgroups representing particular specialties according to structure (Department of Elementary School Principals, Classroom Teachers, etc.) or according to teaching functions determined by subject matter (arithmetic teachers, council for the social studies, etc.). The general representative assembly is supposed to represent all such groups, but in fact tends to be overpopulated in any given convention session with those school personnel able to attend the meeting—usually those in administrative or quasi-administrative posts. Many school districts "reward" teachers or other personnel with administrative posts if they become prominent in "professional" activities. This accounts for the preponderance of administration-oriented delegates and how their disproportionate membership and voice on boards, committees, and commissions, are perpetuated. The AF of T, in its recruitment campaigns, has often capitalized on this imbalance, much to the consternation of the NEA's leadership, who may be powerless to change their own situation, considering the economic facts of life in convention attendance and other professional activity. The serious concern of the leadership of NEA has been its inability to recruit members beyond a bare majority of eligible educators, and to command sufficient respect and authority to obtain its goals. The NEA has also tended to breed a strong interlocking "in-group" that has not always been amenable to change, except on its terms and to the extent that such change benefits the careers of its members. This condition also contributes to NEA's inability to *earn* its leadership role.

Apart from such previously alluded to built-in sociological factors as the pattern of intermittent employment among education's practitioners, other fundamental schisms within NEA impair its effectiveness. The facts are that administrators and teachers do not see things from the same perspective, and neither do southern and northern educators. Rural and urban educators perceive some educational problems quite differently, and the extensive age range within the membership causes additional divisions. Most of these schisms also affect the AF of T, except for the administrator-teacher conflict.

THE QUESTION OF ETHICS

Perhaps nowhere are the schisms in education so easily illustrated as in an examination of the NEA Code of Ethics, a stately document of high purpose and dedication. The *first* section of the *First* Principle of the Code states that a teacher (no other specialty is named) will:

> Deal justly and impartially with students regardless of their physical, mental, emotional, political, economic, social, racial, or religious characteristics.

Achievement of such behavior would virtually nominate a teacher for sainthood; and this canon, despite its noble intent, seems therefore impractical. For example, would a teacher who openly supported segregated schools be considered unethical? The NEA spent years trying to pass a simple resolution supporting the Supreme Court decision against school segregation. Would those who opposed the resolution be considered unethical? Teachers who resist the intrusion of "release time" religious programs by planning important or exciting events for the release time period might also be judged unethical under this canon. The canon fails to define both "justly" and "impartially"; thus, inherent social differences are left to influence dealings according to the biases or even prejudices of a particular practitioner. For example, middle-class teachers surely consider themselves acting "justly" if they insist upon *their* middle-class code of behavior as a proper standard for all children. Are they, therefore, unethical if this code of behavior violates the accepted codes of behavior of other social strata? The first canon is illustrative of further differences within the organization when it fails to indicate who shall be the judge of teacher behavior. Lacking definition, the task has almost automatically reverted to the structural leader, or administrator, and has therefore created a further source of irritation between teachers and administrators.

The second canon sets up further problems. It states, again referring only to teachers, that one should:

> Recognize the differences among students and seek to meet their individual needs.

Any teacher who seriously pursues the intent of this canon soon finds himself in conflict with many present school policies and procedures. For example, the basic organization of elementary and secondary schools on the single criterion of age-grade is an acknowledged violation of individual differences and individual needs. Would an NEA teacher be considered unethical if she opposed this kind of organization imposed by her school board and supported by her NEA administrator? Considering the stress put on the facts of individual differences in most teacher- and administrator-training schools, would a teacher or administrator who did not recognize such differences and behave accordingly be unethical or incompetent?

A code of ethics for a profession must be clear and workable. Education, in dealing with millions of children in thousands of cities and hamlets in all corners of the nation, faces unique problems. As a mass occupation dealing with virtually the entire range of human knowledge, values, and attitudes it lacks the narrower focus of medical activities or the practice of law. To achieve its ethical goals, education requires a greater measure of skill in defining, interpreting, and enforcing its ethical standards. The accomplishment of a national, enforceable code of ethics will be another contribution toward granting education professional status and autonomy.

OTHER OBSTACLES TO AUTONOMY

Crucial decisions concerning the professionalization of education need to be made, but they are often blocked by misunderstandings over function and the decision-making process. The power to make decisions is imperative to any concept of professional autonomy, be it limited or complete autonomy. But power in education has become entangled in the conflicts over "authoritarian" vs. "authoritative," "responsibility" vs. "power," "power over" vs. "power with." These disputes, misunderstandings, or philosophical differences seem inherent in a modern democratic society, but perhaps they can be resolved sufficiently to permit progress toward professionalization in education.

Fischer[8] points out that educators seem prone to confuse "authoritarian" with "authoritative." He clarifies the two terms when he says:

> —it is clear that for one to be *authoritative* concerning some matter, he should have substantial mastery of available knowledge, both substantive and methodological, relative to the task. Such competence facilitates further inquiry into the problem at hand. The role of authoritative behavior is that of furthering the development of ideas and of the individual concerned.

[8] Louis Fischer, "Authoritative or Authoritarian?" *Educational Leadership,* 19, No. 1 (October 1961).

> In contrast, the *authoritarian* person occupies his position by virtue of a special power secured through force, tradition or birth. It is irrelevant whether or not such a person has the knowledge or skill for the task. His main concern is power, not knowledge or human growth. . . . the key consequence of authoritarian behavior is to perpetuate the special position of power over others and to insure their continuing dependency upon the one who wields the power.
>
> The decision or statement we label *authoritative* is made in an open, examinable fashion. . . . . Authoritative statements are characteristically based on the best evidence currently available. As the situation changes or new evidence is gained, a new authoritative statement will supersede the earlier one.
>
> The grounds for *authoritarian* statements, on the other hand, are private and not open to scrutiny by those influenced by the decision. They may or may not be justifiable by logic or empirical evidence.

Conflicts between administrators and teachers are often the result of this misunderstanding. Many teachers resent what to them seems to be the excessive control of their professional practice by the administrators. They resist the notion that because the administrator has been assigned *responsibility* for the operation of a school this gives him leave to assume absolute *power.* Administrators, on the other hand, sometimes adopt the military's single-minded conception of *responsibility,* "accountability"—meaning, if anything goes wrong, it is your neck. It is possible, asserts Wiles,[9] to be more effective as a leader if one is concerned for "power with" rather than "power over," but this does not solve the problem, states Fischer,[10] if leaders "diffuse choice-making power by sharing with those who do not have the preparation requisite for the authoritative behavior needed. Fearing authoritarian behavior in themselves, or the negative label, they (the administrators) proceed to organize, over organize, create study groups, and postpone decisions until outside sources impose decisions on the group."

The authoritarian leader in education, in addition to offending the democratic commitments of his colleagues, does little to increase the professionalization of education, for he eliminates rational discussion and professional autonomy. On the other hand, teachers who approach even authoritative statements with suspicion and mistrust do little to bolster their autonomy or anyone else's, for they regard all decisions with equal malice,

[9] Kimball Wiles, *Supervision for Better Schools,* 2nd ed. (Englewood Cliffs, N.J.: Prentice-Hall, Inc., 1955), pp. 161–178.

[10] Fischer (see note 8).

regardless of the substantive or methodological knowledge backing the statement. Teachers who equate their *singular subjective* experience with adequately researched and verified theory often devaluate their own professional aspirations.

As Fischer has said, the authoritative statement is never final; it is always open to analysis and modification in the light of new evidence. It is, nevertheless, useful in decision making and can be respected and accepted as a guide to action. Educational leaders with integrity will take care to speak authoritatively and will avoid the temptation of becoming authoritarian as they attempt to lead educators toward professionalization, which, by definition, means an occupation that deals *authoritatively* with its particular concerns.

Applying the yardstick of authoritative behavior, it is clear that some of the functions our schools have assumed are not within their competence. Part of the confusion over the professionalization of education lies in the tendency for educators to assume, or at least accept, responsibility for tasks far outside their training, experience, and social function. The intricate problems of juvenile delinquency, the rising divorce rate, alcoholism, the use of narcotics, and a host of other pressing social issues, if accepted by the schools as their legitimate responsibility, confuse the image and function of the professional educator. Is he a sociologist, a psychologist, a probation officer, a marriage counselor, or is he a teacher? Can educators speak authoritatively on these diverse problems? Admittedly, the task of educating today's children and youth brings the educator into direct confrontation with these problems, but so does it cause him to face complicated medical problems which, thus far, he has been reluctant to try to solve. As a licensed *specialist,* he must limit his behavior to the areas which are his specialty and leave the rest to other specialists who are more appropriately trained. The fact that other specialists do not seem to be concerned or fail to take adequate action does not justify the educator's taking over of roles that are inconsistent and inappropriate to his training and proclaimed function. If he is "professional," he will limit his activities to those in which he may speak authoritatively, thereby raising the value of his own training.

It is naturally a problem to obtain a sufficient supply of such "professionals" in the field of education. We have previously discussed the many problems confronting education on matters of supply and demand, and how these problems tend to devaluate the standards that must be upheld if professionalization is to be achieved. A redefinition of the functions and duties of the professional teacher might reveal some partial solutions to this problem. If teaching could be defined closely enough, so that all duties and functions extraneous to that definition could be eliminated or assigned to other personnel, then the present supply of teachers might be more efficiently employed and compromises with professional standards avoided. Most school administrators, for example, have convinced their school boards that they cannot function as administrators if they are required to be clerk-typists too. The school secretary, a subprofessional worker, thus has become an accepted member of the educational enterprise. Neither does the school principal accept responsibility for performing janitorial services or driving the school bus, as once was the case in many schools. Additional personnel have been hired to execute these functions, or technological innovations have reduced the problems involved. But the point is that, over the years, the school administrator has systematically attempted, to rid himself of all functions and duties he did not consider part of his *professional* role.

Such changes are also possible for teachers. Recent experimentation in the use of technical devices indicate that many subprofessional tasks now performed by teachers can be assumed by machines. B. F. Skinner summarized this argument when he stated: "Will machines replace teachers? On the contrary, they are capital equipment to be used by teachers to save time and labor. In assigning certain mechanizable functions to machines, the teacher emerges in his proper role as an indispensable human being. He may teach more students than heretofore—this is probably inevitable if the world-wide demand for education is to be satisfied—but he will do so in fewer hours and with fewer burdensome chores. In return for his greater productivity he can ask society to improve his economic condition."[11] Much hope is also invested in the development of educational television as a technological device to aid the teacher, although television has not yet solved the problem of allowing for individual differences. As in the case of the administrator, subprofessional personnel can be employed to carry out those parts of the teacher's duties which diminish his professional role. Yard supervision, secretarial duties, even assistance in grading papers and recording marks are but a few examples of duties that could be handled by full-time subprofessional employees or even qualified laymen in the

[11] B. F. Skinner, "Teaching Machines," *Science,* 128, No. 3330 (October 1958).

community. Many experiments have been tried in the use of such subprofessionals, and most have reported a significant measure of success without impairing the professional standing of teachers. Even the knotty problem of salaries has been overcome in some of these experiments where the public interest has been viewed from vantage points other than exclusively economic.

NEW APPROACHES TO PROFESSIONALIZATION

As more educators have become aware of the criteria of professionalism and have studied the problems involved—particularly under the leadership of the Teacher Education and Professional Standards (TEPS) Commission of the NEA, some significant steps calculated to achieve progress toward professionalization have been formulated. The first of these moves has been to try and make practitioners more aware of the necessity of *validating their procedures* through research and experimentation. As a result, there has been in recent years a tremendous increase in educational research, which has attracted the attention of not only the best minds in education but that of leading scholars from such allied fields as psychology and sociology. The expanded efforts of the American Educational Research Association (AERA) and its state affiliates has done much to call attention to the research being conducted as well as to enforce higher standards in such research. The activity of AERA has also tended to reduce the time gap between execution of research and dissemination of results to practitioners in the field. In short, education has become increasingly research conscious and has, therefore, occasionally modified its behavior in the direction of a more professional posture.

A second development has been the increasingly favorable attention given to proposals to classify the first two to five years of teaching as a type of "apprentice" period leading to the eventual achievement of *full professional status.* Commensurate rewards in salaries and prestige would presumably accompany the achievement of the higher status. Education has been plagued, as has been mentioned earlier, with a very rapid turnover of personnel, particularly within the first five years of teaching. Colleges freely predict that 60 per cent of their teacher graduates will drop out of the occupation within this initial five-year period. It is reasonable to assume that such an attrition rate can be attributed to value choices in which the commitment to the occupation comes off second best. In some cases, the education major in college was the result of a young girl's need for some respectable and logical reason to seek higher education. In addition, the kinds of learning common to preprofessional training for teachers are perceived as also useful to prospective mothers and suburban housewives. If the real goal of marriage is not achieved by graduation time, then a teaching position for two or three years offers an ample salary for a young lady until she has achieved the goal of matrimony. Some young teachers also plan to gain possession of a teaching license as a form of insurance for later life, should their husbands' support be removed for any of a number of reasons. While no one takes issue with these examples of foresight, it is also felt that the professional teacher must be one to whom a career is a considerable commitment. Consecutive years of service seem to be one appropriate measure of such dedication.

A third development in the direction of achievement of professionalization is the increasing pressure to raise the standards of certification. Almost all states have legislation planned, pending, or passed to raise the minimum training period for teachers, and many states have similarly elevated the requirements for the positions of administrator, supervisor, and other special personnel. In some states, however, the additional requirements seem to have been added to satisfy special interest groups or were designed with little knowledge of the requirements of teaching. One state, for example, has made it possible, under the guise of raising standards, for anyone with virtually any academic major to add a minimal amount of professional training (20 units) and be qualified to teach elementary school. This state may soon find graduates in business administration, Russian musicology, and medieval philosophy attempting to teach first-grade reading with unpredictable results. On the other side of the coin, however, there is powerful resistance to any raising of standards at all from groups who fear a consequent increase in the teacher shortage will result. Close examination of their arguments often reveals that the real fear of these groups is that higher standards will mean higher salaries, and that a high demand for a short supply will raise costs in the procurement and maintenance of a qualified teaching staff.

The general trend toward raising standards has focused much attention on teacher education. Unfortunately, much that has been written in the public press on the subject is misinformed and flagrantly biased. Many of the sweeping reforms, advocated by persons who have never been connected with the occupation, resemble recommendations of major surgery for curing personality defects. Informed sources have great difficulty being heard in this maelstrom of charge and counter charge that has prevailed in some areas. Basically, the public debate has focused on two supposedly valid controversies: (1) traditional versus progressive education and (2) knowledge of subject versus knowledge of methodology. A reasonable review of the facts indicates that calm and responsible people have never advocated "either-or" positions on these issues. Logically, a teacher must know what she is teaching and how to teach it. Logically too, she must call upon the best evidence of research and experience to accomplish these ends *regardless* of whether she is considered "traditional" or "progressive," for both terms imply a purity of definition that does not match reality. The achievement of goals needs to be based upon the best knowledge of all relevant facts. Emotional generalizations from any side of a controversy do little to contribute to workable solutions. Thus, if the occupation of education is seeking professionalization through the raising of standards, it must be scrupulously objective in reviewing its present deficiencies and needs. If groups outside education wish to raise the quality of education, they, too, are enjoined to seek such a goal objectively, knowledgeable of all the facts and realities of this complex enterprise. It is the contention of some that many of the current controversial issues over the improvement of education can be resolved better through research than debate. This position rests on the assumption that many educational problems are the result of lack of knowledge and that research, a primary professional tool, must be employed if such knowledge is to be obtained. In the research process, educators will presumably become more professional, for they will have to become increasingly analytical and, therefore, will modify their decisions and behavior in the light of such analyses.

THE ULTIMATE QUESTION OF AUTONOMY

Just as the ultimate test of a teacher trainee is his ability to put into practice all that he has learned, so the ultimate test of professionalism lies in the day-to-day performance of the tasks of teaching. The quality of decisions a teacher makes is the measure of his degree of professionalization. Whatever he does has consequences and presumably stems from his diagnosis of the complex educational situation in which he finds himself. Not all alternatives are open to him; he must plan and select courses of action within the framework of ends prescribed by others. What the teacher decides to do, what course of action he chooses, is a basic professional act.

If he is required to make no decisions, simply to follow a given set of prescriptions, then he has not yet engaged in any professional activity. In fact, he has relinquished his basic claim to professional status if he allows his autonomy in the decision-making process to be compromised.

In the act of making professional decisions (and we repeat that both teaching and administration involve a ceaseless series of choices among appropriate alternatives), the educator must invoke both his moral and intellectual authority. He, the teacher, must constantly rule on matters of fact—that is, he exercises his intellectual authority. Similarly, he constantly has to decide between good ends and bad ends, between appropriate or inappropriate behavior; thus he exercises his moral authority.

There is, however, considerable debate over the sources of such intellectual and moral authority. The selective awareness of environment by individuals and groups in a predominantly urban society has made the selection of fact from opinion a more difficult task. All people do not perceive "truth" in the same manner, and no individual can be absolutely sure of all the facts in a given situation. Similarly, in the realm of moral authority, a great diversity of standards, customs, and opinions exists; this is inevitable in a culturally pluralistic society. It also seems inevitable that individuals and groups holding differing standards will clash with varying degrees of violence. In this constant struggle, government, as represented by law, stands as a beleaguered referee, but schools seem to be the football.

The sources of authority for educators are multiple. Some believe the schools belong to the parents of the children who inhabit them. Their reasoning is simple: the children are sent to school to learn what their parents want them to learn in order to cope with the world of the future. This might be a simple directive to follow were it not for the wide range of differences among parents. Since these differences represent the full circle of differences in the population, no single segment of opinion among parents is a valid guiding authority. In short, the parents represent the precise pluralism that has made the school the arena for many social disputes.

The community may be another source of authority, but it too speaks with many tongues and differs with other communities. In an era of high mobility, the provincialism implied in full local autonomy is unbelievable. Even state standards seem to smack of isolationism when one reviews the profound differences between some states. For example, education in rural South Dakota and urban New York is so different that it is hard to believe both kinds are present in the same nation. Or compare a rural Louisiana school with a school in San Francisco or in Seattle. Such schools sometimes do not even read the same editions of standard school textbooks. In such a situation, what is fact and what is moral?

Suggestions have been made that a national curriculum be developed,[12] that education be consciously used as an instrument of national goals.[13] But reception to these proposals has been ambivalent, in some cases, and violently negative in others. The historical tradition of local control is deeply embedded in the social scheme. Many people are reluctant to relinquish this control and the many benefits that go with it, in exchange for an unknown national control system that might seem to offer logical solutions to many pressing problems but is untested and fraught with possible antidemocratic dangers. Paradoxically, one of the main expressions of democracy is a profound suspicion of its logical operations. This is to say that Americans operate and accept a representative democracy in almost all matters, but they distrust this same system if it is applied to the field of education.

Still another group views the problem of authority with alarming simplicity. They would simply accept the authority of their particular organized religious group as supreme. It is obvious, however, that diversity in the pursuit of religion plus constitutional edicts separating church and state make this solution impossible. The authority for the educator must, therefore, come from some other source.

In a democratic society, the power to give authority rests in the general population. In many situations, the society has chosen to delegate its power and authority to selected specialists. Medical doctors, for example, are delegated authority to practice their specialty with extensive autonomy; lawyers are similarly granted much autonomy. In both cases, the society has seen fit to accomplish its purposes by delegating its power and authority to experts whose "professional" judgment can be trusted. However, this delegated authority extends only to matters that are within the legitimate sphere of the professional's training and competence—i.e., the crucial test of competence must be passed before the autonomy can be granted. Thus, the source of the authority is the society, but the specific implementation of that authority is expressed by the responsible judgment of the competent practi-

[12] Paul R. Hanna, "Design for a National Curriculum," *Nation's Schools*, September 1958.

[13] Paul R. Hanna, ed., *Education: An Instrument of National Goals* (New York: McGraw-Hill Book Co., Inc., 1962).

tioner. When we say "responsible" judgment, we introduce another key concept. The exercise of independent professional judgment simply means that the professional has autonomy but stands responsible for the consequences of his decisions. He is responsible to the source of authority that granted him his autonomy—namely, the society that delegated a part of its authority to him.

The authority of the educator should logically be derived from this same process of delegating power, if the conditions society demands for its protection are met. In other words, the educator will receive social sanction to be his own source of authority, *as a designated expert,* when he can demonstrate he has sufficient competence to perform expertly in his field of endeavor, and when he is willing to accept responsibility for his professional acts and their consequences. Potentially, we assert, education has already available to it the bodies of knowledge which, if mastered, will permit educators to acquire the expected level of competence. Whether sufficient numbers of people capable of mastering these requirements are available, is another question.

Present practitioners in education have been reluctant to accept full responsibility for their decisions. They have been unwilling, for example, to lay themselves open to malpractice or negligence suits stemming from the consequences of their decisions. The argument has always been that educational practices and their consequences are still too much a matter of personal opinion. Under these conditions, educators have been reluctant to accept personal jeopardy; yet, it is obvious that the *general society* cannot, and will not, engage in the activities necessary to clarify or validate educational practices.

THE IMPLICATIONS FOR EDUCATORS

If education is to become a profession and an academic discipline, with the rights and social respect accorded a profession and a true discipline, then *its practitioners* must *initiate* reforms that will lead to the accomplishment of that goal. These must include creation of standards of competence, effective and uniform certification and accreditation procedures and assure the efficient accomplishment of the goals of education. The doctor is granted autonomy when he proves he has the skills and procedures to heal the wounded and cure the sick. If he fails to heal or to cure, he must stand accountable for the professional decisions he made. If such scrutiny proves him to be without blame, he may proceed in the practice of his profession. If examination proves him negligent in his judgment, he may be asked to surrender his autonomy.

The educator who aspires to professional status can expect to be held to similar standards. He must clarify what is his competence, demonstrate his possession of that competence, and assert his willingness to accept all the risks as well as the privileges of professional autonomy. When society judges these conditions to have been obtained, then and only then, will educators be granted full professional status.

SUMMARY

Education has struggled mightily to attain the status of a profession, but the current criteria of professionalism suggest that education does not yet qualify. Many problems confront educators in their quest for professional status; some of these are within the power of educators to solve.

The more difficult obstacles seem to be the achievement of professional autonomy by public servants, the stabilization of a predominantly female occupation in order to have a comprehensive and cohesive organization, and the development of sufficient areas of agreement on the aims of education, and the functions and standards of competence of educators.

Educators are capable of achieving higher levels of competence, better defined certification, and more universally accepted accreditation standards. They can also achieve unity in organization, and perhaps an enforceable code of ethics. But the degree of commitment to legitimate professional goals seems limited within the ranks of practicing educators. Where this lack of commitment is combined with internal dissension and external criticism, the occupations associated with education face considerable struggle before professionalism can prevail.

SELECTED BIBLIOGRAPHY

Gauerke, Warren E. *Legal and Ethical Responsibilities of School Personnel.* Englewood Cliffs, N.J.: Prentice-Hall, Inc., 1959.

Hanna, Paul R., ed. *Education: An Instrument of National Goals.* New York: McGraw-Hill Book Company, 1962.

Huggett, Albert J., and T. M. Stinnett. *Professional Problems of Teachers.* New York: The Macmillan Company, 1956.

Lieberman, Myron. *Education as a Profession.* Englewood Cliffs, N.J.: Prentice-Hall, Inc., 1956.

National Commission on Teacher Education and Professional Standards. *A Position Paper.* Washington, D.C.: National Education Association, 1963.

National Society for the Study of Education. *Education for the Professions.* Chicago: University of Chicago Press, 1962.

PART IV

CONCLUSIONS AND CASES

CHAPTER 16

CONCLUDING REMARKS

Education, during the latter half of the twentieth century, is a complex enterprise that offers a variety of intellectually challenging careers. It is no longer appropriate to hold that teachers, administrators, school board members or other educational workers run a relatively simple system of institutions in order to pass the settled knowledge of the past on to the future through the current generation of students. According to our thesis, the educational process requires that an endless series of decisions be made by many types of educators who perform different professional roles.

It is vital for educators to understand the culture within which they work, the goals they seek to reach, and the range of environmental factors bearing upon individual behavior. A culture and its educational institutions mutually affect each other; they shape, and in turn are shaped by, each other.

We considered the various aspects of the ideational environment that influence educational decisions. Whether or not one faces them explicitly, *some* ideas are influencing his decisions. The position assumed by the authors is that professional workers become increasingly aware of the ideas and social forces that help shape their beliefs, their decisions, and their behavior. The environment of ideas, so crucial for educators to understand, includes a variety of beliefs drawn from many sources. Some of these beliefs are accepted uncritically from tradition, some are based upon careful examination of alternative philosophic or even theological positions, while other beliefs are grounded in scientific observation and experimentation.

The complexity of educational decisions is such that almost every situation calls for the dovetailing of both scientific and philosophic considerations. The best examples of rational behavior involve carefully considered value alternatives, values confronted with facts as well as the best predictions of the relevant sciences.

Regardless of the question of desirability, so far there exists no decision-making machine for the computerizing of educational problems other than the scheduling of classes, the arrangement of physical facilities, and the management of the bookkeeping aspects of large operations. Furthermore, we have no theory of decision making in education, if we use "theory" in its rigorous scientific sense. We can and do theorize, although, as yet, we lack an overarching theory. Let us briefly distinguish "theory" and "theorizing."

A *theory* is a logically consistent set of statements composed of assumptions or postulates and theorems derived from them. Its assertions must be logically consistent, comprehensive enough to explain all relevant facts, should employ as few basic terms as possible, and should generate testable hypotheses.

Theorizing, on the other hand, occurs whenever we suspend action, however temporarily, and reflect upon or carefully consider the various factors relevant to our action or to our alternative possible courses of action. Theorizing might make use of theory or might not. The construction or use of theory, on the other hand, necessarily involves theorizing.

Our book, we hope, will help serious educators in their theorizing as it bears upon their various professional decisions. By the very nature of the professional task, a recipe for decisions is inappropriate and indefensible. Situational decisions must be made on the basis of materials relevant to the problem at hand. Thus, even in the absence of a full-blown theory of decision making, theorizing is necessary for professional behavior and provides a basis for intelligent action. Let us look briefly at several situations calling for decisions and indicate (1) some of the alternative courses of action and (2) the considerations which would render a chosen action relevant and defensible.

EXAMPLES OF DECISION-MAKING SITUATIONS

SITUATION I

In the second grade of Emerson Elementary School, located in a suburb of a midwestern city, Tommy used the expression "it ain't worth a damn" as he tore up a painting he had just completed. Tommy had been in the class but three days, having arrived with his family from a depressed rural area located within the same state. His expression upset some of the children, one of whom complained about it to the teacher.

The teacher must always choose from among alternative courses of action. Even inaction has educational consequences in this setting and represents one possible alternative for the teacher.

POSSIBILITIES

1. The teacher may decide not to take action at all.

2. The teacher may decide to reprimand Tommy either privately or in front of the other children.

3. The teacher may discuss the incident with Tommy alone, or with the entire class.

4. The teacher may decide to note the incident and postpone action until after further observation and investigation.

RELEVANT CONSIDERATIONS

1. The teacher must have a clear conception of the goals towards which his children should progress. In the absence of such a conception, he cannot decide whether anything should be done about Tommy's expression. In the final analysis, this calls for examination of the values to be perpetuated by the school. Thus the relevance of educational philosophy.

2. Even if the values sought are clear and agreed upon, other considerations enter. Why does Tommy use this expression? Does he have any knowledge of its social unacceptability in this school? Or does he purposely use it to upset the other children and perhaps the teacher?

3. Information about the ethnic, social-class and family background would be relevant to the questions raised in (2) above. Sociologists and anthropologists have provided a significant body of scientific information for the teacher to draw upon for a better understanding of the complex culture in which he, his class, and Tommy are to work and learn together. The more he knows about the factors relevant to the situation, the more effective he should be as a clinician to help his class, and Tommy within the class, to approach the stated goals and aims of his school.

4. What about the social system of his classroom? Often, it is possible to understand the behavior of one child only in light of the complex of social forces within the class or the school as they relate to the child's behavior.

5. The above consideration falls clearly into the area of social psychology. This is evidence of the fact that educational decisions, if they are to be handled adequately, demand that we draw upon several of the so-called "separate disciplines." The relevance of psychology is further clear when the teacher considers the motivational factors as well as the influence of his own behavior on Tommy and on the rest of the class.

SITUATION II

Mr. Martin teaches advanced algebra in an urban high school. George K., one of his students, is barely passing his course at the eleventh-grade level. George has had difficulties in other subject areas as well, but his parents have insisted on his pursuing a college preparatory curriculum. His parents, who are among the civic and business leaders in the community, have always gone out of their way to support the schools and have insisted on entertaining the teachers and administrators of the schools George attended. Mr. Martin has been asked by Mr. K. and by the principal to give George all the extra work necessary to earn a grade of "B" in algebra.

POSSIBILITIES

1. Mr. Martin may choose to give George lots of extra attention and extra work, to enable him to earn a "B" through massive expansion of effort.

2. Mr. Martin may become highly indignant at the principal and the parents and vent his anger at them, or George, or both.

3. Mr. Martin may go to the ethics committee of a local professional association to seek protection against the encroachment upon his academic freedom and professional autonomy.

4. Mr. Martin may choose to continue teaching George as he did before.

RELEVANT CONSIDERATIONS

1. Why is George in Mr. Martin's eleventh-grade algebra class? Should he be there at all, considering his abilities or is he there because of his parents' aspirations for him? Sociologists have given us sound information about the pressures placed upon children and educators by upper-middle-class families.

2. What are the criteria whereby grades are determined? Should they be based on effort, on ability, on achievement, or on some combination of these factors? These questions can be answered only with the aid of philosophic analysis.

3. What are the consequences of following one kind of grading policy or another? This, unlike the previous question, is amenable to scientific investigation.

4. Does Mr. Martin have autonomy in the determination of a grade for George? Ideally yes, within the bounds of the agreed-upon policy

developed by his school system. In the reasonable exercise of his discretion he is likely to be protected against undue pressures.

5. The former consideration relates to the existence, or its lack, of an organization whose task is to protect Mr. Martin if he acts in a professional manner. This, of course, implies an agreement on what professional behavior would be in this situation. Other related factors would include the existence of legal protection through tenure laws; the power status of Mr. K., as well as his willingness to misuse his power; and the extent to which the principal is willing to protect Mr. Martin against undue pressure or influence from a powerful lay figure in the community.

SITUATION III

The school system of Mount Parade needed a substantial amount of money to provide new buildings and teachers for its expanding school-age population. At the local election, the proposals for a bond issue and for a real-property-tax increase were both defeated. The school board called a meeting to consider its next steps.

POSSIBILITIES

1. Imposition of the financial obligation on the community against its vote.

2. Construction of the needed facilities, and spreading of the costs among all the families who have school-age children.

3. Elimination of some existing programs and an increase in class sizes, while carrying on as normal, to satisfy the wishes of the community.

4. Continuation with a pared-down program, while exploring the reasons for community rejection. As soon as seems advisable, securing of voter support of the program.

RELEVANT CONSIDERATIONS

1. The legal limits placed upon the powers of the school board must be considered.

2. In order to explore whether we may wish to attain community support or somehow impose the financial obligation on all or on some of its members, we must re-examine our commitment to a theory of democracy.

3. Was the vote an informed vote? Did the school board enlist the support of the lay citizenry in order to get the facts before the voting public? What does the experience of comparable communities tell us?

4. Would it be desirable and useful to conduct some post-election

studies, to determine more accurately why the voters turned down the requests?

5. What part of the total school program should be eliminated? Temporarily suspended? Should we suspend special programs for the retarded, the gifted, the blind, the deaf, and others?

6. Should we enlarge the enrollment in each existing classroom up to the limits of physical safety and proceed as before?

7. Was the vote a significant protest against some educational policies and practices? Or was it an uninformed vote due to apathy or, perhaps, due to an inadequate public information campaign prior to the election?

SITUATION IV

The teachers and administrators of Lincoln School received communications from members of the local Association for Liberty protesting the upcoming school festival on the grounds that its theme was "Music and Songs from Many Lands" and, consequently, not sufficiently "American." The educators were asked to change the theme or cancel the festival.

POSSIBILITIES

1. Cancelation of the festival because of the controversy.

2. Ignoring of the protests, and proceeding according to the original plans.

3. Invitation to the spokesmen of the Association for Liberty to discuss the entire matter.

4. Invitation to civic leaders and spokesmen for various community groups, including the protesting one, to discuss the situation.

5. Mounting of a campaign attacking the loyalty of the protesting group.

6. Appealing to the school board for decision as the board sees fit.

RELEVANT CONSIDERATIONS

1. What were the objectives of the festival? Are they relevant and appropriate for the school to pursue?

2. Is the decision an appropriate one for joint lay-professional deliberations, or is it one for professional judgment to be backed and supported by a lay board?

3. Is the protesting group worthy of respect? Does it deserve consideration around the conference table along with other groups?

4. How powerful is the protesting group in this community? How

independent is the school board in exercising its decision-making powers?

5. How united are the educators, and how much autonomy have they achieved in making educational decisions?

6. What does it mean to assert that a festival that includes songs from many lands is not "American"?

7. Should there be any censoring of school activities? Who are the appropriate "censors"?

SITUATION V

Three separate groups of teachers, all employed within the same large school district, are attempting to organize the teachers and to represent them in negotiations with the superintendent and the school board. The first is affiliated with the National Educational Association, the second with the American Federation of Teachers; the third is a local organization, claiming independence of any state or national associations. Before the Board of Education, each claims to represent the best interest of the teachers, of the students, and of the community. The board declares that it will discuss matters with a committee of the three organizations, but that it is not willing to negotiate or bargain with any group. What are the possibilities and relevant considerations?

SITUATION VI

Whittier Elementary School is located in the suburbs of a midwestern city. The parents of Ellen, a fourth grader, wish to have her transferred to the other fourth-grade classroom within the same school. In conference with the teacher and the principal, the parents express their respect and confidence. However, they indicate that Ellen is most unhappy about the presence of a Negro boy in the classroom. The parents state that they are not at all prejudiced, that they simply want Ellen to be happy at school and to learn well, and that she can get used to learning in the same classroom with Negroes when she is more mature. What are the possibilities and relevant considerations?

SITUATION VII

In a medium-sized city the Board of Education decides to build a new high school to meet the needs of a growing population. A local group of citizens, organized under the title of "Better Schools for a Better Tomorrow," petitions the Board to eliminate courses in driver education, sewing, typing, cooking, wood- and metalwork from the curriculum of the new school. What are the possibilities and relevant considerations?

SITUATION VIII

Several teachers, members of the Jewish faith, request that the local Board of Education grant them the right not to teach during Jewish religious holidays, without a loss in salary. A board member raises an objection based on the additional costs involved and points out that national holidays, together with Christmas and Easter, are paid vacations for all teachers. What are the possibilities and relevant considerations?

SITUATION IX

Lay leaders of a Mexican-American community approach the teachers and the principal of an elementary school with the request that children who speak Spanish fluently and English poorly, or not at all, be given primary schooling in Spanish. They propose that English instruction for these children be deferred until after they have mastered the basic skills of reading and writing in their mother tongue—Spanish. What are the possibilities and relevant considerations?

SITUATION X

The Board of Education must decide the proper location of new schools to be built in a rapidly growing community. Leaders of several civil-rights groups urge that the schools be so located that the student population of each school will be composed of children from several social classes and various ethnic, racial, and religious backgrounds. What are the possibilities and relevant considerations?

PERVASIVE CONSIDERATIONS

Each of the foregoing situations calls for decisions to be made. While the names and places were changed to ensure anonymity, the illustrations are based on actual occurrences. An endless list could be supplied by the authors, or other educators, precisely because the entire educational process is a complex web of such situations and decisions. It is quite clear that in none of the cases presented would a research study or set of scientific studies provide a clear and unambiguous answer. It is equally clear that nonscientific beliefs, philosophizing, theorizing, or common-sense speculations alone are equally inadequate to solve these problems.

At this stage of educational development we need the combination, the dovetailing, of scientific studies and philosophic analysis. Our theorizing is most defensible when we rely upon both of these powerful sources of beliefs. It may be annoying to the novice, or even to some long-time practitioner, that quick and simple solutions were not provided for our situations. The more mature and insightful student, on the other hand, will realize that education in the United States of America has no single "official" point of view or set of values to be imposed upon all practitioners. While there are long-range goals expressed in high-level abstractions that we agree upon, similar to the magnificent but equally abstract goals of law and medicine, particular situations evoke disagreements and proposals for alternative solutions.

It is possible that in the long run, as we construct more tenable theories and build a larger storehouse of valid and reliable scientific conclusions, large areas of education will lie beyond disagreement. In the meantime, however, intelligent educators will be repeatedly called upon to theorize with the aid of the methods and conclusions to be gleaned from science as well as philosophy. Can anyone ask for a greater challenge?

INDEX

Accreditation of schools, 330-333
Achieved status, 66
Acton, Lord, 123, 182
Adams, E. Merle, Jr., 25
Administrators, 5, 6, 325, 334, 337
(*see also* Educators)
Adult programs, 155
Agricultural workers, 222-224 *passim*
Albany Normal School, 289
American Association of Colleges for Teacher Education, 331
American Association of University Professors, 333
American Association of University Women, 260
American Education Research Association, 340
American Farm Bureau, 253
AFL-CIO, 260
American Federation of Teachers, 260, 327, 333, 334
American Flag Committee, 269
American Legion Auxiliary, 257
Anderson, Nels, 156
Anderson, Robert, 228*n*
Angell, Robert, 30, 140
Analytic assertions, 14-16
Aquinas, St. Thomas, 102
Aristotle, 53, 102, 109-110, 282
Arnstein, George E., 157*n*, 160*n*
Ascoli, Max, 296
Ascribed status, 66
Attitudes, 50 (*see also* Beliefs and assumptions; Values)
Auden, W. H., 136
Automation, 151-163 *passim*
(*see also* Technology)
Axtelle, G., 113*n*

Bacon, Sir Francis, 61, 96
Ball, William B., 201*n*
Barnard, Chester I., 6*n*
Barnard, Henry, 247, 289
Barnes, Harry Elmer, 295*n*
Barnett, Governor, 211
Barnette case, 185
Barr, Arvil S., 317*n*, 318
Beard, Charles, 295
Becker, Carl, 43
Behavioral science and education, 96-98
Beliefs and assumptions, 14-19, 100-102
(*see also* Values)
Bell, Daniel, 117*n*
Bendix, Reinhard, 64*n*, 66*n*
Benjamin, Harold, 7*n*, 281
Benne, Kenneth D., 114*n*
Bentham, Jeremy, 121
Bettelheim, Bruno, 76*n*
Bias, 95-96
Bible reading, 186-188
Bicultural background, 217-220
Bigelow, Karl W., 305
Black, Justice, 187, 190-191
Black, Max, 104*n*
Black Muslims, 224
Blum, Virgil C., 194, 196

Board of education functions, 5
(*see also* Policy)
Bode, Boyd H., 97, 114*n*
Borrowman, Merle L., 300, 303*n*
Brennan, Justice, 188
Bridgman, P. W., 264
Brim, Orville J., Jr., 25-26, 33, 284, 317-318
Brookover, Wilbur B., 72*n*, 310
Broudy, Harry S., 160*n*
Brubacher, John S., 110*n*
Burgess, Ernest W., 76, 77
Butts, R. Freeman, 33, 35*n*, 177*n*, 178*n*, 195, 197, 265*n*, 283, 284*n*, 285*n*, 289*n*
Byers, Loretta, 314

California State Board of Education, 267-268
Calverton, V. F., 29*n*, 295*n*
Calvinist influence, 9, 283-284
Caplow, Theodore, 139-140, 326
Carnegie Foundation for the Advancement of Teaching, 295-296
Cassell, Frank H., 160*n*
Caste, 63-64
Case-study method, 164
Catholic parochial schools, 182
Censorship, 270
Center for the Study of Leisure, University of Chicago, 163
Certification of teachers, 292-293, 294, 329, 341-342
Chamberlain case, 187
Chandler, B. J., 138*n*, 149
Charters, W. W., 72*n*
"Child-benefit" theory, 192-193, 196
Child-labor legislation, 153
Children (*see also* Students):
handicapped, 238
leisure of, 153-154, 172
poverty's impact on, 216
(*see also* Cultural deprivation)
Childs, John L., 97, 113*n*
Church League of America, 257
Civil-rights legislation, 211
Civil-rights movement, 266*n*
Clark, Burton, 234*n*
Clark, Justice, 187, 188, 198
Clayton, Horace R., 67*n*
Class (*see* Social class and stratification)
Class size, 91, 237-238
"Clear and present danger" doctrine, 270
Cochran case, 192
Cohen, Morris R., 61*n*
Coladarci, Arthur P., 9-10
Coleman, Richard P., 66*n*
Coleman, S. J., 72*n*
College competition for students, 302-303
Colleges (*see* Teacher training)
Comenius, 61
Committee for Economic Development, 250
Communication:
and culture change, 94
and democracy, 123
language barriers, 217-220
mass media, 72
technology and, 132
urban mass society and, 91-96
and value conflict, 45-46
Communism, 117-120, 256, 268-270
Community, 27-28
"decline of," 140
social-stratification context, 66
Comprehensive high school, 243
Conant, James B., 73*n*, 96*n*, 197, 206, 236, 243, 302, 306
Conformity, 135-141, 147-148
in curriculum, 263-273 *passim*
loyalty issues, 268-273
and recruitment, 314-315, 316
of teachers, 266, 271-273
Controversial issues in the classroom, 263-278
Cook, James Graham, 212
Cooley, Charles H., 76
Coombs, Jerrold R., 243
Coon, Carleton S., 82*n*
Costello, Frank, 310
Costs of education, 226, 237, 249-254 *passim* (*see also* Financing; Salary)
Cotton, John, 177, 178
Council of Chief State School Officers, 258
Counts, George, 42, 144
Court decisions, 185-198, 208-214 *passim*, 270
Cowar, Thomas A., 158*n*
Crane, Stephen, 328
Cremin, Lawrence A., 35*n*, 112*n*, 177*n*, 178*n*, 265*n*, 283, 284*n*, 289*n*
Crowley, Dean, 181

Cubberly, E. P., 282
Cultural deprivation, 73-74, 204-230
Cultural lag, 42-43
Cultural pluralism, 141-144
  language problems, 217-220
  religion, 176-179, 180-203 *passim*, 220-222
  segregation and, 149
Cultural pyramid, 41
Culture, 21-22, 266-267
  controversial issues, 263-278
  and decision making, 7-8, 11-12, 19
  economic and social relations, 133-134
  and education, 21-47, 61-99 *passim*
  leisure, 163-168, 168-172 *passim*
  mass society, 131-150 (*see also* Urban life)
  segregation and, 208-214 *passim*
  subcultures (*see* Subcultures)
  technology and, 82-83, 151-163, 163-175 *passim*
  values (*see* Values)
Culture change, 39-45, 82 (*see also* Social change; Urban life)
  and communication problems, 94
  family structure and functions, 75-82
  "progress" concept, 41-43 *passim*
Curriculum, 44-45, 57
  child's development and, 275-276
  in colonial America, 283
  comprehensive high school, 243
  control of, 45, 256, 344 (*see also* Policy)
  controversial issues, 263-278
  and cultural deprivation, 226
  grade system, 227-228
  loyalty issues and, 268-273
  morality in, 198-202 *passim*
  national standards, 344
  philosophic bases of, 111-112
  pressures for change, 233-234
  religion in, 179, 188, 198-202 *passim*
  special programs, 236-244 *passim*, 248
  traditional orientation of, 265-266
  UNESCO materials in, 269
  values and, 57-58, 344 (*see also* Goals of education)
  vocational programs, 93-94

Dame schools, 286-287
Darwin, Charles, 96
Daughters of the American Revolution, 257
Davie, James S., 73*n*
Davies, Daniel R., 6*n*
Davis, Allison, 67*n*, 71*n*
Davis, Kingsley, 27, 140
Dawson, William, 258
Decision making, 7-12, 173-174 (*see also* Policy)
  beliefs and assumptions in, 14-19
  communication problems and, 94-96
  consumer culture and, 158-159
  and cultural change, 44-45
  district organization and, 38-39
  "facts" and, 61-62
  and leisure use, 173-174
  levels of, 4-7, 38-39, 44-45
  professional-autonomy issues, 325-326, 336-337, 342-346
  sample cases, 352-358
  science and, 12-14
  value conflicts in, 52-56
Democracy, 120-124
  and controversial issues, 264
  and decision making, 11-12, 344-345
  and education, 113-115, 121, 124, 144-149, 195, 239-244, 266-278 *passim*, 344-345
  equality and conformity issues, 135-141
  in family life, 78-81
  leisure and, 171
  national goals, 239-244 *passim* (*see also* Values)
  resolution of value conflicts, 55-56
  social mobility and, 67
  school's functions in, 266-278 *passim* (*see also* Goals of education)
Demography (*see* Population)
Deutsch, Karl, 139
Dewey, John, 42, 62*n*, 97, 102, 106-107, 109*n*, 110-114 *passim*, 119*n*, 295, 302-306 *passim*
Dialectic view of history, 118
Dictionary of American Slang, 270
Diebold, John, 156, 157
Dierenfeld, R. H., 186
Discrimination in schools, 225-229 (*see also* Segregation)
"Dismissed-time" programs, 192
Dollard, John, 67*n*

Donahue, Wilma, 154*n*
Douglas, Justice, 190
Drake, St. Clair, 67*n*
Dred Scott case, 208
Dropouts, 90-91, 154, 242
Dubois, Cora, 217-218

Ebenstein, William, 115*n*, 117*n*, 121-122
Economic determinism, 117-118
Economic factors, 70-71, 121, 122, 214-220, 226 (*see also* Costs; Financing; Salary; Socioeconomic factors)
Education, 3 (*see also* Schools; Teachers)
  attacks on, 322
  automated instruction, 161-163
  bias vs. prejudice in, 95-96
  under communism, 119-120
  and consumer decision making, 159
  costs, 226, 237, 249-254 *passim*
  cultural deprivation and, 204-230
  and culture transmission and change, 21-47
  curriculum (*see* Curriculum)
  decision making in, 3-21 (*see also* Policy)
  and democracy, 113-115, 121, 124, 144-149, 195, 239-244, 266-278 *passim*
  equality and conformity issues, 135-141 *passim*
  under fascism, 116-117
  federal-state-local control issues, 5, 188-189, 254-260
  financing (*see* Financing)
  formal and informal aspects, 34-35
  geographic variation, 343-344
  goals of (*see* Goals of education)
  history of, 281-307
  and income, 70-71
  indoctrination vs. freedom issues, 266-268
  international competition and, 240-241
  Lancasterian teaching method, 287-288
  leadership in, 336-338 *passim*
  learning theory, 273-275
  and leisure, 167-174 *passim*
  legal requirements, 293
  levels achieved (distribution), 242
Education (continued)
  the liberal tradition, 300-303, 305-306
  Lyceum movement, 290
  mass society and, 131-150 *passim*
  of migrants' children, 222-224
  and occupation, 68, 70, 89-91, 156, 159-160, 233-234
  opportunity for, 70-75 *passim*
  philosophy and, 100-127 *passim* (*see also* Values)
  population growth and, 87-89
  quality of, 146, 189, 195, 222-224 (*see* Quality of education)
  science and, 61-99 *passim*
  and social change, 11
  and social class, 65, 70-75
  and social control, 35
  social foundations of, 61-99 *passim*
  and social mobility, 68
  specialization vs. generalization, 160-161, 300-306 *passim*
  the technical tradition, 303-306
  technology and, 158-163
  and values, 48-60 *passim*, 144-149, 196 (*see also* Culture; Values)
Educational Policies Commission (*see* National Education Association)
Educators, 3-4 (*see also* Administrators; Teachers)
  anti-intellectualism among, 316
  autonomy of, 342-345 (*see also* Professionalism)
  competence of, 275-276, 337-338
  conformist pressures on, 266, 271-273
  public confidence in, 275-276
  social structure of, 336-338 *passim*
  teachers of teachers, 316 (*see also* Teacher training)
Eels, Kenneth, 65*n*
Ehlers, Henry, 181*n*, 183*n*
Elsbree, Willard S., 284*n*, 288*n*, 290, 291*n*, 292*n*
Employment (*see also* Occupation):
  age and, 87
  requirements for, 91-96 *passim*, 156, 159-160, 233-234
  technology and, 155-188
  of women (*see* Women)
  work ethic, 166, 310-312 *passim*
  work satisfaction, 167

Engels, Friedrich, 117
Ennis, Robert, 104*n*
Enrollment:
in Catholic parochial schools, 182
requirements, 189-191 *passim*
Ethnic groups (*see* Cultural pluralism; Segregation; Subcultures; Socioeconomic factors)
Evans, Luther H., 157*n*, 160*n*
Everson case, 193, 196, 197
Experimentalist school of education, 112-114, 273

"Fact," 61, 263 (*see also* Science)
Family life:
changing character of, 75-82
economic level and, 215
and school functions, 81-82
Family size, 79-80, 153
Fascism, 116-117, 240-241
Faubus, Governor, 211
Federal government (*see also* Government control):
financing education, 246-262
and local policy, 5, 188-189, 254-260 *passim*
suspicion of, 255-256
Financing of education, 34-35, 38, 39, 88
federal aid, 246-262
G.I. Bill, 248, 255
"impact" support, 248-249
Lancasterian method, 287-288
National Defense Education Act, 72, 249
parochial schools, 192-193, 194-198, 257, 259-260
population expansion and, 322
religious establishment and, 177-178 *passim*
religious instruction, 190
scholarship programs, 241-242, 255
segregation and, 257-259
state responsibility, 188-189, 247-248
for teacher training, 288
for vocational training, 248
Fischer, Louis, 124*n*, 326-327, 336-338 *passim*
Fithian, P. V., 285
Fitzgerald, Gerald B., 169
Fliegler, Louis A., 233*n*
Ford Foundation, 282
Fox, William, 312*n*
Frohnen, Richard, 194
Frankfurter, Justice, 196
Friends of the Public Schools, 257
Frost, Robert, 320

Gage, N. L., 12*n*, 72*n*
Galbraith, John Kenneth, 214-215
Garcia, Hector, 222
Gardner, Burleigh B., 67*n*, 71*n*
Gardner, Mary R., 67*n*, 71*n*
General Federation of Women's Clubs, 260
Gentile, Giovanni, 116
Geographic isolation of rural schools, 222-224
Geographic mobility:
and dropouts, 154
and financing education, 249
urbanization, 83-96 *passim*
German teacher-training schools, 288
Getzels, J. W., 240
Ghiselin, Bernard, 274
Gifted children, 154, 231-245
G. I. Bill of Rights, 248, 255
Gilbert, Arthur, 184
Gist, Noel P., 28*n*
Goals of education, 109-111, 276-278 (*see also* Values)
in colonial America, 283-284
conflicts about, 52-56 *passim*, 145-146, 239-244 *passim*, 229-306
creativity, 274
critical thinking, 273
democratic society and, 266-278 *passim*
and gifted-student programs, 239-244 *passim*
"social engineering" issue, 144-149 *passim*
social basis of, 29-34 *passim*
teacher's role, 74-75
use of leisure, 167-168
Gobitis case, 185
Goldberg, Justice, 188
Goldwater, Barry, 257
Goodlad, John I., 6*n*, 228*n*
Gottlieb, D., 72*n*
Gottman, Jean, 138

Government control (*see also* Federal government; Policy):
certification, 294, 329, 341-342
financing and, 246-262 *passim*
variations in, 44
and religion, 176-203 *passim*
scholarship programs, 241-242
and teacher training, 296
Grade system, 227-228
"Great Cities Improvement Project," 74
Greenberg, Clement, 148
Greenberg, Simon, 184*n*
Greenhoe, Florence, 309
Griffiths, Daniel E., 5*n*
Gross, Neal, 76*n*

Halevy, Elie, 121*n*
Hall, G. Stanley, 97
Handicapped-children programs, 238
Hanna, Lavonne, 41*n*
Hanna, Paul R., 204*n*, 344*n*
Harbison, Frederick, 159*n*
Harrington, Michael, 214
Harris, Joan R., 88*n*
Havighurst, Robert J., 67*n*, 71, 275
Hegel, 118
Henry, Nelson B., 235*n*
Herrold, Kenneth F., 6*n*
Hersey, John, 242*n*
"Higher Horizons" program, 74
Hill, Samuel E., 159*n*
Hitler, Adolf, 116
Hockwalt, Frederick, 259
Hodgkinson, Harold L., 43*n*
Hollingshead, August B., 64*n*, 72
Holman, Mary V., 313
Holmes, Oliver Wendell, 80, 270
Honeywell, Roy J., 232*n*
Hook, Sidney, 200
Hoos, Ida R., 157*n*
Horne, Herman H., 114
Hullfish, H. Gordon, 14*n*, 100*n*, 113*n*
Human nature, 107-110 *passim*
Hutchins, Robert Maynard, 111, 114

Ideologies, 115-124 (*see also* Values)
Impersonality, 133-134
Income, 70-71, 214, 254
Index of Status Characteristics, 65
Individualism, 120-121, 147-148
education and, 267, 276
leisure and, 170-171
Inductive method, 96
Industrialization, 82-83, 132-135 *passim* (*see also* Technology; Urban life)
and education, 133
and social change, 11, 78-79
In-service teacher training, 294
Institutions, 23-27
special-interest groups and, 30
Intelligence (*see* Gifted children)
Interest groups, 29-31, 140
Investment Bankers Association, 253

James, William, 16*n*, 97
Jackson, Justice, 185, 193
Jackson, P. W., 240
Jefferson, Thomas, 179, 232, 242, 246
Johnson, F. Ernest, 184*n*
Johnson, Lyndon, 194, 215*n*, 226*n*, 256*n*
Jones, Robert E., 317*n*
Jung, Raymond K., 172

Kahl, Joseph A., 48, 64*n*, 67*n*, 69-70
Kalamazoo case of 1872, 247
Kelley, Earl, 264, 275-277 *passim*
Kennedy, John F., 182, 194, 259
Kibbutz, 76
Kilpatrick, William H., 97
Kinney, Lucien C., 324
Kirkorian, Y. H., 96*n*
Kirkpatrick, C., 78*n*
Kleemeier, R. W., 154*n*
Komarovsky, Mirra, 151*n*
Komisar, B. Paul, 243
Krumgold, Joseph, 77*n*
Kuchel, Thomas, 270

Ladies of the Grand Army of the Republic, 257
Lancasterian teaching method, 287-288
Land-grant colleges, 247
Larrabee, Eric, 163*n*, 168
Larrabee, Harold A., 14*n*
Laski, Harold, 309

Lawrence, D. H., 308*n*
League of Women Voters, 260
Learners (*see* Students)
Learning theory, 273-275
Lee, Gordon, 181*n,* 183
Legal factors:
  of federal aid to education, 247-248
  schooling requirements, 293
  segregation, 208-214 *passim*
  tenure, 295
  welfare, 216
Leisure, 151-175 *passim*
Lenin, Nikolai, 117
Lerner, Max, 198, 204, 229
Lexington Normal School, 288
Lewin, Kurt, 31
Lewis, Oscar, 204-205
Lieberman, Myron, 325
Lippmann, Walter, 300
Lipset, Seymour Martin, 64*n,* 66*n*
Lloyd-Jones, Esther, 313
Locke, H. J., 76
Locke, John, 108
Loeb, Martin B., 71
Lucas, Wingate, 257
Lucito, Leonard J., 240-241
Lundberg, George A., 151*n*
Lunt, L. W., 71*n*
Lunt, Paul S., 64*n*
Lusted, Lee B., 158*n*
Lyceum movement, 290
Lynch, Kevin, 146-147

MacIver, Robert M., 29, 30, 165*n,* 166-167
Macmillan, Robert H., 156
Malinowski, Bronislaw, 22, 24
Malthus, 121
Mann, Horace, 186, 247, 265, 288, 290, 291, 293
Maritain, Jacques, 182, 201
Marx, Karl, 117
Mason, W. S., 76*n*
Mass society, 131-150
  education in, 144-149
McAteer, S. Eugene, 216*n*
McCluskey, Neil G., 182, 194, 195-196
McCollum case, 180, 190, 191, 196
McCormick, Paul J., 209
McEachern, A. W., 76*n*
McGill, Ralph, 214
McGrath, Karl, 257
McInerny, Mary A., 151*n*
McIntyre, Cardinal, 194, 196
McLaurin case, 209
Meeker, Marchia, 65*n,* 88*n*
Mendez case, 209
Merrill, Francis E., 21
Meyersohn, Rolf, 163*n,* 168
Michelson, L. C., 154*n*
Migrant workers, 214-216 *passim,* 222-224
Mill, John Stuart, 96
Mills, C. Wright, 22
Mobility (*see* Geographic mobility; Social mobility)
Morrell Act of 1862, 247
Morris, Charles, 94*n*
Motivation:
  and conformity, 138-141 *passim*
  social class and, 72
  of teachers, 311-315
Mulligan, Raymond A., 73*n*
Multiple deprivation, 224-225
Mumford, Lewis, 83*n,* 135, 142-145 *passim*
Munger, Frank, 257*n*
Murphy, Gardner, 195
Murray, John Courtney, 114, 182
Mussolini, Benito, 116
Myrdal, Gunnar, 51*n*

Nagel, Ernest, 61*n,* 96*n*
Nash, Ogden, 166
National Association for the Advancement of Colored People, 258
National Association of Manufacturers, 253
National Catholic Welfare Conference, 259
National Committee for Support of the Public Schools, 251
National Congress of PTAs, 260
National Council for the Accreditation of Teacher Education, 331
National debt, 253
National Defense Education Act, 72, 249
National Economic Council, 257
National Education Association, 75*n,* 88*n,* 91*n,* 145, 167-168, 198-199, 213, 235, 236*n,* 250, 258, 260, 309, 331, 332, 340
  code of ethics, 235-236

National Education
  Association (continued)
  membership in, 327, 333, 334
  origins of, 290
National Grange, 253
National Opinion Research Center, 331*n*
National School Boards Association, 331
National Science Foundation, 249
National Teachers Association, 290
Neibuhr, Reinhold, 180-181
Neibuhr, Richard, 181
Neighborhood-school concept, 210*n*, 212-213
Nelson, Henry, 232*n*
Neumeyer, Esther S., 170*n*
Neumeyer, Martin H., 170
New Britain Normal School, 289
Newgarten, Bernice, 67*n*
Newland, T. E., 239
New leisure, 151-175
New York Board of Regents, 186-187
Nineteenth Women's Patriotic Conference on Defense, 257
Normal schools, 288-289, 293, 294, 304, 331 (*see also* Teacher training)

Occupation (*see also* Employment):
  education and, 70, 89-91
  group standards, 30
  and leisure, 152-155 *passim*, 166
  and social class, 65, 68
  specialization, 133-134, 139-140
  professionalism (*see* Professionalism)
Oden, M. H., 237
Oregon case, 189

Parochial schools, 182, 188-198 *passim*
  federal aid to, 257, 259-260
Parrington, Vernon Louis, 178*n*
Parsons, Talcott, 66*n*
Penn, Lemuel, 211
Per capita income, 254
Philosophy and education, 9, 100-127 *passim*
Pierce, Cyrus, 288-289, 304
Pittenger, Benjamin F., 38
Pius XI, 181
Plato, 61, 102, 108, 109, 232, 242, 282
Plessy-Ferguson decision, 208-209
Policy, 5 (*see also* Decision making)
  communication and, 45-46
  public confidence and, 275-276
  geographic variations, 44
  society and, 31
Population:
  of ethnic subcultures, 206
  family size, 79-80
  growth and mobility, 83-91
  preindustrialization characteristics, 131-132
Powell, Adam Clayton, 258
Prayers in schools, 176-198 *passim*
Prejudice, 95-96, 225-229 (*see also* Segregation)
  religion and school admission, 221
Private schools, 34-35 (*see also* Parochial schools)
Professionalism, 74-75, 324-347
  administrators, 325
  autonomy and, 342-345
  anti-intellectualism and, 316
  automation and, 157, 158, 339
  career patterns, 320-321, 326
  certification, 292-293, 294, 341-342
  competence and, 318, 328-333, 337-338
  criteria of, 324-325
  vs. historical view of teaching, 281-286 *passim*
  and leisure, 152
  memberships, 290-291, 327
  research and, 340-341
  and segregation, 213
  training and, 305-306, 340-342
  and values, 46
Programmed instruction, 161-163
"Progressive-education" issue, 256
Psychological factors:
  development of child, 275-276
  learning theory, 273-275
  and occupational patterns, 92, 311-315
  and teaching competence, 318-319
  poverty and, 216

Quaker schools, 287
Quality of education, 146, 189, 195, 222-224
  federal role, 248, 256

Quality of education (continued)
  geographic variation, 328-333 *passim*
  problems of, 317-321
  teacher competence (*see* Teachers)
  teacher training, 315-316
Quillen, I. J., 41*n*, 95*n*
Quintilian, 61

Randall, John Herman, Jr., 96*n*
Raup, R. Bruce, 97
Recreation (*see* Leisure)
Recruitment of teachers, 281-286 *passim*, 291
  personality needs and, 314
  problems of, 222, 315-317, 321-322
  standards and, 328-333
Redfield, Robert, 48, 141*n*
Reissman, Frank, 74*n*, 206
"Released time," 189-192
Religion:
  church's education functions, 282
  and cultural deprivation, 220-222
  federal-aid issues, 259
  and education, 101, 176-203
  and educator's authority, 344
  in Kennedy-Nixon campaign, 259
  as teacher qualification, 283-285 *passim*
Research:
  and gifted-children programs, 238-239
  on human behavior, 61-62
  on leisure, 168-170
  and professionalism, 340-341
Retirement, 154-155
Reuter, E. B., 313
Rhulman, Jessie, 164*n*
Ricardo, 121
Richey, Robert, 312*n*
Riesman, David, 55*n*, 137, 139, 142, 148, 169*n*, 272
Rickover, Hyman, 145, 240
Robb, Inez, 212
Roberts, Benjamin, 208
Rockefeller Brothers Fund, 250
Rodwin, Lloyd, 146-147
Role, 76
Rosenburg, Bernard, 136
Rousseau, 9, 102
Russell, Bertrand, 102, 119*n*, 165
Russell, James E., 157*n*
Rutledge, Justice, 193, 196, 197
Ruttenberg, Stanley H., 157
Ryan, Mary Perkins, 192
Ryder, N. B., 86*n*, 88*n*, 135

Salary of teachers, 286-288 *passim*, 291-292, 295
Salem witch trials, 265
Schempp case, 187, 198
Schlesinger, Arthur, Jr., 165
Scholarships, 248-249 *passim*
Schooling, 3, 34, 35-39 (*see also* Education)
School districts, 38-39, 91
School year, 153-154
Schools (*see also* Education; Teachers):
  accreditation, 330-333
  admission quotas, 221
  adult programs, 155
  changing functions, 81-82
  class size, 91
  dame schools, 286-287
  discriminatory practices, 225-229
  enrollment data, 88-91 *passim*
  extracurricular activities, 173
  financing (*see* Financing of education)
  grade system, 227-228
  levels of, 38-39 *passim*
  neighborhood districts, 210*n*, 212-213
  parochial schools (*see* Parochial schools)
  religion in, 176-203
  "released time," 189-192
  segregation, 208-214 *passim*, 257-259
  social system of, 227
Science:
  and education, 12-14, 61-69
  ideology of, 123
Scientism, 12-13
Schramm, Wilbur, 161-163
Scobey, Mary-Margaret, 41
Secularism, 201
Segregation, 149, 335
  and cultural deprivation, 208-214
  and federal aid, 257-259
Seligman, E. R. A., 22*n*
"Separate but equal" doctrine, 208-209
Sex factors, 79-80, 92 (*see also* Women)
Sexton, Patricia C., 51*n*, 226*n*
"Shared-time" programs, 192

Sharer, Erwin L., 191
Siegel, Bernard J., 31
Skinner, B. F., 339
Smith, Adam, 121
Smith, B. Othaniel, 104*n*
Smith, Ethel M., 80*n*
Smith-Hughes Act of 1917, 248
Smith, Philip, 14*n,* 100*n,* 102
Snow, Charles P., 233
Social change, 49-50, 265-266, 277
Social-control functions of education, 35
Socialization, 34, 75-82 *passim*
Social mobility, 67-68
Social science and education, 96-98
Social status, stratification, and class, 75-76, 310 (*see also* Socioeconomic factors)
  community variation, 28
  and curriculum, 284
  education and, 70-75
  Marxist view, 117-118
  mobility, 67-68
  and motivation, 72
  population distribution in, 66-67
  studies of, 61-68
  and teacher education, 228-229
  of teachers, 227, 281-286 *passim,* 291-292, 295-296, 309-311
  and values, 68-70
  of women, 78-79
Social values (*see* Values)
Society, 22
  culture and, 22-23
  gifted child's role, 239-244 *passim*
  and individual, 240-244 *passim*
  reform of, 144-149 *passim,* 263-278 *passim* (*see also* Social change)
Society for Constitutional Security, 257
Socioeconomic factors, 65 (*see also* Social status, stratification, and class)
  and children's leisure, 172
  and cultural deprivation, 204-230 *passim*
  and segregation, 208-214 *passim*
Socrates, 282
Southern States Industrial Council, 253
Soviet education, 240-241
Sowards, G. Wesley, 41
Special-interest groups, 29-31
  vs. federal aid, 253-254
  and value conflicts, 141-144 *passim*
Specialization (*see* Education; Occupation)
Spellman, Cardinal, 196
Spencer, Herbert, 41-42, 121
Spindler, George D., 24, 26*n,* 31*n,* 220*n,* 312
Stanford-Binet Intelligence Scale, 235
Stanley, William O., 30*n*, 32, 140
State government education role, 5, 247-248
Status (*see* Social status)
Stereotypes, 106
  occupations and, 30
  of teachers, 308-312 *passim*
Strang, Ruth, 217*n*
Students:
  development patterns, 275
  dropouts, 90-91, 154, 242
  gifted children, 154, 231-245
  pressures on, 154
  role in community life, 266
  views of, 107-110 *passim*
Student-teacher ratio, 237-238
Styles, Lindley J., 313
Subcultures, 26-27
  age and, 94
  bicultural background, 217-220
  deprivation, 204-230
  geographical isolation and, 222-224
  income and, 215
  migrant workers, 222-224
  social class and, 68-69
  social mobility in, 67
  occupation and, 94
  and value conflict, 54-55
Sullivan, John W. N., 12*n*
Summer, Charles, 208
Super, Donald E., 320-321
Superintendent of schools, 5 (*see also* Administrators; Educators)
Supreme Court decisions, 185-198, 208-214 *passim,* 270
Survey ordinance of 1785, 247
Swados, Harvey, 164, 165*n*
Swenson, Jean, 164
Sweatt case, 209
Swett, John, 292-293
Symbols, 94-95
Synthetic assertions, 14-16

Tannenbaum, Abraham J., 232*n*
Tax, Sol, 48*n,* 141*n*

Taylor, Frank S., 82*n*
Teachers (*see also* Educators):
  vs. administrators, 337
  assignment of, 225
  certification, 292-293, 294, 329, 341-342
  class origins, 309-311
  colonial schoolmaster, 284-286
  competence, 281-286 *passim,* 289, 291-293, 317-321, 322, 325, 326
  decision making, 5, 6
  and goals of education, 74-75
  motivation of, 311-315
  numbers of, 88
  organizations, 290-291 (*see also* National Education Association)
  personality factors, 311-315
  personal life, 292
  political activity, 266
  professionalism (*see* Professionalism)
  recruitment of (*see* Recruitment)
  salary, 286-288 *passim,* 291-292, 296
  shortage of, 321-322
  specialization, 294, 320, 337-339
  status of, 227, 281-286 *passim,* 291-292, 295-296, 309-311
  stereotype of, 308-309
  tenure, 295
  training of (*see* Teacher training)
  turnover, 292, 340
  value orientations of, 309-315 *passim*
  women, 289, 304, 320
Teachers College, Columbia University, 269
Teacher training, 282-287 *passim,* 288-290, 291-293 *passim,* 296-298
  accreditation and, 330-333 *passim*
  class bias, 228-229
  content of, 342
  in-service programs, 294
  normal schools, 288-289, 293, 294, 304, 331
  and recruitment problems, 315-316
  and professionalism, 340-342
  "refresher" programs, 321
  "student teaching" phase, 298-299, 305
  technical tradition, 332
  teachers of teachers, 316
Teaching, 327-328 (*see also* Education; Quality)
Teaching machines, 161-163, 339
Teaching materials, 294, 295
Technology:
  and culture, 82-83
  educational demands of, 233-234
  and leisure, 153, 155-158
  and professional work, 157, 158
  teaching machines, 161-163, 339
  and unemployment, 155
Tenure, 295
Terman, Lewis M., 234-237 *passim,* 240
Terrien, Frederic, 313
Thayer, V. T., 179*n,* 197, 199-202 *passim*
Thomas, Donald R., 75*n,* 88, 206, 223, 312
Thomas, Lawrence, 56*n,* 109*n,* 113*n,* 123, 324
Thomas, Maurice, 197
Thomas, W. I., 30
Thurber, James, 308
Tibbetts, C., 154*n*
Torrance, E. P., 240
Tumin, Melvin, 204*n,* 207*n*
Tyler, E. B., 305

Ulrich, Robert, 35*n*
Unemployment, 154, 155
  of migrant workers, 211-216 *passim*
UNESCO materials, 269
U.S. Chamber of Commerce, 253
U.S. Office of Education, 249
Urban life and urbanization, 83-96 *passim,* 132-135 *passim,* 222
  and child labor, 153
  communication problems, 91-96
  and conformity, 135-141 *passim*
  mass education, 144-149
  and value conflicts, 141-144 *passim*

Van Dusen, Henry P., 180
Van Til, William, 161
Value conflicts, 45-46, 48-60, 141-144
  and education of gifted children, 236-244 *passim*
  personal vs. professional views, 74-75
  resolution of, 52-56
Values, 48-49
  bias vs. prejudice, 95-96
  church-state separation, 177-178, 179, 180-185
  communism, 117-120

community and, 30
conformity issues (*see* Conformity)
cultural lag, 42-43
curriculum coverage, 198-202 *passim*
and decision making, 8-9
democracy (*see* Democracy)
education and, 144-149 *passim*
of education (*see* Goals of education)
fascism, 115-117
federal-aid issues, 261
individualism (*see* Individualism)
and leisure use, 166, 168-172
mass media and, 72
national goals, 236-244 *passim*
"progress" concept, 41-42, 43
quality vs. economy in education, 289
segregation and, 209
social class and, 68-70
and social process, 23, 49-50
special-interest groups and, 29-31 *passim*
of teachers, 74-75, 309-315 *passim,* 335-336
urban life, 135-141
work ethic, 166, 310-312 *passim*
Vocational guidance, 93
Vocational training, 160-161, 248

Wallace, Governor, 211
Ward, Lester, 42
Ward, Virgil S., 237
Waring, Thomas R., 211
Warner, W. Lloyd, 28, 64*n,* 65*n,* 71, 206, 310
Warren, Earl, 209-210
Watt, James, 82
Webber, Irving L., 164
Weigel, Gustave, 105-106
Wernick, Murray, 159*n*
Western Library Institute and College of Professional Teachers, 290
Wheel of Progress, 257
Whitehead, A. N., 102, 324, 327
White House Conference on Education, 250
White, Victor, 182
Whyte, William H., Jr., 137, 272
Wiles, Kimball, 5*n,* 337
Williams, George, 301, 303
Williams, Roger, 177, 178
Wilson, Charles H., 298
Wilson, Woodrow, 196
Witty, Paul, 235, 237
Wolfe, D., 242*n*
Women:
leisure of, 153
marriage and career, 320-321
membership in National Education Association, 290
and professionalism problems, 326
status of, 78-79
in teaching, 287, 289, 290, 320
Wood, John T., 269*n*
Woodring, Paul, 301, 302
Work-success ethic, 166, 310-312 *passim*

Zelomek, A. Wilbert, 165, 169*n*
Zintz, Miles, 206
Znaniecki, Florian, 30
Zorach case, 190-191